D1062939

Also by G. Scott Thomas

Sports
A Brand New Ballgame
The Best (and Worst) of Baseball's Modern Era
Leveling the Field

History
Presidential Election Record Book 2020
Counting the Votes
A New World to Be Won
Advice From the Presidents
The United States of Suburbia
The Pursuit of the White House

Demographics
Dreamtowns
Micropolitan America
The Rating Guide to Life in America's Fifty States
Where to Make Money
The Rating Guide to Life in America's Small Cities

Cooperstown at the Crossroads

Cooperstown at the Crossroads

The Checkered History (and Uncertain Future) of Baseball's Hall of Fame

G. Scott Thomas

 NIAWANDA BOOKS

Cooperstown at the Crossroads: The Checkered History (and Uncertain Future) of Baseball's Hall of Fame

Copyright © 2022 by G. Scott Thomas

All rights reserved. No part of this book may be reproduced, distributed, or transmitted in any form or by any means, including photocopying, recording, or other electronic or mechanical methods, without the prior written permission of the publisher, except in the case of brief quotations embodied in critical reviews and certain other noncommercial uses permitted by copyright law. For permission requests, write the publisher at the address below.

Niawanda Books
949 Delaware Road
Buffalo, NY 14223

Printed in the United States of America

First Edition
10 9 8 7 6 5 4 3 2 1

Contents

Cooperstown at the Crossroads

CHAPTER ONE

January

THE SHOW BEGAN WITH tape of a brick building at night, light streaming from three sets of glass doors at the rear of a small central courtyard. The camera zoomed smoothly toward the middle entrance, which magically swiveled open, followed a moment later by the interior doors, beckoning the audience into the most famous structure in Cooperstown, New York.

Fans across the country, eager to learn the results of the National Baseball Hall of Fame's annual election, had been awaiting this invitation for months. The swinging doors welcomed them to the sport's cable channel, MLB Network, whose election coverage would run from four to eight o'clock, with the formal announcement coming around the midpoint. The player or players chosen this evening, Tuesday, January 25, 2022, would be inducted at a ceremony in Cooperstown six months hence, a rite bestowing eternal membership in the pantheon of baseball's all-time greats.

"America has few honors greater than enshrinement in the Hall of Fame of its National Game," Zev Chafets wrote in his 2009 book, *Cooperstown Confidential*. "The title HoF that the approximately sixty living members are entitled to add to their signatures confers upon them the closest American equivalent of knighthood."[1] The stakes were high, the anticipation intense.

The safest way for MLB Network to cover this historic occasion— this dubbing of baseball's newest knights—was to flavor its four-hour program with a blend of nostalgia and reverence. The opening shot drawing the audience into the Hall of Fame seemed to match that approach perfectly.

But one aspect of the introductory segment was at odds. The accompanying music bore no resemblance to the evocative soundtracks of classic baseball movies. It had none of the heart-tugging majesty of *Field of Dreams* or the soaring fanfares of *The Natural*. Chuck D, leader of the famed hip-hop group Public Enemy, began rapping to a persistent beat as images of Hall of Fame candidates suddenly flashed across the screen. His words were far from celebratory. They were angry.

> *We get Papi, Sheffield, Druw, and Jimmy*
> *But no Barry, Roger, Manny, or Sammy*
> *See the last dance for types like Schilling*
> *But Cobb, Landis, Cap Anson in the hall still chillin'* [2]

Those four lines contained much to unpack.

The players in Chuck D's first line had emerged as stars in the final decade of the twentieth century or the early years of the twenty-first. Right fielder Gary Sheffield retired in late 2009, which meant 2022 was his eighth year on the Hall of Fame ballot. (Anybody who plays at least ten years in the big leagues becomes eligible for the hall after a five-year waiting period.) Center fielder Andruw Jones, who last played in 2012, was facing voters for the fifth time, and a pair of 2016 retirees, designated hitter David "Big Papi" Ortiz and shortstop Jimmy Rollins, were newcomers to the process. All were expected to draw considerable support, though it was unknown if any would be approved by at least 75 percent of the 394 voters, the threshold for Hall of Fame induction.

It was the next five—left fielders Barry Bonds and Manny Ramirez, right fielder Sammy Sosa, and pitchers Roger Clemens and Curt Schilling—who commanded the most attention on this cold January day. There was no disputing their greatness. Bonds had blasted 762 home runs, the highest total ever, surpassing such famed sluggers as Henry Aaron and Babe Ruth. Clemens had won 354 games, putting him ninth among all pitchers in big-league history. Their three colleagues had not risen to the same exalted level, yet still boasted impressive statistics widely deemed to be worthy of Cooperstown: 609 homers for Sosa, 555 for Ramirez, and 216 wins for Schilling.

But few observers expected these five stars to reach 75 percent in the 2022 election. Their problem, as everybody knew, was reputational. Ramirez had twice been suspended for using steroids or related performance-enhancing drugs, commonly known as PEDs.[3] Bonds, Clemens, and Sosa were widely suspected of similar abuse, though their records were free of convictions or suspensions. Schilling was an outlier, a vocal critic of PEDs and the players who took them, though he had a different problem. He had become infamous for obnoxious behavior on social media and in his dealings with reporters. The latter shortcoming had proved harmful to his cause, since sportswriters, specifically members of the Baseball Writers' Association of America, were the sole participants in the Hall of Fame election.

The prospects of these five controversial figures were muddled by the obscurity of the hall's admission standards. Voters were merely pointed toward Rule 5, often called the "character clause." It was brief and somewhat vague: "Voting shall be based upon the player's record, playing ability, integrity, sportsmanship, character, and contributions to the team(s) on which the player played."[4] A majority of the BBWAA's members initially interpreted Rule 5 as barring anyone suspected of steroid abuse, a view backed by several legendary players. "There's no place in the Hall of Fame for people who cheat," Henry Aaron said emphatically.[5] Bonds and Clemens, who would have been heartily welcomed to the hall in 2013 without their PED baggage, finished below 40 percent in their first three years on the ballot.

But attitudes were changing. "They never flunked a drug test," USA Today's Bob Nightengale wrote of the two superstars. "Never were suspended. And are the only ones who spent millions of dollars clearing their name in federal court. They instead are guilty in the court of public opinion."[6] That, in Nightengale's opinion, failed to constitute a violation of Rule 5. He annually voted for both pariahs, as did a growing number of his BBWAA counterparts. Bonds and Clemens moved in tandem, climbing above 50 percent in 2017, then 60 percent in 2020. But they had little time remaining to reach the magic percentage of 75.

Chuck D had hinted at the urgency attached to the 2022 election with his mention of a "last dance." The hall's rules stipulated that no candidate could remain on the ballot for more than a decade. If he failed to achieve three-quarters support in ten elections, a player's fate would be shunted off to an unwieldy and unpredictable committee system, a last-ditch opportunity to gain admission. This hazy prospect now faced Bonds, Clemens, Schilling, and Sosa, all of whom had first appeared on the BBWAA ballot in 2013.

And what of the final three names in Chuck D's stanza? The rapper had reached back more than a century for his rapid evocation of "Cobb, Landis, Cap Anson in the hall still chillin'." Center fielder Ty Cobb, who starred from 1905 to 1928, was one of the five immortals knighted in the Hall of Fame's very first election in 1936. First baseman Cap Anson, who retired way back in 1897, joined the elite club in 1939. And Kenesaw Mountain Landis, baseball's original commissioner, was ushered into Cooperstown upon his death in 1944.

These three men were united not only by their exalted status in baseball's early history, but also by a contemptible defect. Cobb and Anson were virulent racists, vocally determined to maintain what they saw as the lily-white purity of the major leagues. Landis had been their surreptitious compatriot. He shunned their public vitriol, yet quietly and effectively enforced the sport's color line.

The status of Cobb, Anson, and Landis in Cooperstown went undisputed until 2013, when the PED controversy awakened interest in the character clause, which coincidentally had been stapled into the Hall of Fame's guidelines the year that Landis died.[7] Members of the BBWAA began questioning the relative severity of personal flaws. Was it worse to be a steroid abuser or a racist? A few critics began calling for action against any inductees who had sought to prevent integration. "It might be appropriate for the Hall of Fame to consider removing or at least adding an asterisk to a few of those plaques," wrote historian David Gordon in 2018.[8]

This debate worried the hall's administrators, especially once the Black Lives Matter movement swept the nation in 2020. They went so far as to post a sign that admitted the commissioner's error: "As the most powerful person in baseball, Landis had the greatest ability to effect change, but his lack of overt action in promoting integration gave tacit approval to maintaining the status quo of a segregated system."[9]

But they did not remove his plaque—or those of Cobb and Anson—from the hall's atrium.

The beat kept pounding, and Chuck D pivoted back to contemporary times. He dropped the names of Pete Rose, the game's all-time hit leader whose gambling had disqualified him from Cooperstown, and Alex Rodriguez, another PED abuser who was listed on the ballot for the first time. And then he wrapped up his lament, folding his arms and dropping his head (adorned with a New York Yankees cap) as he spat out two final questions, voicing the confusion and unrest that plagued the baseball world on what was supposed to be one of its happiest days.

"Where does it start?" asked Chuck D. "And when does it end?"[10]

THE RAPPER FADED FROM the screen, and MLB Network's Studio 21 came to life. Host Greg Amsinger briefly welcomed viewers, then turned to analyst Harold Reynolds. What headline, asked Amsinger, would the coming announcement generate? What would baseball fans be discussing tomorrow?

"Will Bonds and Clemens get in? Let's be honest. That's the headline," said Reynolds.[11]

He was correct, of course. If the Hall of Fame had been allowed to set the tone, this January 25th would have been an unadulterated celebration of on-field excellence. But the clouds glimpsed by Chuck D had already settled over the studio, darkening the tone of MLB Network's program. It was destined to be as much a dreary debate of drug policy as a joyous festival.

Two other analysts shared the studio with Amsinger and Reynolds. Tom Verducci did his best to redirect the discussion, noting that the list of candidates was rich with talent. "Six players from the five hundred home-run club are on this ballot," he pointed out. "Three players who had the most home runs at their positions in the history of baseball—left field, second base, DH. And two of the top fifteen strikeout pitchers of all time. These are some of the biggest names, the biggest showmen in baseball history—on the ballot today."

Colleague Bob Costas leaned in from the right side of the screen. "But a majority of those names you mentioned are compromised, to one extent or another, by a connection to performance-enhancing drugs," he said. "That's always been part of the story."[12]

It had indeed been a major theme for two decades. Years of rumors and innuendoes had finally forced Major League Baseball to confront its drug problem back in 2003, when it tested 1,438 players for steroids. The intent was merely to determine the extent of the abuse. Nobody was to be disciplined, and all results were supposed to remain anonymous. But inevitable leaks revealed that 104 players had tested positive. A subsequent investigation headed by former U.S. Senator George Mitchell, commonly known as the Mitchell Report, identified eighty-nine players who had allegedly taken PEDs.[13]

The public demanded details, and it got them. Sources revealed the names of those who had tested positive in 2003, grand juries and congressional investigations uncovered others, and Mitchell willingly supplied his 409-page report to the press in 2007. The former legislator urged baseball to "look ahead to the future," but disillusioned fans preferred to gaze back at the past. They bemoaned the fact that some of the game's greatest players had been accused of PED abuse, led by Barry Bonds and Roger Clemens, then at the end of historic careers.[14]

Both superstars denied the accusations from the start. Bonds: "They can test me every day if they choose to."[15] Clemens: "I did not take steroids, human growth hormone, or any other banned substances at any time in my baseball career or, in fact, my entire life."[16] Those stands eventually caused both players to be indicted—Bonds for perjury and obstruction of justice, Clemens for making false statements to Congress—yet neither was permanently scarred by the legal system. Bonds's conviction for obstruction was overturned on appeal. Clemens's first trial ended with a mistrial, the second with an acquittal.[17]

That left the BBWAA with a dilemma that lingered into 2022. The records of Bonds and Clemens were officially unblemished—no PED suspensions, no criminal convictions—yet both were widely believed to have perpetrated fraud, to have enhanced their statistics by illegal and immoral means. Did they belong in Cooperstown, or had they run afoul of Rule 5?

Bonds was especially belligerent in his own defense: "Do the best players in the game deserve to be in the Hall of Fame? Yes. Everything that everyone has accomplished in baseball is in [the record] book. Correct? So if that's correct, then [I] need to be in there. End of story."[18]

Few of the BBWAA's members saw the choice in such stark terms. Some, such as *USA Today*'s Nightengale, suspected that Bonds and Clemens had cheated, yet nonetheless voted for both, given that they had not been formally punished for PED abuse. Others steadfastly ignored the pair. "I cannot vote for two people who, by all appearances, shamelessly made a mockery of the game for their own benefit," wrote Mark Faller of the *Arizona Republic*.[19] And still others complained that it was impossible to make a choice without guidance from Major League Baseball. "This is 2022, and the league still has not truly reckoned with its past," wrote *Los Angeles Times* columnist Bill Shaikin. "The league punted the matter to the Hall of Fame, and in turn the hall punted to the baseball writers."[20]

Such criticism did not faze the hall's president, Josh Rawitch, who steadfastly refused to be pinned down. "Once you try to start giving guidance on character in one instance, you probably have to start giving it in all instances," he said. "We just think it's far more important to leave that up to the electorate, whether that's the BBWAA or the Era Committees, because it means something different to every person."[21]

This lack of clarity spawned a PED controversy that had engulfed the hall since Bonds and Clemens became eligible in 2013. The BBWAA's members grappled annually with questions that lacked easy answers. Did any of the leading candidates take PEDs? If so, did the drugs artificially enhance their performances? And if the answer to the first two questions was yes, should the guilty players be disqualified from Cooperstown? A voter needed the skills of a detective, a scientist, and an ethicist to fill out a ballot.

This massive headache would not be subsiding anytime soon. It was true that Bonds and Clemens would no longer be the BBWAA's concern after 2022, no matter what happened to them this evening, but a new generation of PED cases was surfacing. Alex Rodriguez, one of only nine batters to hit more than six hundred home runs, was on the ballot for the first time. His election to the Hall of Fame would have been a certainty today, if not for his admission of steroid use in the early

2000s and his subsequent yearlong suspension in 2014.[22]

Harold Reynolds discussed Rodriguez's candidacy as the first half of MLB Network's four-hour show drew to a close: "Putting up the numbers, the controversies, everything else, he put it all together, really. Fielding, hitting, all that."

"What kind of support do you think he gets?" asked Greg Amsinger. "We're moments away from finding out."

Reynolds thought for a moment. "I'll be interested to see if he gets 30 percent. I don't see him getting over that much, and I think it's because of [the] suspension. It's one thing to have the whispers. It's another thing to have it *there*."[23]

THE PICTURESQUE VILLAGE OF Cooperstown sits peacefully on the south shore of Otsego Lake, seventy-five miles west of New York's capital, Albany, the nearest city of any prominence. The foothills of the Catskill Mountains rise above Cooperstown's small business district and its well-tended brick buildings. Baseball is omnipresent. Stores sell baseball memorabilia, caps, cards, and books. Team pennants hang from the walls of a pizzeria. A baseball mural adorns the entrance to a grocery store.

The National Baseball Hall of Fame and Museum occupies half of a sizable block on the south side of Main Street, a quarter-mile from the point where the Susquehanna River descends from the lake. The hall opened its doors to visitors in 1939, three years after its first election, and it almost immediately became a place of veneration, baseball's version of the Holy Land.

"Every time I go to Cooperstown, I am filled with patriotic fervor, for here is enshrined the American spirit which has made us a great nation," an early honoree, Connie Mack, gushed a decade after the grand opening.[24] His reverence has been echoed down the years by subsequent inductees. "I cannot fully express how much it means to be here as a Hall of Famer," said Tom Seaver. "It is the most exclusive club or at least one of the most exclusive clubs in our country."[25] Fellow pitcher Don Sutton's awe bordered on religious devotion. "If you don't feel an aura that's almost spiritual when you walk through the Hall of Fame, then check tomorrow's obituary," he said. "You're in it."[26]

Bronze plaques honoring players, managers, executives, and umpires—there were 333 at the beginning of 2022—line the oak walls of a high-ceilinged gallery toward the rear of the Hall of Fame's main building. The museum offers three floors of exhibits, but the plaques on the first floor are indisputably the main attraction, luring a steady stream of baseball fans to Cooperstown no matter the season, even during the cold upstate New York winter.

It was here in the gallery, with the plaques of baseball immortals arrayed behind him, that the hall's president finally stepped to the podium at 6:15. "Tonight," said Josh Rawitch, "we are pleased to announce the addition of one new member to the Hall of Fame fraternity."

Only one. Knowledgeable fans immediately suspected that David Ortiz was the BBWAA's sole choice, leaving Bonds and Clemens short of induction for the tenth straight year. But Rawitch sustained the suspense a moment longer, telling the TV audience that the unidentified winner "will be honored alongside Bud Fowler, Gil Hodges, Jim Kaat, Minnie Minoso, Tony Oliva, and Buck O'Neil at our induction ceremonies on July 24 at the Clark Sports Center here in Cooperstown."[27]

It was a reminder that today's election, despite the ballyhoo, was not the only source of honorees for the class of 2022. The Hall of Fame's idiosyncratic voting system vested equal power in the BBWAA and four sixteen-member panels. The latter, each known as an Era Committee, met at multiyear intervals. They were named for the time frames they encompassed: Early Baseball (prior to 1950), Golden Days (1950 to 1969), Modern Baseball (1970 to 1987), and Today's Game (1988 to the present). The hall's schedule had called for the first two groups, Early Baseball and Golden Days, to gather on December 5, 2021, in Orlando, where they debated the merits of twenty candidates previously rejected by similar committees and/or the BBWAA. The six names recited by Rawitch had received the necessary stamps of approval.

Defenders of the Era Committees liken them to an appeals court, a body empowered to grant new life to any deserving candidate who has been spurned by the sportswriters. Yet the parallel is inexact. An appellate court is still subject to review by the Supreme Court, while the separate versions of the Era Committee answer to no one. Their decisions are final, carrying the same weight as any BBWAA election. If twelve of the sixteen panel members agree, a candidate is instantly elevated to the Hall of Fame.

This committee process, according to critics, is ripe for abuse. It's difficult to mount an effective campaign for a candidate in a BBWAA election, given the large number of sportswriters participating (usually around four hundred) and the private nature of the voting (a secret ballot, unless a writer chooses to make it public). But the sixteen committee members meet and vote in a single room. Persuasion and pressure can easily sway the outcome. "The panel's selection process has often resembled a bunch of ex-players arguing for, and eventually electing, their best friends or cronies," wrote James Vail, an author who analyzed the hall's elections.[28]

The Era Committees swing into action only after a candidate's BBWAA eligibility has expired, which means that anyone anointed in those small rooms has endured a lengthy wait for admission. No one in the class of 2022 had been delayed longer than Cooperstown resident Bud Fowler, a second baseman and pitcher believed to be the first black player to compete side by side with whites in professional leagues. Fowler had died more than a century earlier in 1913. Three of his fellow inductees were also deceased: first baseman and manager Gil Hodges (as of 1972), first baseman, manager, coach, and scout Buck O'Neil (2006), and left fielder Minnie Minoso (2015).[29]

O'Neil was a veteran of the Negro leagues, America's pre-integration outlet for black ballplayers. He thereby escaped the scrutiny of the BBWAA, which had never included Negro leaguers in its pool of candidates. Hodges climbed as high as 50 percent in the annual balloting prior to his death, then inched upward to 63 percent before being dropped from the ballot in 1983. Minoso didn't fare nearly as well, peaking at 21 percent in 1988 and suffering elimination in 1999.

The disconnect was striking. The BBWAA had persistently deemed Hodges and Minoso to be unworthy of Cooperstown, yet the Era Committees happily added them to the class of 2022. Informed observers were divided on their merits, though several caustically blamed the writers for having botched both cases. "It is, quite frankly, shocking and appalling that he was not elected while he was alive," author Joe Posnanski said of Minoso.[30]

The two living honorees, pitcher Jim Kaat and right fielder Tony Oliva, both starred for the Minnesota Twins in the 1960s and early 1970s, and both were eighty-three years old. Oliva noted that the hall often seemed to wait for a player to die before honoring him, the inevitable result of a bizarre system that pitted the same candidates against each other year after year, creating an electoral logjam. "The phone rang, and I said, 'Ohhhhh. I'm alive!' That was a big relief," Oliva joked at a December 6 press conference.[31] He had topped out at 47 percent in BBWAA elections, despite winning three American League batting titles. Kaat never even reached 30 percent, though he had notched 283 victories.

All six men chosen by the Era Committees had been fine players—nobody could dispute that—but an unspoken question hovered in the air: Were they truly of Cooperstown caliber? Unanimity was impossible. Hordes of discerning fans lined up on the affirmative and negative sides, heatedly debating the relative merits of the new inductees. There was one point, however, on which both blocs could agree: The annual selections by the committees tended to be less compelling than the BBWAA's choices.

"Each year when the committee votes, informed fans can usually be found under their beds, awaiting another dread announcement that somebody like Tookie Gilbert or Marv Throneberry has just been declared a baseball immortal," wrote John Leo in a *New York Times* essay in 1988.[32] He exaggerated for humorous effect, but his point was valid. The writers, who were given first crack at the candidates, immediately picked the brightest stars, leaving the borderline cases for the appellate courts.

Kaat admitted as much during his post-selection press conference. "There's got to be degrees of the Hall of Fame," he said. "I think they probably have a back row for me, and I'll wave to those guys up there."[33]

THE TIME HAD COME to reveal the sole winner of the BBWAA's election, the seventh newcomer to Cooperstown's plaque gallery.

"Our final member of the 2022 class is a feared slugger who performed his best on the biggest stage, winning three world championships," Rawitch announced. "Today, David Ortiz becomes the fourth Dominican-born member of the National Baseball Hall of Fame."[34]

Greg Amsinger and Harold Reynolds made no pretense of impartiality in MLB Network's studio. Both applauded.

"This is great news," said Amsinger. "We all are huge fans of David Ortiz, not just as a player, but as a human being. What a wonderful person. And for him to be a first-ballot Hall of Famer, this is a great day."[35]

Ortiz was renowned both for his power at the plate and the engaging smile he flashed almost everywhere else. His statistics were definitely at a Hall of Fame level—541 home runs and 1,768 runs batted in during a 20-year career with the Minnesota Twins and Boston Red Sox—but it helped that he seemed so nice. His sunny personality contrasted with the tight-lipped surliness of the alleged steroid twins who had dominated MLB Network's discussion to this point. "There's a likability factor with David Ortiz that there isn't with the others," Tony Kornheiser, cohost of ESPN's *Pardon the Interruption*, would say the next day. "People like Big Papi, and they don't like Bonds and Clemens."[36]

Perhaps that explained Ortiz's ability to shed his own PED baggage in his very first year on the ballot. The Red Sox star had been one of the 104 players who tested positive in 2003, when baseball was conducting its supposedly anonymous survey. The story broke in 2009, and Ortiz swiftly declared his innocence. "Based on the way I have lived my life," he said, "I am surprised to learn I tested positive."[37] He suggested that careless consumption of over-the-counter supplements might be to blame, but insisted he had never taken steroids.

What was unusual about Ortiz's case was the support he received from the baseball establishment. Bonds and Clemens had been equally vehement in their denials, and they, like Ortiz, had never tested positive after Major League Baseball implemented its formal testing program in 2004. But Ortiz was embraced, while the other two were shunned. The former executive director of the players' union, Michael Weiner, and MLB commissioner Rob Manfred helped clear his path to Cooperstown. Weiner suggested that Ortiz's 2003 test had yielded a false positive, and Manfred agreed it was "entirely possible" that Ortiz had never taken a banned substance.[38]

The BBWAA released the full results a few moments after Rawitch's announcement. The standings showed Ortiz above the 75 percent threshold with eleven votes to spare. None of the other twenty-nine candidates came close to induction:

1. David Ortiz, 307 (77.92%)
2. Barry Bonds, 260 (65.99%)
3. Roger Clemens, 257 (65.23%)
4. Scott Rolen, 249 (63.20%)
5. Curt Schilling, 231 (58.63%)
6. Todd Helton, 205 (52.03%)
7. Billy Wagner, 201 (51.02%)
8. Andruw Jones, 163 (41.37%)
9. Gary Sheffield, 160 (40.61%)
10. Alex Rodriguez, 135 (34.26%)
11. Jeff Kent, 129 (32.74%)
12. Manny Ramirez, 114 (28.93%)
13. Omar Vizquel, 94 (23.86%)
14. Sammy Sosa, 73 (18.53%)
15. Andy Pettitte, 42 (10.66%)
16. Jimmy Rollins, 37 (9.39%)
17. Bobby Abreu, 34 (8.63%)
18. Mark Buehrle, 23 (5.84%)
19. Torii Hunter, 21 (5.33%)
20. Joe Nathan, 17 (4.31%)
21. Tim Hudson, 12 (3.05%)
22. Tim Lincecum, 9 (2.28%)
23. Ryan Howard, 8 (2.03%)
24. Mark Teixeira, 6 (1.52%)
25. Justin Morneau, 5 (1.27%)
25. Jonathan Papelbon, 5 (1.27%)
27. Prince Fielder, 2 (0.51%)
27. A.J. Pierzynski, 2 (0.51%)
29. Carl Crawford, 0 (0.00%)
29. Jake Peavy, 0 (0.00%)

The BBWAA's election was commonly—and incorrectly—believed to be a referendum on the relative worthiness of each candidate. Scott

Rolen, who played third base for four clubs, primarily the Philadelphia Phillies and St. Louis Cardinals, was backed by 63.2 percent of the 394 participating writers in 2022. The results implied a binary choice, with the 249 Rolen supporters checking a Yes box on the ballot and the other 145 opting for an adjacent No.

But that wasn't the way it worked, not at all. The Hall of Fame, contrary to popular belief, does not ask voters to pass direct judgment on individual candidates.

It might seem logical to pose the same question for each of the thirty nominees: Do you consider Player A worthy of induction? How about Player B? Player C? But the hall has always staged a head-to-head competition, limiting each BBWAA member to ten affirmative votes. If a writer believes that seventeen candidates are deserving, he must make a series of tough choices: Was Player A better than Player B? How about C vs. D? E vs. F? A Rolen supporter might very well ignore the sole box next to his name, reserving those ten valuable votes for players who seem more qualified or have been waiting longer for admission.

This system has created a sizable logjam, unnecessarily delaying many inductions for years, even decades. Consider a random example from half a century earlier, the election of 1972. Three new honorees were chosen by the BBWAA that year—Sandy Koufax, Yogi Berra, and Early Wynn—with no other candidate coming close. Yet thirteen of the also-rans on 1972's ballot would eventually be welcomed to the Hall of Fame, including Duke Snider (21 percent in 1972), Nellie Fox (16 percent), and Richie Ashburn (3 percent). Those three would be delayed another eight, twenty-five, and twenty-three years, respectively. Did their records improve during their lengthy exiles? Of course not. The system had simply forced them to wait their turn.

Rolen was one of several contenders currently stuck in the doldrums. He had debuted on the ballot in 2018, finishing in seventeenth place. The voters advanced him to thirteenth the following year, then to seventh in 2020 and fourth place in 2021 and 2022. Rolen's eventual induction seemed inevitable, but it would not occur before he had paid sufficient dues. First baseman Todd Helton, relief pitcher Billy Wagner, and right fielder Gary Sheffield were in the same predicament. All three had joined Rolen in the top ten each year since 2020, and all three would return in 2023 and, if necessary, in 2024 to face the voters again.

Those former stars could console themselves with dreams of future elections, but half of 2022's thirty candidates would never again be listed on a BBWAA ballot. The bottom eleven—from Joe Nathan on down—fell short of the 5 percent threshold for retention. All had been fine players, and some had even been the very best for brief periods. Ryan Howard and Justin Morneau were the Most Valuable Players of their leagues; Tim Lincecum and Jake Peavy won Cy Young Awards. But all eleven were automatically excluded from future elections.

The 5 percent requirement was implemented in 1979 to clear deadwood from the ballot. But history suggests a dark byproduct, the elimination of deserving candidates before they gather electoral momentum. The case of Ralph Kiner is instructive. The famed slugger floundered below 4 percent in his first two elections, 1960 and 1962. If the mandatory cutoff had existed, Kiner would have been booted. But the system back then gave him time to climb through the ranks, and he finally topped the golden line of 75 percent in 1975, a phoenix-like rise that could not be duplicated today.

Four high-profile contenders from the 2022 ballot were being eliminated for a different reason. Bonds, Clemens, Schilling, and Sosa had reached the end of their ten-year eligibility periods. Their fates would be decided by an Era Committee in a year yet to be determined, perhaps in a painful series of many meetings over many years.

The ceiling for eligibility had been more generous until 2014, when the Hall of Fame's board unexpectedly approved a reduction from fifteen years to ten. "It's become evident, especially over the past thirty years or so, that the likelihood of election after ten years is incredibly minimal," explained Jeff Idelson, then the hall's president.[39]

But his assertion flew in the face of three counterexamples from the previous eight years. The BBWAA had elected reliever Bruce Sutter (class of 2006) on his thirteenth try, starting pitcher Bert Blyleven (2011) in his fourteenth year, and left fielder Jim Rice (2009) on his fifteenth and final appearance on the ballot.

The more likely explanation for 2014's reduction was the specter of Bonds and Clemens, who had become eligible for the hall the previous year. The board was obviously concerned that the controversial duo might slowly gain support, perhaps even reaching 75 percent by 2027, the original end of their eligibility. The cut to ten years removed them from consideration just as both men crossed 65 percent for the first time.

"Do you think the hall saw that coming when it rewrote the rules?" asked Jayson Stark, a veteran baseball writer for *The Athletic*. "I know how I'd answer that."[40]

DAVID ORTIZ HAD PLAYED it cool all day, an act belied by a video that MLB Network played at 7:05.

Ortiz had donned a festive, multicolored shirt at his home in the Dominican Republic that afternoon, and he had spoken calmly and philosophically about his chances of making it to the Hall of Fame. "There's things in life you have no control over," he told a reporter. "I think I did okay, and hopefully at some point it happens."[41]

But none of this nonchalance was evident on the video. The short clip was taken shortly after six o'clock, just minutes before Josh Rawitch's announcement. Ortiz was sitting rigidly in a chair, the epitome of tension, when the telephone rang. BBWAA secretary/treasurer Jack O'Connell came on the line. Ortiz put him on speaker and stared grimly at the phone cupped in his massive hands. "I'm calling you from Cooperstown, New York," said O'Connell, "to let you know the baseball writers have elected you to the National Baseball Hall of Fame."

Ortiz immediately shouted "Yes!" and sprang to his feet, pumping both arms over his head. He bent to his right, simultaneously hugging his father and former Red Sox teammate Pedro Martinez, himself a Hall of Famer. Family members and friends surrounded Ortiz, clapping, cheering, and waving Dominican flags.[42]

The other twenty-nine candidates—and the public—remained in the dark until Rawitch finally uttered Ortiz's name at 6:20. Many of the runners-up hastened to join the applause. Barry Bonds jumped on Instagram: "Congratulations Big Papi on your induction into the Hall of Fame! Well deserved...I love you my brother." Curt Schilling, who had played four seasons with Ortiz in Boston, posted a message on

Twitter: "David Ortiz deserved a 1st ballot induction! Congratulations my friend you earned it!"[43]

Roger Clemens took a different tack, releasing an upbeat statement about his personal situation. He professed a lack of interest in the election results: "My family and I put the HOF in the rear view mirror ten years ago." But this suggestion of insouciance was contradicted by the sheer length of his message—140 words, a veritable screed on Twitter—and by the gratitude he expressed to the writers who voted for him. Clemens closed with a wish that even his detractors could endorse: "Hopefully everyone can now close this book and keep their eyes forward focusing on what is really important in life."[44]

MLB Network did its best to comply in its final hour of coverage. Greg Amsinger and his three companions devoted themselves to Ortiz's twenty-year career. They combed through reams of his statistics, marveled at video clips of his powerful home runs, dissected his batting style with analysts and former players, and interviewed Cooperstown's newest inductee by video link.

But old habits die hard. The four panelists in Studio 21 also wandered back to previous subjects, speaking once again about Bonds and Clemens, even speculating about the timetable for their eventual consideration by an Era Committee. The discussion pivoted shortly before eight o'clock to another star of questionable reputation, Pete Rose, who had been banned from the hall in 1991 before becoming eligible for the ballot. "Nobody wants to nominate him for Citizen of the Year," said Bob Costas. "But, when you look at steroid guys and other transgressors, why wasn't he ever able to be considered?"[45]

And so MLB Network's program ended as it had begun, placing the emphasis on controversy and debate, rather than quality and celebration. That's not to say the announcers were wrong. Harold Reynolds had been deadly accurate with his opening prediction. The next day's headlines would indeed focus more on Bonds and Clemens than on Ortiz.

This unfortunate imbalance admits to only one conclusion: The National Baseball Hall of Fame finds itself in a dark quandary.

"As the keepers of the game's history, the Hall of Fame helps you relive your memories and celebrate baseball history," its website promises.[46]

Yet the hall has turned its back on important aspects of that history. It has chosen to exclude the all-time leaders in hits (Rose) and home runs (Bonds), as well as the pitcher with the most Cy Young Awards (Clemens), even as its plaque gallery honors other men with infamous reputations.

This dilemma is compounded by the unwillingness of the hall's leaders to express a definitive opinion on the PED controversy, which will continue to rage for years to come, certainly as long as Alex Rodriguez remains a candidate. "We just think it's far more important to leave that up to the electorate," Rawitch had said, offering no guidance whatsoever to the perplexed members of the BBWAA.[47]

And then there are those other problems that were so clearly evident on January 25, 2022. The unnecessary complexity of the Hall of Fame's two-tiered voting system, not to mention its surprising ineffectiveness at choosing inductees of the highest quality. The overly restrictive nature of its rules and thresholds. And the lengthy logjam of contenders, a waiting list that serves no real purpose. "What I've done is either enough or it isn't enough," Harmon Killebrew said after falling twelve votes short of election in 1983.[48] He would qualify for induction the following year on his fourth try, but his point remains as valid now as it was four decades ago.

The National Baseball Hall of Fame has delighted millions of visitors since swinging open its doors in 1939, yet its shortcomings have frustrated legions of players, writers, and fans. Legendary sportswriter Red Smith became so exasperated that he once suggested scrapping the hall.[49] Dave Kindred, the lead columnist of the *Sporting News*, echoed the sentiment with an incendiary twist in 2000. "There's nothing wrong with baseball's Hall of Fame," he wrote, "that couldn't be fixed by blowing it up and starting over."[50]

That seems a step too far, but reform is clearly needed. If the hall maintains its present course, its eventual destination might be national indifference—or even complete irrelevance.

Chuck D had posed a germane question in the first minutes of MLB Network's telecast: "When does it end?" Those four words captured the public's impatience with the endless talk about steroids and Rose's gambling and other off-field controversies, as well as a broad desire to refocus on the players—and the game—loved by tens of millions of fans. When, indeed, would the Hall of Fame finally cut through all of the nonsense to reclaim its status as a national shrine?[51]

The best response is another question: Why not now?

CHAPTER TWO

Yardsticks

IF EARL AVERILL HAD reacted in the typical manner, he would have been ecstatic when notified of his election to the Hall of Fame in 1975. But he was different. He was tired and bitter.

Averill had waited more than three decades for the call from Cooperstown, fervently believing that his record warranted a speedier induction. He had batted .318 between 1929 and 1941, spending the bulk of that time—ten full seasons and a small part of another—in center field for the Cleveland Indians. His greatest year was 1936, when he pushed his average up to .378 and led the American League with 232 hits and 15 triples. Averill finished among the top ten vote-getters for the AL's Most Valuable Player Award on four occasions, and he had the distinction of being the only outfielder named to the first six All-Star teams (1933-1938) in either league.[1]

But the Hall of Fame electorate never seemed to be very impressed. Averill received a grand total of thirty-six votes from the BBWAA between 1949 and 1962, peaking at a measly 5.3 percent in 1958. He then bounced to the Veterans Committee, a forerunner of the Era Committees, which kicked his name around for a decade before finally granting admission.

Averill was one of six players to amass at least two thousand hits in the major leagues from 1929 through 1941. The other five were welcomed to the plaque gallery between 1949 and 1956, yet he was kept outside for another nineteen years. Averill insisted in his induction speech that he wasn't resentful—despite evidence to the contrary—though he did admit to confusion. "It's based on the fact that statistics alone are not enough to gain a player such recognition," he said. "What right does anyone have to ignore cold hard facts in favor of looking for some intangible item to keep a person out of Cooperstown?"[2]

Red Ruffing understood completely. The right-handed starting pitcher had been a mainstay of the New York Yankees' rotation, winning 219 games between 1930 and 1942. The only big-league pitcher credited with more victories over that 13-year period was Carl Hubbell with 221. But a broader perspective gave the edge to Ruffing, whose total career, including stops with the Red Sox and White Sox, spanned 22 seasons and 273 wins. Hubbell's respective totals were 16 and 253.

The BBWAA saw it differently. The writers punched Hubbell's ticket in 1947, his third year of eligibility, giving him 87 percent of their votes. Ruffing was unable to crawl above 15 percent until his eighth year on the ballot. He finally sneaked into the hall on his fifteenth and final try, winning a rare runoff election in 1967.

"I was a little bitter," he admitted. "If they put men in for their record, I think I should have been in before. I was wondering if it was a popularity contest, or if they were going on a man's record." Ruffing, like Averill, contended that statistics were the only yardsticks that could accurately measure a player's Hall of Fame credentials, and he considered length of service to be especially important. "I think if a man plays twenty years in the major leagues, he should be in automatically," Ruffing said.[3]

Both men were understandably annoyed by the long delays they had endured, but they went too far in portraying themselves as victims of an ingrained bias against statistics. Averages, rates, and totals were important ingredients in the recipe for the hall's first honorees in 1936, and they remain essential today. "Statistics have always played a large role in determining who gets into the Hall of Fame—and, in fact, they should, because statistics, carefully considered, provide awfully good evidence about the quality of a player's contribution," wrote Bill James, who was instrumental in marrying baseball with data analysis.[4]

The real question is this: Should the Hall of Fame act on Averill's and Ruffing's complaints by making statistics—"cold hard facts," as the former called them—the only criteria for induction? It's a tempting concept, isn't it? And it's one that has already been adopted by another sport.

The Ladies Professional Golf Association uses a simple mechanism to determine which players are admitted to the LPGA Hall of Fame. Any candidate was required to meet a pair of qualifying standards—playing at least ten years on the tour and winning a major championship—until the former condition was eliminated in 2022. Any qualifier must accumulate twenty-seven points for induction. Each victory in a regular tournament counts for one point; each title in a designated major tourney is worth two. Single points are awarded for winning the Player of the Year Award or the Vare Trophy. The former is the LPGA's version of baseball's MVP; the latter goes to the woman with the best scoring average in a given year. (An Olympic gold medal is also worth one point as of 2022).[5]

It would seem to be an ideal system—stringent, yet equally applicable to all candidates; rigorous, though easy for fans to understand.

But here's the problem: It's an incredibly difficult benchmark to meet. Only twenty-five women were inducted into the LPGA's hall between 1967 and 2021, the equivalent of one every 2.2 years. Not a single player made the grade during the eight years following 2007. Inbee Park, who finally reached twenty-seven points in 2016, remained the most recent inductee until the standards were loosened six years later.[6]

That doesn't sound like a system that would cure Cooperstown's ills. If anything, a rigid statistical threshold would extend the Hall of Fame's waiting list of qualified candidates, a line that is already too long. And it would do nothing to resolve those never-ending complaints about fairness. Critics unhappy with the current election structure are unlikely to be appeased by an artificial point requirement.

Let's face it. Subjectivity plays an important role in the hall's induction process, as it should. Bill James, the ultimate numbers guy, has long conceded the point. "There are things in baseball which can't be measured in statistics or which aren't well measured in statistics," he wrote.[7]

Cooperstown's class of 2022 proved the truth of James's observation. Gil Hodges was a fine first baseman, but what may have put him over the top with the Golden Days Committee was the glorious world title he won as manager of the New York Mets in 1969. Jim Kaat enhanced his pitching reputation with a fine second career as a base-ball broadcaster, ultimately spending more years in press boxes than his twenty-five seasons on big-league mounds. "Worthiness of the Baseball Hall of Fame does not end with a playing career," wrote Tom Verducci. "Other contributions to the game also matter. Character also matters. *Fame* also matters."[8]

So we can forget about adapting the LPGA's scheme to fit Cooperstown's needs. An automatic induction threshold simply would not work for baseball. Yet the concept of a simple point system might still have its uses. This book, for instance, intends to assess the players currently in line for admission to the Hall of Fame, as well as those who already reside within. Assigning a point value to each player would facilitate those comparisons.

Such a system, as I see it, should have four objectives:

• It should measure a player's performance over three spans: short (each season individually), midrange (five consecutive years), and long (an entire career).

• It should encompass all aspects of the game: batting, fielding, and pitching.

• It should use traditional averages and counting stats, though it should not ignore newer analytics.

• It should somehow level the statistical field, so that different eras can be compared fairly.

I kept these goals in mind as I developed such a point system, which I'm calling quality score (QS). It's a single number that encapsulates a player's full range of on-field achievements. QS is plotted on a one-hundred-point scale, though nobody has ever attained a triple-digit score. The highest QS in baseball history is not tied to Babe Ruth, Cy Young, Henry Aaron, Barry Bonds, or any of the usual suspects. It belongs to Honus Wagner, the incomparable shortstop for the Pittsburgh Pirates, who retired in 1917 and was one of the first five players elected to the Hall of Fame in 1936. Wagner finished his amazing twenty-one-year career with a QS of ninety-eight.

I must stress one thing at the very start: QS is not a binary indicator. It does not render a yes-or-no verdict on a specific Hall of Fame candidate. (Remember those important subjective considerations that we discussed a few paragraphs back? They're beyond its scope.) QS is a yardstick that provides a quick and valuable indication of a player's relative standing among his peers. Let's take a closer look at how it's derived—and what it means.

I'VE CALCULATED QUALITY SCORES for 873 men who played big-league ball between 1871 and 2020. This pool includes all 268 players who have already been inducted into the Hall of Fame, as well as 605 plausible contenders. (Yes, David Ortiz was the 340th person elected to the hall, yet just the 268th player. The remaining seventy-two honorees were managers, executives, and umpires.)

How did I decide which players to rate? We'll deal with that question after we tackle two other tasks: defining the major leagues and explaining the chosen time span.

Most of us think of the majors as an umbrella that covers only two leagues, the American and the National. But several circuits of similar quality and scope functioned during the early decades of baseball history, a group that swelled retroactively in December 2020, when Commissioner Rob Manfred conferred major status upon the long-defunct Negro leagues.[9] Here is the full list of thirteen major leagues:

- American Association (1882-1891)
- American League (1901 to the present)
- American Negro League (1929)
- East-West League (1932)
- Eastern Colored League (1923-1928)
- Federal League (1914-1915)
- National Association (1871-1875)
- National League (1876 to the present)
- Negro American League (1937-1948)
- Negro National League (1920-1931, 1933-1948)
- Negro Southern League (1932)
- Players League (1890)
- Union Association (1884)

If you're a true student of baseball history, you'll notice that I snuck one entry into the list. Purists have long contended that the National Association does not deserve big-league status. The Special Baseball Records Committee issued a determination along those lines in 1968, condemning the NA for its "erratic schedule and procedures."[10] The committee ruled that all National Association statistics should be kept out of the official record book.

I don't have a dog in this fight. I do know that the NA was considered to be the nation's premier professional league in its time, but if the historians wish to exclude it, that's fine by me. Except for one thing.

If you stop in front of Cap Anson's plaque in the Hall of Fame's central atrium, you'll read that he "was [a] .300 class hitter 20 years, batting champion 4 times." If you go to the hall's website, you'll find this: "When he retired after the 1897 season at the age of 45, Anson owned big league records for games, hits, at-bats, doubles, and runs. He finished with 3,435 hits, becoming the first player ever to cross the 3,000-hit line."[11]

Anson starred in the National Association throughout its five-year history, departing in 1876 for the National League's Chicago franchise, where he remained for the rest of his career. He batted .300 or better in twenty-four of his twenty-seven seasons, yet his plaque seems to confine itself to his NL tenure. Nineteen (not twenty) of Anson's .300 seasons occurred in that league, as did all four batting titles. But the website is more generous. Anson had 3,012 hits in the National League. His total climbs to 3,435 only if the National Association is included. The sport's statistical oracle, Baseball Reference, also credits Anson with 3,435 hits.[12]

That's good enough for me. If baseball's ultimate arbiters now appear to recognize the National Association as a major league, so will I. That decision, in turn, explains why my ratings begin in 1871. I selected 2020 as my endpoint because, first, it's a nice round number, and second, anybody who retires after 2020 won't be eligible for the Hall of Fame until well after this book is published.

The playoffs raise another dilemma. Many Hall of Famers have cemented their legends in the World Series. Let your mind drift back to Babe Ruth and his controversial "called shot" against the Cubs in 1932, Willie Mays and his sensational over-the-shoulder catch of Vic Wertz's blast in 1954, Bill Mazeroski and his walk-off homer to send the Yankees packing in 1960, and Reggie Jackson and his three home runs on three consecutive swings in 1977. Shouldn't such postseason heroics be folded into my ratings?

I pondered this question long and hard, finally deciding that fairness required me to confine QS to regular-season statistics.

A surprisingly large number of Hall of Famers never appeared in the World Series—or any postseason series—through no fault of their own. George Sisler batted a torrid .340 over his fifteen-year career. Was he any less a hitter because he spent all but three of those seasons with the miserable St. Louis Browns? Ernie Banks won a pair of MVP trophies. Was his excellence diminished because he wore the uniform of the lowly Chicago Cubs for nearly two decades? And what about Luke Appling, Rod Carew, Ken Griffey Jr., Fergie Jenkins, Ralph Kiner, Ted Lyons, Phil Niekro, Gaylord Perry, Ron Santo, Frank Thomas, and Billy Williams? Great players all, yet their combined total of World Series games was zero. It wouldn't be right to reduce their quality scores because of the inadequacies of their teams.

More than twenty thousand men have played big-league ball since 1871. I saw no reason to generate a QS for each and every one, since the vast majority finished well short of Cooperstown's standards. I used a series of statistical tests to build my list of 873 plausible finalists, welcoming to the pool anybody who reached one or more of my five benchmarks. The details follow.

One-Year Test

THE HALL OF FAME's guidelines are vague in many respects—remember Rule 5?—but not when it comes to downplaying the value of a single outstanding season.

This is Rule 6: "No automatic elections based on performances such as a batting average of .400 or more for one year, pitching a perfect game, or similar outstanding achievement shall be permitted."[13] There goes Don Larsen's hope of ever getting a plaque. Roger Maris's, too, since his primary claim to fame was those sixty-one homers in 1961.

But don't misunderstand. It's still important for a candidate to impress the voters with an outstanding season or two or three, provided that those peak years highlight an otherwise strong career. "One of the most dependable patterns in Hall of Fame voting, both in the BBWAA vote and from the Veterans Committee, is that players who have big seasons are much more likely to be selected than are players of equal overall accomplishment, but greater consistency," wrote Bill James.[14]

This point was dramatized by contemporary right-handed pitchers Don Drysdale and Milt Pappas. Their records were virtually identical. Drysdale wrapped up his career in 1969 with 209 wins against 166 losses; Pappas finished four years later with a mark of 209-164. Their similarity was confirmed by Baseball Reference, which compares the statistics for each big-league player against the corresponding numbers for everybody else who made it to the majors, more than twenty thousand players over a century and a half. The closest match for Drysdale, says the website, was Pappas.[15]

Yet the BBWAA failed to see the resemblance. The writers elected Drysdale to the hall in 1984 on his tenth try. They eliminated Pappas in his initial year on the ballot, 1979, giving him just five votes.

Why the disparity? Drysdale's highlights were more impressive—and certainly more memorable. The righty with the blazing fastball won the Cy Young Award in 1962, while topping the majors in victories (25) and strikeouts (232). He led the big leagues in strikeouts on two other occasions (1959 and 1960) and qualified for eight All-Star teams. Pappas never finished higher than ninth in Cy Young balloting, never won more than seventeen games in a season, never led the majors in any stat but wild pitches, and was named to two All-Star squads.

Pappas, to be fair, does deserve a footnote in Hall of Fame history. He was initially left off of 1979's BBWAA ballot, but he demanded that the snub be overturned. "What are they doing to me?" he complained. "I won 209 games." The BBWAA eventually relented and added his name. His protest ultimately did Pappas no good—he drew just 1.2 percent support—though it did inspire the current practice of listing every eligible retiree who played at least ten years in the majors.[16]

The larger lesson of the Drysdale-Pappas comparison is obvious. Hall of Fame voters put major stock in breakout seasons, which is why I created my one-year test. I awarded points for league-leading performances in the following nineteen categories each season:

Five Points

- Most Valuable Player Award (all players)
- Wins above replacement (all players)

Four Points

- Wins above replacement (position players)

Three Points

- Batting average (batters)
- Defensive wins above replacement (position players)
- Earned-run average (pitchers)
- Home runs (batters)
- Runs batted in (batters)
- Strikeouts (pitchers)
- Wins (pitchers)

Two Points

- Cy Young Award (pitchers)
- Hits (batters)
- Reliever of the Year Award (pitchers)
- Runs scored (batters)
- Saves (pitchers)
- Slugging average (batters)
- Strikeouts per walk (pitchers)
- Walks and hits per innings pitched (pitchers)
- Wins above replacement (pitchers)

Allow me to explain the logic that undergirds this point pyramid. Baseball's ultimate award, the MVP, and the game's all-inclusive statistic, WAR, constitute the apex. A separate rating of WAR for position players—everybody but pitchers—sits a rung below. The three-point level features the Triple Crown stats for batters (BA, HR, RBI) and pitchers (ERA, SO, W) and WAR for fielders. Nearly half of the categories—nine of nineteen—form the base, doling out two points apiece for a pair of pitching awards and lesser stats for pitchers and hitters. If two or more players tie in any category, each co-leader receives the full amount of points.

A few tweaks were necessary. Most Valuable Players were named spasmodically in the 1910s and 1920s, but the award wasn't firmly established until 1931. The Cy Young Award was created in 1956, though only one annual winner was selected. The current practice of celebrating the top pitcher in each league wasn't instituted until 1967. And don't forget the eleven leagues other than the American and National. They never gave out MVPs or Cy Young Awards at all.

How did I fill the gaps? By declaring that the overall WAR leader was the MVP for a given league that did not hand out a trophy in a particular season, and by giving the Cy Young Award to the pitcher with the highest WAR (including, ironically, Cy Young himself on six occasions) in similar years. My system still distributed points for overall and pitching WAR in any season that lacked formal awards, so those categories essentially counted twice.

The Reliever of the Year Award posed a problem, too. It has been handed out annually in both leagues since 1976, with a brief hiatus in 2013. I extended it back to 1961 (roughly the time when relief pitchers began to attain their current importance) and also filled the 2013 holes by substituting the reliever with a league's highest WAR in each season.

If you perused the point list, you might have been struck by an apparent disparity. Pitching WAR (two points) has been assigned only half the value of WAR for position players (four). Why? Because the top pitcher in terms of WAR is likely to win either Cy Young or Reliever of the Year recognition, too, thereby boosting his combined haul to four points. There is no corresponding award for position players. (Everybody—pitchers and batters alike—is eligible to be the MVP.)

Let's examine Mickey Mantle's superlative performance in 1956 to see the one-year test in action. The Yankees center fielder was named the American League's Most Valuable Player (5 points) after piling up 11.2 wins above replacement (5 points for leading all AL players in WAR, another 4 for topping the position players). He won the Triple Crown with 52 homers, 130 runs batted in, and a .353 batting average (3 points apiece). He also paced the AL by scoring 132 runs and slugging .705 (2 points each).

Mantle's total haul in 1956 was twenty-seven points. That's an exceptionally high sum for a single year, roughly double the fourteen points, say, that Mike Trout earned during his impressive 2014 season. The Angels center fielder won the American League's MVP Award that year, while leading the AL in WAR for position players, runs scored, and runs batted in.

Trout's list of honors was not as lengthy as Mantle's, though an important distinction must be made. Trout played in a fifteen-club league, almost twice the size of Mantle's eight-team circuit. Competition for awards and statistical leadership obviously becomes more intense when a league adds teams and players. Seventy-seven batters achieved the necessary number of plate appearances to qualify for the batting title in 2014, surpassing 1956's number of qualifiers (forty-one) by 87.8 percent. That's remarkably close to the 87.5 percent difference between the number of clubs that took the field in those two seasons.

The obvious solution is to adjust the point totals to reflect the relative level of competition. An award in 2014, for example, should be weighted 87.5 percent more heavily than the same honor in 1956. Here's the formula:

Final points = Raw points • (Number of clubs / 8)

The American and National Leagues contained eight clubs apiece during the first six decades of the twentieth century, so I chose that number for my base. I adjusted the points for leagues of every size, even as tiny as the five-team Eastern Colored League of 1928. There was no need to get complicated, so I rounded each multiplier (the number of clubs divided by 8) to a single decimal place, such as 1.9 for a 15-team league, and similarly rounded each final answer. Here are the resulting point structures for the different league sizes that we've seen since 1950:

Clubs: 8

5 base points: 5.0 converted points
4 base points: 4.0 converted points
3 base points: 3.0 converted points
2 base points: 2.0 converted points

Clubs: 10

5 base points: 6.5 converted points
4 base points: 5.2 converted points
3 base points: 3.9 converted points
2 base points: 2.6 converted points

Clubs: 12

5 base points: 7.5 converted points
4 base points: 6.0 converted points
3 base points: 4.5 converted points
2 base points: 3.0 converted points

Clubs: 14

5 base points: 9.0 converted points
4 base points: 7.2 converted points
3 base points: 5.4 converted points
2 base points: 3.6 converted points

Clubs: 15

5 base points: 9.5 converted points
4 base points: 7.6 converted points
3 base points: 5.7 converted points
2 base points: 3.8 converted points

Clubs: 16

5 base points: 10.0 converted points
4 base points: 8.0 converted points
3 base points: 6.0 converted points
2 base points: 4.0 converted points

Trout's MVP trophy in 2014's 15-club American League was worth 5 base points, which translated to 9.5 converted points, as you can see above. His leadership in the other three categories brought 7.6 converted points for WAR for position players, 5.7 for runs batted in, and 3.8 for runs scored. Grand total: 26.6 points, virtually the same as Mantle's 1956 output.

So that's the one-year test, though I must admit it's a bit of a misnomer. Yes, the points reflect single-season excellence, but a player's rating is not based on his peak performance. It's determined by the sum of all point totals throughout his career. The following list shows the twenty-five point leaders of all time. Hall of Famers in this list—and all other lists in this chapter—are designated by asterisks.

One-Year Test Sums

1. Barry Bonds, 257.5
2. Babe Ruth, 218.0*
3. Roger Clemens, 208.4
4. Cy Young, 200.0*
5. Alex Rodriguez, 194.4
6. Walter Johnson, 192.0*
7. Albert Pujols, 188.0
8. Rogers Hornsby, 179.0*
9. Randy Johnson, 158.4*
10. Willie Mays, 155.4*
11. Josh Gibson, 153.7*
12. Christy Mathewson, 140.0*
13. Clayton Kershaw, 138.8
14. Ted Williams, 136.0*
15. Mike Trout, 135.7
16. Lefty Grove, 135.0*
17. Mike Schmidt, 133.5*
18. Pete Alexander, 133.0*
19. Ty Cobb, 130.0*
20. Pedro Martinez, 125.0*
21. Honus Wagner, 123.0*
22. Kid Nichols, 117.5*
23. Greg Maddux, 112.6*
24. Stan Musial, 112.0*
25. Justin Verlander, 108.5

And what of Don Drysdale and Milt Pappas, whom we compared at the beginning of this section? Both finished well down the list, but that doesn't mean their results were comparable. Drysdale amassed 25.6 points during his career, a sum roughly 10 times larger than Pappas's 2.6. Bill James was right. Peak performances really do matter.

I'll come back to the one-year test later in this chapter, explaining its role in the generation of quality scores. But we need to discuss other yardsticks first.

Five-Year Test

LET ME TELL YOU about a pitcher. He's a young guy—just twenty-five years old—who possesses a supersonic fastball and a curve that drops off the table. An amazing prospect, though he has a serious problem.

His control is erratic on his best days, nonexistent on his worst. He has been knocking around the majors for 6 years, and his stats are decidedly unimpressive: 36-40 with an ERA of 4.10.

What are his odds of making the Hall of Fame? Zero, wouldn't you say?

You might think again if I told you that Sandy Koufax was the pitcher in question.

Koufax followed that mediocre 1955-1960 period with one of the most astonishing six-year streaks in big-league history. He went 129-47 with a 2.19 ERA—*yes, 2.19!*—in 211 starts between 1961 and 1966, winning an MVP Award and 3 Cy Young Awards. And that was back when the pitchers in both leagues competed for a single Cy.

An arthritic elbow forced Koufax to retire prior to his thirty-first birthday, but nobody doubted that he was destined for Cooperstown. Nobody but the man himself. "I'm a little surprised I got so many votes," he said upon his first-ballot election in 1972. "I didn't have as many good years as many people who are in the Hall of Fame. My career lasted twelve years, but only six were good ones."[17]

Those six seasons weren't just good, of course. They were exceptional. And they demonstrated how a multiyear run of excellence can elevate the candidacy of any Hall of Fame hopeful.

Hence my five-year test, which distills a century and a half of major-league statistics into seventy midrange groups. Each of these bites is confined to a single league. Fifty-eight of them are precisely half a decade long, starting with the National Association's run from 1871 to 1875, and ending with the final five years of my study period (2016-2020) in the American and National Leagues.

These are the twelve exceptions:

• Five leagues survived for a single year: the Union Association (1884), Players League (1890), American Negro League (1929), East-West League (1932), and Negro Southern League (1932).

• The Federal League played two seasons, 1914 to 1915.

• I divided three circuits with longer lifespans into six-year groups, a total of six such fragments in all. The Eastern Colored League was an easy decision, since it existed for exactly six years (1923-1928). The

Negro American League endured for twelve seasons, which I split into 1937-1942 and 1943-1948, a simpler move than creating a trio of four-year slivers. The same consideration led me to divide the Negro National League into three six-year spans (1920-1925, 1926-1931, 1938-1943) and a pair of five-year groups.

My aim was to identify the top batters and pitchers in each of these seventy groups. I began by setting eligibility thresholds: 2 plate appearances per game for hitters, 1 start every 10.8 games for starters, and 1 appearance every 5.4 games for relievers. These rates translate to the following 5-season standards under the current 162-game slate: 1,620 trips to the plate, 75 starts, or 150 relief appearances, each of which could be met by even a part-time player. Previous leagues played schedules of different lengths, of course, so I adjusted their thresholds accordingly.

The resulting groups of eligible batters ranged from as many as 102 in the American League's 1976-1980 cohort to as few as 30 for the Negro National League from 1944 to 1948. Pitchers reached a maximum of 142 for the National League's 2006-2010 group and a minimum of 20 in both the National Association (1871-1875) and the Negro American League (1937-1942).

Allow me to hastily append an asterisk to the 2006-2010 total I just mentioned. I began dividing pitchers into separate collections of starters and relievers as of 1961-1965, a policy I continued through the most recent half-decade, 2016-2020. (Almost all pitchers who qualified prior to 1961 were starters, so no subdivision was necessary in those earlier years.) The National League actually had 62 starters and 80 relievers in its respective 2006-2010 groups, yielding the previously mentioned total of 142.

I generated six sets of statistics for each batting and pitching group and converted them to rates, allowing for easy and fair comparisons of the eligible players. Only a couple of the stats listed below require explanation. Bases per out (BPO) is a ratio of the bases that a batter attained (through hits, walks, hit batsmen, stolen bases, and sacrifices) to the outs he made. Wins and saves are added at a two-to-one ratio, then converted to a rate per thirty games. Early Wynn, for example, notched precisely 100 wins and 7 saves while pitching 187 games in the American League between 1951 and 1955. He received 207 points (200 for the wins, 7 for the saves), which worked out to 33.21 points per 30 games.

Five-Year Test (Batters)
- Batting average
- Slugging average
- Bases per out
- Runs scored per five hundred plate appearances
- Runs batted in per five hundred plate appearances
- Wins above replacement per five hundred plate appearances

Five-Year Test (Pitchers)
- Wins plus saves per thirty games
- Earned-run average
- Walks and hits per inning pitched
- Strikeouts per nine innings
- Strikeouts per walk
- Wins above replacement per one hundred innings

There's no reason to go into great detail about how I ranked the players in each group. Suffice it to say that I used standard deviations and z-scores. What's important is that I wound up with a top-to-bottom list. I then assigned a point total to each player, based on the percentage of competitors that he outranked.

Let's look at the American League between 2006 and 2010. A total of 101 batters crossed the eligibility threshold for that group, with the best scores going to the 10 hitters listed below. Each is shown with the percentage of contestants that he surpassed. Joe Mauer, for instance, finished in fourth place, putting him ahead of ninety-seven of the other one hundred hitters, precisely 97.0 percent.

Five-Year Test (American League Batters, 2006-2010)
1. Alex Rodriguez, 100.0%
2. Miguel Cabrera, 99.0%
3. Josh Hamilton, 98.0%
4. Joe Mauer, 97.0%
5. David Ortiz, 96.0%
6. Evan Longoria, 95.0%
7. Jim Thome, 94.0%

8. Kevin Youkilis, 93.0%
9. Mark Teixeira, 92.0%
10. Manny Ramirez, 91.0%

I converted each player's percentage into his final score for the given five-year test. Rodriguez earned the maximum of 100.0 points in the AL's 2006-2010 cohort, while Mauer picked up 97.0. All scores were rounded to one decimal place. If a league existed for less than five years, its results were downgraded accordingly. Maximum scores were set at forty points for the two-year Federal League and twenty points for any of the five leagues that lasted a single season.

A total of 164 group champions emerged from the battery of five-year tests—70 batters, 46 pre-1961 pitchers, and separate post-1960 sets of 24 starters and 24 relievers. I see no reason to list them all, but I have assembled a shorter rundown of repeat winners. The sixteen batters and thirteen pitchers shown below earned one hundred points on multiple five-year tests. All but four of these superstars have been enshrined in Cooperstown.

Five-Year Test Champions (Batters)

Josh Gibson, 3*
Stan Musial, 3*
Babe Ruth, 3*
Ross Barnes, 2
Barry Bonds, 2
Dan Brouthers, 2*
Willard Brown, 2*
Oscar Charleston, 2*
Ty Cobb, 2*
Rogers Hornsby, 2*
Chuck Klein, 2*
Mickey Mantle, 2*
Willie Mays, 2*
Alex Rodriguez, 2
Honus Wagner, 2*
Ted Williams, 2*

Five-Year Test Champions (Pitchers)

Satchel Paige, 4*
Walter Johnson, 3*
Mariano Rivera, 3*

Pete Alexander, 2*
Bert Blyleven, 2*
Dennis Eckersley, 2*
Rich Gossage, 2*
Lefty Grove, 2*
Randy Johnson, 2*
Clayton Kershaw, 2
Pedro Martinez, 2*
Christy Mathewson, 2*
Dazzy Vance, 2*

The five-year test is an ideal indicator of midrange excellence, as demonstrated by its ability to capture Sandy Koufax's sudden emergence as the preeminent pitcher of his time. Koufax skyrocketed from 31.0 points in the National League's 1956-1960 rankings to a perfect score of 100.0 in 1961-1965.

But what about the players who were highly regarded, yet never quite reached the top? Phil Niekro won 318 games during a career that stretched from 1964 to 1987. The knuckleballer's victory total was certainly impressive, though Niekro didn't dominate hitters the way Koufax did. He made just five All-Star teams in twenty-four seasons, and he never picked up a Cy Young Award.

Niekro qualified for a quartet of five-year tests, always failing to reach the ninety-point barrier. He earned 76.2, 87.0, 83.3, and 43.2 points, respectively, during the half-decades between 1966 and 1985. The first three scores were well above average, to be sure, though they fell short of being extraordinary.

Our perspective changes, however, if we add Niekro's results. His five-year tests yielded a sum of 289.7 points, a figure surpassed by only 29 pitchers in history. My standings show Christy Mathewson (296.4) just ahead of Niekro, and Carl Hubbell (288.1) just behind. That's an imposing set of Hall of Fame bookends.

So, as we can see, the five-year test is useful in a second way. It not only quantifies a player's performance at his peak, but it also singles out the batters and pitchers who were able to reel off strong half-decades in consecutive order. The following chart shows the twenty-five players with the highest sums on five-year tests.

Five-Year Test Sums

1. Babe Ruth, 483.4*
2. Cap Anson, 451.6*
3. John Smoltz, 431.8*
4. Jim O'Rourke, 400.1*
5. Satchel Paige, 400.0*
6. Turkey Stearnes, 399.1*
7. Walter Johnson, 392.9*
8. Willie Mays, 392.7*
9. Henry Aaron, 392.4*
10. Ty Cobb, 390.8*
11. Barry Bonds, 387.9
12. Roger Clemens, 387.7
13. Greg Maddux, 387.3*
14. Stan Musial, 386.5*
15. Mel Ott, 385.2*
16. Frank Robinson, 383.0*
17. Honus Wagner, 382.3*
18. Nap Lajoie, 381.4*
19. Mike Schmidt, 381.3*
20. Pete Alexander, 379.1*
21. Paul Molitor, 378.9*
22. Fergie Jenkins, 377.4*
23. Mike Mussina, 376.0*
24. Bullet Rogan, 375.2*
25. Alex Rodriguez, 374.5

Fifty-eight players amassed more than three hundred points on their five-year tests. Only six of the thirty-six batters and two of the twenty-two pitchers can't be found in Cooperstown's plaque gallery, and most of their exclusions are easily explained. You know all about the problems plaguing Barry Bonds, Alex Rodriguez, Roger Clemens, and Pete Rose. Adrian Beltre won't be eligible for the Hall of Fame ballot until 2024, and Miguel Cabrera will have to wait even longer.

The other two outsiders, Paul Hines and Jesse Orosco, simply seem to have faded into unwarranted obscurity. Hines, a hard-hitting outfielder, retired in 1891 and died in 1935. Orosco, the all-time leader in games pitched, received a single vote in his only BBWAA election in 2009.

Hall of Fame Monitor

I WANTED TO INCLUDE one test that had been developed by somebody else, just in case my biases or inaccuracies were excluding qualified candidates from the pool. I settled on the Hall of Fame monitor, which has an impeccable family tree. It was invented by Bill James, the high priest of sabermetrics, and it was popularized by Baseball Reference, a statistical repository of inestimable value.

The monitor assesses the likelihood that a player will eventually be inducted into the Hall of Fame. It allocates points for winning awards or reaching statistical benchmarks during a single season or a career. The formula is lengthy, so I won't delineate it here. If you're interested, it can be seen on Baseball Reference's website.

There are two thresholds to keep in mind. Any player who earns at least 130 points on the Hall of Fame monitor is labeled a virtual cinch for induction, while anybody who lands between 100 and 129 points is rated as a good possibility. Below are the twenty-five players with the highest scores.

Hall of Fame Monitor

1. Stan Musial, 452*
2. Ty Cobb, 445*
3. Henry Aaron, 421*
4. Babe Ruth, 411*
5. Alex Rodriguez, 390
6. Willie Mays, 376*
7. Walter Johnson, 364*
8. Ted Williams, 354*
9. Lou Gehrig, 352*
10. Rogers Hornsby, 350*
11. Barry Bonds, 340
12. Cy Young, 338*
13. Derek Jeter, 337*
14. Roger Clemens, 332
15. Randy Johnson, 331*
15. Albert Pujols, 331
17. Jimmie Foxx, 314*
18. Honus Wagner, 313*
19. Pete Rose, 311
20. Christy Mathewson, 303*

21. Mickey Mantle, 301*
22. Tony Gwynn, 279*
23. Charlie Gehringer, 277*
24. Tim Keefe, 271*
25. Joe DiMaggio, 269*

No prediction formula is flawless, a rule that holds true in this case. The Hall of Fame monitor has been wrong about roughly one of every seven candidates that it classifies as highly qualified. The 130-point threshold has been crossed by 108 eligible batters and 56 eligible pitchers, but only 94 of the former and 47 of the latter have been rewarded with induction. The respective accuracy rates are 87 and 84 percent—not perfect by any means, yet pretty good when you consider the numerous quirks in the hall's election system.

The Pool

I DECIDED TO CAST a wide net when I started the process of generating quality scores. I gathered statistics for every big leaguer who ever won an award or led a statistical category listed among the criteria for the one-year test, or who amassed enough plate appearances or innings pitched to qualify for any five-year test, or who scored at least eighty points on the Hall of Fame monitor.

The grand total: 5,267 players, which was way, way too many. I wanted to focus on current or prospective Hall of Famers, but this massive horde contained such small fry as Eufemio Abreu, Ace Adams, Chuffy Alexander, Mel Almada, Whitey Alpermann, and Jerry Augustine, just to mention a few names atop the alphabetical list.

So I drained the pool and removed the bottom feeders. The only players who were allowed to keep swimming were those who met or exceeded a predetermined level of excellence on any of my tests, which were applied in this order:

• The 268 players in the Hall of Fame automatically qualified.

• Another 222 candidates scored at least 15 points on the one-year test over the course of their careers, bringing the pool's population to 490.

• An additional 256 achieved a peak score of 90 or better on a single five-year test, which meant they ranked among the top 10 percent of their league's batters or pitchers for half a decade. They increased the membership to 746.

• Seventy-four candidates qualified by totaling 200 points or more when all of their five-year test results were added, boosting the pool to 820.

• Fifty-three members made it on the fifth and final test by receiving at least eighty points from the Hall of Fame monitor. The total number of qualifiers: 873.

A player automatically joined the pool as soon as he met a single standard, but don't be misled by my step-by-step winnowing process. Most candidates succeeded on multiple tests. A total of 110 Hall of Famers passed all 5 benchmarks, another 98 players reached 4 of the 5 thresholds, and an additional 109 candidates attained the required marks on 3 tests.

The resulting list is a comprehensive roster of the game's greatest players. I'm not going to waste space by listing all 873 pool members—a rundown that would take several pages—but I can provide a quick summary.

Each player was assigned a primary position, which usually was a simple process. (Yet not always. Frank Thomas is listed by the Hall of Fame as a first baseman, though you could make a strong case for him as a designated hitter. The same dichotomy applies to shortstop Ernie Banks, who spent several seasons at first base.) The two largest groups in the pool are starting pitchers (296) and relief pitchers (100), who collectively account for 45 percent of the membership.

Eighty-three first basemen carry the banner for the off-mound position with the greatest representation. Next come the outfielders (seventy-eight in right field, sixty-five in center, sixty-one in left), followed by the remaining infielders (fifty-five shortstops, forty-eight at third base, thirty-nine at second base). There are thirty-nine catchers in the pool, equaling the number of second basemen. Last place belongs to the newest position, designated hitter, with nine.

Not everybody in the pool is eligible for the Hall of Fame at this time. A total of 764 players had retired by the end of 2016, including the 268 who have already been inducted. That leaves 496 outsiders who had met the cutoff by 2022. But the other 109 players remained active in 2017 and beyond, many of them into the following decade. They won't be showing up on the ballot anytime soon.

Adjusted Statistics

You know what old-timers are like. They're contemptuous of the way baseball has evolved since their era. They insist that modern players are unskilled and modern salaries are exorbitant. Listen to a former third baseman: "Baseball today is not what it should be. It makes me weep to think of the men of the old days and the boys of today. It's positively a shame—and they are getting big money for it, too." A Hall of Fame center fielder chimes in: "The great trouble with baseball today is that most of the players are in the game for the money."[18]

Who might these faultfinders be? A couple of discontented, underpaid stars from the 1960s or 1970s, moaning about the twenty-first century version of the game?

Not even close. Both critics—Bill Joyce and Ty Cobb—passed from the ranks of the living more than sixty years ago. They were sounding off in 1916 and 1925, respectively.

It has always been this way. Every baseball generation expresses a low opinion of the ones that follow. Hall of Famer Reggie Jackson is a recent addition to the chorus. "I struck out more times than anyone in the history of the game, almost twenty-six hundred times, but I did it over twenty years," Jackson said in 2021. "That's 125 strikeouts per year. A leadoff guy today strikes out 125 times. It's not productive. The game has changed so much, and for the worse."[19]

These disgruntled old-timers occasionally make a valid point, but much of their criticism flies in the face of observation. Athletes are steadily raising the bar in sports that are easily measurable. Runners and swimmers are completing their races more quickly. High jumpers and pole vaulters are soaring higher. Why would baseball players, in defiance of this trend, actually be getting worse?

That's what ESPN's David Schoenfield wondered, so he sat down after the 2018 season and watched tapes of two postseason games from four decades earlier. He found much to like in the previous version of baseball, especially the brisker pace of play. But Schoenfield also came to admire the skill of modern players: "If anything, after watching 1978 baseball, you'll realize this about the game in 2018: (1) Hitting is much more difficult now, given how hard the pitchers throw. (2) Pitching is much more difficult now, given how much better the hitters are."[20]

Jimmy Lanier was in a unique position to understand this clash between old and new. Lanier served as a batboy in the 1920s for the Detroit Tigers, a team managed by none other than Cobb, who, though nearly forty, still roamed center field and hit for an exceptional average (.378 in 1925). Lanier later moved to Atlanta, becoming such a devoted Braves fan that he regularly watched them on television into his nineties.

"All these young stars today are so wonderful, and the playing conditions are so much better now," he told an Atlanta reporter. "But the players in Mr. Cobb's day had all the abilities they have now, all of the same basic abilities. I think if you would take the 2000 Braves and put them in Detroit in 1925, with all the conditions of that day, and if you would take the 1925 Tigers and switch them over to today's equipment and conditions, there wouldn't be much difference, in my opinion."[21]

It would be magnificent if we could put Lanier's theory to the test, but alas, time travel has not yet made the leap from fantasy to reality. What we're left with, as he noted, are statistics that were generated in dramatically different environments. The 1925 Tigers played only in the daytime, the 2000 Braves mostly at night. The Tigers played only on grass, the Braves sometimes on artificial turf. The Tigers played only against whites, the Braves against players of all races. The Tigers traveled by train, the Braves by jet. The Tigers rarely faced relief pitchers, the Braves often did.

It's no wonder that the stats vary so greatly from generation to generation. The Tigers and the other seven American League teams hit sixty-seven homers per club and collectively batted .292 in 1925. The Braves and the other 15 National League teams in 2000 nearly tripled the home-run count to 188 per club, but sliced the overall batting average by 26 points to .266. How could we possibly compare these disparate seasons fairly and accurately?

There is a way—statistical adjustment.

Here's a quick glimpse of the theory in action: Atlanta piled up 479 extra-base hits in 2000, dwarfing Detroit's total of 411 in 1925. A neophyte would instantly deduce that the Braves possessed a more potent lineup, though a balanced comparison suggests a different story. Batters for the typical National League club amassed 511 extra-base hits in 2000, putting the Braves 6.3 percent below the norm. The Tigers finished just 0.7 percent under 1925's American League average of 414 extra-base hits per team. We can adjust Detroit's total to fit into Atlanta's season by keeping the Tigers 0.7 percent below the NL's benchmark for 2000. That gives us these results on a level field: 507 extra-base hits for the Tigers, 479 for the Braves.

I don't want to turn this into a mathematics textbook, so I'll explain the overall adjustment process as briefly as possible. My aim is to convert all statistics—no matter what season they were generated—into their 2011-2020 equivalents. You've already seen the basic principle above, so let's dig deeper into the recipe for batters, interspersed with examples from Robin Yount's performance for the Milwaukee Brewers in 1981. If you're interested, read on. If not, you'll probably be happier if you skip the bulleted paragraphs.

• Adjust a batter's number of games so that it conforms to a 162-game schedule. Yount played 96 of Milwaukee's 109 games in the strike-shortened 1981 season. That's the rounded equivalent of 143 games over a full year.

• Calculate a batter's adjusted number of plate appearances. Yount made 411 PAs in 1981, an average of 4.28 per game. That yields a rounded total of 612 appearances in 143 games.

• Calculate a ratio that compares a batter with the league's other players in the same category. Let's use hits as an example. Yount produced 103 hits in 411 appearances, equaling 0.2506 hits per PA. All other American League players in 1981 had 12,913 hits in 56,457 appearances, translating to 0.2287 hits per PA. (Note that these calculations are based on plate appearances, not at-bats.) Yount's 1981 rate was 9.58 percent higher than the figure for the rest of the league, so his adjusted rate will be set 9.58 percent above the 2011-2020 average of 0.2267 hits per PA. That puts Yount at 0.2484 hits per appearance, yielding a rounded total of 152 adjusted hits in 612 appearances. The same process is used to adjust statistics in most other categories.

• Calculate a player's at-bats by subtracting his adjusted totals for walks, hit batsmen, sacrifice hits, and sacrifice flies from his adjusted number of plate appearances. Then calculate his batting average. Yount's 152 adjusted hits came in 563 adjusted at-bats, giving him a 1981 batting average of .270 on the 2011-2020 scale. (His real-life average was .273.)

• Extra-base hits are trickier, though the process begins with a familiar step. Calculate ratios for doubles, triples, and home runs, comparing a batter to the outputs of all other players. But the results often fail to conform to the batter's expected slugging average, so a bit of statistical tinkering is required. (The changes are usually minor, and any explanation would be lengthy and boring, so I ask for your trust.) Yount actually hit fifteen doubles, five triples, and ten homers in 1981, but his adjusted totals (in 2011-2020 terms) are twenty-six doubles, six triples, and twenty-two home runs.

Nothing better demonstrates the impact of statistical adjustment than the list of top home-run hitters. We're familiar with the actual standings—Barry Bonds controversially taking the lead, runner-up Henry Aaron nevertheless being considered the real champ by legions of fans, Babe Ruth sitting third with the still-iconic number of 714. These were the top twenty-five sluggers at the end of 2020, when my study period concluded:

Home Runs (Actual)

1. Barry Bonds, 762
2. Henry Aaron, 755*
3. Babe Ruth, 714*
4. Alex Rodriguez, 696
5. Albert Pujols, 662
6. Willie Mays, 660*
7. Ken Griffey Jr., 630*
8. Jim Thome, 612*

9. Sammy Sosa, 609
10. Frank Robinson, 586*
11. Mark McGwire, 583
12. Harmon Killebrew, 573*
13. Rafael Palmeiro, 569
14. Reggie Jackson, 563*
15. Manny Ramirez, 555
16. Mike Schmidt, 548*
17. David Ortiz, 541*
18. Mickey Mantle, 536*
19. Jimmie Foxx, 534*
20. Willie McCovey, 521*
20. Frank Thomas, 521*
20. Ted Williams, 521*
23. Ernie Banks, 512*
23. Eddie Mathews, 512*
25. Mel Ott, 511*

Adjustment converts everybody's totals to 2011-2020 equivalents, resulting in dramatic increases for batters who played in eras where home runs were not as common as today. It's often forgotten how absurdly anomalous Babe Ruth's tremendous power was for his time. He reached his peak with sixty home runs for the Yankees in 1927, a year in which the other American League *teams* averaged forty homers apiece. Ruth's count consequently soars after adjustment to 1,144.

Henry Aaron and his compatriots from the 1950s and 1960s also batted in a difficult environment, which is why their totals are higher on the list below. Negro leaguers played much shorter seasons, so they benefit from the adjustment to a 162-game schedule. That explains the presence of Turkey Stearnes in third place, Mule Suttles in sixth, and Josh Gibson in ninth. Here are the adjusted standings, which give a true representation of baseball's greatest sluggers, certainly much better than the previous list:

Home Runs (Adjusted)

1. Babe Ruth, 1,144*
2. Henry Aaron, 934*
3. Turkey Stearnes, 877*
4. Barry Bonds, 868
5. Jimmie Foxx, 823*
6. Mule Suttles, 820*

7. Willie Mays, 815*
8. Lou Gehrig, 810*
9. Josh Gibson, 794*
9. Mel Ott, 794*
11. Ted Williams, 778*
12. Mike Schmidt, 728*
13. Frank Robinson, 700*
14. Mickey Mantle, 695*
15. Reggie Jackson, 693*
16. Alex Rodriguez, 692
17. Harmon Killebrew, 688*
18. Albert Pujols, 682
19. Stan Musial, 680*
20. Ken Griffey Jr., 677*
21. Sammy Sosa, 659
22. Rogers Hornsby, 652*
23. Ty Cobb, 644*
24. Willie McCovey, 642*
25. Oscar Charleston, 634*

Now on to the pitchers. We'll follow Bob Feller's 1946 season for the Cleveland Indians through the adjustment process. Here are the steps:

• Adjust a pitcher's games pitched and games started so they fit a 162-game schedule. Feller appeared in 48 games and made 42 starts in 1946 (when the Indians played 156 games), which translate to the rounded equivalents of 50 games and 44 starts in 162 games.

• Determine the adjusted number of relief appearances by subtracting adjusted starts from adjusted games. The result for Feller, based on calculations in the previous step, is six games in relief.

• If the adjusted number of starts is greater than thirty-five, reduce it to that figure, which corresponds to the largest number of games started by any pitcher between 2011 and 2020. Feller's GS total for 1946 is consequently cut to thirty-five.

• Add the adjusted games as a starter (thirty-five) and reliever (six) to get a pitcher's adjusted total of games (forty-one for Feller).

• Adjust the total of innings pitched. Begin by multiplying a pitcher's actual starts by six, then add his actual number of relief appearances. (Why? Because the typical starter in 2011-2020 worked roughly six innings, while the typical reliever went a single inning.) That gives Feller 258 points. Divide his actual total of innings in 1946 (371⅓) by his points (258) and multiply by 6. The result is his estimated innings per start—in this case, 8.6. That's 26.47 percent longer than the ratio for all starters in 1946 (6.8 innings), so his adjusted innings per start will be 26.47 percent longer than the 2011-2020 standard of 5.7 innings. That gives Feller 7.2 innings per adjusted start, or 252 innings in 35 starts. His six relief appearances are set at 26.47 percent longer than an inning, or a rounded sum of eight innings. Feller's adjusted total of innings pitched is 260.

• Adjust a pitcher's wins and losses. Divide actual wins (26) by actual games (48) to determine a ratio, which was 0.54 wins per game for Feller. Multiply the ratio by the adjusted number of games (forty-one) to get the adjusted win total (twenty-two). The latter figure is capped at thirty-five. Repeat the process for losses.

• Calculate a ratio that compares a pitcher with the league's other pitchers in the same category. Let's use earned runs as an example. Feller allowed 90 earned runs in 371⅓ innings in 1946, equaling 0.2424 earned runs per inning. All other American League pitchers that season allowed 4,216 earned runs in 10,690⅔ innings, translating to 0.3944 ER per IP. Feller's 1946 rate was 38.54 percent lower than the figure for the rest of the league, so his adjusted rate will be set 38.54 percent below the 2011-2020 average of 0.4542 earned runs per inning. That puts Feller at 0.2792 ER per IP, yielding a rounded total of 73 adjusted earned runs in 260 adjusted innings, giving him an earned-run average of 2.53 on the 2011-2020 scale. (His real-life ERA was 2.18.) The same process is used to adjust statistics in most other categories.

• Strikeouts pose the same problem for pitchers as extra-base hits do for batters, and similar care is required. The formula for strikeouts actually works on parallel tracks. It calculates strikeouts per inning, comparing a pitcher's average to the average for all other pitchers during the same season. It performs the same calculation and comparison for all outs resulting from batted balls (grounders, flies, foulouts). These two figures are brought into balance through a series of additional steps, similar to those I used for extra-base hits, thereby determining a pitcher's adjusted strikeouts. Extra-base hits and strikeouts are direct components of other statistics, which is why these additional moves are needed. Strikeouts must conform with innings pitched, since each strikeout equals one-third of an inning.

This last category demonstrates the impact of adjusted statistics on historical perspective. We live in a free-swinging age, of course, and the strikeout totals prove it. Pitchers are inducing more third strikes than ever. The all-time list of strikeout leaders is consequently tilted toward the modern era:

Strikeouts (Actual)

1. Nolan Ryan, 5,714*
2. Randy Johnson, 4,875*
3. Roger Clemens, 4,672
4. Steve Carlton, 4,136*
5. Bert Blyleven, 3,701*
6. Tom Seaver, 3,640*
7. Don Sutton, 3,574*
8. Gaylord Perry, 3,534*
9. Walter Johnson, 3,509*
10. Greg Maddux, 3,371*
11. Phil Niekro, 3,342*
12. Fergie Jenkins, 3,192*
13. Pedro Martinez, 3,154*
14. Bob Gibson, 3,117*
15. Curt Schilling, 3,116
16. CC Sabathia, 3,093
17. John Smoltz, 3,084*
18. Justin Verlander, 3,013
19. Jim Bunning, 2,855*
20. Mickey Lolich, 2,832
21. Mike Mussina, 2,813*
22. Cy Young, 2,803*
23. Max Scherzer, 2,784
24. Frank Tanana, 2,773
25. Zack Greinke, 2,689

Are these really the twenty-five greatest strikeout artists of all time? Of course not. Recent decades have featured a growing number of swings and misses, which is why this list is saturated with pitchers who were active at some point during the past half-century. Walter Johnson and Cy Young are the only members of the top twenty-five who retired before 1971.

Now look at the adjusted list below. The three leaders remain the same—though in a slightly different order—and you might be surprised that their strikeout totals have increased. Yes, Nolan Ryan, Roger Clemens, and Randy Johnson all played in an environment favorable to fastball pitchers, but all three retired prior to 2011-2020, the ten-year period with the steepest strikeout rate of all. Their totals consequently rose when adjusted to that decade's standards.

But they didn't come close to Walter Johnson's increase of nearly 61 percent. The Big Train, the famed fireballer of the early twentieth century, moves up to fourth place on the adjusted list. Fellow old-timers Young, Lefty Grove, Dazzy Vance, and Pete Alexander are among the twenty-five adjusted leaders, as are such strikeout kings of later eras as Bob Feller, Warren Spahn, and Bob Gibson, as well as the great Negro leaguer, Satchel Paige. The result is a more realistic roster of baseball's greatest strikeout pitchers:

Strikeouts (Adjusted)

1. Nolan Ryan, 6,949*
2. Roger Clemens, 5,729
3. Randy Johnson, 5,723*
4. Walter Johnson, 5,632*
5. Steve Carlton, 5,131*
6. Bert Blyleven, 4,816*
7. Tom Seaver, 4,643*
8. Don Sutton, 4,618*
9. Cy Young, 4,604*
10. Gaylord Perry, 4,439*
11. Lefty Grove, 4,329*
12. Phil Niekro, 4,185*
13. Greg Maddux, 4,069*
14. Satchel Paige, 3,971*
15. Bob Feller, 3,967*
16. Fergie Jenkins, 3,932*
17. Red Ruffing, 3,925*
18. Warren Spahn, 3,922*
19. Dazzy Vance, 3,902*
20. Frank Tanana, 3,859
21. Pete Alexander, 3,797*

22. Early Wynn, 3,796*
23. Bob Gibson, 3,785*
24. Pedro Martinez, 3,702*
25. John Smoltz, 3,667*

This section has run for quite awhile, and I'd like to wrap it up. But I still need to discuss an omission from my adjustment process, an exclusion that will irritate the purists.

I consciously decided not to use ballpark factors, those coefficients that purportedly counteract a stadium's statistical biases toward batters or pitchers. Denver's Coors Field, with its high altitude, is the epitome of a hitter's park, while San Diego's Petco Park, with its vast outfield, has long been a haven for pitchers. Adding a ballpark factor to any adjustment formula will supposedly make any such inequalities disappear.

If you perused the step-by-step procedure to calculate the factor for a given stadium, you would instantly be convinced of its efficacy, which certainly was true in my case. It's so complicated that the explanation in *Total Baseball*, the old baseball encyclopedia, consumes twenty-four inches of small type, encompassing twenty-two separate formulas. Something that byzantine must be incredibly precise, wouldn't you think?[22]

I no longer do. I have come to doubt the accuracy or consistency of ballpark factors. Consider an extreme example. The Dodgers played in a football stadium, the Los Angeles Memorial Coliseum, during their first four seasons in California. A gigantic 40-foot screen was erected above the left-field fence, which loomed just 250 feet from home plate, while the wall in right-center field was 440 feet away, rising in the vicinity of the football end zone.[23]

This lopsided configuration clearly favored right-handed power hitters. San Francisco center fielder Willie Mays ran into fellow slugger Duke Snider in the runway before the Coliseum's first game in 1958. Snider had blasted forty homers for the Brooklyn Dodgers in 1957, the third-highest total in the National League, putting him directly ahead of Mays, who finished fourth with thirty-five. Mays, who batted from the right side, told the left-handed Snider to gaze into the distance. "Look where that right-field fence is, Duke," Mays laughed. "And look what they gave me—250 feet. They sure fixed you up good. You couldn't reach it with a cannon."[24]

The ballpark factor for the Coliseum that first year was 105, indicating that the stadium consistently favored hitters by 5 percent. But the impact was hardly uniform. The Dodgers' new home clearly didn't suit Snider, who managed to clear the Coliseum's distant fence just 6 times in 183 plate appearances in 1958. Mays hit nearly as many homers in Los Angeles—five—even though the Giants played only eleven games there all year. It seems illogical to adjust the stats for both lefties and righties by the same 5 percent under such disparate circumstances.

Another problem is the tendency of factors to vary from year to year, even if nothing in the stadium has changed. Coors Field, for example, posted an amazingly high ballpark factor of 124 in 2012, which was recalibrated to 110 the following year, then bumped back to 120 in 2014. The experts suggest that three years of factors should be averaged to smooth out such deviations, which sounds to me like a statistical dodge, a makeshift effort to fix a concept that is obviously flawed.

I have a different suggestion: Let's ignore ballpark factors until somebody improves them dramatically.

Quality Scores

We now have the necessary tools to generate quality scores for the 873 players who qualified for the pool. I've developed separate formulas for batters and pitchers. They are similar in form, and they produce scores on the same one-hundred-point scale. Here are the informal equations:

QS for Batters = 25% Tests + 15% WAR + 10% Fielding + 50% Adjusted

QS for Pitchers = 25% Tests + 15% WAR + 60% Adjusted

I posed four objectives early in this chapter. I suggested that the QS should measure a player's performance over short, midrange, and long spans; it should encompass all aspects of the game; it should blend traditional averages and counting stats with newer analytics; and it should level the statistical field to allow fair comparisons of different eras. These formulas accomplish all four goals.

Let's turn first to the pool's 477 non-pitchers, interchangeably known as batters or position players. They're ranked in the following eighteen categories, which are listed with their maximum scores in parentheses:

Tests

- One-year test sum (ten points)
- Five-year test peak (five points)
- Five-year test sum (five points)
- Hall of Fame monitor (five points)

WAR

- Wins above replacement for position players (ten points)
- Wins above replacement per five hundred plate appearances (five points)

Fielding

- Defensive wins above replacement (five points)
- Defensive wins above replacement per one hundred games (five points)

Adjusted

- Batting average (five points)
- Slugging average (five points)
- Bases per out (five points)
- Runs scored per five hundred plate appearances (five points)
- Runs batted in per five hundred plate appearances (five points)
- Bases (five points)
- Runs scored (five points)
- Hits (five points)
- Home runs (five points)
- Runs batted in (five points)

You already know about the tests, but explanations are necessary for a few other categories.

WAR comes in various forms, including an overall version that quantifies all aspects of a player's performance, as well as separate WARs that are confined to pitching, everything but pitching, or fielding. The latter two, known as position-player WAR and defensive WAR, are elements of the QS formula for batters. (Several websites generate their own WAR totals, sometimes differing in their results. I rely solely on Baseball Reference, the ultimate source for all things statistical.)

The adjusted statistics are split between five averages and rates, which are listed first, and five counting stats. The only one that might be unfamiliar is bases, which is the number of bases that a batter reached with singles, doubles, triples, homers, walks, hit batsmen, stolen bases, sacrifice hits, and sacrifice flies. (It's true that a hitter can't get on base with the latter two, but he does gain a base for his team, which is why he is credited.)

The pitching formula is slightly different. It excludes fielding, which is not as important a skill for pitchers as for position players. I've filled the resulting gap by increasing the total value of the adjusted component to sixty points. Each of the adjusted stats consequently carries a maximum score of six.

These are the sixteen categories in which the pool's 396 pitchers are rated:

Tests
- One-year test sum (ten points)
- Five-year test peak (five points)
- Five-year test sum (five points)
- Hall of Fame monitor (five points)

WAR
- Wins above replacement for pitchers (ten points)
- Wins above replacement per one hundred innings pitched (five points)

Adjusted
- Earned-run average (six points)
- Wins or saves per thirty games (six points)
- Hits per inning (six points)
- Walks per inning (six points)
- Strikeouts per inning (six points)
- Strikeouts per walk (six points)
- Outs (six points)
- Games started or relieved (six points)
- Wins or saves (six points)
- Strikeouts (six points)

Each pitcher in the pool is classified as a starter or a reliever, depending on his dominant role during his career. Three of the adjusted categories have been subdivided accordingly. The 296 starters are evaluated for wins per 30 games, games started, and total wins, while the 100 relievers are analyzed for saves per 30 games, games relieved, and total saves. (It should be noted that each pitcher's QS is based on his entire body of work, regardless of his classification. Warren Spahn started 665 games over 21 seasons, so he is naturally listed as a starter. But the results of his eighty-five relief appearances are included in his stats.)

The first six adjusted statistics for pitchers are averages and rates, while the latter four are totals. The categories themselves seem to be self-explanatory, with the possible exception of outs, a stat that isn't commonly recorded. It's the total number of batters retired by a given pitcher, with extra credit for double plays and runners caught stealing.

We now proceed to the climax of this lengthy chapter, the generation of quality scores for all 873 members of the pool.

The score within a category is determined by the top-to-bottom rankings of all eligible players. The four tests bring batters and pitchers together in one massive group. The eighty-seven players who do the best on a given test—the highest 10 percent—receive the maximum of five points. (The one-year test has a ten-point ceiling, so its raw scores are doubled.) The reward descends for each subsequent increment of 10 percent in the standings, concluding with a single point for anybody between 351st and 437th place. Players in the bottom half of the test rankings—those between 438th and 873rd—receive nothing.

The same principle is used for the categories that fall under the heading of WAR, fielding, and adjusted statistics. The key difference is that the 477 batters, 296 starting pitchers, and 100 relievers are rated in separate groups. Players are ranked from best to worst in each category, with points awarded on a descending scale to those in the upper half.

The following chart shows the ranks that correspond to each point level. Batters are graded solely on a five-point scale, but starters and relievers have maximums of five or six in different categories:

Overall Tests (873)

5 points: 1st to 87th
4 points: 88th to 175th
3 points: 176th to 262nd
2 points: 263rd to 350th
1 point: 351st to 437th

Batters (477)

5 points: 1st to 48th
4 points: 49th to 96th
3 points: 97th to 144th
2 points: 145th to 192nd
1 point: 193rd to 240th

Starters (296, Scale #1)

5 points: 1st to 30th
4 points: 31st to 59th
3 points: 60th to 89th
2 points: 90th to 118th
1 point: 119th to 148th

Starters (296, Scale #2)

6 points: 1st to 25th
5 points: 26th to 49th
4 points: 50th to 74th
3 points: 75th to 99th
2 points: 100th to 124th
1 point: 125th to 148th

Relievers (100, Scale #1)

5 points: 1st to 10th
4 points: 11th to 20th
3 points: 21st to 30th
2 points: 31st to 40th
1 point: 41st to 50th

Relievers (100, Scale #2)

6 points: 1st to 8th
5 points: 9th to 17th
4 points: 18th to 25th
3 points: 26th to 33rd
2 points: 34th to 42nd
1 point: 43rd to 50th

I previously noted that the scores on this chart must be doubled for the one-year test. The same rule applies to the separate rankings of WAR for position players and pitchers, which carry maximums of ten points. All other scores can be obtained directly from the chart.

Here's how the formula works, using Honus Wagner as an example:

• Tests: If you flip back to the early pages of this chapter, you'll find lists of the top twenty-five players on three of the four tests. Wagner is embedded in all three. He ranks 17th for his five-year sum (382.3), 18th on the Hall of Fame monitor (313), and 21st for his one-year sum (123.0). The first two results earn five points apiece, and the latter is doubled to ten. Wagner draws another five points for his five-year peak of precisely one hundred, the highest possible mark. Total: twenty-five points.

• WAR: Only twenty-one position players in big-league history have piled up more than one hundred wins above replacement. Wagner's 130.8 WAR puts him seventh in that elite group, good for 10 points. And he ranks 19th with 5.56 WAR per 500 plate appearances, harvesting another 5. Total: fifteen points.

• Fielding: Wagner played a key position, shortstop, and he played it for two decades. That combination of essentiality and longevity yielded a career total of 21.3 defensive wins above replacement, which ranks 35th in the pool and earns 5 points. But the first evidence of a slight flaw emerges in the ratio of defensive WAR per 100 games. Wagner's 0.76 per 100 is good, yet not great. It ranks 77th among all 477 position players, which falls in the 4-point range. Total: nine points.

• Adjusted: The process of statistical adjustment allows us to see Wagner in a new light. We know that he was adept at the plate, as evidenced by his eight National League batting titles and .328 career average. But we don't think of him as a power hitter, given that he launched only 101 homers in his career. His lifetime slugging average was .467, which wouldn't have ranked among the fifty best rates in the major leagues in 2021. But Wagner's adjusted numbers demonstrate his true power, with 565 homers and a .565 slugging average at 2011-2020 levels. He earns five points in nine of the ten adjusted categories. The exception is 4 points for his 78.07 runs scored per 500 plate appearances, where he ranks 62nd. Total: forty-nine points.

And that's how Wagner ran up the highest quality score of all time—ninety-eight points. Only eleven players in big-league history have reached or passed ninety on the QS scale. Nine have been enshrined in Cooperstown. The two exceptions—you guessed it—are Barry Bonds and Roger Clemens. Here's a full rundown of the 100 best quality scores of all time (actually 104 with ties). Each player is listed with his primary position in parentheses, and Hall of Famers are denoted by asterisks:

Top Quality Scores

1. Honus Wagner (SS), 98*
2. Rogers Hornsby (2B), 96*
2. Walter Johnson (SP), 96*
4. Willie Mays (CF), 95*
5. Mike Schmidt (3B), 91*
6. Barry Bonds (LF), 90
6. Roger Clemens (SP), 90
6. Ty Cobb (CF), 90*
6. Lefty Grove (SP), 90*
6. Nap Lajoie (2B), 90*
6. Babe Ruth (RF), 90*
12. Randy Johnson (SP), 89*
12. Mariano Rivera (RP), 89*
12. Ted Williams (LF), 89*
15. Henry Aaron (RF), 87*
15. Lou Gehrig (1B), 87*
15. Christy Mathewson (SP), 87*
15. Stan Musial (LF), 87*
19. Pete Alexander (SP), 86*
19. Dan Brouthers (1B), 86*
19. Cy Young (SP), 86*
22. Jimmie Foxx (1B), 85*
22. Frank Robinson (RF), 85*
22. Alex Rodriguez (SS), 85
22. Tris Speaker (CF), 85*
26. Mickey Mantle (CF), 84*
26. Pedro Martinez (SP), 84*
28. Cap Anson (1B), 83*
28. Tom Seaver (SP), 83*
30. Greg Maddux (SP), 82*
30. Kid Nichols (SP), 82*
32. Mel Ott (RF), 81*
33. Oscar Charleston (CF), 80*
33. Albert Pujols (1B), 80
35. Turkey Stearnes (CF), 79*
36. Joe DiMaggio (CF), 78*
36. Carl Hubbell (SP), 78*
36. Curt Schilling (SP), 78
39. Roger Connor (1B), 77*

39. Trevor Hoffman (RP), 77*
39. Billy Wagner (RP), 77
39. Willie Wells (SS), 77*
43. Josh Gibson (C), 76*
43. Larry Walker (RF), 76*
45. Clayton Kershaw (SP), 75
46. Bob Gibson (SP), 74*
46. Justin Verlander (SP), 74
48. Ed Delahanty (LF), 73*
48. Satchel Paige (SP), 73*
50. Eddie Collins (2B), 72*
50. Ken Griffey Jr. (CF), 72*
50. Warren Spahn (SP), 72*
53. Bob Feller (SP), 70*
53. Nolan Ryan (SP), 70*
53. Carl Yastrzemski (LF), 70*
56. Bert Blyleven (SP), 69*
56. George Brett (3B), 69*
56. Roberto Clemente (RF), 69*
56. Tim Keefe (SP), 69*
56. Mike Mussina (SP), 69*
56. Robin Roberts (SP), 69*
62. Jeff Bagwell (1B), 68*
62. Sam Crawford (RF), 68*
62. Fergie Jenkins (SP), 68*
62. Al Kaline (RF), 68*
62. Buck Leonard (1B), 68*
67. Miguel Cabrera (1B), 67
67. Steve Carlton (SP), 67*
67. Harry Heilmann (RF), 67*
67. Dazzy Vance (SP), 67*
71. Johnny Mize (1B), 66*
71. Manny Ramirez (LF), 66
73. Rickey Henderson (LF), 65*
73. Reggie Jackson (RF), 65*
73. John Smoltz (SP), 65*
73. Mule Suttles (1B), 65*
77. Chipper Jones (3B), 64*
77. Joe Morgan (2B), 64*
77. Cal Ripken Jr. (SS), 64*
80. Max Scherzer (SP), 63
80. Al Simmons (LF), 63*
80. Don Sutton (SP), 63*
83. Wade Boggs (3B), 62*

83. Roy Halladay (SP), 62*
83. Juan Marichal (SP), 62*
83. Francisco Rodriguez (RP), 62
83. Frank Thomas (1B), 62*
88. Dennis Eckersley (SP), 61*
88. Charlie Gehringer (2B), 61*
88. Craig Kimbrel (RP), 61
88. Gaylord Perry (SP), 61*
92. Johnny Bench (C), 60*
92. Eddie Mathews (3B), 60*
92. Lee Smith (RP), 60*
92. Duke Snider (CF), 60*
96. Willard Brown (CF), 59*
96. Rod Carew (2B), 59*
96. Rollie Fingers (RP), 59*
96. Zack Greinke (SP), 59
96. Willie McCovey (1B), 59*
96. Willie Stargell (LF), 59*
96. Mike Trout (CF), 59
96. Rube Waddell (SP), 59*
96. Ed Walsh (SP), 59*

Honus Wagner was chosen as one of the Hall of Fame's five charter members, though he didn't receive the most votes in the BBWAA's 1936 election. That honor went to Ty Cobb, much to the displeasure of some of his contemporaries. "Cobb! A great hitter, a sensational baserunner, and a dynamic personality on the diamond, yes," said Jack Meyers, a catcher in the National League from 1909 to 1917. "But he was a poor outfielder, did not possess a good arm, and was never known as a team player."

And who did Meyers consider the greatest player in the sixty-five-year history of major-league baseball? "Old Honus was a ballplayer's player," Meyers said. "He did everything well. We used to marvel at his all-round ability. We considered him an artist, rather than just a player." Wagner was unsurpassed in Meyers's estimation, and he retains that distinction in today's quality-score standings, holding a two-point lead over his closest rivals.[25]

I've analyzed the quality scores for all 873 pool members at considerable length, and I'm pleased with the results, not just at the top, but throughout the standings. The correlation between QS and Hall of Fame membership is a strong one. Anybody with a score of sixty or better is a virtual lock for induction. Ninety-five pool members reached that threshold by 2020, though seven continued to play after 2016, thereby delaying their candidacies for the hall. All but six of the eligible eighty-eight have been enshrined in Cooperstown. We're sadly familiar with the reasons why Barry Bonds (QS of ninety), Roger Clemens (ninety), Alex Rodriguez (eighty-five), Curt Schilling (seventy-eight), and Manny Ramirez (sixty-six) have been excluded. The only other high-level outsider is Billy Wagner (seventy-seven).

The odds of induction dwindle as quality scores decline, a linkage shown on the chart below. I have delineated four ranges. Keep in mind that they refer only to the likelihood of being elected to the Hall of Fame. Anybody who runs up a quality score of forty-four is indeed an excellent player, yet his chances of making it to Cooperstown are marginal. This chart is limited to the 764 pool members who were eligible for the hall as of 2022; the other 109 players will get their chances in the years to come.

Excellent

QS range: 60 to 100
Eligible players in pool: 88
Hall of Famers: 82 (93.2%)

Good

QS range: 45 to 59
Eligible players in pool: 95
Hall of Famers: 68 (71.6%)

Marginal

QS range: 30 to 44
Eligible players in pool: 136
Hall of Famers: 53 (39.0%)

Poor

QS range: 0 to 29
Eligible players in pool: 445
Hall of Famers: 65 (14.6%)

I'm convinced that the quality score is a fair and accurate measure of a player's accomplishments. It applies just as well to the old-timers who retired in the nineteenth century as to the stars of the twenty-first. But I must admit to one shortcoming. QS does not treat all Negro leaguers equitably.

There's a great story about Ray Dandridge, a hard-hitting, smooth-fielding third baseman who played in the Mexican League for several years. Higher salaries had lured a few white major leaguers, including Danny Gardella and Max Lanier, to Mexico in 1946. The tale was told in different ways—sometimes Gardella was the impressed onlooker, other times it was Lanier—but the gist was always the same. The white player watched in amazement as his black counterpart blasted a series of deep flies in batting practice.

"Man, where did you come from?" Gardella/Lanier finally asked with a touch of awe.

Dandridge paused for a moment and looked at him coolly. "Same country you did," he said.[26]

The problem, of course, was that Dandridge and all black players were still barred from the American and National Leagues in 1946, rendering them anonymous to most white players and fans in the United States. Dandridge was thirty-five when the New York Giants finally signed him for their AAA club in Minneapolis in 1949. He batted a robust .362, yet the call to the majors never came. "They said he was too old," recalled Monte Irvin, a black star who did make it to New York. "I asked what difference it made if he could play."

Dandridge played only 246 games in the Negro leagues, a pittance next to the 8 seasons he spent in Mexico, where the money was better. Even his stay in AAA ball was longer, eventually stretching past five hundred games. The owner of the Giants, Horace Stoneham, was afraid that he might offend white fans by adding another black player to his roster, so the aging Dandridge remained in Minneapolis. "I know it was the old quota system," Irvin said sadly.[27]

Quality scores, of course, aren't based on statistics from Mexico or the minors. Those 246 games in the Negro leagues constituted Dandridge's major-league career, a very small sample indeed. His skills were indisputably of big-league caliber—a judgment affirmed by his 1987 election to the Hall of Fame—but circumstances kept him from his rightful place. The resulting quality score of eight points isn't a true measure of the man.[28]

The same problem afflicts black ballplayers who came along too early. John Henry Lloyd turned thirty-six in 1920, the first year of major status for the Negro leagues. He had already gained fame in the black community for his skill at the plate and his wide range as a shortstop. He was commonly called the Honus Wagner of Negro baseball, a nickname seconded by the idol himself. "I am honored to have John Lloyd called the Black Wagner," said white Honus. "It is a privilege to have been compared with him."[29]

Lloyd played 433 games in the Negro leagues, a majority of them after passing his 40th birthday. He batted a robust .349 between 1921 and 1929, yet contemporaries believed he had been a greater star in earlier seasons that weren't covered by the major-league umbrella. Lloyd was inducted by the Hall of Fame in 1977, though his QS (fifteen points) reflects only the output of his twilight years.[30]

Most Negro leaguers fare much better under the quality-score system, especially those who attained stardom between the 1920s and 1940s. QS fully reflects the greatness of such Hall of Famers as Oscar Charleston (eighty points), Turkey Stearnes (seventy-nine), Willie Wells (seventy-seven), Josh Gibson (seventy-six), Satchel Paige (seventy-three), Buck Leonard (sixty-eight), and Mule Suttles (sixty-five). All are ensconced in the excellent classification, right where they deserve to be.

We'll refer to quality scores through the remainder of this book, as we assess the members of the Hall of Fame and the candidates who aspire to join them. Who truly belongs in Cooperstown? Who doesn't? QS won't give us a definitive answer—it's not designed for such heavy duty—but it will help point the way.

Earl Averill might have liked the concept of the quality score. The unhappy member of the hall's class of 1975, whom we met at the beginning of this chapter, stressed his belief in statistics and "cold hard facts." QS would seem to be right up his alley. It's based on a wide range of stats that cover every aspect of a player's career, and it's a strong indicator of a player's Hall of Fame worthiness.

There's just one problem. My formula gives Averill a quality score of twenty-six points, thereby classifying him as a poor candidate for induction. Perhaps he shouldn't have been quite so angry about the long wait he endured before Cooperstown finally opened its doors.

The more appropriate emotion, it seems, would have been gratitude.

CHAPTER THREE

Elections

THE NATIONAL BASEBALL HALL OF FAME was built on a false foundation.

The sport's early leaders were fanatically determined to prove that theirs was an all-American pastime. They scoffed at claims that baseball had evolved from the English game of rounders, though they could offer no proof to the contrary. So they empaneled a committee in 1905 to dig up the necessary documentation. Abraham Mills, a former president of the National League, was designated the chairman, and his task force became known as the Mills Commission.

The subsequent investigation was haphazard, yet effective. The key piece of evidence acquired by the commission was a letter from Abner Graves, a seventy-one-year-old mining engineer from Colorado. Graves had grown up in Cooperstown, New York, and he recalled being present at a seminal event in 1839. He wrote that Abner Doubleday, a student at a nearby private school, had used a stick to draw a diamond in the dirt, thereby creating the structure for a game that Doubleday called "base ball."

There were a few problems with the old man's story. Graves would have been only five years old when he allegedly witnessed history being made. Doubleday attended the United States Military Academy, not a Cooperstown school, in 1839. And Mills himself had been well acquainted with Doubleday in adulthood, yet had never heard his friend claim to be the inventor of baseball.[1]

No matter. The Mills Commission issued a brief report in December 1907 that certified the sport's American origins. "The first scheme for playing baseball, according to the best evidence obtainable to date, was devised by Abner Doubleday at Cooperstown, N.Y., in 1839," the panel concluded.[2]

The creation myth was thereby stamped as fact, and Doubleday was glorified as the first man of baseball. "Abner was Adam," insisted Ken Smith, a New York sportswriter who would one day become the Hall of Fame's director. Smith proceeded to embroider the legend, portraying Doubleday as the Johnny Appleseed of baseball, a vagabond who spread the word about his new game from town to town. "He was not only the inventor, but a crusader," Smith wrote.[3]

It took a quarter-century—change has always come slowly to base-ball—but a campaign was finally launched to honor Doubleday and his supposed invention. The sport's self-proclaimed bible, the *Sporting News*, took the lead. "In the little city of Cooperstown, N.Y., is a plot of ground that should represent to baseball what Plymouth Rock means to the United States, Bunker Hill to New England, and the Alamo to Texas—a hallowed spot venerated for its historic associations," the newspaper trumpeted in a 1934 editorial. But its subsequent paragraph was shrouded in gloominess: "What has baseball done to perpetuate the historic site? Nothing."[4]

Alexander Cleland believed he had the perfect solution. Cle-land worked for Stephen Clark, an heir to a portion of the Singer sewing-machine fortune, a man of substantial wealth who happened to have been born in Cooperstown. Cleland suggested to his boss that Doubleday's historic site would be the ideal place for a baseball museum, though he set the bar awfully low. "Hundreds of visitors would be attracted to the shopping district right in the heart of Coo-perstown each year," Cleland cautiously predicted.[5]

Clark instructed his aide to run the idea past baseball's leaders, which is how Cleland ended up in the office of Ford Frick, the new president of the National League. "By happy chance, I had visited the National Hall of Fame at New York University a few days before Cle-land's visit," Frick recalled. "I was much impressed, and had a notion that a Baseball Hall of Fame would be great for the game."[6]

The NYU facility, officially known as the Hall of Fame for Great Americans, had been conceived thirty-five years earlier as a New World equivalent of Great Britain's Westminster Abbey or France's Pantheon, a shrine to the nation's greatest artists, authors, educators, inventors, politicians, scientists, and soldiers. It wasn't actually a hall, but a 630-foot colonnade, an outdoor sculpture gallery that formed a semicircle around the university's library in the Bronx. Bronze busts of the honorees lined both sides of the walkway.

The initial class of twenty-nine great Americans had been chosen by a panel of one hundred college presidents, editors, historians, and lawyers in 1900. A new election was conducted each half-decade. A candidate for induction was required to meet three stipulations. He or she must have been born in the United States, must have been deceased for at least twenty-five years, and must have drawn at least fifty-one votes from the one hundred electors. Sixty-nine busts adorned the Hall of Fame for Great Americans on the day in 1935 that the National League's president paid his visit.[7]

Frick believed that New York University's concept could be adapted to baseball, and Cleland and his boss were easily persuaded to expand their modest plans. Clark pledged to construct a National Baseball Hall of Fame and Museum in Cooperstown, and Frick promised in turn that the major leagues would provide logistical and financial support. Cleland enlisted the Baseball Writers' Association of America to choose the hall's members, a much simpler procedure than piecing together a large selection panel, which is what NYU did every five years.[8]

The first annual election was held in 1936, and three more were conducted before Clark's structure was finally ready for its grand opening on June 12, 1939, just in time to celebrate the centennial of the game's purported invention. The nation's most prestigious newspaper happily parroted the myth. "Baseball had a birthday party today in this pretty village where Abner Doubleday marked out baselines with a walking stick and thus originated the sport one hundred years ago," began the front-page story in the *New York Times*.[9]

One of Abner's descendants, Lieutenant Daniel Doubleday, was among the estimated ten thousand fans who jammed Main Street to view the opening ceremony. The crowd cheered as ten inductees were introduced, emerging one at a time through the Hall of Fame's front doors and striding to an adjacent podium. (Twenty-five men had been elected to the hall by the middle of 1939, but fourteen were deceased. A slow train delivered the eleventh living member, Ty Cobb, after the ceremony was over.) Connie Mack was the first to speak—"because I was the oldest, no doubt," he said—and Babe Ruth was the last.[10] "They started something here," Ruth said. "And the kids are keeping the ball rolling. I hope some of you kids will be in the Hall of Fame. I'm very glad that in my day I was able to earn my place."[11]

It fell to Commissioner Kenesaw Mountain Landis to give the benediction. Landis had been been strangely unexcited about the Cooperstown project from the beginning, perhaps because it wasn't his idea, but he played the role of good soldier on this festive day. "Nowhere, other than at its birthplace, could this museum be appropriately situated," Landis told the crowd. Microphones on the podium carried his words to a nationwide radio audience. The Doubleday myth had been confirmed on a grand scale.[12]

But not everybody believed. Frick would later recall having met Abraham Mills—he of the Mills Commission—at a large dinner in 1926, thirteen years before the Hall of Fame swung open its doors. Somebody asked the old chairman if he had truly unearthed any evidence that linked the national pastime and Cooperstown. His response came as a surprise. "None at all, young man," said Mills. "None at all, so far as the actual origin of baseball is concerned." The chairman's confession shook some of his listeners, though not Frick, who already presumed that baseball was a souped-up version of rounders. "That the game is a product of evolution cannot be denied," he wrote in his 1973 memoirs.[13]

Historians eventually revealed the slipshod nature of the Mills Commission's research, and baseball's creation myth lost most of its adherents. But the emergence of the truth didn't lessen Frick's enthusiasm for the Hall of Fame he had conceived in 1935 or the community where it had been built. Tiny Cooperstown, he contended, was the ideal place to celebrate a sport that had been popularized a century earlier in small towns throughout America.

Residents of the village gradually came to accept the judgment of history. They still called their local ballpark Doubleday Field, and one of their favorite restaurants on Main Street was still known as the Doubleday Cafe. But they grudgingly conceded that Abner Doubleday had never drawn a baseball diamond in the mud with a stick, that baseball had not been created in one of their parks. "It's an origin story that's a myth," Cooperstown mayor Jeff Katz, himself an author of baseball books, told a visitor in 2014. "But we're such a perfect setting for that myth. Baseball wasn't invented here. But it should have been."[14]

THE REST OF THIS chapter is devoted to breakdowns of the eighty-four Hall of Fame elections between 1936 and 2022. Each capsule begins with a four-part summary, which is followed by a discussion of the results.

Here's a quick guide to the summaries:

Hall of Fame Summary

New inductees: The number of honorees elected in the given year.

Category: The Hall of Fame places each inductee in one of four categories: player, manager, pioneer/executive, or umpire. This is the split for the year.

Election: The respective number of honorees elected in the year by the BBWAA or by a committee.

Player QS average: The average quality score for the year's newly inducted players. (QS, of course, is calculated only for players, not for the other categories.) Separate averages for the BBWAA and committee inductees are provided in parentheses.

Hall of Famers to date: The number of inductees from 1936 through the given year.

Category: The all-time number of players, managers, pioneers/ executives, and umpires admitted to the hall.

Election: The methods by which all Hall of Famers since 1936 were selected.

Player QS average: The average quality score for all players in the Hall of Fame, with separate BBWAA and committee averages in parentheses.

Inductees

Name: The inductees in a given year are listed in alphabetical order. Each name is followed by the information listed below.

Category: Player, manager, pioneer/executive, or umpire.

Position: A player's primary position is designated by the Hall of

Fame. It is the position at which he is judged to have had the greatest impact, usually (though not always) the one he played most frequently.

QS: Quality score for a player. It's followed in parentheses by the corresponding range: excellent (60-100), good (45-59), marginal (30-44), or poor (0-29). The range describes the player's likelihood of being elected to the Hall of Fame, not his skill level. (QS does not accurately reflect the records of a few Negro leaguers, as the previous chapter explained.)

Career: Basic statistics are provided for each player and manager, beginning with the span of his major-league career within his category. (The span for a manager, for instance, covers only his managerial career, not his time as a player.) Batters are listed with totals for games, home runs, runs batted in, and batting average. Pitchers are listed with totals for games, wins and losses, saves, and earned-run average. Managers are listed with wins and losses, league pennants, and World Series titles. (All statistics are actual, not adjusted.)

Election: BBWAA or a committee.

BBWAA Election Summary

Voters: The number of BBWAA members who participated in the election.

Votes needed for induction: A candidate must receive at least 75 percent of the votes to be elected. This was the resulting threshold for the year.

Candidates receiving votes: The number who drew at least one vote.

Candidates elected: The number who drew at least 75 percent of the votes.

Candidates inducted in future: Vote-getters who were not elected that year, but who were subsequently inducted into the Hall of Fame.

BBWAA Top Ten

Rank: The ten highest vote-getters in the BBWAA election are listed in order. Each candidate is described by the information listed below.

Name: The name of the candidate.

Votes: The raw total of votes that he received.

Percentage: The percentage of voters who supported the candidate.

Asterisk: If a candidate was elected to the Hall of Fame, his line ends with an asterisk.

Any election system is destined to evolve as the decades pass. Consider the method for choosing the president of the United States. The Founding Fathers vested all power in the Electoral College, a tiny group of political and financial elites, because they had little faith in the common man. "It would be [as] unnatural to refer the choice of a proper character for chief magistrate to the people," scoffed George Mason of Virginia, "as it would to refer a trial of colors to a blind man."[15] But the right to vote was gradually extended to most white men by 1840, then to black men (in theory, at least) with the ratification of the Fifteenth Amendment in 1870, then to women through the Nineteenth Amendment fifty years later. The franchise is now so widespread that more than 158 million Americans participated in the 2020 presidential election.

Choices of uneven quality are an inevitable byproduct of any method of selection. The nation's voters have picked such truly distinguished presidents as George Washington, Abraham Lincoln, and Franklin Roosevelt. But they have also saddled the country with such nonentities as Zachary Taylor, James Buchanan, and Warren Harding, not to mention a few disasters of a more recent variety.

The stakes may be lower, but the National Baseball Hall of Fame's election system is no exception to these universal rules, as the subsequent year-by-year summaries will demonstrate. We'll trace the evolution of the hall's procedures, a timeline that has been dotted with dozens of changes, both minor and momentous. We'll also have an opportunity to cheer the voters' successful choices and bemoan their failures. And, if we look closely enough, we'll detect several ways to make important improvements in the Hall of Fame in the years to come.

1936

Hall of Fame Summary

New inductees: 5
Category: Player 5
Election: BBWAA 5
Player QS average: 92.2 (BBWAA 92.2)

Inductees

- Ty Cobb. **Category:** Player. **Position:** CF. **QS:** 90 (excellent). **Career:** 1905-1928, G 3,034, HR 117, RBI 1,944, BA .366. **Election:** BBWAA.
- Walter Johnson. **Category:** Player. **Position:** P. **QS:** 96 (excellent). **Career:** 1907-1927, G 802, W-L 417-279, SV 34, ERA 2.17. **Election:** BBWAA.
- Christy Mathewson. **Category:** Player. **Position:** P. **QS:** 87 (excellent). **Career:** 1900-1916, G 636, W-L 373-188, SV 30, ERA 2.13. **Election:** BBWAA.
- Babe Ruth. **Category:** Player. **Position:** RF. **QS:** 90 (excellent). **Career:** 1914-1935, G 2,503, HR 714, RBI 2,214, BA .342. **Election:** BBWAA.
- Honus Wagner. **Category:** Player. **Position:** SS. **QS:** 98 (excellent). **Career:** 1897-1917, G 2,794, HR 101, RBI 1,732, BA .328. **Election:** BBWAA.

BBWAA Election Summary

Voters: 226
Votes needed for induction: 170
Candidates receiving votes: 47
Candidates elected: 5
Candidates inducted in future: 35

BBWAA Top Ten

1. Ty Cobb, 222 (98.23%)*
2. Babe Ruth, 215 (95.13%)*
2. Honus Wagner, 215 (95.13%)*
4. Christy Mathewson, 205 (90.71%)*
5. Walter Johnson, 189 (83.63%)*
6. Nap Lajoie, 146 (64.60%)
7. Tris Speaker, 133 (58.85%)
8. Cy Young, 111 (49.12%)
9. Rogers Hornsby, 105 (46.46%)
10. Mickey Cochrane, 80 (35.40%)

THIS SHOULD HAVE BEEN a simple year—the simplest of all—for the Hall of Fame's voters. They were starting from scratch in 1936, so their pool of candidates was unlimited. Every player who participated in the first sixty-five years of big-league competition was in the mix.

It's hard to dispute the electorate's eventual choices. Four of the five inductees boasted quality scores of ninety or better. The outlier, Christy Mathewson, had a score of eighty-seven. The average QS of 92.2 remains the highest for any multiplayer class in the hall's history.

But the election process failed to meet expectations in 1936, despite the pristine circumstances. The Hall of Fame's brain trust entered the inaugural year with a vague plan to elect as many as ten charter members. The BBWAA was instructed to skim the cream from the post-1900 period, an assignment it completed with its five selections. A seventy-eight-member Old-Timers Committee was asked to identify the best players from the nineteenth century, a task it bungled badly.[16]

The problem was a lack of clarity about which players belonged to which group. Baseball's winningest pitcher, Cy Young, was the prime case in point. He had played in both centuries, notching 286 victories between 1890 and 1900, then another 225 from 1901 to 1911, yielding his famous total of 511 wins. If anybody was worthy of a plaque in Cooperstown, it was Young.

But nobody from the Hall of Fame bothered to decide if the BBWAA or the committee had prior claim, so Young received only 49.1 percent support from the former and 41.7 percent from the latter, well short of the 75 percent threshold. A substantial number of voters on each side had assumed that Young's fate was the responsibility of the other. The same confusion hampered seven other players whose careers straddled the turn of the century. They also drew votes from both groups, but not enough from either.

The Old-Timers Committee proved to be remarkably picky in general. Its members split their votes among fifty-seven candidates, giving bare majorities to only two, Cap Anson and Buck Ewing, who tied for first place at 50.6 percent. Both fell twenty votes short of election, so the first three decades of big-league ball went unrepresented in the Hall of Fame's charter class.

The BBWAA's election also had its critics. It was widely assumed that the greatest players would be universally acclaimed by the 226 voters. Each writer, after all, was allowed to support as many as ten candidates, affording ample space to include the all-time favorites. The first hundred ballots were unfolded and counted, and all contained the names of Babe Ruth and Ty Cobb. Then came a piece of paper with no mention of Ruth. "The [tabulation] committee was amazed," wrote an unidentified *New York Times* reporter. "Vote counting stopped momentarily for a discussion on how anyone could leave the great Ruth off the list of immortals."[17] A ballot without Cobb's name was soon discovered.

The press bemoaned the lack of unanimity. John Kieran of the *Times* suggested that a handful of voters had penalized Ruth and Cobb for their "deliberate or carefree antics" as young men. "The Babe was no model of deportment when he came roistering along the road to fame some fifteen years ago. The fiery Cobb made plenty of enemies during his baseball career," the columnist conceded. He suggested that the recalcitrant voters had held the stars to a higher standard. "To them, Ruth and Cobb may have failed in the character test," Kieran wrote, thereby making the first connection between the Hall of Fame and the C-word that would become so famous in the twenty-first century.[18]

Ruth and Honus Wagner were spurned by eleven voters apiece, tying for second place. Cobb, who was left off of only four ballots, emerged as the top vote-getter. His share of 98.23 percent, which would remain the record until 1992, elevated him to the status of first among equals, the unofficial leader of the five immortals.

One other aspect of the 1936 election was obscured by the parallel controversies stirred up by the Old-Timers Committee's confusion and the BBWAA's lack of total agreement. Abner Doubleday, still highly acclaimed as baseball's founding father, was somehow left out of the class of 1936, yet nobody seemed to notice—or care. It was a curious omission indeed.

1937

Hall of Fame Summary

New inductees: 8
Category: Player 3, Manager 2, Pioneer/Executive 3
Election: BBWAA 3, Committee 5
Player QS average: 87.0 (BBWAA 87.0)
Hall of Famers to date: 13
Category: Player 8, Manager 2, Pioneer/Executive 3
Election: BBWAA 8, Committee 5
Player QS average: 90.3 (BBWAA 90.3)

Inductees

- Morgan Bulkeley. **Category:** Pioneer/Executive. **Election:** Centennial Commission.
- Ban Johnson. **Category:** Pioneer/Executive. **Election:** Centennial Commission.
- Nap Lajoie. **Category:** Player. **Position:** 2B. **QS:** 90 (excellent). **Career:** 1896-1916, G 2,480, HR 82, RBI 1,599, BA .338. **Election:** BBWAA.
- Connie Mack. **Category:** Manager. **Career:** 1894-1950, W-L 3,731-3,948, Pennants 9, Titles 5. **Election:** Centennial Commission.
- John McGraw. **Category:** Manager. **Career:** 1899-1932, W-L 2,763-1,948, Pennants 10, Titles 3. **Election:** Centennial Commission.
- Tris Speaker. **Category:** Player. **Position:** CF. **QS:** 85 (excellent). **Career:** 1907-1928, G 2,789, HR 117, RBI 1,531, BA .345. **Election:** BBWAA.
- George Wright. **Category:** Pioneer/Executive. **Election:** Centennial Commission.
- Cy Young. **Category:** Player. **Position:** P. **QS:** 86 (excellent). **Career:** 1890-1911, G 906, W-L 511-315, SV 18, ERA 2.63. **Election:** BBWAA.

BBWAA Election Summary

Voters: 201
Votes needed for induction: 151
Candidates receiving votes: 113
Candidates elected: 3
Candidates inducted in future: 49

BBWAA Top Ten

1. Nap Lajoie, 168 (83.58%)*
2. Tris Speaker, 165 (82.09%)*
3. Cy Young, 153 (76.12%)*
4. Pete Alexander, 125 (62.19%)

5. Eddie Collins, 115 (57.21%)
5. Willie Keeler, 115 (57.21%)
7. George Sisler, 106 (52.74%)
8. Ed Delahanty, 70 (34.83%)
9. Rube Waddell, 67 (33.33%)
10. Jimmy Collins, 66 (32.84%)

KENESAW MOUNTAIN LANDIS HAD no patience for sloppiness, so the bulky and bumbling Old-Timers Committee was eliminated one year after its creation. It was replaced by the grandly titled Centennial Commission, which comprised Commissioner Landis, the presidents of the American and National Leagues, and three other functionaries. "They were, in short, the people who held the power in baseball at the time," wrote Bill James, "and pretty much could do whatever the hell they wanted to." Which is what they did.[19]

Some of the commission's five choices in 1937 were indisputably sound, notably those of Connie Mack and John McGraw, who were considered baseball's greatest managers to that point. Mack and McGraw had piled up a total of nineteen pennants and eight World Series titles. But Landis & Co. also made one of the most absurd selections in Hall of Fame history, Morgan Bulkeley, who had been appointed as president of the National League in 1876 after his name was drawn from a hat. Bulkeley served for a single year as a figurehead for William Hulbert, the real power behind the NL, and then left to pursue a political career. He left no imprint on baseball.[20]

The BBWAA made amends to Cy Young by electing him to the hall with 153 votes, 2 above the threshold. The writers also admitted Nap Lajoie and Tris Speaker, the pair who had finished immediately behind the five immortals in the 1936 election. All three of the BBWAA's 1937 choices were excellent, as evidenced by their quality scores of eighty-five or better.

1938

Hall of Fame Summary

New inductees: 3
Category: Player 1, Pioneer/Executive 2
Election: BBWAA 1, Committee 2
Player QS average: 86.0 (BBWAA 86.0)
Hall of Famers to date: 16
Category: Player 9, Manager 2, Pioneer/Executive 5
Election: BBWAA 9, Committee 7
Player QS average: 89.8 (BBWAA 89.8)

Inductees

- Pete Alexander. **Category:** Player. **Position:** P. **QS:** 86 (excellent). **Career:** 1911-1930, G 696, W-L 373-208, SV 32, ERA 2.56. **Election:** BBWAA.
- Alexander Cartwright. **Category:** Pioneer/Executive. **Election:** Centennial Commission.
- Henry Chadwick. **Category:** Pioneer/Executive. **Election:** Centennial Commission.

BBWAA Election Summary

Voters: 262
Votes needed for induction: 197
Candidates receiving votes: 120
Candidates elected: 1
Candidates inducted in future: 53

BBWAA Top Ten

1. Pete Alexander, 212 (80.92%)*
2. George Sisler, 179 (68.32%)
3. Willie Keeler, 177 (67.56%)
4. Eddie Collins, 175 (66.79%)
5. Rube Waddell, 148 (56.49%)
6. Frank Chance, 133 (50.76%)
7. Ed Delahanty, 132 (50.38%)
8. Ed Walsh, 110 (41.98%)
9. Johnny Evers, 91 (34.73%)
10. Jimmy Collins, 79 (30.15%)

A SPECIAL URGENCY IMPELLED the induction of Grover Cleveland Alexander in 1938. The great pitcher, who was commonly known as Pete, had finished back in the pack in the BBWAA's initial election, supported by just 24 percent of the electorate. But an Associated Press dispatch revealed during the 1937 voting period that Alexander was "now reported near death." A surge of sympathy vaulted him to 62 percent, and the writers finished the job by making him their only Hall of Fame choice in 1938.[21]

It was the first occasion, though certainly not the last, of death (either recent or impending) swaying the Hall of Fame's voters. Yet the report proved to be false. Alexander clearly deserved his plaque—he had a QS of eighty-six—and there was no denying the harshness of his life. He was an alcoholic who rotated through a series of sanitariums and boarding houses, never able to hold a job after his baseball days. But he did not die until 1950, when he was claimed either by an epileptic seizure or a heart attack.[22]

It was certainly no consolation, but Alexander's tribulations gave him a perspective that would be sorely lacking in several egomaniacal honorees who later crossed Cooperstown's doorstep. "I'm in the Hall of Fame, and I'm proud to be there," he once said. "But I can't eat the Hall of Fame."[23]

The Centennial Commission chipped in with a pair of intriguing and commendable choices in 1938. Alexander Cartwright was credited with establishing many of the game's basic rules, such as setting the bases ninety feet apart and limiting games to nine innings. His plaque dubbed him the "father of modern baseball," hinting that the sport's leaders privately doubted the Doubleday myth they peddled in public. Henry Chadwick was a journalist who was hailed as the inventor of the box score and the author of baseball's first rulebook. "Of all the contributions baseball writers have made to the game, his was probably the greatest," said Ford Frick, a former sportswriter himself.[24]

1939

Hall of Fame Summary

New inductees: 10
Category: Player 7, Pioneer/Executive 3
Election: BBWAA 4, Committee 6
Player QS average: 57.7 (BBWAA 61.5, Committee 52.7)
Hall of Famers to date: 26
Category: Player 16, Manager 2, Pioneer/Executive 8
Election: BBWAA 13, Committee 13
Player QS average: 75.8 (BBWAA 81.1, Committee 52.7)

Inductees

- Cap Anson. **Category:** Player. **Position:** 1B. **QS:** 83 (excellent). **Career:** 1871-1897, G 2,524, HR 97, RBI 2,075, BA .334. **Election:** Centennial Commission.
- Eddie Collins. **Category:** Player. **Position:** 2B. **QS:** 72 (excellent). **Career:** 1906-1930, G 2,826, HR 47, RBI 1,299, BA .333. **Election:** BBWAA.
- Charles Comiskey. **Category:** Pioneer/Executive. **Election:** Centennial Commission.
- Candy Cummings. **Category:** Pioneer/Executive. **Election:** Centennial Commission.
- Buck Ewing. **Category:** Player. **Position:** C. **QS:** 33 (marginal). **Career:** 1880-1897, G 1,315, HR 71, RBI 883, BA .303. **Election:** Centennial Commission.
- Lou Gehrig. **Category:** Player. **Position:** 1B. **QS:** 87 (excellent). **Career:** 1923-1939, G 2,164, HR 493, RBI 1,995, BA .340. **Election:** BBWAA.
- Willie Keeler. **Category:** Player. **Position:** RF. **QS:** 45 (good). **Career:** 1892-1910, G 2,123, HR 33, RBI 810, BA .341. **Election:** BBWAA.
- Old Hoss Radbourn. **Category:** Player. **Position:** P. **QS:** 42 (marginal). **Career:** 1881-1891, G 527, W-L 310-194, SV 2, ERA 2.68. **Election:** Centennial Commission.
- George Sisler. **Category:** Player. **Position:** 1B. **QS:** 42 (marginal). **Career:** 1915-1930, G 2,055, HR 102, RBI 1,178, BA .340. **Election:** BBWAA.
- Al Spalding. **Category:** Pioneer/Executive. **Election:** Centennial Commission.

BBWAA Election Summary

Voters: 274
Votes needed for induction: 206
Candidates receiving votes: 108

Candidates elected: 4^
Candidates inducted in future: 53
^: Collins, Keeler, and Sisler were chosen in the BBWAA's 1939 general
  election. Gehrig was chosen in a special election in December 1939.

<u>BBWAA Top Ten</u>

1. George Sisler, 235 (85.77%)*
2. Eddie Collins, 213 (77.74%)*
3. Willie Keeler, 207 (75.55%)*
4. Rube Waddell, 179 (65.33%)
5. Rogers Hornsby, 176 (64.23%)
6. Frank Chance, 158 (57.66%)
7. Ed Delahanty, 145 (52.92%)
8. Ed Walsh, 132 (48.18%)
9. Johnny Evers, 107 (39.05%)
10. Miller Huggins, 97 (35.40%)

SIXTEEN MEN WERE ADMITTED to the Hall of Fame in its first three elections. Most of the choices—with the obvious exception of the nondescript Morgan Bulkeley—were beyond reproach. The honorees included nine players, all with quality scores of eighty-five or better, putting them in the upper half of the excellent range.

Cooperstown's standards began to loosen in 1939 in a couple of ways.

The first was the sheer size of the class of '39, which contained ten members. It remains to this day the third-largest group of inductees in a single year.

The second was a new willingness to honor men with lesser accomplishments. The quality scores for four of the seven players admitted in 1939 were lower than fifty points. Buck Ewing, to be fair, had been a very good catcher for several clubs in the nineteenth century, but his QS was just thirty-three points, roughly one-third of Honus Wagner's ninety-eight.

Nine of 1939's ten honorees were elected to the hall during the regular round of voting. Lou Gehrig was added in December. The first baseman for the New York Yankees, the famed Iron Horse, had played his final game seven months earlier, ending a record streak of 2,130 consecutive appearances. He had mysteriously grown feeble, too weak to play big-league ball. Doctors at the Mayo Clinic soon diagnosed him with amyotrophic lateral sclerosis. They gave him no more than three years to live.[25]

The BBWAA conducted a special election during baseball's winter meetings in Cincinnati. The writers voted unanimously to suspend the rules and immediately admit Gehrig to the Hall of Fame. Their resolution expressed a desire to "commemorate the year in which he achieved his record."[26] Gehrig's QS of eighty-seven surpassed the scores for all six players who had been elected earlier in the year.

The BBWAA made another important decision in Cincinnati. The writers canceled their annual voting schedule, replacing it with a three-year cycle, apparently under the theory that too many men were being inducted into the Hall of Fame much too quickly. The next election was set for 1942.[27]

The Centennial Commission also suspended operations, though no reason was given. Baseball had just celebrated its hundredth birthday, so the panel's name was no longer relevant, and Kenesaw Mountain Landis seemed to believe that the panel itself was somehow lacking. He would eventually reconstitute the Old-Timers Committee as a replacement, though not for another five years.

1942

Hall of Fame Summary

New inductees: 1
Category: Player 1
Election: BBWAA 1
Player QS average: 96.0 (BBWAA 96.0)
Hall of Famers to date: 27
Category: Player 17, Manager 2, Pioneer/Executive 8
Election: BBWAA 14, Committee 13
Player QS average: 76.9 (BBWAA 82.1, Committee 52.7)

Inductees

- Rogers Hornsby. **Category:** Player. **Position:** 2B. **QS:** 96 (excellent). **Career:** 1915-1937, G 2,259, HR 301, RBI 1,584, BA .358. **Election:** BBWAA.

BBWAA Election Summary

Voters: 233
Votes needed for induction: 175
Candidates receiving votes: 72
Candidates elected: 1
Candidates inducted in future: 44

BBWAA Top Ten

1. Rogers Hornsby, 182 (78.11%)*
2. Frank Chance, 136 (58.37%)
2. Rube Waddell, 136 (58.37%)
4. Ed Walsh, 113 (48.50%)
5. Miller Huggins, 111 (47.64%)
6. Ed Delahanty, 104 (44.64%)
7. Johnny Evers, 91 (39.06%)
8. Wilbert Robinson, 89 (38.20%)
9. Mickey Cochrane, 88 (37.77%)
10. Frankie Frisch, 84 (36.05%)

SPORTSWRITERS DESERVED TO TAKE a bow in 1942. They elected Rogers Hornsby to the Hall of Fame, even though he had treated most of them with contempt throughout his twenty-three year career.

Hornsby clearly belonged in Cooperstown. His credentials were impeccable: seven batting titles, a pair of Triple Crowns, and a career batting average of .358 (adjusted to .329 on the 2011-2020 scale). His score of ninety-six points tied him with Walter Johnson for second place in the all-time QS rankings.

The problem was that Hornsby also led the majors in sarcasm, snide remarks, and all-around ornery behavior. Everybody was a target for his barbed remarks or chilly silences—baseball executives, reporters, opponents, even his teammates. John Drebinger of the *New York Times* tried to put a gloss on this persistently antisocial behavior. He wrote that Hornsby, "blunt and outspoken to a fault, somehow could never keep his peace with the so-called 'stuffed shirts' in baseball front offices."[28]

But Drebinger was writing the day after Hornsby's election had been announced. He was trying to be nice, portraying the new inductee as an anti-establishment rebel. The truth was that almost everybody who came into contact with Hornsby disliked him, a pattern that never changed. Dozens of contemporaries willingly spoke of their hatred.

Space is limited, so let's randomly call on two critics from different decades, a pair of players who had Hornsby as a manager. Second baseman Billy Herman, himself a future Hall of Famer, broke in under Hornsby with the Chicago Cubs in 1931. "He was a very cold man," said Herman. "He ignored me completely, and I figured it was because I was a rookie. But then I realized he ignored everybody."[29] Shortstop Joe DeMaestri, who played eleven seasons in the majors, made Hornsby's acquaintance on the 1952 St. Louis Browns. He recalled the old man as "the worst manager and the worst person I ever played for."[30]

I'm not saying that obnoxious characters should be kept out of the Hall of Fame. Rule 5 didn't exist in 1942, but even if it had, it should never have been stretched that far.

My point is something different, something that was ignored in the contemporary accounts of Hornsby's election. A player with his tremendous record—probably the greatest second baseman in history—barely eked into the Hall of Fame. He received only 182 votes, exceeding the threshold by 7. Fifty-one writers knew of his excellence, yet deliberately left him off their ballots.

Hornsby once conceded that he was "rough and hard-boiled and demanding."[31] These traits, he said, were byproducts of his love of baseball. Well, the BBWAA showed him in 1942 that it also knew something about tough love. Hornsby was too talented to bar from Cooperstown, but his rocky path to induction was an object lesson for Hall of Fame candidates whose resumés weren't as shiny. An uncivil relationship with the press could have unhappy consequences on election day.

1944

Hall of Fame Summary

New inductees: 1
Category: Pioneer/Executive 1
Election: Committee 1
Hall of Famers to date: 28
Category: Player 17, Manager 2, Pioneer/Executive 9
Election: BBWAA 14, Committee 14
Player QS average: 76.9 (BBWAA 82.1, Committee 52.7)

Inductees

- Kenesaw Mountain Landis. **Category:** Pioneer/Executive. **Election:** Old-Timers Committee.

STEPHEN CLARK, THE FOUNDER of the Hall of Fame, was installed by Kenesaw Mountain Landis as chairman of a reincarnated Old-Timers Committee in August 1944. The panel comprised six members in all, including three club presidents and two sportswriters. There was idle talk about a preliminary meeting, but none had been scheduled prior to the arrival of sad news from Chicago.[32]

The commissioner suffered a fatal coronary thrombosis on November 25, 1944, five days after his seventy-eighth birthday. Baseball plunged into mourning. "Landis lifted the sport to the highest plane it has ever achieved and built for himself a monument that will endure as long as the game itself," insisted the *Sporting News*.[33] Even Clark Griffith, the perpetually cranky owner of the Washington Senators, seemed to be deeply affected by the loss. "We are beholden to him for so much," Griffith said.[34]

The course of action was clear. The Old-Timers Committee had no option but to follow the Gehrig precedent and elect Landis to the Hall of Fame immediately. Clark assembled his colleagues in early December, and they did just that.

Selected aspects of Landis's record were glossed over in the haste to enshrine him. Many owners—no matter what they said in public—privately disparaged his cold demeanor, erratic temper, and dictatorial behavior. They also conceded that Landis's accomplishments had been limited in scope. The former federal judge had served as baseball's commissioner for nearly a quarter of a century (1920-1944), yet had done little to advance the sport.

It was true that he had permanently banned the Black Sox for fixing the 1919 World Series, an act always depicted with Landis in the role of Superman, singlehandedly rescuing the national pastime. But baseball's enhanced popularity in the 1920s owed more to the incandescence of its new stars, especially Babe Ruth, and the robust health of the economy than to any ruling issued by the commissioner.[35]

Landis accomplished little of a constructive nature after handing down the Black Sox decision. The years passed, and he made no effort to improve baseball's administration or expand its audience. Owners often asked for guidance on complicated issues. "Do it, and I'll rule on it," he invariably replied. He always thought of himself as a judge, not a leader.[36]

America's population soared by 30 percent during his tenure—adding thirty-two million residents—yet Landis did nothing to extend baseball's footprint.[37] The same sixteen clubs played in the same ten Northeastern and Midwestern cities when he took office and when he died. He instinctively opposed most innovations, including night baseball and farm systems, though he was not always able to block them. Civil rights emerged as an important issue in his later years, yet Landis quietly worked to forestall integration of the major leagues.[38]

His successor as commissioner, Happy Chandler, was one of the few who looked behind the myth, who realized that enshrining Landis in the Hall of Fame was like giving a lifetime achievement award to a steady, albeit uninspired, employee. "I knew Old Man Landis," Chandler once said. "I knew him well. He was a nice old man—but nothing special."[39]

1945

Hall of Fame Summary

New inductees: 10
Category: Player 9, Manager 1
Election: Committee 10
Player QS average: 43.6 (Committee 43.6)
Hall of Famers to date: 38
Category: Player 26, Manager 3, Pioneer/Executive 9
Election: BBWAA 14, Committee 24
Player QS average: 65.4 (BBWAA 82.1, Committee 45.8)

Inductees

- Roger Bresnahan. **Category:** Player. **Position:** C. **QS:** 12 (poor). **Career:** 1897-1915, G 1,446, HR 26, RBI 530, BA .279. **Election:** Old-Timers Committee.
- Dan Brouthers. **Category:** Player. **Position:** 1B. **QS:** 86 (excellent). **Career:** 1879-1904, G 1,676, HR 107, RBI 1,301, BA .342. **Election:** Old-Timers Committee.
- Fred Clarke. **Category:** Player. **Position:** LF. **QS:** 45 (good). **Career:** 1894-1915, G 2,246, HR 67, RBI 1,015, BA .312. **Election:** Old-Timers Committee.
- Jimmy Collins. **Category:** Player. **Position:** 3B. **QS:** 19 (poor). **Career:** 1895-1908, G 1,725, HR 65, RBI 983, BA .294. **Election:** Old-Timers Committee.
- Ed Delahanty. **Category:** Player. **Position:** LF. **QS:** 73 (excellent). **Career:** 1888-1903, G 1,837, HR 101, RBI 1,466, BA .346. **Election:** Old-Timers Committee.
- Hugh Duffy. **Category:** Player. **Position:** CF. **QS:** 38 (marginal). **Career:** 1888-1906, G 1,737, HR 106, RBI 1,302, BA .326. **Election:** Old-Timers Committee.
- Hughie Jennings. **Category:** Player. **Position:** SS. **QS:** 21 (poor). **Career:** 1891-1918, G 1,284, HR 18, RBI 840, BA .312. **Election:** Old-Timers Committee.
- King Kelly. **Category:** Player. **Position:** RF. **QS:** 49 (good). **Career:** 1878-1893, G 1,456, HR 69, RBI 950, BA .307. **Election:** Old-Timers Committee.
- Jim O'Rourke. **Category:** Player. **Position:** LF. **QS:** 49 (good). **Career:** 1872-1904, G 1,999, HR 62, RBI 1,208, BA .310. **Election:** Old-Timers Committee.
- Wilbert Robinson. **Category:** Manager. **Career:** 1902-1931, W-L 1,399-1,398, Pennants 2, Titles 0. **Election:** Old-Timers Committee.

BBWAA Election Summary

Voters: 247
Votes needed for induction: 186
Candidates receiving votes: 95
Candidates elected: 0
Candidates inducted in future: 56

BBWAA Top Ten

1. Frank Chance, 179 (72.47%)
2. Rube Waddell, 154 (62.35%)
3. Ed Walsh, 137 (55.47%)
4. Johnny Evers, 134 (54.25%)
5. Roger Bresnahan, 133 (53.85%)
5. Miller Huggins, 133 (53.85%)
7. Mickey Cochrane, 125 (50.61%)
8. Jimmy Collins, 121 (48.99%)
9. Ed Delahanty, 111 (44.94%)
10. Clark Griffith, 108 (43.72%)

IF LOGIC HAD PREVAILED, the BBWAA would have elected several players to the Hall of Fame in 1945. A substantial backlog had developed during the previous five years, a half-decade in which the writers elevated Rogers Hornsby and no one else. The quality scores for thirteen of 1945's candidates exceeded sixty points—putting them in the excellent range—and the marks for another twenty contenders were classified as good (forty-five to fifty-nine points). This wealth of talent apparently overwhelmed the writers, who scattered their votes among ninety-five players, including fifty-six who would ultimately be admitted to Cooperstown.

The latter figure confirmed the outstanding quality of the year's field. No other Hall of Fame election from 1936 to 2022 encompassed such a large number of future inductees. Yet the writers spurned every single candidate in 1945. Frontrunner Frank Chance fell seven votes short of the 75 percent threshold. Nobody else came within thirty votes.

The void was filled by a suddenly vigorous Old-Timers Committee, which previously had done nothing but rubber-stamp the ascension of Kenesaw Mountain Landis. The panel announced an extensive list of ten honorees in 1945, headed by a pair of unassailable selections, Dan Brouthers and Ed Delahanty, who had ranked among the greatest hitters in the late nineteenth century.

But several of the committee's other choices were head-scratchers. Shortstop Hughie Jennings (twenty-one points), third baseman Jimmy Collins (nineteen), and catcher Roger Bresnahan (twelve) became the first inductees with quality scores under thirty, landing them in the lowest range on the QS scale.

Sympathy played a role in their inductions. The committee met just four months after Bresnahan died, two years after Collins passed away. Influential patrons were also important. Collins had played for Connie Mack, the dominant member of the Old-Timers Committee, while Jennings had been a close friend of Hall of Fame manager John McGraw. Unusual factors proved to be instrumental, too. Much was made of Bresnahan's 1907 invention of shinguards for catchers.[40]

Another McGraw acolyte, Wilbert Robinson, was the only manager inducted in 1945. Robinson had been a solid catcher for the Baltimore Orioles in the 1890s, but his selection was tied specifically to the eighteen seasons (1914-1931) he spent at the helm of the Brooklyn Dodgers. The committee ignored his unimpressive managerial record—1,399 wins against 1,398 losses (just one game above .500) with no World Series titles—and indulged its fond memories of the easygoing rascal known to one and all as Uncle Robbie. "His conversation was a continuous flow of homely philosophy, baseball lore, and good humor," John Kieran happily recalled.[41]

This was the first election conducted under Rule 5, the clause that added "integrity, sportsmanship, [and] character" to the list of necessary virtues for induction.[42] Nobody paid much attention. It would have been considered absurd to suggest the removal of Cap Anson because of his racism or Rogers Hornsby because of his misanthropy. A few writers even gave game-fixers a pass. Shoeless Joe Jackson, infamous for his involvement in the Black Sox scandal, would receive two votes in 1946.

1946

Hall of Fame Summary

New inductees: 11
Category: Player 10, Pioneer/Executive 1
Election: Committee 11
Player QS average: 33.9 (Committee 33.9)
Hall of Famers to date: 49
Category: Player 36, Manager 3, Pioneer/Executive 10
Election: BBWAA 14, Committee 35
Player QS average: 56.6 (BBWAA 82.1, Committee 40.4)

Inductees

- Jesse Burkett. **Category:** Player. **Position:** LF. **QS:** 51 (good). **Career:** 1890-1905, G 2,067, HR 75, RBI 952, BA .338. **Election:** Old-Timers Committee.
- Frank Chance. **Category:** Player. **Position:** 1B. **QS:** 26 (poor). **Career:** 1898-1914, G 1,288, HR 20, RBI 596, BA .296. **Election:** Old-Timers Committee.
- Jack Chesbro. **Category:** Player. **Position:** P. **QS:** 13 (poor). **Career:** 1899-1909, G 392, W-L 198-132, SV 5, ERA 2.68. **Election:** Old-Timers Committee.
- Johnny Evers. **Category:** Player. **Position:** 2B. **QS:** 12 (poor). **Career:** 1902-1929, G 1,784, HR 12, RBI 536, BA .270. **Election:** Old-Timers Committee.
- Clark Griffith. **Category:** Pioneer/Executive. **Election:** Old-Timers Committee.
- Tommy McCarthy. **Category:** Player. **Position:** RF. **QS:** 1 (poor). **Career:** 1884-1896, G 1,273, HR 44, RBI 732, BA .292. **Election:** Old-Timers Committee.
- Joe McGinnity. **Category:** Player. **Position:** P. **QS:** 39 (marginal). **Career:** 1899-1908, G 465, W-L 246-142, SV 24, ERA 2.66. **Election:** Old-Timers Committee.
- Eddie Plank. **Category:** Player. **Position:** P. **QS:** 58 (good). **Career:** 1901-1917, G 623, W-L 326-194, SV 23, ERA 2.35. **Election:** Old-Timers Committee.
- Joe Tinker. **Category:** Player. **Position:** SS. **QS:** 21 (poor). **Career:** 1902-1916, G 1,806, HR 31, RBI 785, BA .262. **Election:** Old-Timers Committee.
- Rube Waddell. **Category:** Player. **Position:** P. **QS:** 59 (good). **Career:** 1897-1910, G 407, W-L 193-143, SV 5, ERA 2.16. **Election:** Old-Timers Committee.

- Ed Walsh. **Category:** Player. **Position:** P. **QS:** 59 (good). **Career:** 1904-1917, G 430, W-L 195-126, SV 35, ERA 1.82. **Election:** Old-Timers Committee.

BBWAA Election Summary

Voters: 202
Votes needed for induction: 152
Candidates receiving votes: 76
Candidates elected: 0
Candidates inducted in future: 46

BBWAA Top Ten

1. Frank Chance, 144 (71.29%)
2. Johnny Evers, 130 (64.36%)
3. Miller Huggins, 129 (63.86%)
4. Rube Waddell, 122 (60.40%)
5. Ed Walsh, 115 (56.93%)
6. Frankie Frisch, 104 (51.49%)
7. Carl Hubbell, 101 (50.00%)
8. Mickey Cochrane, 80 (39.60%)
9. Clark Griffith, 73 (36.14%)
10. Lefty Grove, 71 (35.15%)

COOPERSTOWN'S WAITING LIST HAD grown so lengthy by 1946 that it could not be ignored. "Getting into baseball's Hall of Fame has been a more difficult task than getting into the Union League Club or into heaven," conceded Arthur Daley, a columnist for the *New York Times*.[43]

The BBWAA offered a pair of solutions. It scrapped its three-year cycle in favor of annual elections. And it pledged to stage a second contest—a runoff election—if all of a given year's candidates failed to reach 75 percent.

These changes had no immediate impact. Frank Chance remained the BBWAA's top vote-getter, but he once again failed to attain the magic number. Chance had fallen seven votes short of induction in 1945. He finished eight votes shy in 1946's initial election. A breakthrough was widely anticipated in the runoff, yet Chance's share inexplicably plummeted from 71.3 percent to 57.0 percent. No other candidate topped 42 percent in the second contest. The writers had struck out once again.

The Old-Timers Committee rode to the rescue, making Chance one of its eleven Hall of Fame selections. The panel, for good measure, added the other two members of the Cubs' double-play combination—"Tinker to Evers to Chance"—that had been immortalized in a 1910 poem by Franklin P. Adams.[44]

A case could be made for the induction of Chance, whose QS of twenty-six was not particularly impressive, yet who had managed the Cubs to four pennants and two world titles while also starring at first base. But the selections of shortstop Joe Tinker (twenty-one points) and second baseman Johnny Evers (twelve) were laughable. Adams had acclaimed the fielding skills of the Chicago triumvirate—"trio of bear cubs, and fleeter than birds"—though his poetic license was blatant. Tinker, Evers, and Chance had been teammates for eleven seasons (1902-1912), a span in which the Cubs never led the National League in double plays.[45] "Almost singlehandedly, that poem was later to carry those three players into baseball's holy of holies, the Hall of Fame in Cooperstown," admitted Ford Frick.[46]

Four of the Old-Timers Committee's choices in 1946 were indisputable. Left fielder Jesse Burkett and pitchers Eddie Plank, Rube Waddell, and Ed Walsh all had quality scores higher than fifty points. But five of the new inductees were mired in the poor range with QS readings below thirty. A total of nineteen players were admitted to the hall during the committee's 1945-1946 orgy. They carried an average quality score of 38.5, only half as good as the average QS of 76.9 for their seventeen predecessors inducted between 1936 and 1942.

The worst selection in 1946 was inexplicably bad. Tommy McCarthy had been an outfielder for five clubs over thirteen seasons in the previous century. He was certainly fast—stealing as many as ninety-three bases in a season—but had otherwise failed to distinguish himself. McCarthy's quality score of one point—*one!*—is still the lowest for any member of the Hall of Fame.

Critics pinned the blame on chauvinism. The real name of the committee's most powerful member, Connie Mack, was Cornelius McGillicuddy. It was perhaps no coincidence that the classes of 1945 and 1946 abounded with Irish surnames: Bresnahan, Collins, Delahanty, Duffy, Kelly, McGinnity, O'Rourke, Walsh, and yes, McCarthy. "The new immortals sounded like a roll call at a meeting of the Ancient Order of Hibernians," moaned Zev Chafets.[47]

The baseball establishment watched 1946's selection process with distaste. The BBWAA was unable to elect anybody, while the Old-Timers Committee was inclined to elect everybody, or so it seemed. The *Sporting News* threw up its hands in frustration. "It appears," said one of its editorials, "that the entire Hall of Fame scheme is in need of a complete overhauling."[48]

1947

Hall of Fame Summary

New inductees: 4
Category: Player 4
Election: BBWAA 4
Player QS average: 58.8 (BBWAA 58.8)
Hall of Famers to date: 53
Category: Player 40, Manager 3, Pioneer/Executive 10
Election: BBWAA 18, Committee 35
Player QS average: 56.9 (BBWAA 76.9, Committee 40.4)

Inductees

- Mickey Cochrane. **Category:** Player. **Position:** C. **QS:** 21 (poor). **Career:** 1925-1937, G 1,482, HR 119, RBI 830, BA .320. **Election:** BBWAA.
- Frankie Frisch. **Category:** Player. **Position:** 2B. **QS:** 46 (good). **Career:** 1919-1937, G 2,311, HR 105, RBI 1,244, BA .316. **Election:** BBWAA.
- Lefty Grove. **Category:** Player. **Position:** P. **QS:** 90 (excellent). **Career:** 1925-1941, G 616, W-L 300-141, SV 54, ERA 3.06. **Election:** BBWAA.
- Carl Hubbell. **Category:** Player. **Position:** P. **QS:** 78 (excellent). **Career:** 1928-1943, G 535, W-L 253-154, SV 33, ERA 2.98. **Election:** BBWAA.

BBWAA Election Summary

Voters: 161
Votes needed for induction: 121
Candidates receiving votes: 39
Candidates elected: 4
Candidates inducted in future: 25

BBWAA Top Ten

1. Carl Hubbell, 140 (86.96%)*
2. Frankie Frisch, 136 (84.47%)*
3. Mickey Cochrane, 128 (79.50%)*
4. Lefty Grove, 123 (76.40%)*
5. Pie Traynor, 119 (73.91%)
6. Charlie Gehringer, 105 (65.22%)
7. Rabbit Maranville, 91 (56.52%)
8. Dizzy Dean, 88 (54.66%)
9. Herb Pennock, 86 (53.42%)
10. Charles Bender, 72 (44.72%)

THE BBWAA HAD BEEN decidedly unproductive—enshrining only one candidate since 1939—so the Hall of Fame began to tighten the screws.

The baseball writers had been allowed to vote for anybody who played at any point in the twentieth century, even those who had not yet retired. (Joe DiMaggio, Bill Dickey, Joe Gordon, Hank Greenberg, and Johnny Vander Meer were among the active players who received votes in 1945.) The hall's brain trust suspected that the younger, less knowledgeable voters were unfamiliar with many of the candidates, while their older colleagues were overburdened by the dizzying array of options.

The hall decided to make reductions on both sides. It shrank the electorate in 1947 by stripping the voting rights of any writer who hadn't been a member of the BBWAA for at least a decade. And it narrowed the field by imposing a one-year retirement requirement on candidates in 1946 and adding a quarter-century eligibility window the following year. That final step restricted 1947's ballot to players who had retired between 1921 and 1945.[49]

The changes appeared to have the desired effect, as the writers broke out of their slump by electing four candidates in 1947. The player who most deserved the honor, strangely enough, received the least support. Lefty Grove, the greatest left-handed pitcher over the first seven decades of big-league ball, squeaked above the 75 percent line with just two votes to spare. Thirty-eight writers somehow left Grove off their ballots, despite his three hundred victories, nine earned-run-average titles, consecutive Triple Crowns (wins, ERA, and strikeouts) in 1930 and 1931, and QS of ninety points.

The relative youth of the four inductees increased the Hall of Fame's attractiveness to the ticket-buying public. Most fans—even those in their teens and twenties—had closely followed the achievements of Grove, Mickey Cochrane, Frankie Frisch, and Carl Hubbell, all of whom had retired within the past decade. The honorees from the previous two years seemed like fossils by comparison. The nineteen players admitted in 1945 and 1946 had been retired for an average of thirty-six years, limiting their fan bases to the middle-aged and elderly.

Not everybody was happy with the alterations to the voting system.

Fewer than half of the BBWAA's eligible members—just 161 in all—cast ballots in 1947. It was easily the worst turnout for any Hall of Fame election to date, dipping below the previous ebb of 201 participants in 1937. Dan Daniel, the esteemed columnist for the *New York World-Telegram*, suggested that his fellow journalists consider terminating their formal affiliation with the Hall of Fame "unless all the writers are eligible and their field of choice is less restricted."[50]

1948

Hall of Fame Summary

New inductees: 2
Category: Player 2
Election: BBWAA 2
Player QS average: 22.0 (BBWAA 22.0)
Hall of Famers to date: 55
Category: Player 42, Manager 3, Pioneer/Executive 10
Election: BBWAA 20, Committee 35
Player QS average: 55.2 (BBWAA 71.5, Committee 40.4)

Inductees

- Herb Pennock. **Category:** Player. **Position:** P. **QS:** 28 (poor). **Career:** 1912-1934, G 617, W-L 241-162, SV 37, ERA 3.60. **Election:** BBWAA.
- Pie Traynor. **Category:** Player. **Position:** 3B. **QS:** 16 (poor). **Career:** 1920-1937, G 1,941, HR 58, RBI 1,273, BA .320. **Election:** BBWAA.

BBWAA Election Summary

Voters: 121
Votes needed for induction: 91
Candidates receiving votes: 106
Candidates elected: 2
Candidates inducted in future: 50

BBWAA Top Ten

1. Herb Pennock, 94 (77.69%)*
2. Pie Traynor, 93 (76.86%)*
3. Al Simmons, 60 (49.59%)
4. Charlie Gehringer, 52 (42.98%)
4. Bill Terry, 52 (42.98%)
6. Paul Waner, 51 (42.15%)
7. Jimmie Foxx, 50 (41.32%)
8. Dizzy Dean, 40 (33.06%)
8. Harry Heilmann, 40 (33.06%)
10. Bill Dickey, 39 (32.23%)

HERB PENNOCK MADE A dramatic exit. The fifty-three-year-old general manager of the Philadelphia Phillies collapsed as he entered New York's Waldorf-Astoria Hotel to attend a National League meeting in January 1948, and there he died, the victim of a cerebral hemorrhage.[51]

Pennock's death was widely publicized, not due to his executive position, but because of his starring role as a pitcher for the great New York Yankees in the 1920s and early 1930s. He had hovered on the fringe of Hall of Fame consideration for a decade—first receiving votes in 1937—though several pitchers appeared to be more deserving of induction. Kid Nichols, Dazzy Vance, Mordecai Brown, and Pud Galvin all had quality scores of forty-five points or better, seemingly putting them in line ahead of Pennock and his QS of twenty-eight.

But two important factors favored Pennock in 1948. He had played in the nation's premier media market, New York, where he enjoyed the enhanced acclaim that was denied those who spent their careers in smaller cities, as Nichols, Brown, and Galvin had done. And he died during the BBWAA's annual voting period, his name suddenly propelled to the forefront of the Hall of Fame discussion.

It wasn't overly surprising when Pennock's election was announced a month later. He vaulted from ninth place in 1947 to the very top of the standings in 1948. Accompanying him to Cooperstown was Pie Traynor, a longtime member of the Pittsburgh Pirates, who also jumped the line at his position. Traynor's QS (sixteen points) was a fraction of the scores for other third basemen still outside the hall, notably Home Run Baker (forty-nine) and Deacon White (forty-seven).

The writers continued to sulk in 1948. More than 300 ballots were sent to BBWAA members, but only 121 were returned, which remains the lowest number of participants in any Hall of Fame election. Traynor consequently set the all-time record for the fewest votes received by a new inductee, only ninety-three.[52]

1949

Hall of Fame Summary

New inductees: 3
Category: Player 3
Election: BBWAA 1, Committee 2
Player QS average: 64.7 (BBWAA 61.0, Committee 66.5)
Hall of Famers to date: 58
Category: Player 45, Manager 3, Pioneer/Executive 10
Election: BBWAA 21, Committee 37
Player QS average: 55.8 (BBWAA 71.0, Committee 42.6)

Inductees

- Mordecai Brown. **Category:** Player. **Position:** P. **QS:** 51 (good). **Career:** 1903-1916, G 481, W-L 239-130, SV 49, ERA 2.06. **Election:** Old-Timers Committee.
- Charlie Gehringer. **Category:** Player. **Position:** 2B. **QS:** 61 (excellent). **Career:** 1924-1942, G 2,323, HR 184, RBI 1,427, BA .320. **Election:** BBWAA.
- Kid Nichols. **Category:** Player. **Position:** P. **QS:** 82 (excellent). **Career:** 1890-1906, G 621, W-L 362-208, SV 16, ERA 2.96. **Election:** Old-Timers Committee.

BBWAA Election Summary

Voters: 153
Votes needed for induction: 115
Candidates receiving votes: 98
Candidates elected: 1
Candidates inducted in future: 51

BBWAA Top Ten

1. Charlie Gehringer, 102 (66.67%)^
2. Mel Ott, 94 (61.44%)
3. Al Simmons, 89 (58.17%)
4. Dizzy Dean, 88 (57.52%)
5. Jimmie Foxx, 85 (55.56%)
6. Bill Terry, 81 (52.94%)
7. Paul Waner, 73 (47.71%)
8. Hank Greenberg, 67 (43.79%)
9. Bill Dickey, 65 (42.48%)
10. Harry Heilmann, 59 (38.56%)

^: *Gehringer was chosen in a subsequent runoff election.*

THE FOUR ELECTIONS PRIOR to 1949 had lowered the Hall of Fame's standards dramatically. A few outstanding players were inducted in the span between 1945 and 1948, but Lefty Grove, Carl Hubbell, Dan Brouthers, and Ed Delahanty were outnumbered by Tommy McCarthy and his ilk. The quality scores for eleven of the twenty-five players admitted to Cooperstown during the four-year period were rated as poor. The average QS for all enshrined players had been an impressive 76.9 points as late as 1944, but it dived 28 percent to 55.2 points once 1948's election results were factored in.

This downward trend was arrested in 1949, when the BBWAA and the Old-Timers Committee made three admirable selections.

The writers initially reverted to their indecisive ways, leaving front-runner Charlie Gehringer thirteen votes short of induction. But they pushed the longtime Tigers second baseman up to 85 percent in the runoff. He was joined in the class of '49 by a pair of well-regarded pitchers, Kid Nichols and Mordecai Brown, both of whom were chosen by the committee. Brown was certainly deserving of the honor, as evidenced by his quality score of fifty-one points, though his candidacy undoubtedly received a boost from his death a year prior to the panel's election.[53]

1950

Hall of Fame Summary

New inductees: 0
Hall of Famers to date: 58
Category: Player 45, Manager 3, Pioneer/Executive 10
Election: BBWAA 21, Committee 37
Player QS average: 55.8 (BBWAA 71.0, Committee 42.6)

BBWAA Election Summary

Voters: 168
Votes needed for induction: 126
Candidates receiving votes: 100
Candidates elected: 0
Candidates inducted in future: 48

BBWAA Top Ten

1. Mel Ott, 115 (68.45%)
2. Bill Terry, 105 (62.50%)
3. Jimmie Foxx, 103 (61.31%)
4. Paul Waner, 95 (56.55%)
5. Al Simmons, 90 (53.57%)
6. Harry Heilmann, 87 (51.79%)
7. Dizzy Dean, 85 (50.60%)
8. Bill Dickey, 78 (46.43%)
9. Rabbit Maranville, 66 (39.29%)
10. Hank Greenberg, 64 (38.10%)

THE HALL OF FAME quietly scuttled its runoff provision at the start of the new year, even though the value of such an election had been proven in 1949. A runoff would have been equally useful in 1950, when the BBWAA once again failed to give the required level of support to any of the contenders.[54]

Not that there was a shortage of decent candidates. Eight eligible retirees boasted quality scores higher than 60 points, led by a pair of renowned sluggers, Jimmie Foxx (85 points) and Mel Ott (81), who had blasted 1,045 home runs between them. The average QS for 1950's top 10 vote-getters was 53.3, a figure that exceeded the scores for more than half of the players (23 of 45) who had already been inducted. All ten of 1950's leaders would eventually be admitted to the plaque gallery, as would an additional thirty-eight hopefuls who received votes the same year, though all would have to wait.

Frustration was brewing among the top candidates, who were unhappily aware that death was often the best route to electoral success. One aspirant conveyed his exasperation in a letter to the *Sporting News*. "Must a man die to gain the Roll of Honor of the game to which he gave his best years?" asked the former star. "Are the writers waiting for time to mow down our outstanding candidates before they can vote them into the Hall of Fame?" The paper declined to identify its correspondent, but assured readers that he "should have been elected years ago."[55]

The hall proceeded with its annual ceremony on July 24, 1950, despite the lack of new inductees. Several thousand fans jammed into Cooperstown to witness the grand opening of a new wing, which contained additional displays of memorabilia. A reporter suggested that the contractors had failed to leave enough space for plaques, given that only ten open slots remained. Hall of Fame director Bob Quinn said there was no reason to worry. "At the present rate," he said, "it will take a long time to fill it up."[56]

1951

Hall of Fame Summary

New inductees: 2
Category: Player 2
Election: BBWAA 2
Player QS average: 83.0 (BBWAA 83.0)
Hall of Famers to date: 60
Category: Player 47, Manager 3, Pioneer/Executive 10
Election: BBWAA 23, Committee 37
Player QS average: 57.0 (BBWAA 72.0, Committee 42.6)

Inductees

- Jimmie Foxx. **Category:** Player. **Position:** 1B. **QS:** 85 (excellent).
  Career: 1925-1945, G 2,317, HR 534, RBI 1,922, BA .325. **Election:**
  BBWAA.
- Mel Ott. **Category:** Player. **Position:** RF. **QS:** 81 (excellent). **Career:**
  1926-1947, G 2,730, HR 511, RBI 1,860, BA .304. **Election:** BBWAA.

BBWAA Election Summary

Voters: 226
Votes needed for induction: 170
Candidates receiving votes: 86
Candidates elected: 2
Candidates inducted in future: 44

BBWAA Top Ten

1. Mel Ott, 197 (87.17%)*
2. Jimmie Foxx, 179 (79.20%)*
3. Paul Waner, 162 (71.68%)
4. Harry Heilmann, 153 (67.70%)
5. Bill Terry, 148 (65.49%)
6. Dizzy Dean, 145 (64.16%)
7. Bill Dickey, 118 (52.21%)
8. Al Simmons, 116 (51.33%)
9. Rabbit Maranville, 110 (48.67%)
10. Ted Lyons, 71 (31.42%)

ONLY THREE PLAYERS HAD hit more than five hundred home runs as of 1951. The all-time leader, of course, was Babe Ruth with 714. The runners-up were Jimmie Foxx with 534 and Mel Ott with 511.

Ruth was rightfully enshrined in the Hall of Fame in his first year of eligibility, drawing votes from more than 95 percent of 1936's participating writers. Most observers wondered why he wasn't elected unanimously. But his fellow sluggers had a different fate. They were forced to wait for induction.

Foxx played first base for four clubs, primarily the Philadelphia Athletics and Boston Red Sox, between 1925 and 1945. He swatted at least thirty homers in twelve different seasons, peaking at fifty-eight in 1932. He was only twenty-eight years old when the hall conducted its first election, yet he was so highly regarded that twenty-one writers voted for him. Foxx's support would ebb and flow in the years to come, finally attaining a significant level in 1948 at 41 percent. He steadily clawed his way toward 75 percent after that, crossing the threshold at last in 1951.

Ott was also a feared slugger, though not quite as prodigious as Foxx. He spent his entire twenty-two year career (1926-1947) as an outfielder for the New York Giants, reaching the thirty-homer mark eight times. He became eligible for the Hall of Fame in 1949, though his gaudy statistics and New York connections proved to be insufficient for immediate induction. Ott fell short in his first two elections before joining Foxx in the class of '51.

Neither delay made any sense, especially given the absence of other compelling candidates. The BBWAA had elected just one player in 1949, Charlie Gehringer, and none at all in 1950. Foxx and Ott were the only contenders on either ballot whose quality scores exceeded eighty points, yet they were forced to step aside for Gehringer and his sixty-one points, then were rebuffed again the following year. "No one can quarrel with the [1951] election of Ott and Foxx, whose elections were perhaps too long delayed," conceded J.G. Taylor Spink, the publisher of the *Sporting News*.[57]

The writers had fallen into a curious habit, refusing to approve any candidate in his first year of eligibility. The immortal five of 1936 were exceptions to the rule, of course, but all seventeen players chosen in the BBWAA's regular elections between 1937 and 1951 had been forced to face the voters multiple times. Eight placed higher than eighty points on the QS scale—including Lefty Grove, Rogers Hornsby, and Nap Lajoie at ninety points or better—yet every single one had been required to bide his time.

Impatience was growing with the BBWAA's excessive caution and outright pickiness, a discontent voiced by the *Sporting News* in a separate editorial. "In electing Mel and Jimmie after the washout of 1950 and the single choice of 1949," it said, "the writers rallied out of the slough. But they have quite a way to go yet in a just and comprehensive approach to the Hall of Fame problem."[58]

1952

Hall of Fame Summary

New inductees: 2
Category: Player 2
Election: BBWAA 2
Player QS average: 59.0 (BBWAA 59.0)
Hall of Famers to date: 62
Category: Player 49, Manager 3, Pioneer/Executive 10
Election: BBWAA 25, Committee 37
Player QS average: 57.1 (BBWAA 71.0, Committee 42.6)

Inductees

- Harry Heilmann. **Category:** Player. **Position:** RF. **QS:** 67 (excellent). **Career:** 1914-1932, G 2,147, HR 183, RBI 1,543, BA .342. **Election:** BBWAA.
- Paul Waner. **Category:** Player. **Position:** RF. **QS:** 51 (good). **Career:** 1926-1945, G 2,549, HR 113, RBI 1,309, BA .333. **Election:** BBWAA.

BBWAA Election Summary

Voters: 234
Votes needed for induction: 176
Candidates receiving votes: 75
Candidates elected: 2
Candidates inducted in future: 40

BBWAA Top Ten

1. Harry Heilmann, 203 (86.75%)*
2. Paul Waner, 195 (83.33%)*
3. Bill Terry, 155 (66.24%)
4. Dizzy Dean, 152 (64.96%)
5. Al Simmons, 141 (60.26%)
6. Bill Dickey, 139 (59.40%)
7. Rabbit Maranville, 133 (56.84%)
8. Dazzy Vance, 105 (44.87%)
9. Ted Lyons, 101 (43.16%)
10. Gabby Hartnett, 77 (32.91%)

HARRY HEILMANN WAS CONFINED to his deathbed in the early summer of 1951, wearily battling the lung cancer that would soon claim his life, when an unlikely angel arrived to lift his spirits. Ty Cobb, typically a cheerless fellow, brought news that was as joyous as it was unexpected. The Old-Timers Committee had just conducted a special meeting,

Cobb told his old Detroit teammate, and it had voted Heilmann into the Hall of Fame.[59]

Heilmann died on July 9, 1951, believing to the end that he had just become the hall's newest member. It wasn't true. Cobb concocted the story in an uncharacteristic act of charity. He reasoned that Heilmann had come close to victory in the BBWAA's 1951 election—finishing fourth at 67.7 percent—and undoubtedly would cross the finish line in the coming year.

He was right. Heilmann clearly had the necessary credentials for induction, highlighted by a .342 lifetime batting average, 6 seasons above .350, and 2,660 hits in 17 years as a big leaguer. But it was his death that sealed the deal, boosting his support by nineteen percentage points in 1952 and lifting him into the plaque gallery with twenty-seven votes to spare.

Paul Waner rapped 3,152 hits in his 20-year career—exceeding Heilmann by 492—and he finished at least 4 percentage points ahead of Heilmann in each of the 4 previous Hall of Fame elections. But Waner was saddled with an electoral disadvantage in 1952—he was still alive—so he drew eight fewer votes than Heilmann, though still a sufficient number for induction. "I had given up hope," Waner told reporters, "but at last I have realized my life's ambition."[60]

An old right fielder for the Washington Senators, Sam Rice, was named on a single ballot in 1952, miring him in a tie for fifty-eighth place. Not that anybody paid attention. It was the fifth year in which Rice had received just one vote, the sure sign of a dead-end candidacy. No eventual Hall of Famer ever received so little support from the BBWAA over such a protracted period. But Rice would defy the odds with a surprising burst of momentum in the years to come. His plaque would be unveiled in 1963.

1953

Hall of Fame Summary

New inductees: 8
Category: Player 4, Pioneer/Executive 2, Umpire 2
Election: BBWAA 2, Committee 6
Player QS average: 43.8 (BBWAA 55.5, Committee 32.0)
Hall of Famers to date: 70
Category: Player 53, Manager 3, Pioneer/Executive 12, Umpire 2
Election: BBWAA 27, Committee 43
Player QS average: 56.1 (BBWAA 69.8, Committee 41.8)

Inductees

- Ed Barrow. **Category:** Pioneer/Executive. **Election:** Veterans Committee.
- Charles Bender. **Category:** Player. **Position:** P. **QS:** 32 (marginal). **Career:** 1903-1925, G 459, W-L 212-127, SV 34, ERA 2.46. **Election:** Veterans Committee.
- Tommy Connolly. **Category:** Umpire. **Election:** Veterans Committee.
- Dizzy Dean. **Category:** Player. **Position:** P. **QS:** 48 (good). **Career:** 1930-1947, G 317, W-L 150-83, SV 31, ERA 3.02. **Election:** BBWAA.
- Bill Klem. **Category:** Umpire. **Election:** Veterans Committee.
- Al Simmons. **Category:** Player. **Position:** LF. **QS:** 63 (excellent). **Career:** 1924-1944, G 2,215, HR 307, RBI 1,828, BA .334. **Election:** BBWAA.
- Bobby Wallace. **Category:** Player. **Position:** SS. **QS:** 32 (marginal). **Career:** 1894-1918, G 2,383, HR 34, RBI 1,121, BA .268. **Election:** Veterans Committee.
- Harry Wright. **Category:** Pioneer/Executive. **Election:** Veterans Committee.

BBWAA Election Summary

Voters: 264
Votes needed for induction: 198
Candidates receiving votes: 83
Candidates elected: 2
Candidates inducted in future: 40

BBWAA Top Ten

1. Dizzy Dean, 209 (79.17%)*
2. Al Simmons, 199 (75.38%)*
3. Bill Terry, 191 (72.35%)
4. Bill Dickey, 179 (67.80%)

5. Rabbit Maranville, 164 (62.12%)
6. Dazzy Vance, 150 (56.82%)
7. Ted Lyons, 139 (52.65%)
8. Joe DiMaggio, 117 (44.32%)
9. Charles Bender, 104 (39.39%)
9. Gabby Hartnett, 104 (39.39%)

THE OLD-TIMERS COMMITTEE fell out of favor after its spasm of inductions in 1945 and 1946. It wisely receded to the background, waiting until 1949 to admit two new members and then vanishing completely. "The committee has not held an actual meeting for years," Dan Daniel reported in February 1953. He asked one of the panel members, Mel Webb, to recall the date of its last session. It had been so long ago, Webb replied, that he had no idea.[61]

The old committee's final box score was unimpressive. The group had admitted twenty-four men to the plaque gallery, including a manager, two executives, and twenty-one players. The average quality score for the players, 41.1 points, was in the marginal range. It was 40 percent lower than the average QS of 69.0 for the other 28 players admitted to Cooperstown from 1936 through 1952.

Baseball's new commissioner, Ford Frick, decided it was time for a fresh start. He disbanded the Old-Timers Committee in the summer of 1953 and replaced it with an eleven-member Veterans Committee. J.G. Taylor Spink was installed as chairman, an unusually clever move by Frick. Spink's *Sporting News* had been carping for years about the hall's selection process, so the commissioner challenged him to clean up the mess.[62]

The panel didn't hold its first meeting until September, eight months after the writers voted pitcher Dizzy Dean and left fielder Al Simmons into the hall. Simmons was at Hialeah Park Race Track in Florida when the BBWAA announced its election results. The call from Cooperstown came just after he cashed winning tickets from three straight races. Simmons's luck with the Hall of Fame was equally strong. He tiptoed across the threshold with a single vote more than the required 198.[63]

The Veterans Committee's initial picks were as uninspiring as most of the choices made by the Old-Timers Committee. The new group admitted the first two umpires to the hall, judiciously selecting one from each league. It added a nineteenth-century manager (Harry Wright), a president of the New York Yankees (Ed Barrow), and a couple of players with identical (and relatively low) quality scores of thirty-two points, Charles Bender and Bobby Wallace.

Frick seemed especially happy about the selection of Wallace, who had played shortstop for three clubs between 1894 and 1918, spending fifteen of those years with the St. Louis Browns. "It looked as if his card was hidden in the old-timers' deck," said the commissioner, "and I am pleased this new committee dug it up."[64] Wallace had batted a fairly anemic .268 over his career, the equivalent of .261 when adjusted to 2011-2020 levels. Committee members didn't explain why they picked him instead of an eligible shortstop with a higher quality score, notably George Davis (fifty-one points) or John Ward (thirty-seven).

1954

Hall of Fame Summary

New inductees: 3
Category: Player 3
Election: BBWAA 3
Player QS average: 28.3 (BBWAA 28.3)
Hall of Famers to date: 73
Category: Player 56, Manager 3, Pioneer/Executive 12, Umpire 2
Election: BBWAA 30, Committee 43
Player QS average: 54.6 (BBWAA 65.7, Committee 41.8)

Inductees

- Bill Dickey. **Category:** Player. **Position:** C. **QS:** 27 (poor). **Career:** 1928-1946, G 1,789, HR 202, RBI 1,209, BA .313. **Election:** BBWAA.
- Rabbit Maranville. **Category:** Player. **Position:** SS. **QS:** 21 (poor). **Career:** 1912-1935, G 2,670, HR 28, RBI 884, BA .258. **Election:** BBWAA.
- Bill Terry. **Category:** Player. **Position:** 1B. **QS:** 37 (marginal). **Career:** 1923-1936, G 1,721, HR 154, RBI 1,078, BA .341. **Election:** BBWAA.

BBWAA Election Summary

Voters: 252
Votes needed for induction: 189
Candidates receiving votes: 53
Candidates elected: 3
Candidates inducted in future: 30

BBWAA Top Ten

1. Rabbit Maranville, 209 (82.94%)*
2. Bill Dickey, 202 (80.16%)*
3. Bill Terry, 195 (77.38%)*
4. Joe DiMaggio, 175 (69.44%)
5. Ted Lyons, 170 (67.46%)
6. Dazzy Vance, 158 (62.70%)
7. Gabby Hartnett, 151 (59.92%)
8. Hank Greenberg, 97 (38.49%)
9. Joe Cronin, 85 (33.73%)
10. Max Carey, 55 (21.83%)

THE VETERANS COMMITTEE WOULD NOT wear out its welcome, as the Old-Timers Committee had done with its infamous deluge of inductions in 1945 and 1946. The Hall of Fame clamped tight restrictions on the new panel, limiting its meetings to odd-numbered years.[65]

That put the pressure squarely on the writers in 1954, and they responded with three new Hall of Famers.

The top vote-getter, Rabbit Maranville, had been riding the Cooperstown roller coaster since 1937, drawing at least 10 percent support in fourteen consecutive elections despite a weak quality score of twenty-one points. He inched up to 62.1 percent and fifth place by 1953, though his prospects remained in doubt. The clincher came on January 5, 1954, when Maranville died of a heart attack as BBWAA members were voting. He shot up to 82.9 percent in the results announced two weeks later.

The gregarious, fun-loving Maranville played a smooth, wide-ranging shortstop. There were no reliable statistical tools as of 1954 to assess his fielding skills, though analysts would later credit him with 30.8 defensive wins above replacement, making him one of only six Hall of Famers to exceed 30 dWAR. Batting was an entirely different matter. Maranville's career average of .258 was the lowest for any Hall of Fame position player elected to that point, and it remains the third-lowest today.

The other two inductees, like Maranville, blended solid reputations with surprisingly low quality scores. New York Yankees catcher Bill Dickey (twenty-seven points) was inducted just eight years after his retirement, the shortest wait ever for a player whose QS was in the poor range. New York Giants first baseman Bill Terry lingered for eighteen years after his 1936 retirement, even though his quality score was higher (thirty-seven points) and he had famously batted .401 in 1930.

Terry was held back by his prickly, abrasive personality. "The dislike for Winsome Will Terry among the Gentlemen of the Press has not diminished one iota down through the years," Arthur Daley wrote in 1947, and many writers still refused to vote for him in 1954.[66] Fifty-seven left him off their ballots.

An Associated Press reporter encountered Terry's unique brand of charm after 1954's election results were announced. The reporter called the new Hall of Famer at home. "I have nothing to say about it," Terry barked. The bewildered AP man asked, "Nothing at all?" Terry snapped back, "I have no comment to make." He mellowed a bit, fortunately for all concerned, by the time the induction ceremony rolled around.[67]

1955

Hall of Fame Summary

New inductees: 6
Category: Player 6
Election: BBWAA 4, Committee 2
Player QS average: 45.3 (BBWAA 53.3, Committee 29.5)
Hall of Famers to date: 79
Category: Player 62, Manager 3, Pioneer/Executive 12, Umpire 2
Election: BBWAA 34, Committee 45
Player QS average: 53.7 (BBWAA 64.2, Committee 40.9)

Inductees

- Home Run Baker. **Category:** Player. **Position:** 3B. **QS:** 49 (good). **Career:** 1908-1922, G 1,575, HR 96, RBI 991, BA .307. **Election:** Veterans Committee.
- Joe DiMaggio. **Category:** Player. **Position:** CF. **QS:** 78 (excellent). **Career:** 1936-1951, G 1,736, HR 361, RBI 1,537, BA .325. **Election:** BBWAA.
- Gabby Hartnett. **Category:** Player. **Position:** C. **QS:** 33 (marginal). **Career:** 1922-1941, G 1,990, HR 236, RBI 1,179, BA .297. **Election:** BBWAA.
- Ted Lyons. **Category:** Player. **Position:** P. **QS:** 35 (marginal). **Career:** 1923-1946, G 594, W-L 260-230, SV 25, ERA 3.67. **Election:** BBWAA.
- Ray Schalk. **Category:** Player. **Position:** C. **QS:** 10 (poor). **Career:** 1912-1929, G 1,762, HR 11, RBI 593, BA .253. **Election:** Veterans Committee.
- Dazzy Vance. **Category:** Player. **Position:** P. **QS:** 67 (excellent). **Career:** 1915-1935, G 442, W-L 197-140, SV 12, ERA 3.24. **Election:** BBWAA.

BBWAA Election Summary

Voters: 251
Votes needed for induction: 189
Candidates receiving votes: 65
Candidates elected: 4
Candidates inducted in future: 31

BBWAA Top Ten

1. Joe DiMaggio, 223 (88.84%)*
2. Ted Lyons, 217 (86.45%)*
3. Dazzy Vance, 205 (81.67%)*
4. Gabby Hartnett, 195 (77.69%)*
5. Hank Greenberg, 157 (62.55%)

6. Joe Cronin, 135 (53.78%)
7. Max Carey, 119 (47.41%)
8. Ray Schalk, 113 (45.02%)
9. Edd Roush, 97 (38.65%)
10. Hank Gowdy, 90 (35.86%)

THE HALL OF FAME QUIETLY altered its eligibility standards in 1954, henceforth requiring candidates to be retired for five seasons, not one. The change had no immediate impact, since any contender who received at least one hundred votes in 1953 was grandfathered into the system. That's why Joe DiMaggio was able to secure a plaque in 1955, even though he had completed only three years of retirement.[68]

The writers and the Veterans Committee combined to admit six new members, the greatest number in any year between 1953 and 1964. Four of 1955's honorees had their credentials stamped by the BBWAA. The writers would not again give 75 percent support to four players in a single election until 2015, sixty years in the future.

All six members of the class of 1955 were still alive, contradicting the voters' seeming preference for deceased candidates. Photos taken at the induction ceremony on July 25 showed the forty-year-old, dark-haired DiMaggio posing with five middle-aged and elderly men, Home Run Baker being the oldest at sixty-nine.[69] They were greeted by Cooperstown's largest crowd since 1939, eager to cheer the first postwar star admitted to the hall. "It was obvious from the reaction of the thousands of visitors who crammed every vantage point that Jolting Joe was the chief hero of the occasion," wrote Joseph Sheehan in the *New York Times*.[70]

The BBWAA's four choices were solid and defensible, but the Veterans Committee's selections inspired a pair of disparate questions.

Home Run Baker was among the forty-seven players who received votes in the hall's initial election in 1936, yet had cooled his heels for almost two decades while a pair of third basemen with lower quality scores (Jimmy Collins and Pie Traynor) were inducted. Why had he been forced to wait so long?

Ray Schalk hit only .253 in his eighteen-year career as a catcher, mostly with the Chicago White Sox. His batting average was the lowest for any position player in the hall—then or now—and his quality score of ten points was second-lowest at that time to Tommy McCarthy's single point. Cynics suggested that Schalk was inducted as a reward for being one of the Clean Sox who steered clear of the fixing of the 1919 World Series. Could that possibly have been the reason?

The two men understood their respective situations, as indicated by their reactions to the committee's announcement. Baker said, "I'm not exactly surprised." Schalk said, "You've taken my breath away."[71]

1956

Hall of Fame Summary

New inductees: 2
Category: Player 2
Election: BBWAA 2
Player QS average: 44.5 (BBWAA 44.5)
Hall of Famers to date: 81
Category: Player 64, Manager 3, Pioneer/Executive 12, Umpire 2
Election: BBWAA 36, Committee 45
Player QS average: 53.4 (BBWAA 63.1, Committee 40.9)

Inductees

- Joe Cronin. **Category:** Player. **Position:** SS. **QS:** 36 (marginal). **Career:** 1926-1945, G 2,124, HR 170, RBI 1,424, BA .301. **Election:** BBWAA.
- Hank Greenberg. **Category:** Player. **Position:** 1B. **QS:** 53 (good). **Career:** 1930-1947, G 1,394, HR 331, RBI 1,274, BA .313. **Election:** BBWAA.

BBWAA Election Summary

Voters: 193
Votes needed for induction: 145
Candidates receiving votes: 106
Candidates elected: 2
Candidates inducted in future: 40

BBWAA Top Ten

1. Hank Greenberg, 164 (84.97%)*
2. Joe Cronin, 152 (78.76%)*
3. Red Ruffing, 97 (50.26%)
4. Edd Roush, 91 (47.15%)
5. Lefty Gomez, 89 (46.11%)
6. Hack Wilson, 74 (38.34%)
7. Max Carey, 65 (33.68%)
8. Tony Lazzeri, 64 (33.16%)
9. Kiki Cuyler, 55 (28.50%)
10. Hank Gowdy, 49 (25.39%)

DAN DANIEL BELIEVED HE HAD broken Cooperstown's code. "Since the writers follow the pattern of one year very closely in the next canvass," he wrote in February 1955, "it would appear almost certain that the 1956 election will enshrine Hank Greenberg and Joe Cronin."[72]

Daniel was wrong about the trend, yet correct in his prediction. The writers had inducted both of the previous runners-up (the two candidates who came closest to 75 percent without reaching it) only three times from 1942 to 1955, which hardly constituted a pattern. But two of those three matches had occurred in 1954 and 1955, and the streak would continue in 1956 with the elevation of Greenberg and Cronin, who shot up to 85.0 and 78.8 percent, respectively.

A large gap separated the two winners from the rest of the field. Red Ruffing was the only other contender to reach 50 percent, and he barely made it. Several deserving candidates inexplicably failed to attract much support. Right fielder Chuck Klein, a slugger whose quality score of fifty points nearly equaled Greenberg's fifty-three, floundered in twelfth place at 22.8 percent. A pair of contenders who outrated both of 1956's honorees fared even worse. Left fielder Joe Medwick (QS of fifty-six points) was mired at 16.1 percent, shortstop Arky Vaughan (fifty-seven) at 4.7 percent.

One other oddity was tucked into the upper echelon of 1956's standings, though nobody could have known at the time.

Hank Gowdy, a catcher for the Boston Braves and New York Giants between 1910 and 1930, finished in tenth place in 1956, just as he had in 1955. His popularity with the voters was almost impossible to figure. Gowdy had been a relatively weak hitter (twenty-one career homers) who was remembered for a critical error in the final inning of the final game of the 1924 World Series. He missed a seemingly easy foul pop after getting entangled in the face mask he had just discarded—"I thought my foot was being held in a bear trap"—thereby opening the door for the Washington Senators to snatch the world championship from Gowdy's Giants.[73]

The BBWAA conducted seventeen Hall of Fame elections from 1936 through 1956, with fifty-five different players finishing among the top ten vote-getters at some point over that period. Fifty-four eventually received plaques in Cooperstown, a process completed with the induction of Tony Lazzeri in 1991. The only exception—the only top-ten contender from 1936 to 1956 who remains outside the Hall of Fame to this day—was Hank Gowdy.

1957

Hall of Fame Summary

New inductees: 2
Category: Player 1, Manager 1
Election: Committee 2
Player QS average: 68.0 (Committee 68.0)
Hall of Famers to date: 83
Category: Player 65, Manager 4, Pioneer/Executive 12, Umpire 2
Election: BBWAA 36, Committee 47
Player QS average: 53.6 (BBWAA 63.1, Committee 41.8)

Inductees

- Sam Crawford. **Category:** Player. **Position:** RF. **QS:** 68 (excellent). **Career:** 1899-1917, G 2,517, HR 97, RBI 1,523, BA .309. **Election:** Veterans Committee.
- Joe McCarthy. **Category:** Manager. **Career:** 1926-1950, W-L 2,125-1,333, Pennants 9, Titles 7. **Election:** Veterans Committee.

TWENTY-ONE PLAYERS, EXECUTIVES, AND UMPIRES were admitted to the Hall of Fame between 1951 and 1955. It wasn't the biggest number of inductions in a half-decade—thirty plaques had been commissioned in the hectic span from 1945 to 1949—but the baseball establishment still fretted that the pace was much too rapid.

So the hall tinkered with its election rules once again, implementing a two-year rotation. Its decree, which was handed down in July 1956, took effect in 1957. The Veterans Committee would continue to meet in odd-numbered years, restricted to a maximum of two honorees. The writers would vote only in years that ended in even numerals, though they were now graced with a wider window. The BBWAA would be allowed to scrutinize players who had retired as long as thirty years in the past, instead of twenty-five. One final adjustment mandated that any nominated player must have been a big leaguer for at least ten seasons. There previously had been no minimum.[74]

These alterations left 1957 wide open for the Veterans Committee, which quickly bagged its two-man limit. Sam Crawford, a fleet outfielder for the Cincinnati Reds and Detroit Tigers from 1899 to 1917, still ranks as baseball's all-time leader in triples (309). Joe McCarthy managed the Chicago Cubs to a National League pennant in 1929, then directed the New York Yankees to seven world titles between 1932 and 1943.

"They are worthy additions to a glorious company," editorialized the *Sporting News*. The paper's publisher also happened to be the chairman of the selection committee, yet nobody could really dispute the quality of 1957's inductees.[75]

1958

Hall of Fame Summary

New inductees: 0
Hall of Famers to date: 83
Category: Player 65, Manager 4, Pioneer/Executive 12, Umpire 2
Election: BBWAA 36, Committee 47
Player QS average: 53.6 (BBWAA 63.1, Committee 41.8)

BBWAA Election Summary

Voters: 266
Votes needed for induction: 200
Candidates receiving votes: 154
Candidates elected: 0
Candidates inducted in future: 42

BBWAA Top Ten

1. Max Carey, 136 (51.13%)
2. Edd Roush, 112 (42.11%)
3. Red Ruffing, 99 (37.22%)
4. Hack Wilson, 94 (35.34%)
5. Kiki Cuyler, 90 (33.83%)
5. Sam Rice, 90 (33.83%)
7. Tony Lazzeri, 80 (30.08%)
8. Luke Appling, 77 (28.95%)
9. Lefty Gomez, 76 (28.57%)
10. Burleigh Grimes, 71 (26.69%)

THE BBWAA FAILED TO ELECT anybody to the hall in 1958, an outcome cheerfully endorsed by most baseball executives and sportswriters.

Commissioner Ford Frick: "I'm not surprised, and I'm not unhappy. This will make those who are already in the Hall of Fame gain in stature and prestige."[76]

BBWAA president Bob Broeg, the sports editor of the *St. Louis Post-Dispatch*: "I was almost certain no one would make it, and that's a healthy sign."

Dick Hackenberg of the *Chicago Sun-Times*: "Failure to elect anyone to the Hall of Fame emphasizes the great honor which goes with election."[77]

Arthur Daley of the *New York Times*: "This is as it should be. Once the baseball pantheon loses its exclusiveness, it loses its value and becomes merely a hang-out for old-timers."[78]

And so on and so forth. The din of this self-congratulatory applause drowned out any serious analysis of 1958's nonsensical voting results. Several eligible candidates boasted solid credentials. Three had quality scores of fifty points or better—Joe Medwick, Chuck Klein, Arky Vaughan—and merited serious consideration for immediate induction. Close behind were another five players with solid scores between forty-two and forty-nine points (Lefty Gomez, Red Ruffing, Goose Goslin, Red Faber, and Luke Appling).

So who was the top vote-getter? That distinction fell to Max Carey, an outfielder who led the National League in stolen bases ten times, yet had never been considered one of his era's greats. Carey's QS of twenty-four points fit into the poor range, but he trounced 1958's three best candidates, no matter that their quality scores were more than twice as strong. Medwick finished fourteenth, Klein twenty-first, and Vaughan sixty-fourth. A former BBWAA president, Joe Cashman of the *Boston Record*, was one of the few who found the results absurd. "When Max Carey was revealed as the leader," he said, "that really floored me."[79]

Carey fell sixty-four votes short of induction, though he finished comfortably ahead of runner-up Edd Roush, another outfielder with a quality score of twenty-four.

1959

Hall of Fame Summary

New inductees: 1
Category: Player 1
Election: Committee 1
Player QS average: 40.0 (Committee 40.0)
Hall of Famers to date: 84
Category: Player 66, Manager 4, Pioneer/Executive 12, Umpire 2
Election: BBWAA 36, Committee 48
Player QS average: 53.4 (BBWAA 63.1, Committee 41.8)

Inductees

- Zack Wheat. **Category:** Player. **Position:** LF. **QS:** 40 (marginal). **Career:** 1909-1927, G 2,410, HR 132, RBI 1,248, BA .317. **Election:** Veterans Committee.

THE VETERANS COMMITTEE FACED a daunting task in 1959. Its members were handed an extensive menu of Hall of Fame candidates, forty-four in all. Thirty-five were players who had finished their careers prior to the Great Depression. Four managers and five umpires were also on the list.

The rules stipulated that only two of these contenders could be elected, which seemed to presage a lengthy meeting. A participant suggested that a secret ballot might winnow the field and accelerate the process. Each member was told to write his top three choices in order.

The strategy worked, partially at least. Zack Wheat, a longtime out-fielder for the Brooklyn Dodgers, was listed first on ten of the eleven slips of paper. A motion was quickly approved to make his election unanimous.

One down, one to go. The committee debated the merits of the remaining old-timers, though it made no headway. Another secret vote was eventually called, with each panelist writing down a single name. No candidate received more than three votes, far short of the necessary nine.[80]

Hall of Fame committees historically had been free and easy with their admission passes, inducting at least five candidates on five different occasions between 1937 and 1953, peaking with the absurdly high total of eleven honorees in 1946. But the Veterans Committee showed unusual restraint in 1959. It chose only Wheat, opting to leave its second slot unoccupied.

1960

Hall of Fame Summary

New inductees: 0
Hall of Famers to date: 84
Category: Player 66, Manager 4, Pioneer/Executive 12, Umpire 2
Election: BBWAA 36, Committee 48
Player QS average: 53.4 (BBWAA 63.1, Committee 41.8)

BBWAA Election Summary

Voters: 269
Votes needed for induction: 202
Candidates receiving votes: 134
Candidates elected: 0
Candidates inducted in future: 40

BBWAA Top Ten

1. Edd Roush, 146 (54.28%)
2. Sam Rice, 143 (53.16%)
3. Eppa Rixey, 142 (52.79%)
4. Burleigh Grimes, 92 (34.20%)
5. Jim Bottomley, 89 (33.09%)
6. Red Ruffing, 86 (31.97%)
7. Red Faber, 83 (30.86%)
8. Luke Appling, 72 (26.77%)
8. Kiki Cuyler, 72 (26.77%)
8. Hack Wilson, 72 (26.77%)

THE FRONTRUNNER IN THE previous BBWAA election, Max Carey, did not make the ballot in 1960. He had retired in 1929, which meant he was now outside the thirty-year window. The Veterans Committee would eventually decide Carey's fate. The writers would have to find another favorite.

They elevated Edd Roush to the top position, though with no particular enthusiasm. The center fielder for the Cincinnati Reds and New York Giants fell fifty-six votes short of victory. Another summer would slip by without an induction ceremony in Cooperstown.

There was none of the bravado that accompanied 1958's shutout. Panic was the order of the day in 1960. "If the Hall of Fame is to be kept in business, a new system of voting must be devised," insisted BBWAA secretary Hy Hurwitz, who supervised the hall's elections.[81] The *Sporting News* chimed in with a caustic editorial: "The latest Hall of Fame election fiasco, in which no one commanded the necessary number of votes, points up the urgent need for revision of the rules."[82]

The problem wasn't a shortage of acceptable candidates. Forty of 1960's vote-getters would eventually make it to Cooperstown, a larger number of future inductees than any subsequent election would involve. Responsibility for the hall's woes could be traced to two other factors—1956's rule changes and the writers' shortcomings.

The attempt to slow the pace of inductions, as mandated in July 1956, had been more effective than anticipated. Only two players and a manager were welcomed to the plaque gallery in the four years from 1957 through 1960. Neither of the inducted players had been active since 1927, which meant that nobody under the age of thirty-five had seen them play. It wasn't the best way to attract younger fans to Cooperstown.

The writers didn't help matters with their lazy and inattentive voting habits. They scattered their support among 134 players in 1960, including such nonentities as Mule Haas, Bubbles Hargrave, Charley O'Leary, Sibby Sisti, and Gus Suhr. Six BBWAA members wrote in the name of Lefty Grove, an undeniably great pitcher who was nonetheless ineligible. The reason was simple: Grove had been inducted thirteen years earlier.[83]

The best candidate on 1960's ballot, as determined by quality score, was first baseman Johnny Mize, whose sixty-six points fit into the excellent range. The writers inexplicably spurned him. Mize received only forty-five votes and finished in thirteenth place. The QS ratings for all of the top ten vote-getters, on the other hand, were lower than forty-five points, consigning them to the marginal or poor range.

The hall slapped a pair of bandages on these problems in August 1960. It freed the Veterans Committee to resume annual meetings as of 1961, though still with a two-induction limit. And it revived the BBWAA's runoff provision, which had been abandoned a decade earlier. The writers would continue to vote only in even-numbered years. If they failed to pick an honoree, a second election involving the leading candidates would be conducted.[84]

1961

Hall of Fame Summary

New inductees: 2
Category: Player 2
Election: Committee 2
Player QS average: 36.5 (Committee 36.5)
Hall of Famers to date: 86
Category: Player 68, Manager 4, Pioneer/Executive 12, Umpire 2
Election: BBWAA 36, Committee 50
Player QS average: 52.9 (BBWAA 63.1, Committee 41.4)

Inductees

- Max Carey. **Category:** Player. **Position:** CF. **QS:** 24 (poor). **Career:** 1910-1929, G 2,476, HR 70, RBI 802, BA .285. **Election:** Veterans Committee.
- Billy Hamilton. **Category:** Player. **Position:** CF. **QS:** 49 (good). **Career:** 1888-1901, G 1,594, HR 40, RBI 742, BA .344. **Election:** Veterans Committee.

THE HALL OF FAME's frustration would simmer for another two decades before boiling over. Not until 1979 would its leaders take decisive action to discourage writers from voting for players who had no hope of being inducted, the likes of Mule Haas, Bubbles Hargrave, and Sibby Sisti. An annual minimum of 5 percent would be imposed, barring from future BBWAA ballots any candidate who fell below the line.

If such a rule had existed in the 1930s and 1940s, it's highly unlikely that Max Carey would be a member of the hall today.

Nothing about Carey's record stamped him as a Hall of Famer. Not his weak quality score of twenty-four points, not his pedestrian batting average of .285 (the equivalent of just .267 at 2011-2020 levels), and certainly not his complete lack of power (seventy career home runs).

The writers initially showed little interest in Carey, giving him less than 3 percent support in every election between 1937 and 1947. A 5 percent requirement would have wiped him from the BBWAA's slate, leaving him to the mercy of the Veterans Committee after thirty years of retirement. The committee was already inundated with candidates whose records were more impressive than Carey's. Why would it take up the cause of somebody who had been so swiftly rejected by the writers?

But the 5 percent rule was still far in the future, so Carey's bandwagon had ample time to gather momentum. He inexplicably clawed his way into the writers' top ten by 1954, then to seventh place in 1955 and 1956, and finally—miracle of miracles—all the way to first place (though far short of 75 percent) in 1958, his last year of BBWAA eligibility.

This phoenix-like rise guaranteed Carey's eventual induction. Top-five status in one of the writers' elections amounted to an automatic admission ticket, even if it sometimes fell to the committee to give the final approval. Eighty-nine players, including Carey, would make top-five appearances during the first half-century of BBWAA voting (1936 through 1985). All eighty-nine can be found in the plaque gallery today.

The Veterans Committee did its duty in 1961, electing Carey on its first ballot, then adding nineteenth-century speedster Billy Hamilton (QS of forty-nine) on its second pass.[85] The panel bypassed two old-timers whose quality scores were in the excellent range—first baseman Roger Connor (seventy-seven points) and pitcher Tim Keefe (sixty-nine)—as well as eight other contenders who boasted higher scores than both of the new inductees.

1962

Hall of Fame Summary

New inductees: 4
Category: Player 3, Manager 1
Election: BBWAA 2, Committee 2
Player QS average: 47.3 (BBWAA 59.0, Committee 24.0)
Hall of Famers to date: 90
Category: Player 71, Manager 5, Pioneer/Executive 12, Umpire 2
Election: BBWAA 38, Committee 52
Player QS average: 52.7 (BBWAA 62.9, Committee 40.9)

Inductees

- Bob Feller. **Category:** Player. **Position:** P. **QS:** 70 (excellent). **Career:** 1936-1956, G 570, W-L 266-162, SV 22, ERA 3.25. **Election:** BBWAA.
- Bill McKechnie. **Category:** Manager. **Career:** 1915-1946, W-L 1,896-1,723, Pennants 4, Titles 2. **Election:** Veterans Committee.
- Jackie Robinson. **Category:** Player. **Position:** 2B. **QS:** 48 (good). **Career:** 1945-1956, G 1,416, HR 141, RBI 761, BA .313. **Election:** BBWAA.
- Edd Roush. **Category:** Player. **Position:** CF. **QS:** 24 (poor). **Career:** 1913-1931, G 1,967, HR 68, RBI 981, BA .323. **Election:** Veterans Committee.

BBWAA Election Summary

Voters: 160
Votes needed for induction: 120
Candidates receiving votes: 79
Candidates elected: 2
Candidates inducted in future: 36

BBWAA Top Ten

1. Bob Feller, 150 (93.75%)*
2. Jackie Robinson, 124 (77.50%)*
3. Sam Rice, 81 (50.63%)
4. Red Ruffing, 72 (45.00%)
5. Eppa Rixey, 49 (30.63%)
6. Luke Appling, 48 (30.00%)
7. Phil Rizzuto, 44 (27.50%)
8. Burleigh Grimes, 43 (26.88%)
9. Hack Wilson, 39 (24.38%)
10. Joe Medwick, 34 (21.25%)

JACKIE ROBINSON INTEGRATED THE Hall of Fame in 1962, just fifteen years after he broke the big-league color barrier.

Coverage of his victory gave surprisingly little play to the racial angle. The *Sporting News* briefly described Robinson as "the first Negro big leaguer," its only reference to the hue of his skin. The bulk of its story lauded other personal attributes, including "great competitor," "daring, brilliant base-runner," and "successful businessman."[86] The dispatch from United Press International waited until the eleventh paragraph to state the obvious: "He will be the first Negro in the Hall of Fame."[87]

That was the way Robinson wanted it. He had asked the writers to judge him solely as a ballplayer, not as a racial pioneer, and they appeared to take him at his word. The hall did the same. Robinson's sixty-word plaque made no mention of his trailblazing role, an omission that would later seem absurd. (A new plaque, affixed to the gallery wall in 2008, would hail him for the "tremendous courage and poise" he displayed in integrating the majors.)[88]

Robinson eked into the hall with only four votes to spare, much too tight a margin for such a historic figure. Did racial prejudice dampen his vote total? Almost certainly. But the BBWAA's finicky behavior in that era must also be taken into account. The writers seemed to pride themselves on rejecting new candidates, an informal rule that they actually lifted in Robinson's case. He and the only player to receive more votes in 1962, fireballing pitcher Bob Feller, became the first honorees since 1936 to be elected in their initial year of eligibility. It might even be said that Robinson was treated more fairly than Dizzy Dean, another high-profile personality who carried precisely the same QS (forty-eight points), yet was forced to slog through nine elections before being admitted in 1953.

The Veterans Committee added center fielder Edd Roush and manager Bill McKechnie to 1962's induction ceremony. The sixty-eight-year-old Roush had drawn votes in nineteen BBWAA elections before passing into the committee's purview, a quarter-century grind that clearly dispirited him. "It's all right, but sometimes these things come too late," he said when notified of his selection. "It takes them too long to vote on these players."[89]

The hall's rules stipulated that each candidate must fit into one of four categories—player, manager, umpire, or pioneer/executive. Journalist Henry Chadwick had been inducted in 1938 as a representative of the fourth group, though he was considered a special case.[90] Writers were not typically deemed to be Hall of Fame material, so the BBWAA proposed an alternative in October 1962, a career achievement award that would be given a separate display in Cooperstown. (Stories in future years would tell of award winners being enshrined in the "writers' wing," an entirely fictitious structure.) The hall's president, Paul Kerr, approved the plan, and the writers named J.G. Taylor Spink as the first honoree.[91]

1963

Hall of Fame Summary

New inductees: 4
Category: Player 4
Election: Committee 4
Player QS average: 35.5 (Committee 35.5)
Hall of Famers to date: 94
Category: Player 75, Manager 5, Pioneer/Executive 12, Umpire 2
Election: BBWAA 38, Committee 56
Player QS average: 51.8 (BBWAA 62.9, Committee 40.3)

Inductees

- John Clarkson. **Category:** Player. **Position:** P. **QS:** 56 (good). **Career:** 1882-1894, G 531, W-L 328-178, SV 5, ERA 2.81. **Election:** Veterans Committee.
- Elmer Flick. **Category:** Player. **Position:** RF. **QS:** 31 (marginal). **Career:** 1898-1910, G 1,483, HR 48, RBI 756, BA .313. **Election:** Veterans Committee.
- Sam Rice. **Category:** Player. **Position:** RF. **QS:** 24 (poor). **Career:** 1915-1934, G 2,404, HR 34, RBI 1,077, BA .322. **Election:** Veterans Committee.
- Eppa Rixey. **Category:** Player. **Position:** P. **QS:** 31 (marginal). **Career:** 1912-1933, G 692, W-L 266-251, SV 14, ERA 3.15. **Election:** Veterans Committee.

THE HALL OF FAME'S BOARD loosened the shackles on the Veterans Committee for a second time in July 1962.

The first slackening had occurred two years earlier, when the hall authorized the panel to resume annual meetings. The committee's freedom was now enhanced in a pair of ways: the removal of its two-induction limit and the widening of its pool of candidates. The latter was accomplished by shrinking the BBWAA's eligibility window from twenty-five years to fifteen. Any candidate who had been retired at least twenty years would have his fate determined by the committee, not the writers, beginning in 1963.[92]

Edd Roush wasn't explicitly given credit for these alterations, though his 1962 lament had obviously struck home. "Waiting thirty years after a man becomes inactive, and five years to vote him in, is too long," he had said, and the baseball establishment evidently agreed.[93]

The Veterans Committee celebrated its emancipation with four inductions in 1963. Pitcher John Clarkson, who had died in 1909, was clearly overdue with a QS of fifty-six points. The others—outfielders Elmer Flick and Sam Rice and pitcher Eppa Rixey—were debatable choices at best. Their quality scores ranged between 24 and 31 points, far below the average of 51.8 points for the 75 players enshrined in Cooperstown.

The seventy-one-year-old Rixey, who had retired thirty years earlier, joked about the obscurity into which he had descended by 1963. "They selected me to the hall?" he asked with a chuckle. "They're really scraping the bottom of the barrel, aren't they?"[94] Rixey was reported to be in good health when elected, but he suffered a fatal heart attack just thirty-two days later.[95]

1964

Hall of Fame Summary

New inductees: 7
Category: Player 6, Manager 1
Election: BBWAA 1, Committee 6
Player QS average: 39.7 (BBWAA 42.0, Committee 39.2)
Hall of Famers to date: 101
Category: Player 81, Manager 6, Pioneer/Executive 12, Umpire 2
Election: BBWAA 39, Committee 62
Player QS average: 50.9 (BBWAA 62.4, Committee 40.2)

Inductees

- Luke Appling. **Category:** Player. **Position:** SS. **QS:** 42 (marginal). **Career:** 1930-1950, G 2,422, HR 45, RBI 1,116, BA .310. **Election:** BBWAA.
- Red Faber. **Category:** Player. **Position:** P. **QS:** 42 (marginal). **Career:** 1914-1933, G 669, W-L 254-213, SV 27, ERA 3.15. **Election:** Veterans Committee.
- Burleigh Grimes. **Category:** Player. **Position:** P. **QS:** 31 (marginal). **Career:** 1916-1934, G 616, W-L 270-212, SV 18, ERA 3.53. **Election:** Veterans Committee.
- Miller Huggins. **Category:** Manager. **Career:** 1913-1929, W-L 1,413-1,134, Pennants 6, Titles 3. **Election:** Veterans Committee.
- Tim Keefe. **Category:** Player. **Position:** P. **QS:** 69 (excellent). **Career:** 1880-1893, G 600, W-L 342-225, SV 2, ERA 2.63. **Election:** Veterans Committee.
- Heinie Manush. **Category:** Player. **Position:** LF. **QS:** 17 (poor). **Career:** 1923-1939, G 2,008, HR 110, RBI 1,183, BA .330. **Election:** Veterans Committee.
- John Ward. **Category:** Player. **Position:** SS. **QS:** 37 (marginal). **Career:** 1878-1894, G 1,827, HR 26, RBI 869, BA .275. **Election:** Veterans Committee.

BBWAA Election Summary

Voters: 201
Votes needed for induction: 151
Candidates receiving votes: 58
Candidates elected: 1
Candidates inducted in future: 21

BBWAA Top Ten

1. Luke Appling, 142 (70.65%)^
2. Red Ruffing, 141 (70.15%)

3. Roy Campanella, 115 (57.21%)
4. Joe Medwick, 108 (53.73%)
5. Pee Wee Reese, 73 (36.32%)
6. Lou Boudreau, 68 (33.83%)
7. Al Lopez, 57 (28.36%)
8. Chuck Klein, 56 (27.86%)
9. Johnny Mize, 54 (26.87%)
10. Mel Harder, 51 (25.37%)
10. Johnny Vander Meer, 51 (25.37%)
^: *Appling was chosen in a subsequent runoff election.*

IT SEEMED LIKE OLD TIMES in 1964. An unrestrained committee was welcoming hordes of inductees to Cooperstown, while a conflicted BBWAA was struggling to pick anybody at all. A time traveler might have thought it was 1945 or 1946.

The writers came first on the calendar, conducting their election in January. Two contenders battled for the lead: Luke Appling, a twenty-year shortstop for the Chicago White Sox, and Red Ruffing, a pitcher who had divided his twenty-two-season career between the Boston Red Sox and New York Yankees. Both fell just short of 75 percent—Appling by nine votes, Ruffing by ten—so a runoff was held, with Appling emerging victorious in mid-February. "I don't care if I made it on the second, third, or fortieth round or had to crawl to get in," he said happily.[96]

The Veterans Committee tapped five players and a manager to join Appling. Two were especially deserving. Tim Keefe, a nineteenth-century pitcher, won 342 games while posting a quality score (69 points) in the excellent range. John Ward, often referred to by his full name of John Montgomery Ward, was a shortstop and pitcher whose QS (thirty-seven) failed to reflect his historic value. The Columbia Law School graduate organized the first players' union in 1885 and founded the short-lived Players League five years later.[97] Ward was labor's preeminent spokesman in baseball's early years, accusing owners of engaging in "the manipulation of a traffic in players, a sort of speculation in livestock, by which they are bought, sold, and transferred like so many sheep."[98]

The inductee with the lowest quality score, Heinie Manush (seventeen points), benefited from statistical inflation. Nobody could deny that he was a capable hitter—he won the American League's batting title in 1926—but he wasn't nearly as skilled as his .330 career average might indicate. It was Manush's good fortune to play from 1923 to 1939, the heart of the lively ball era, when batters held a decided advantage over pitchers. His lifetime average, when translated to 2011-2020 levels, dropped to .298, still respectable, but hardly exceptional.

1965

Hall of Fame Summary

New inductees: 1
Category: Player 1
Election: Committee 1
Player QS average: 45.0 (Committee 45.0)
Hall of Famers to date: 102
Category: Player 82, Manager 6, Pioneer/Executive 12, Umpire 2
Election: BBWAA 39, Committee 63
Player QS average: 50.8 (BBWAA 62.4, Committee 40.3)

Inductees

- Pud Galvin. **Category:** Player. **Position:** P. **QS:** 45 (good). **Career:** 1875-1892, G 705, W-L 365-310, SV 2, ERA 2.85. **Election:** Veterans Committee.

THE VETERANS COMMITTEE'S PERIOD of unrestrained freedom—its flurry of ten inductions in two years—proved to be short-lived. Hall of Fame officials had given the panel some slack in 1963 and 1964 "because of the heavy backlog of old-time greats," as Dan Daniel explained. But such leniency was no longer considered necessary, so the committee's two-induction limit was reimposed in 1965.[99]

First baseman Roger Connor, with a quality score of seventy-seven points, topped 1965's list of candidates. Connor had batted .316 for five clubs between 1880 and 1897. Seven other contenders had impressive scores of fifty points or better.

But the committee skipped all of them. It selected just one name from its lengthy list, Pud Galvin, the only pitcher besides Cy Young to win and lose at least three hundred games apiece. His QS was forty-five. Galvin had last taken the mound in 1892 for the St. Louis Browns and had died in 1902.[100]

The BBWAA didn't hold an election—1965 was an odd-numbered year—which meant that Galvin was the sole honoree at July's induction ceremony. It was difficult to scrape up representatives for the newest Hall of Famer, who was so ancient that nine of his eleven children had already passed away. His remaining survivors, a son and daughter both in their seventies, journeyed to Cooperstown to accept Galvin's plaque, though few fans joined them. Attendance at the hall's brief program was generously estimated to be thirty-five hundred, but it appeared much smaller to most reporters.[101]

1966

Hall of Fame Summary

New inductees: 2
Category: Player 1, Manager 1
Election: BBWAA 1, Committee 1
Player QS average: 89.0 (BBWAA 89.0)
Hall of Famers to date: 104
Category: Player 83, Manager 7, Pioneer/Executive 12, Umpire 2
Election: BBWAA 40, Committee 64
Player QS average: 51.3 (BBWAA 63.0, Committee 40.3)

Inductees

- Casey Stengel. **Category:** Manager. **Career:** 1934-1965, W-L 1,905-1,842, Pennants 10, Titles 7. **Election:** Veterans Committee.
- Ted Williams. **Category:** Player. **Position:** LF. **QS:** 89 (excellent). **Career:** 1939-1960, G 2,292, HR 521, RBI 1,839, BA .344. **Election:** BBWAA.

BBWAA Election Summary

Voters: 302
Votes needed for induction: 227
Candidates receiving votes: 49
Candidates elected: 1
Candidates inducted in future: 19

BBWAA Top Ten

1. Ted Williams, 282 (93.38%)*
2. Red Ruffing, 208 (68.87%)
3. Roy Campanella, 197 (65.23%)
4. Joe Medwick, 187 (61.92%)
5. Lou Boudreau, 115 (38.08%)
6. Al Lopez, 109 (36.09%)
7. Enos Slaughter, 100 (33.11%)
8. Pee Wee Reese, 95 (31.46%)
9. Marty Marion, 86 (28.48%)
10. Johnny Mize, 81 (26.82%)

THE *SPORTING NEWS* DID SOME quick math in January 1966—two weeks before the BBWAA's election results were to be announced—and it was disheartened by its calculations.

The Hall of Fame had inducted 102 members to that point, including 82 players. If the current pace continued, the editors warned, 176 players would be enshrined in Cooperstown by 2000.

"Perhaps it is possible to think of 176 names as 'immortals' of the diamond," the paper grumbled, "but we have our doubts." It urged the hall to tighten its standards to "maintain the prestige that goes with selection." (Imagine the editors' indignation if they had known the actual number of players who would be inducted by the turn of the century—201.)

The *Sporting News* said nothing of the real reason for the inflated membership, namely the eagerness of Hall of Fame committees to admit candidates with minimal credentials. Eighteen players with quality scores in the poor range (twenty-nine points or less) were already on display in the plaque gallery. Most of them, thirteen in all, had been welcomed by the Old-Timers Committee or the Veterans Committee. "Overloading the Hall of Fame is the surest way to ruin its status," warned the editors, oblivious to the massive overloading that had already occurred.[102]

The hall itself seemed aware of the problem. President Paul Kerr announced that the Veterans Committee would not hold its scheduled meeting in 1966 because of a perceived lack of deserving candidates. "We have caught up with the backlog," he said with satisfaction.[103]

There was no suspense about the writers' election. Boston Red Sox left fielder Ted Williams was predicted to be an easy winner in his first year on the ballot, a verdict justified by his .344 batting average, 521 home runs, and exalted quality score of 89 points. Williams had never been friendly with the press—he mockingly called reporters the "knights of the keyboard"—yet he drew 282 of a possible 302 votes.[104] "Only twenty rockheads yielded to personal prejudice and stubbornly refused to name him anywhere on their ten-place ballots," wrote Arthur Daley.[105]

The hall unexpectedly announced a rule change in February. It lifted the five-year retirement requirement for any manager, executive, or umpire who had left the majors after turning sixty-five. Seniors would henceforth be eligible just six months after retiring, an alteration that cleared a path for seventy-five-year-old Casey Stengel, who had stepped down as the New York Mets' manager the year before.[106]

A special election was secretly conducted by mail in early March. The Veterans Committee swiftly approved Stengel, who was informed at an impromptu ceremony prior to the Mets' first intrasquad game of the spring. The loquacious ex-manager was briefly rendered speechless, but soon reverted to form. "I guess I could say a thousand things," said Stengel, and he proceeded to do precisely that.[107]

The presence of two marquee names attracted more than ten thousand fans to the induction festivities on July 25. Reporters estimated the crowd to be the largest since 1939's grand opening, even bigger than the horde that had greeted Joe DiMaggio in 1955. The star at the podium was not Stengel, who rattled on for twenty-one minutes, but Williams, who offered a heartfelt plea for the admission of Negro leaguers. "I hope that Satchel Paige and Josh Gibson somehow will be inducted here as symbols of the great Negro players who are not here because they were not given a chance," he said.[108]

1967

Hall of Fame Summary

New inductees: 3
Category: Player 2, Pioneer/Executive 1
Election: BBWAA 1, Committee 2
Player QS average: 27.0 (BBWAA 44.0, Committee 10.0)
Hall of Famers to date: 107
Category: Player 85, Manager 7, Pioneer/Executive 13, Umpire 2
Election: BBWAA 41, Committee 66
Player QS average: 50.7 (BBWAA 62.6, Committee 39.6)

Inductees

- Branch Rickey. **Category:** Pioneer/Executive. **Election:** Veterans Committee.
- Red Ruffing. **Category:** Player. **Position:** P. **QS:** 44 (marginal). **Career:** 1924-1947, G 624, W-L 273-225, SV 18, ERA 3.80. **Election:** BBWAA.
- Lloyd Waner. **Category:** Player. **Position:** CF. **QS:** 10 (poor). **Career:** 1927-1945, G 1,993, HR 27, RBI 598, BA .316. **Election:** Veterans Committee.

BBWAA Election Summary

Voters: 292
Votes needed for induction: 219
Candidates receiving votes: 47
Candidates elected: 1
Candidates inducted in future: 19

BBWAA Top Ten

1. Joe Medwick, 212 (72.60%)
1. Red Ruffing, 212 (72.60%)^
3. Roy Campanella, 204 (69.86%)
4. Lou Boudreau, 143 (48.97%)
5. Ralph Kiner, 124 (42.47%)
6. Enos Slaughter, 123 (42.12%)
7. Al Lopez, 114 (39.04%)
8. Marty Marion, 90 (30.82%)
9. Johnny Mize, 89 (30.48%)
9. Pee Wee Reese, 89 (30.48%)
^: *Ruffing was chosen in a subsequent runoff election.*

CONTEMPORARIES AGREED THAT BRANCH RICKEY was the greatest general manager the game had ever seen. "He is the smartest baseball man in the country," said the ornery Rogers Hornsby, who disliked almost everyone else he ever met.[109] The immortal boss of the Philadelphia Athletics, Connie Mack, suggested "from my long years of intimate acquaintance with Rickey and knowing his great ability" that he would make an ideal president of the United States.[110]

Rickey's induction was warranted by two trailblazing actions alone—his creation of baseball's first farm system for the St. Louis Cardinals during the 1920s and 1930s, and his integration of the sport by signing Jackie Robinson for the Brooklyn Dodgers. "If Branch Rickey doesn't belong in the Hall of Fame," editorialized the *Sporting News*, "they had better padlock the place and throw away the key."[111]

Yet a technicality had kept him outside. Rickey served a dozen years on the Veterans Committee, which was prohibited from electing any of its members. His death in December 1965 removed that obstacle, so the panel stamped his papers at its next regular meeting in January 1967, a decision that was unanimously hailed. But the committee's other selection was puzzling. "I'm sure happy to be in there with Paul," said Lloyd Waner, a center fielder for the Pittsburgh Pirates whose older brother had been enshrined fifteen years earlier.[112] Paul, with a quality score of fifty-one, had been an obvious choice. That wasn't the case with Lloyd (ten points), who tied Ray Schalk for the second-lowest QS for any inductee to that point.

The Hall of Fame authorized the BBWAA to conduct an election in 1967, temporarily suspending the ban on odd-numbered years.[113] Red Ruffing, who had attained fame as a pitcher for the New York Yankees' great squads in the 1930s and early 1940s, tied for the lead with Joe Medwick, a solid hitter for four clubs, primarily the Cardinals and Dodgers. Both received 212 votes, leaving them 7 short of induction. It was only fitting that Ruffing triumphed in the subsequent runoff election, since he had been languishing on the ballot since 1948, a lengthy wait that made him "a little bitter," he admitted.[114] Medwick had been in line since 1956.

1968

Hall of Fame Summary

New inductees: 3
Category: Player 3
Election: BBWAA 1, Committee 2
Player QS average: 39.3 (BBWAA 56.0, Committee 31.0)
Hall of Famers to date: 110
Category: Player 88, Manager 7, Pioneer/Executive 13, Umpire 2
Election: BBWAA 42, Committee 68
Player QS average: 50.3 (BBWAA 62.4, Committee 39.2)

Inductees

- Kiki Cuyler. **Category:** Player. **Position:** RF. **QS:** 19 (poor). **Career:** 1921-1938, G 1,879, HR 128, RBI 1,065, BA .321. **Election:** Veterans Committee.
- Goose Goslin. **Category:** Player. **Position:** LF. **QS:** 43 (marginal). **Career:** 1921-1938, G 2,287, HR 248, RBI 1,612, BA .316. **Election:** Veterans Committee.
- Joe Medwick. **Category:** Player. **Position:** LF. **QS:** 56 (good). **Career:** 1932-1948, G 1,984, HR 205, RBI 1,383, BA .324. **Election:** BBWAA.

BBWAA Election Summary

Voters: 283
Votes needed for induction: 213
Candidates receiving votes: 48
Candidates elected: 1
Candidates inducted in future: 14

BBWAA Top Ten

1. Joe Medwick, 240 (84.81%)*
2. Roy Campanella, 205 (72.44%)
3. Lou Boudreau, 146 (51.59%)
4. Enos Slaughter, 129 (45.58%)
5. Ralph Kiner, 118 (41.70%)
6. Johnny Mize, 103 (36.40%)
7. Allie Reynolds, 95 (33.57%)
8. Marty Marion, 89 (31.45%)
9. Arky Vaughan, 82 (28.98%)
10. Pee Wee Reese, 81 (28.62%)

Joe Medwick was a patient man. He had come within seven votes of the 75 percent threshold in the 1967 BBWAA election, only to lose to Red Ruffing in a runoff. Yet he remained upbeat. "I'm not discouraged," he told reporters with a smile.[115] The hard-hitting left fielder's faith was rewarded in 1968, when the writers elected him with twenty-seven votes to spare.

Medwick's quality score of fifty-six points stamped him as a solid Hall of Famer. The Veterans Committee, as it so often did, added a pair of honorees whose scores were a good bit lower.

Goose Goslin, a left fielder who spent the majority of his eighteen-year career with the Washington Senators, was a decent selection, as indicated by his QS of forty-three. But Kiki Cuyler, an outfielder for four National League clubs, was a questionable choice. His career batting average of .321 looked impressive, though its 2011-2020 equivalent was just .288. Cuyler's QS was an unexceptional nineteen points. Twenty-one eligible outfielders possessed higher scores, led by Sam Thompson (fifty-two points) and Chuck Klein (fifty).

The 1968 election marked the resumption of annual voting by the BBWAA, which had been confined to even-numbered years between 1956 and 1966. The writers had been given a one-time exemption in 1967 to atone for minor irregularities on 1966's ballot, but the resulting burst of publicity pleased the Hall of Fame's board.[116] It subsequently passed a reform package that reinstated yearly BBWAA elections, eliminated (once again) the runoff provision, and created a screening committee to remove shaky candidates before each winter's list was mailed to the writers. "We are trying to eliminate votes for mediocre players, which cropped up in recent years because their names happened to be on the ballots," said the group's president, Bob Addie of the *Washington Post*.[117]

1969

Hall of Fame Summary

New inductees: 4
Category: Player 4
Election: BBWAA 2, Committee 2
Player QS average: 45.3 (BBWAA 60.0, Committee 30.5)
Hall of Famers to date: 114
Category: Player 92, Manager 7, Pioneer/Executive 13, Umpire 2
Election: BBWAA 44, Committee 70
Player QS average: 50.1 (BBWAA 62.3, Committee 38.9)

Inductees

- Roy Campanella. **Category:** Player. **Position:** C. **QS:** 33 (marginal). **Career:** 1937-1957, G 1,430, HR 260, RBI 1,017, BA .283. **Election:** BBWAA.
- Stan Coveleski. **Category:** Player. **Position:** P. **QS:** 34 (marginal). **Career:** 1912-1928, G 450, W-L 215-142, SV 21, ERA 2.89. **Election:** Veterans Committee.
- Waite Hoyt. **Category:** Player. **Position:** P. **QS:** 27 (poor). **Career:** 1918-1938, G 674, W-L 237-182, SV 53, ERA 3.59. **Election:** Veterans Committee.
- Stan Musial. **Category:** Player. **Position:** LF. **QS:** 87 (excellent). **Career:** 1941-1963, G 3,026, HR 475, RBI 1,951, BA .331. **Election:** BBWAA.

BBWAA Election Summary

Voters: 340
Votes needed for induction: 255
Candidates receiving votes: 46
Candidates elected: 2
Candidates inducted in future: 16

BBWAA Top Ten

1. Stan Musial, 317 (93.24%)*
2. Roy Campanella, 270 (79.41%)*
3. Lou Boudreau, 218 (64.12%)
4. Ralph Kiner, 137 (40.29%)
5. Enos Slaughter, 128 (37.65%)
6. Johnny Mize, 116 (34.12%)
7. Marty Marion, 112 (32.94%)
8. Allie Reynolds, 98 (28.82%)
9. Joe Gordon, 97 (28.53%)
10. Johnny Vander Meer, 95 (27.94%)
10. Early Wynn, 95 (27.94%)

LAWRENCE RITTER'S FIRST BOOK, *Money and Economic Activity*, was far from being a bestseller. His next venture did considerably better.

The New York University economics professor was a diehard baseball fan. He hit the road in the early 1960s—eventually traveling seventy-five thousand miles—as he tracked down elderly men who had played in the major leagues prior to the Great Depression. He found twenty-two who were happy to talk, most of whom had been active in the dead-ball era before 1920. "My role was strictly that of catalyst, audience, and chronicler," Ritter said. "I asked and listened, and the tape recorder did the rest."[118]

The resulting book, *The Glory of Their Times*, became a national sensation in 1966, establishing a template for dozens of oral histories compiled by future authors. Novelist Wilfrid Sheed hailed *Glory* as "quite simply the best sports book in recent memory."[119] The *New York Times* was equally enthusiastic. "If there is a youngster over fifty who does not respond to it," said its reviewer, "he must have a heart of stone."[120]

Three of Ritter's subjects—Paul Waner, Sam Crawford, and Edd Roush—had already been enshrined in the Hall of Fame. Several others were borderline candidates who had faded from public memory. *The Glory of Their Times* revived their campaigns. The book undoubtedly played a role in the Veterans Committee's 1968 selection of Goose Goslin, and it was considerably more influential in the panel's 1969 choice of Stan Coveleski, whose quality score (thirty-four) trailed Goslin's by nine points.

The committee's second honoree in 1969, pitcher Waite Hoyt, counterbalanced a QS smaller than Coveleski's—just twenty-seven points—with a profile that was appreciably larger. Hoyt had been the winningest pitcher on the 1927 New York Yankees, considered by many experts to be the greatest club in big-league history. He remained in the public eye as a longtime broadcaster for the Cincinnati Reds.[121] The panel tapped Hoyt and Coveleski instead of five pitchers who had retired at least twenty years earlier with quality scores of forty-five or better, spanning a timeline from nineteenth-century ace Amos Rusie (fifty-five points) to 1930s star Lefty Gomez (forty-nine).

The BBWAA's two selections were as solid as the Veterans Committee's picks were dubious. Stan Musial and Roy Campanella were both three-time winners of the National League's Most Valuable Player Award. Musial, who batted .331 over twenty-two seasons with the St. Louis Cardinals, carried the second-highest QS (eighty-seven) of any inductee since 1948. Campanella's score was limited to thirty-three points because of misfortunes at both ends of his career. Segregation kept him from joining the Brooklyn Dodgers until he was twenty-six, and a paralyzing auto accident ended his playing days a decade later.

1970

Hall of Fame Summary

New inductees: 4
Category: Player 3, Pioneer/Executive 1
Election: BBWAA 1, Committee 3
Player QS average: 18.7 (BBWAA 31.0, Committee 12.5)
Hall of Famers to date: 118
Category: Player 95, Manager 7, Pioneer/Executive 14, Umpire 2
Election: BBWAA 45, Committee 73
Player QS average: 49.1 (BBWAA 61.6, Committee 37.8)

Inductees

- Lou Boudreau. **Category:** Player. **Position:** SS. **QS:** 31 (marginal). **Career:** 1938-1952, G 1,646, HR 68, RBI 789, BA .295. **Election:** BBWAA.
- Earle Combs. **Category:** Player. **Position:** CF. **QS:** 14 (poor). **Career:** 1924-1935, G 1,455, HR 58, RBI 633, BA .325. **Election:** Veterans Committee.
- Ford Frick. **Category:** Pioneer/Executive. **Election:** Veterans Committee.
- Jesse Haines. **Category:** Player. **Position:** P. **QS:** 11 (poor). **Career:** 1918-1937, G 555, W-L 210-158, SV 11, ERA 3.64. **Election:** Veterans Committee.

BBWAA Election Summary

Voters: 300
Votes needed for induction: 225
Candidates receiving votes: 46
Candidates elected: 1
Candidates inducted in future: 15

BBWAA Top Ten

1. Lou Boudreau, 232 (77.33%)*
2. Ralph Kiner, 167 (55.67%)
3. Gil Hodges, 145 (48.33%)
4. Early Wynn, 140 (46.67%)
5. Enos Slaughter, 133 (44.33%)
6. Johnny Mize, 126 (42.00%)
7. Marty Marion, 120 (40.00%)
8. Pee Wee Reese, 97 (32.33%)
8. Red Schoendienst, 97 (32.33%)
10. George Kell, 90 (30.00%)

IT WAS A SEEMINGLY INNOCUOUS piece of news, warranting just two lines in a *Sporting News* story about a Hall of Fame board meeting in the summer of 1966. "They also named Frank Frisch to the veterans' selection committee," it said, then moved on to other developments.[122]

The appointment would prove to be of seismic importance. Frisch was a Hall of Famer himself, elected by the BBWAA in 1947 after nineteen years as a second baseman with the New York Giants and St. Louis Cardinals. He had been one of the few college-educated players prior to World War II—popularly known as the "Fordham Flash"—yet he was as intense and hard-edged as anybody in the game. "Frisch screamed and he hollered and he used all the four-letter words," recalled a St. Louis teammate, Leo Durocher, who was no shrinking violet himself.[123]

Such a well-respected and powerful personality was destined to emerge as the dominant member of the Veterans Committee, a status that Frisch attained by 1970. Three of his fellow panelists were sportswriters who had covered him as a player in New York and St. Louis—Dan Daniel, Fred Lieb, and J. Roy Stockton—and they happily followed his lead. Frisch would consolidate his power with the appointment of ex-teammate Bill Terry to the committee in 1971, followed a year later by another St. Louis sportswriter, Bob Broeg.[124]

The stage was set for a multiyear string of terrible Hall of Fame selections. Frisch and his cohorts began their reign by picking Yankees center fielder Earle Combs and Cardinals pitcher Jesse Haines in 1970. Their quality scores were pitiful—just fourteen points for Combs, only eleven for Haines—but other factors worked in their favor. Combs had been a member of the fabled '27 Yankees, and Haines had played with Frisch in St. Louis for eleven seasons.

A minor adjustment to the rules gave the Veterans Committee a third slot to fill in 1970, specifically reserved for a manager, umpire, or executive.[125] The honor went to former commissioner Ford Frick, an amiable ex-sportswriter whose credo was as brief as it was stodgy: "Change the status quo only when there is a compelling reason for a change."[126] Frick had accomplished little during his fourteen years as the game's supreme boss (1951-1965), much to the displeasure of critics such as maverick owner Bill Veeck. "Ford Frick does not try to do the wrong thing," Veeck once said. "Given the choice between doing something right or something wrong, Frick will usually begin by doing as little as possible."[127]

The only BBWAA choice in 1970, shortstop Lou Boudreau, had managed and starred for Veeck's 1948 world-champion Cleveland Indians. Boudreau was the American League's MVP that season, though the quality score for his entire fifteen-year career was just thirty-one points. The three players inducted in 1970 carried an average QS of 18.7, which remains the worst figure for any Hall of Fame class to this day.

1971

Hall of Fame Summary

New inductees: 8
Category: Player 7, Pioneer/Executive 1
Election: Committee 8
Player QS average: 30.9 (Committee 30.9)
Hall of Famers to date: 126
Category: Player 102, Manager 7, Pioneer/Executive 15, Umpire 2
Election: BBWAA 45, Committee 81
Player QS average: 47.8 (BBWAA 61.6, Committee 37.0)

Inductees

- Dave Bancroft. **Category:** Player. **Position:** SS. **QS:** 16 (poor). **Career:** 1915-1930, G 1,913, HR 32, RBI 591, BA .279. **Election:** Veterans Committee.
- Jake Beckley. **Category:** Player. **Position:** 1B. **QS:** 37 (marginal). **Career:** 1888-1907, G 2,392, HR 87, RBI 1,581, BA .308. **Election:** Veterans Committee.
- Chick Hafey. **Category:** Player. **Position:** LF. **QS:** 13 (poor). **Career:** 1924-1937, G 1,283, HR 164, RBI 833, BA .317. **Election:** Veterans Committee.
- Harry Hooper. **Category:** Player. **Position:** RF. **QS:** 20 (poor). **Career:** 1909-1925, G 2,309, HR 75, RBI 816, BA .281. **Election:** Veterans Committee.
- Joe Kelley. **Category:** Player. **Position:** LF. **QS:** 37 (marginal). **Career:** 1891-1908, G 1,853, HR 65, RBI 1,194, BA .317. **Election:** Veterans Committee.
- Rube Marquard. **Category:** Player. **Position:** P. **QS:** 20 (poor). **Career:** 1908-1925, G 536, W-L 201-177, SV 20, ERA 3.08. **Election:** Veterans Committee.
- Satchel Paige. **Category:** Player. **Position:** P. **QS:** 73 (excellent). **Career:** 1927-1965, G 391, W-L 118-80, SV 44, ERA 2.70. **Election:** Negro Leagues Committee.
- George Weiss. **Category:** Pioneer/Executive. **Election:** Veterans Committee.

BBWAA Election Summary

Voters: 360
Votes needed for induction: 270
Candidates receiving votes: 48
Candidates elected: 0
Candidates inducted in future: 16

BBWAA Top Ten

1. Yogi Berra, 242 (67.22%)
2. Early Wynn, 240 (66.67%)
3. Ralph Kiner, 212 (58.89%)
4. Gil Hodges, 180 (50.00%)
5. Enos Slaughter, 165 (45.83%)
6. Johnny Mize, 157 (43.61%)
7. Pee Wee Reese, 127 (35.28%)
8. Marty Marion, 123 (34.17%)
8. Red Schoendienst, 123 (34.17%)
10. Allie Reynolds, 110 (30.56%)

YOGI BERRA WON THREE American League Most Valuable Player Awards in eighteen seasons with the New York Yankees, also finishing among the top four vote-getters on four other occasions. Early Wynn, who pitched for three AL clubs, notched precisely three hundred victories and capped his career with a Cy Young Award at age thirty-nine. Ralph Kiner of the Pittsburgh Pirates led the National League in home runs seven straight years from 1946 to 1952.

These three stars—the top contenders on 1971's ballot—appeared to be ironclad Hall of Famers, yet the BBWAA rebuffed them. Berra fell twenty-eight votes shy of 75 percent. Wynn and Kiner missed by thirty and fifty-eight votes, respectively. "I can't tell you how I really feel," said Wynn. "The language would be too embarrassing."[128]

A few writers made the usual effort to defend the indefensible. "It shows that our guys take this thing seriously, that they have some kind of standards, that they're just not going to be steamrollered into anything," bragged Joe Falls of the *Detroit Free Press*.[129] It was a weak excuse for barring three candidates who possessed better credentials than dozens of the hall's existing members.

The Veterans Committee filled the void with a flood of honorees, seven in all. The hall granted Frankie Frisch's gang a one-year waiver from its three-bag limit, opening the door for six players and longtime executive George Weiss, a former general manager of the Yankees and president of the Mets.[130]

The typical fan, sad to say, probably knew more about Weiss than any of the on-field inductees. Two of the hall's newest members had quality scores in the marginal range: thirty-seven points apiece for first base-man Jake Beckley and left fielder Joe Kelley, both of whom had retired more than six decades earlier. The other four newcomers carried scores of twenty points or less—establishing them as poor candidates—though other considerations impelled their inductions. Right fielder Harry Hooper and pitcher Rube Marquard, both at twenty points, had been featured in *The Glory of Their Times.* Shortstop Dave Bancroft (sixteen) and left fielder Chick Hafey (thirteen) had been Frisch's teammates.[131]

The average quality score for the six players chosen by the Veterans Committee was miserably low, just 23.8 points, easily the worst QS for any Hall of Fame class with five or more honorees. But an unanticipated factor—a controversy sparked five years earlier by Ted Williams—rescued 1971 from the pit of mediocrity.

Williams's 1966 plea for the admission of Negro leaguers had gained adherents in the years that followed. Dick Young, an acerbic columnist for the *New York Daily News,* emerged as the movement's unofficial leader. "Why Waite Hoyt and Stan Coveleski, and not Satchel Paige?" Young asked pointedly at 1969's induction ceremony.[132] His question was almost impossible to answer, given that several Hall of Famers had already acknowledged Paige's supremacy. Dizzy Dean, who rarely exhibited humility, credited the black pitcher with having "the greatest stuff I ever saw."[133] Bob Feller chimed in: "The prewar Paige was the best pitcher I ever saw."[134]

Hard-liners insisted that Paige and his fellow Negro leaguers hadn't met the Hall of Fame's simplest requirement, ten years of service in a recognized major league. Young roared back: "Was that their fault, gentlemen? The answer, of course, is obvious."[135] The new commissioner, Bowie Kuhn, jumped aboard the bandwagon as it gathered momentum. The Hall of Fame capitulated in stages, initially pledging to honor Negro leaguers in a separate display, eventually agreeing to extend full-fledged recognition to at least one old-time black player per year.

A special Negro Leagues Committee was created, and it made Paige its first selection. His QS of 73 points not only drove 1971's average score up to 30.9, but it put the year's white inductees firmly in the shade.[136]

1972

Hall of Fame Summary

New inductees: 8
Category: Player 7, Pioneer/Executive 1
Election: BBWAA 3, Committee 5
Player QS average: 50.0 (BBWAA 48.3, Committee 51.3)
Hall of Famers to date: 134
Category: Player 109, Manager 7, Pioneer/Executive 16, Umpire 2
Election: BBWAA 48, Committee 86
Player QS average: 48.0 (BBWAA 60.8, Committee 37.9)

Inductees

- Yogi Berra. **Category:** Player. **Position:** C. **QS:** 48 (good). **Career:** 1946-1965, G 2,120, HR 358, RBI 1,430, BA .285. **Election:** BBWAA.
- Josh Gibson. **Category:** Player. **Position:** C. **QS:** 76 (excellent). **Career:** 1930-1946, G 598, HR 165, RBI 725, BA .374. **Election:** Negro Leagues Committee.
- Lefty Gomez. **Category:** Player. **Position:** P. **QS:** 49 (good). **Career:** 1930-1943, G 368, W-L 189-102, SV 10, ERA 3.34. **Election:** Veterans Committee.
- Will Harridge. **Category:** Pioneer/Executive. **Election:** Veterans Committee.
- Sandy Koufax. **Category:** Player. **Position:** P. **QS:** 53 (good). **Career:** 1955-1966, G 397, W-L 165-87, SV 9, ERA 2.76. **Election:** BBWAA.
- Buck Leonard. **Category:** Player. **Position:** 1B. **QS:** 68 (excellent). **Career:** 1935-1948, G 587, HR 95, RBI 550, BA .345. **Election:** Negro Leagues Committee.
- Early Wynn. **Category:** Player. **Position:** P. **QS:** 44 (marginal). **Career:** 1939-1963, G 691, W-L 300-244, SV 16, ERA 3.54. **Election:** BBWAA.
- Ross Youngs. **Category:** Player. **Position:** RF. **QS:** 12 (poor). **Career:** 1917-1926, G 1,211, HR 42, RBI 592, BA .322. **Election:** Veterans Committee.

BBWAA Election Summary

Voters: 396
Votes needed for induction: 297
Candidates receiving votes: 46
Candidates elected: 3
Candidates inducted in future: 13

BBWAA Top Ten

1. Sandy Koufax, 344 (86.87%)*
2. Yogi Berra, 339 (85.61%)*
3. Early Wynn, 301 (76.01%)*
4. Ralph Kiner, 235 (59.34%)
5. Gil Hodges, 161 (40.66%)
6. Johnny Mize, 157 (39.65%)
7. Enos Slaughter, 149 (37.63%)
8. Pee Wee Reese, 129 (32.58%)
9. Marty Marion, 120 (30.30%)
10. Bob Lemon, 117 (29.55%)

IT TURNED OUT THAT Yogi Berra and Early Wynn were worthy of Hall of Fame recognition after all. Both crossed the 75 percent threshold in 1972, a year after missing by a substantial margin. Berra improved by 18.4 percentage points from 1971, Wynn by 9.3. Nobody could explain why the writers found the two stars so much more appealing after the passage of just twelve months.

"I would have been happier if I'd made it the first year," said Wynn, who had been eligible since 1969. "I don't think I'm as thrilled as I would have been if that had happened."[137]

The BBWAA's top vote-getter, Sandy Koufax, did make it to Cooperstown in his first year on the ballot, only the fifth player to do so since 1937. He expressed shock at the depth of his support, almost 87 percent. "I didn't have as many good years as many people who are in the Hall of Fame," he said, and it was true.[138] But no pitcher in the game had come close to Koufax's dominance between 1961 and 1966. The call from Cooperstown came a few days after his thirty-sixth birthday.

Five additional honorees were named by the hall's two committees, whose output varied dramatically in quality.

The Veterans Committee's three choices were predictably unexciting. Lefty Gomez deserved his honor, though the same could have been said of eight retired pitchers with quality scores of fifty points or better. They remained outside the gallery as Gomez (forty-nine points) entered. It helped tremendously that he had pitched thirteen of his fourteen seasons for the high-profile Yankees. The selections of former American League president Will Harridge and right fielder Ross Youngs stirred no enthusiasm. Youngs's victory would have been impossible to fathom, given his meager QS of twelve points, if not for one simple fact. Two of his teammates on the New York Giants had been Frankie Frisch and Bill Terry, the opinionated duo in charge of the Veterans Committee.

The Negro Leagues Committee, on the other hand, advanced two excellent candidates, catcher Josh Gibson (seventy-six points) and first baseman Buck Leonard (sixty-eight).[139] Gibson's QS was the third-highest for any inductee since 1956, trailing only Ted Williams and Stan Musial. One of the Hall of Fame's original immortals, Walter Johnson, had insisted long ago that Gibson could have starred for any American or National League team. "He can do everything," said the white pitcher. "He hits the ball a mile. And he catches so easy he might as well be in a rocking chair." But segregation was in full force when Johnson spoke, causing him to add a sad postscript: "Too bad this Gibson is a colored fellow."[140]

1973

Hall of Fame Summary

New inductees: 6
Category: Player 5, Umpire 1
Election: BBWAA 2, Committee 4
Player QS average: 40.8 (BBWAA 70.5, Committee 21.0)
Hall of Famers to date: 140
Category: Player 114, Manager 7, Pioneer/Executive 16, Umpire 3
Election: BBWAA 50, Committee 90
Player QS average: 47.7 (BBWAA 61.2, Committee 37.1)

Inductees

- Roberto Clemente. **Category:** Player. **Position:** RF. **QS:** 69 (excellent). **Career:** 1955-1972, G 2,433, HR 240, RBI 1,305, BA .317. **Election:** BBWAA.
- Billy Evans. **Category:** Umpire. **Election:** Veterans Committee.
- Monte Irvin. **Category:** Player. **Position:** LF. **QS:** 29 (poor). **Career:** 1938-1956, G 1,032, HR 137, RBI 688, BA .304. **Election:** Negro Leagues Committee.
- George Kelly. **Category:** Player. **Position:** 1B. **QS:** 5 (poor). **Career:** 1915-1932, G 1,622, HR 148, RBI 1,020, BA .297. **Election:** Veterans Committee.
- Warren Spahn. **Category:** Player. **Position:** P. **QS:** 72 (excellent). **Career:** 1942-1965, G 750, W-L 363-245, SV 28, ERA 3.09. **Election:** BBWAA.
- Mickey Welch. **Category:** Player. **Position:** P. **QS:** 29 (poor). **Career:** 1880-1892, G 565, W-L 307-210, SV 4, ERA 2.71. **Election:** Veterans Committee.

BBWAA Election Summary

Voters: 380
Votes needed for induction: 285
Candidates receiving votes: 44
Candidates elected: 2^
Candidates inducted in future: 15
^: *Spahn was chosen in the BBWAA's 1973 general election. Clemente was chosen in a special election in March 1973.*

BBWAA Top Ten

1. Warren Spahn, 316 (83.16%)*
2. Whitey Ford, 255 (67.11%)
3. Ralph Kiner, 235 (61.84%)
4. Gil Hodges, 218 (57.37%)

5. Robin Roberts, 213 (56.05%)
6. Bob Lemon, 177 (46.58%)
7. Johnny Mize, 157 (41.32%)
8. Enos Slaughter, 145 (38.16%)
9. Marty Marion, 127 (33.42%)
10. Pee Wee Reese, 126 (33.16%)

WARREN SPAHN MADE HIS final big-league appearance on October 1, 1965, retiring with 363 victories to his credit. He ranked—then and now—as the winningest left-handed pitcher in baseball history. Nobody doubted that he would be elected to the Hall of Fame in his first year of eligibility, 1971.

But the hall's voting rules haven't always been governed by common sense. Spahn found it difficult to stay off the mound after becoming a coach and then a manager in the minor leagues. He inserted himself to pitch a handful of innings in 1966 and 1967. The hall promptly reclassified him as an active player and pushed his eligibility date to 1973, as if the voters needed additional time to assess his outings for the Mexico City Tigers and Tulsa Oilers. "I wasn't aware it would delay my chances, but it didn't matter," Spahn said equably. "I wasn't in shape, and I didn't do very well, but I enjoyed the competition."[141]

Spahn finally received his due from the BBWAA in January 1973. A second superstar, right fielder Roberto Clemente of the Pittsburgh Pirates, was added to the hall in a special election two months later, following his death in a plane crash. A total of 424 writers voted by mail, with 92.7 percent approving Clemente's induction.[142] That made 1973 the first year since 1955 in which the writers tapped two players with quality scores in the excellent range. Spahn's QS was seventy-two points, Clemente's sixty-nine.

The two committees produced four additional inductees, none of them compelling. One of the choices could best be called outrageous. George "Highpockets" Kelly had been a first baseman between 1915 and 1932 for five National League teams, primarily the Giants. One of his infield mates in New York was—yes—Frankie Frisch. "He was a line-drive hitter," enthused Frisch, "and he had a better arm than any of today's stars. What an arm!"[143]

Throwing ability, of course, is hardly a prime requisite for a first baseman, though batting skill is. The sad truth is that Old Highpockets didn't rip as many liners as his pal remembered. Kelly's batting average, when adjusted to 2011-2020 levels, was a pedestrian .261. "He wasn't a Hall of Famer on the best day of his life," snorted Bill James.[144] Kelly's quality score of five points put him below every inductee between 1936 and 1973 except Tommy McCarthy, the infamous one-point wonder.

1974

Hall of Fame Summary

New inductees: 6
Category: Player 5, Umpire 1
Election: BBWAA 2, Committee 4
Player QS average: 50.4 (BBWAA 69.0, Committee 38.0)
Hall of Famers to date: 146
Category: Player 119, Manager 7, Pioneer/Executive 16, Umpire 4
Election: BBWAA 52, Committee 94
Player QS average: 47.8 (BBWAA 61.5, Committee 37.1)

Inductees

- Cool Papa Bell. **Category:** Player. **Position:** CF. **QS:** 34 (marginal). **Career:** 1922-1946, G 1,199, HR 57, RBI 593, BA .325. **Election:** Negro Leagues Committee.
- Jim Bottomley. **Category:** Player. **Position:** 1B. **QS:** 28 (poor). **Career:** 1922-1937, G 1,991, HR 219, RBI 1,422, BA .310. **Election:** Veterans Committee.
- Jocko Conlan. **Category:** Umpire. **Election:** Veterans Committee.
- Whitey Ford. **Category:** Player. **Position:** P. **QS:** 54 (good). **Career:** 1950-1967, G 498, W-L 236-106, SV 11, ERA 2.75. **Election:** BBWAA.
- Mickey Mantle. **Category:** Player. **Position:** CF. **QS:** 84 (excellent). **Career:** 1951-1968, G 2,401, HR 536, RBI 1,509, BA .298. **Election:** BBWAA.
- Sam Thompson. **Category:** Player. **Position:** RF. **QS:** 52 (good). **Career:** 1885-1906, G 1,410, HR 126, RBI 1,308, BA .331. **Election:** Veterans Committee.

BBWAA Election Summary

Voters: 365
Votes needed for induction: 274
Candidates receiving votes: 44
Candidates elected: 2
Candidates inducted in future: 14

BBWAA Top Ten

1. Mickey Mantle, 322 (88.22%)*
2. Whitey Ford, 284 (77.81%)*
3. Robin Roberts, 224 (61.37%)
4. Ralph Kiner, 215 (58.90%)
5. Gil Hodges, 198 (54.25%)
6. Bob Lemon, 190 (52.05%)
7. Enos Slaughter, 145 (39.73%)

8. Pee Wee Reese, 141 (38.63%)
9. Eddie Mathews, 118 (32.33%)
10. Phil Rizzuto, 111 (30.41%)
10. Duke Snider, 111 (30.41%)

THE 1974 GATHERING OF THE Veterans Committee lacked a familiar presence. Frankie Frisch had been badly injured in a car accident while traveling from the previous year's meeting in Florida to his home in Rhode Island, dying after five weeks in the hospital. He left behind a dreary legacy of Hall of Fame misfires. The committee had admitted twenty-two candidates—seventeen players, four executives, and an umpire—during Frisch's seven years of service. The quality scores for more than two-thirds of the honored players (twelve of seventeen) were in the poor range.[145]

Several of Frisch's acolytes remained on the committee, and they paid tribute in 1974 by approving another St. Louis candidate with meager credentials. Jim Bottomley was a first baseman best known for his positive attitude—hence his nickname of "Sunny Jim"—and for driving home twelve runs in a single game in 1924.[146] His quality score of twenty-eight points trailed six other first basemen eligible for committee selection, notably Roger Connor (seventy-seven) and Johnny Mize (sixty-six).

The headliners in the class of 1974 were center fielder Mickey Mantle and pitcher Whitey Ford, best friends and teammates on the New York Yankees. "I'm closer to Whitey than to any other man in the world," Mantle said.[147] He was elected by the BBWAA in his first year on the ballot, Ford in his second.

An enormous crowd swarmed to the Hall of Fame's induction ceremonies on August 12, 1974, eager for lighthearted fun in that summer of political turmoil. Richard Nixon had resigned as president just three days earlier, replaced in the White House by Gerald Ford. Thousands of New York fans made the four-hour drive to Cooperstown in search of diversion. They cheered Mickey and Whitey—and paid little attention to the other four honorees.

Mantle drew the biggest ovation, but it was the impish Ford who stole the show. He smiled as he looked over the crowd from the podium.

"Between what happened in Washington last week and what happened here in Cooperstown today," he said, "I'd have to say it was a pretty good week for the Fords."[148]

1975

Hall of Fame Summary

New inductees: 5
Category: Player 4, Manager 1
Election: BBWAA 1, Committee 4
Player QS average: 24.3 (BBWAA 40.0, Committee 19.0)
Hall of Famers to date: 151
Category: Player 123, Manager 8, Pioneer/Executive 16, Umpire 4
Election: BBWAA 53, Committee 98
Player QS average: 47.0 (BBWAA 61.1, Committee 36.4)

Inductees

- Earl Averill. **Category:** Player. **Position:** CF. **QS:** 26 (poor). **Career:** 1929-1941, G 1,669, HR 238, RBI 1,164, BA .318. **Election:** Veterans Committee.
- Bucky Harris. **Category:** Manager. **Career:** 1924-1956, W-L 2,158-2,219, Pennants 3, Titles 2. **Election:** Veterans Committee.
- Billy Herman. **Category:** Player. **Position:** 2B. **QS:** 26 (poor). **Career:** 1931-1947, G 1,922, HR 47, RBI 839, BA .304. **Election:** Veterans Committee.
- Judy Johnson. **Category:** Player. **Position:** 3B. **QS:** 5 (poor). **Career:** 1923-1936, G 709, HR 25, RBI 457, BA .304. **Election:** Negro Leagues Committee.
- Ralph Kiner. **Category:** Player. **Position:** LF. **QS:** 40 (marginal). **Career:** 1946-1955, G 1,472, HR 369, RBI 1,015, BA .279. **Election:** BBWAA.

BBWAA Election Summary

Voters: 362
Votes needed for induction: 272
Candidates receiving votes: 37
Candidates elected: 1
Candidates inducted in future: 14

BBWAA Top Ten

1. Ralph Kiner, 273 (75.41%)*
2. Robin Roberts, 263 (72.65%)
3. Bob Lemon, 233 (64.36%)
4. Gil Hodges, 188 (51.93%)
5. Enos Slaughter, 177 (48.90%)
6. Hal Newhouser, 155 (42.82%)

7. Pee Wee Reese, 154 (42.54%)
8. Eddie Mathews, 148 (40.88%)
9. Phil Cavarretta, 129 (35.64%)
9. Duke Snider, 129 (35.64%)

THE NEW MEMBERS WELCOMED to the Hall of Fame in 1975 seemed to be an exasperated bunch.

Exhibit A was center fielder Earl Averill, who unleashed the anger that had accumulated during thirty-four long years of retirement. He contended that his statistics had warranted induction much earlier, though he had been forced to wait until the Veterans Committee came calling. "What right does anyone have to ignore cold hard facts in favor of looking for some intangible item to keep a person out of Cooperstown?" he asked during his acceptance speech.[149]

Others expressed their frustration more mildly. Slugger Ralph Kiner was the BBWAA's only choice in 1975, finally making it in his thirteenth year on the ballot. He received a single vote more than the required 272. "It was getting tougher and tougher because a lot of people who saw me play have died," said Kiner. "It's like Casey Stengel says: 'Most people my age are dead.'"[150] Third baseman Judy Johnson, picked by the Negro Leagues Committee, was succinct. "I thought I had been forgotten," he said.[151]

There was a touch of exaggeration in all of their comments. Averill's stats weren't as overwhelming as he believed. His quality score was just twenty-six points. Kiner wasn't the senior citizen he portrayed himself to be. He was only fifty-two years old. And Johnson hadn't been forgotten, not by contemporaries of all races who truly knew baseball. Connie Mack had once said that color was the only factor preventing him from being a big-league star. "Judy, it's a shame you're a Negro," Mack told him. "You could name your own price."[152]

Johnson was a solid addition to the plaque gallery despite his quality score of five points, a figure artificially depressed by segregation. But it was difficult to rationalize the Veterans Committee's designation of Bucky Harris as a Hall of Fame manager. Harris did have two factors in his favor. He had always been popular with his players—"If you can't play for Bucky, you don't belong in the major leagues," said Joe

DiMaggio[153]—and he had won world titles with the Washington Senators in 1924 and the Yankees in 1947. But Harris was much more familiar with defeat than victory. Less than a third of the clubs he managed—nine of twenty-nine—finished higher than fifth place. His career winning percentage was a run-of-the-mill .493.

1976

Hall of Fame Summary

New inductees: 6
Category: Player 5, Umpire 1
Election: BBWAA 2, Committee 4
Player QS average: 50.0 (BBWAA 44.5, Committee 53.7)
Hall of Famers to date: 157
Category: Player 128, Manager 8, Pioneer/Executive 16, Umpire 5
Election: BBWAA 55, Committee 102
Player QS average: 47.1 (BBWAA 60.5, Committee 37.1)

Inductees

- Oscar Charleston. **Category:** Player. **Position:** CF. **QS:** 80 (excellent). **Career:** 1920-1941, G 915, HR 143, RBI 853, BA .364. **Election:** Negro Leagues Committee.
- Roger Connor. **Category:** Player. **Position:** 1B. **QS:** 77 (excellent). **Career:** 1880-1897, G 1,998, HR 138, RBI 1,323, BA .316. **Election:** Veterans Committee.
- Cal Hubbard. **Category:** Umpire. **Election:** Veterans Committee.
- Bob Lemon. **Category:** Player. **Position:** P. **QS:** 20 (poor). **Career:** 1941-1958, G 460, W-L 207-128, SV 22, ERA 3.23. **Election:** BBWAA.
- Freddie Lindstrom. **Category:** Player. **Position:** 3B. **QS:** 4 (poor). **Career:** 1924-1936, G 1,438, HR 103, RBI 779, BA .311. **Election:** Veterans Committee.
- Robin Roberts. **Category:** Player. **Position:** P. **QS:** 69 (excellent). **Career:** 1948-1966, G 676, W-L 286-245, SV 25, ERA 3.41. **Election:** BBWAA.

BBWAA Election Summary

Voters: 388
Votes needed for induction: 291
Candidates receiving votes: 32
Candidates elected: 2
Candidates inducted in future: 11

BBWAA Top Ten

1. Robin Roberts, 337 (86.86%)*
2. Bob Lemon, 305 (78.61%)*
3. Gil Hodges, 233 (60.05%)
4. Enos Slaughter, 197 (50.77%)
5. Eddie Mathews, 189 (48.71%)
6. Pee Wee Reese, 186 (47.94%)
7. Nellie Fox, 174 (44.85%)

8. Duke Snider, 159 (40.98%)
9. Phil Rizzuto, 149 (38.40%)
10. George Kell, 129 (33.25%)
10. Red Schoendienst, 129 (33.25%)

THE SIX HALL OF FAME INDUCTEES in 1976 varied widely in skill and popularity. Three had quality scores in the excellent range, making this the first year since 1939 with such a large number of honorees at sixty points or higher on the QS scale. But the other three choices were uninspiring, including an umpire and two players with scores of twenty points or less.

The BBWAA got the ball rolling in January with its election of pitcher Robin Roberts, who carried a QS of sixty-nine. Roberts won at least twenty games in six different seasons for the Philadelphia Phillies, peaking with twenty-eight victories in 1952. He made it to Cooperstown in his fourth year of eligibility. "When you miss getting in, the reaction is to feel that you men who vote are doing a terrible job," he joked when a BBWAA representative called. "But when you get in, you've done a good job."[154]

The Negro Leagues Committee did an excellent job. It picked center fielder Oscar Charleston, only the fourth inductee in a quarter-century with a QS of at least eighty points. "The greatest ballplayer I've ever seen was Oscar Charleston. When I say this, I'm not overlooking Ruth, Cobb, Gehrig, and all of them," said Bernie Borgan, a longtime scout for the St. Louis Cardinals. Buck O'Neil, whose lengthy career straddled the Negro leagues and the integrated majors, described Charleston as "Ty Cobb, Babe Ruth, and Tris Speaker rolled into one."[155]

The Veterans Committee did something unusual in 1976, selecting a candidate in the excellent range for the first time since 1964. First baseman Roger Connor (seventy-seven points) had been retired for seventy-nine years and dead for forty-five. "Not even the members of the committee knew much more about Connor than what appears in the record books," admitted New York sportswriter Jack Lang.[156] The books revealed that Connor had batted higher than .325 in seven seasons and had hit more home runs than anybody else in the dead-ball era, achievements worthy of enshrinement.

But the Veterans Committee couldn't shake its bad habits completely. The panel had become fixated on the Cardinals and New York Giants, electing nine players from those two clubs between 1970 and 1975, eight of them with quality scores in the poor range. Why not add one more? The latest honoree was a third baseman for the Giants, Freddie Lindstrom, who carried a pathetically low QS of four points. Sportswriters had found Lindstrom so unimpressive that they gave him a grand total of twenty-two votes in the BBWAA's elections between 1936 and 1962. That didn't bother the committee, which ushered him into Cooperstown on a unanimous roll call.

1977

Hall of Fame Summary

New inductees: 6
Category: Player 5, Manager 1
Election: BBWAA 1, Committee 5
Player QS average: 32.0 (BBWAA 57.0, Committee 25.8)
Hall of Famers to date: 163
Category: Player 133, Manager 9, Pioneer/Executive 16, Umpire 5
Election: BBWAA 56, Committee 107
Player QS average: 46.6 (BBWAA 60.4, Committee 36.5)

Inductees

- Ernie Banks. **Category:** Player. **Position:** SS. **QS:** 57 (good). **Career:** 1953-1971, G 2,528, HR 512, RBI 1,636, BA .274. **Election:** BBWAA.
- Martin Dihigo. **Category:** Player. **Position:** SS. **QS:** 21 (poor). **Career:** 1923-1945, G 397, HR 68, RBI 309, BA .307. **Election:** Negro Leagues Committee.
- John Henry Lloyd. **Category:** Player. **Position:** 2B. **QS:** 15 (poor). **Career:** 1921-1929, G 433, HR 16, RBI 308, BA .349. **Election:** Negro Leagues Committee.
- Al Lopez. **Category:** Manager. **Career:** 1951-1969, W-L 1,410-1,004, Pennants 2, Titles 0. **Election:** Veterans Committee.
- Amos Rusie. **Category:** Player. **Position:** P. **QS:** 55 (good). **Career:** 1889-1901, G 463, W-L 246-174, SV 5, ERA 3.07. **Election:** Veterans Committee.
- Joe Sewell. **Category:** Player. **Position:** SS. **QS:** 12 (poor). **Career:** 1920-1933, G 1,903, HR 49, RBI 1,054, BA .312. **Election:** Veterans Committee.

BBWAA Election Summary

Voters: 383
Votes needed for induction: 288
Candidates receiving votes: 34
Candidates elected: 1
Candidates inducted in future: 11

BBWAA Top Ten

1. Ernie Banks, 321 (83.81%)*
2. Eddie Mathews, 239 (62.40%)
3. Gil Hodges, 224 (58.49%)
4. Enos Slaughter, 222 (57.96%)
5. Duke Snider, 212 (55.35%)
6. Don Drysdale, 197 (51.44%)

7. Pee Wee Reese, 163 (42.56%)
8. Nellie Fox, 152 (39.69%)
9. Jim Bunning, 146 (38.12%)
10. George Kell, 141 (36.81%)

MIDDLE INFIELDERS RULED IN 1977. The only player elected by the BBWAA, the eternally cheerful Ernie Banks, had established his reputation as a hard-hitting shortstop for the Chicago Cubs before switching to first base in his twilight seasons. The other five inductees included another pair of shortstops (Martin Dihigo and Joe Sewell) and second baseman John Henry Lloyd. They were joined by pitcher Amos Rusie and manager Al Lopez.

Banks was the featured attraction at the annual festivities in Cooperstown, which only seemed fair. His quality score (fifty-seven points) topped the class of 1977, and his popularity with the fans was off the charts. "The whole theory of my life is sunshine," he said with a smile.[157]

Rusie seemed to fit a sadly familiar stereotype—yet another New York Giant enshrined by the Veterans Committee—but there was no denying his worthiness. The right-hander was reputedly the fastest pitcher of the nineteenth century, the Bob Feller or Nolan Ryan of his era. "The giant simply drove the ball at you with the force of a cannon. It was like a white streak tearing past you," recalled a terrified opponent, Jimmy Ryan.[158] Rusie's QS of fifty-five put him just two points behind Banks.

The other inductees in 1977 weren't as impressive on paper. The low quality scores for Dihigo and Lloyd, both tapped by the Negro Leagues Committee, were easily explained as a byproduct of segregation. Both stars passed the eye test, as fellow Hall of Famers willingly testified. "You take your Ruths, Cobbs, and DiMaggios. Give me Dihigo, and I bet I'd beat you almost every time," Buck Leonard said.[159] Babe Ruth had been equally effusive about Lloyd, once naming the second baseman as the greatest player he had ever seen.[160]

The other two picks by the Veterans Committee were more difficult to understand. Sewell was renowned for his amazing bat control—striking out just 114 times in 8,333 trips to the plate—yet otherwise seemed below Hall of Fame standards, as indicated by his QS of 12 points.

Lopez, the ninth manager admitted to the hall, possessed a winning percentage of .584, which was certainly impressive. But he never won a World Series, a flaw he shared with only one other manager already enshrined, Wilbert Robinson.

1978

Hall of Fame Summary

New inductees: 3
Category: Player 2, Pioneer/Executive 1
Election: BBWAA 1, Committee 2
Player QS average: 48.5 (BBWAA 60.0, Committee 37.0)
Hall of Famers to date: 166
Category: Player 135, Manager 9, Pioneer/Executive 17, Umpire 5
Election: BBWAA 57, Committee 109
Player QS average: 46.6 (BBWAA 60.4, Committee 36.5)

Inductees

- Addie Joss. **Category:** Player. **Position:** P. **QS:** 37 (marginal). **Career:** 1902-1910, G 286, W-L 160-97, SV 5, ERA 1.89. **Election:** Veterans Committee.
- Larry MacPhail. **Category:** Pioneer/Executive. **Election:** Veterans Committee.
- Eddie Mathews. **Category:** Player. **Position:** 3B. **QS:** 60 (excellent). **Career:** 1952-1968, G 2,391, HR 512, RBI 1,453, BA .271. **Election:** BBWAA.

BBWAA Election Summary

Voters: 379
Votes needed for induction: 285
Candidates receiving votes: 35
Candidates elected: 1
Candidates inducted in future: 11

BBWAA Top Ten

1. Eddie Mathews, 301 (79.42%)*
2. Enos Slaughter, 261 (68.87%)
3. Duke Snider, 254 (67.02%)
4. Gil Hodges, 226 (59.63%)
5. Don Drysdale, 219 (57.78%)
6. Jim Bunning, 181 (47.76%)
7. Pee Wee Reese, 169 (44.59%)
8. Richie Ashburn, 158 (41.69%)
8. Hoyt Wilhelm, 158 (41.69%)
10. Nellie Fox, 149 (39.31%)

THE WRITERS COULD SEE what was going on, and they weren't happy. They passed a resolution in the summer of 1977, condemning the Veterans Committee's eagerness to admit marginal candidates to the Hall of Fame. Jack Lang, the BBWAA's secretary/treasurer, criticized "the flaunting manner" in which the panel approved nominees who had previously been ignored by the writers. Jesse Haines, George Kelly, Freddie Lindstrom, and Joe Sewell came to mind. None had risen higher than 8.5 percent in any BBWAA election, yet the committee had ushered all four into the hall.[161]

Statistics from the previous decade (1968-1977) buttressed the writers' complaint. The Veterans Committee had admitted 24 players with an average QS of 27.8 points. The BBWAA's output was lower in quantity (15 inductions), but much higher in quality (54.5 points). The writers threatened to boycott the 1978 election if something wasn't done.

Peace (of a sort) was finally brokered in October 1977, when the Hall of Fame slapped a partial restriction on the Veterans Committee. The panel would be allowed to consider a postwar player—one who retired in 1946 or later—only if he had received at least one hundred votes in a single BBWAA election. This alteration ostensibly gave the upper hand in the selection process to the writers, yet their control was far from absolute. All pre-1946 retirees remained fair game for the committee, which meant that Haines, Kelly, Lindstrom, and Sewell still would have been eligible, had they not already been enshrined.

Three smaller adjustments were made to the Veterans Committee in advance of its 1978 meeting. It was expanded to eighteen members, it was limited to two honorees per year (down from three), and it was handed the responsibility for inducting old-time black players.[162] The latter assignment came after the Negro Leagues Committee unexpectedly disbanded, releasing a statement that it could not reach 75 percent agreement on any black players besides the nine it had inducted since 1971.[163] Critics—and there were many—accused the sport's white leaders of applying pressure. "Nine blacks have been named, and that's a full team, and baseball is tired of doing penance," grumbled columnist Red Smith.[164]

The voting process in 1978 went surprisingly well despite all of the pre-election fireworks. Hard-hitting third baseman Eddie Mathews and innovative executive Larry MacPhail were solid choices, though yet another rule change was necessary before pitcher Addie Joss could be admitted. Joss piled up 160 wins and 37 quality points between 1902 and 1910 for the Cleveland Naps. But he died of tubercular meningitis on the opening day of what would have been his tenth season, leaving him a year short of the Hall of Fame's service requirement. The hall's board opted to waive it in his case.[165]

Outstanding baseball writers had been honored since 1962 with the J.G. Taylor Spink Award, which was named after its first recipient. A roster of annual winners was engraved on a plaque in one of Cooperstown's secondary galleries. Play-by-play announcers were extended the same privilege in 1978. Two New York pioneers, Mel Allen and Red Barber, were named the first winners of the Ford C. Frick Award for Broadcasting Excellence, with their names suitably etched on a new plaque.[166] The "broadcasters' wing" of the Hall of Fame, which would be mentioned in occasional news accounts, was just as fanciful as the writers' wing.

1979

Hall of Fame Summary

New inductees: 3
Category: Player 2, Pioneer/Executive 1
Election: BBWAA 1, Committee 2
Player QS average: 62.5 (BBWAA 95.0, Committee 30.0)
Hall of Famers to date: 169
Category: Player 137, Manager 9, Pioneer/Executive 18, Umpire 5
Election: BBWAA 58, Committee 111
Player QS average: 46.8 (BBWAA 61.0, Committee 36.4)

Inductees

- Warren Giles. **Category:** Pioneer/Executive. **Election:** Veterans Committee.
- Willie Mays. **Category:** Player. **Position:** CF. **QS:** 95 (excellent). **Career:** 1948-1973, G 3,005, HR 660, RBI 1,909, BA .301. **Election:** BBWAA.
- Hack Wilson. **Category:** Player. **Position:** CF. **QS:** 30 (marginal). **Career:** 1923-1934, G 1,348, HR 244, RBI 1,063, BA .307. **Election:** Veterans Committee.

BBWAA Election Summary

Voters: 432
Votes needed for induction: 324
Candidates receiving votes: 38
Candidates elected: 1
Candidates inducted in future: 11

BBWAA Top Ten

1. Willie Mays, 409 (94.68%)*
2. Duke Snider, 308 (71.30%)
3. Enos Slaughter, 297 (68.75%)
4. Gil Hodges, 242 (56.02%)
5. Don Drysdale, 233 (53.94%)
6. Nellie Fox, 174 (40.28%)
7. Hoyt Wilhelm, 168 (38.89%)
8. Maury Wills, 166 (38.43%)
9. Red Schoendienst, 159 (36.81%)
10. Jim Bunning, 147 (34.03%)

MILT PAPPAS FELT HE WAS being shortchanged. The BBWAA's screening committee had sifted through the records of twenty-four players who retired in 1973 after at least ten years of big-league service. The screeners plucked two—center fielder Willie Mays and shortstop Luis Aparicio—to join a bunch of holdovers on 1979's Hall of Fame ballot. It discarded the rest, including Pappas, a pitcher who had won 209 games over 17 seasons. "I can understand Mays, of course," Pappas said unhappily, "but my career paralleled Aparicio's."[167]

Pappas filed a complaint with the BBWAA, which surprised almost everybody by ruling in his favor. Jerome Holtzman of the *Chicago Sun-Times* led a successful drive to abolish the screening committee and add all twenty-two rejected candidates to the 1979 ballot. He convinced his fellow writers that every ten-year player deserved at least one shot at the hall.

Not all of them welcomed the opportunity. Catcher Jeff Torborg, who batted .214 for the Los Angeles Dodgers and California Angels between 1964 and 1973, immediately petitioned the BBWAA to have his name removed for a second time. "I don't want to hear all those snickers when I don't get any votes," Torborg said laughingly.[168]

Pappas's victory came with a caveat. The BBWAA still felt it needed a mechanism to limit the number of eligible players, so it replaced the screening committee with a 5 percent threshold. A player could remain on the ballot for as many as fifteen years—stretching to the end of his BBWAA window—if at least 5 percent of the writers supported him each year. A single slip below 5 percent would result in elimination.

That was the fate awaiting Pappas and his colleagues. Twenty-two votes were required in 1979 to qualify for the 1980 ballot. Pappas got five. The other twenty-one candidates rescued by the BBWAA received a grand total of fifteen. All were disqualified from future consideration.

This sideshow did not detract from the election of Mays, who received 94.7 percent support from the writers, the highest share for any candidate in forty-two years. The longtime star for the New York and San Francisco Giants possessed a magnificent quality score of ninety-five points, unsurpassed by any inductee since Rogers Hornsby in 1942. Bowie Kuhn introduced the forty-eight-year-old Mays at the induction ceremony on August 5, 1979. "He never gave the fans a penny of short change," the commissioner shouted, and the crowd roared its agreement.[169]

The hall's other new members seemed insignificant in comparison. Hack Wilson (QS of thirty points) was a hard-hitting center fielder for four National League clubs, primarily the Cubs. His career was unusually short—he played more than 120 games in only 6 seasons—and his defensive deficiencies were glaring. Yet Wilson held one of baseball's golden marks, the one-year record for runs batted in (191), which was the first fact mentioned on his plaque. It was also the likely reason for his selection by the Veterans Committee, even though Rule 6 specifically prohibited the induction of any player based on accomplishments confined to a single season.[170]

The committee's other choice, former National League president Warren Giles, was even less impressive. Giles was a pleasant man with nothing exceptional on his resumé. "I thought Warren was a jolly, kind of dumb guy," said Red Smith. "Friendly, very likable. Kind of a dummy."[171] Giles's Hall of Fame plaque amounted to an award for long and faithful service, the equivalent of a gold watch.

1980

Hall of Fame Summary

New inductees: 4
Category: Player 3, Pioneer/Executive 1
Election: BBWAA 2, Committee 2
Player QS average: 59.3 (BBWAA 64.0, Committee 50.0)
Hall of Famers to date: 173
Category: Player 140, Manager 9, Pioneer/Executive 19, Umpire 5
Election: BBWAA 60, Committee 113
Player QS average: 47.1 (BBWAA 61.1, Committee 36.6)

Inductees

- Al Kaline. **Category:** Player. **Position:** RF. **QS:** 68 (excellent). **Career:** 1953-1974, G 2,834, HR 399, RBI 1,582, BA .297. **Election:** BBWAA.
- Chuck Klein. **Category:** Player. **Position:** RF. **QS:** 50 (good). **Career:** 1928-1944, G 1,753, HR 300, RBI 1,201, BA .320. **Election:** Veterans Committee.
- Duke Snider. **Category:** Player. **Position:** CF. **QS:** 60 (excellent). **Career:** 1947-1964, G 2,143, HR 407, RBI 1,333, BA .295. **Election:** BBWAA.
- Tom Yawkey. **Category:** Pioneer/Executive. **Election:** Veterans Committee.

BBWAA Election Summary

Voters: 385
Votes needed for induction: 289
Candidates receiving votes: 32
Candidates elected: 2
Candidates inducted in future: 11

BBWAA Top Ten

1. Al Kaline, 340 (88.31%)*
2. Duke Snider, 333 (86.49%)*
3. Don Drysdale, 238 (61.82%)
4. Gil Hodges, 230 (59.74%)
5. Hoyt Wilhelm, 209 (54.29%)
6. Jim Bunning, 177 (45.97%)
7. Red Schoendienst, 164 (42.60%)
8. Nellie Fox, 161 (41.82%)
9. Maury Wills, 146 (37.92%)
10. Richie Ashburn, 134 (34.81%)

The statistics for Al Kaline and Duke Snider were of Hall of Fame caliber. The two outfielders collectively rapped more than 800 home runs and 5,100 hits: 399 homers and 3,007 hits for Kaline, 407 homers and 2,116 hits for Snider. Their quality scores were in the excellent range: sixty-eight points for Kaline, sixty for Snider.

The only question was why it took so long for Snider to gain admission. Kaline won BBWAA approval on his first attempt in January 1980, five years and three months after his final game for the Detroit Tigers. But Snider endured an agonizing eleven-year climb from 17.0 percent support in 1970 to 86.5 percent in 1980. He remained upbeat the entire time, even after falling just sixteen votes short the previous year, 1979, when only Willie Mays was elected by the writers. "Willie really more or less deserves to be in by himself, the great player he was," Snider said modestly.[172]

Chuck Klein was superior to the typical Veterans Committee selection. The panel inducted forty-seven players between 1953 and 1980. Only six had quality scores higher than Klein's mark of fifty points. But critics called the right fielder a product of his environment, specifically the nine seasons he played for the Phillies in Philadelphia's tiny Baker Bowl. Klein's affinity for the stadium's 280-foot right-field fence was obvious. He won the Triple Crown in 1933 with 28 homers, 120 runs batted in, and a .368 batting average. His splits were 20/81/.467 at home, just 8/40/.280 on the road. "He needs the Baker Bowl as much as the Phillies need him in it," concluded Sam Murphy of the *New York Sun*.[173]

The committee's other choice was truly baffling. Tom Yawkey had owned the Boston Red Sox between 1933 and 1976, presiding over long periods of mediocrity while dragging his heels on integration. The Red Sox waited until 1959 to employ a black player, the last big-league club to do so. There was nothing in Yawkey's record that made him even vaguely worthy of induction.[174]

But Yawkey had one strength, a pleasant disposition. "I never remember anyone ever saying anything bad about him personally," marveled a fellow owner, Walter O'Malley of the Los Angeles Dodgers.[175] Two of Yawkey's former players, Birdie Tebbetts and Joe Cronin, served on the Veterans Committee. (Cronin had also been a manager and general manager of the Red Sox.) The pair pushed their friend through. "He never bothered anybody," Cronin said in defense of Yawkey's selection. "He had a great feel for the players and often would drop in the clubhouse to talk to a player who might be having some problems."[176] It was a very thin reed indeed.

1981

Hall of Fame Summary

New inductees: 3
Category: Player 2, Pioneer/Executive 1
Election: BBWAA 1, Committee 2
Player QS average: 70.0 (BBWAA 74.0, Committee 66.0)
Hall of Famers to date: 176
Category: Player 142, Manager 9, Pioneer/Executive 20, Umpire 5
Election: BBWAA 61, Committee 115
Player QS average: 47.4 (BBWAA 61.3, Committee 37.0)

Inductees

- Rube Foster. **Category:** Pioneer/Executive. **Election:** Veterans Committee.
- Bob Gibson. **Category:** Player. **Position:** P. **QS:** 74 (excellent). **Career:** 1959-1975, G 528, W-L 251-174, SV 6, ERA 2.91. **Election:** BBWAA.
- Johnny Mize. **Category:** Player. **Position:** 1B. **QS:** 66 (excellent). **Career:** 1936-1953, G 1,884, HR 359, RBI 1,337, BA .312. **Election:** Veterans Committee.

BBWAA Election Summary

Voters: 401
Votes needed for induction: 301
Candidates receiving votes: 32
Candidates elected: 1
Candidates inducted in future: 12

BBWAA Top Ten

1. Bob Gibson, 337 (84.04%)*
2. Don Drysdale, 243 (60.60%)
3. Gil Hodges, 241 (60.10%)
4. Harmon Killebrew, 239 (59.60%)
5. Hoyt Wilhelm, 238 (59.35%)
6. Juan Marichal, 233 (58.10%)
7. Nellie Fox, 168 (41.90%)
8. Red Schoendienst, 166 (41.40%)
9. Jim Bunning, 164 (40.90%)
10. Maury Wills, 163 (40.65%)

"OUTSTANDING" IS AN ADJECTIVE often tossed around at the Hall of Fame—not always with justification—but it truly applied in 1981. The hall inducted two players that year, both with excellent quality scores. The average QS for pitcher Bob Gibson (seventy-four) and first baseman Johnny Mize (sixty-six) was precisely seventy points. That made 1981 only the fourth year in the hall's history—and the first since 1951—in which a multiplayer class posted an average score of seventy or better.

The third inductee in 1981 was equally esteemed. Rube Foster was a pitcher, manager, and executive who became known as the "father of Negro baseball" after he founded the Negro National League in 1920, creating the first circuit for black ballplayers that would later be classified a major league itself.[177] White contemporaries had long noted Foster's skill on the field and in the dugout. "He never did the wrong thing. Rube Foster would have been a sensation in the big leagues," said Jewel Ens, who managed the Pittsburgh Pirates from 1929 to 1931.[178]

Foster was the first Negro leaguer to be inducted by the Veterans Committee, which had assumed responsibility for that sphere in 1978.[179] Three of his black colleagues remained outside Cooperstown despite excellent quality scores: center fielder Turkey Stearnes (seventy-nine points), shortstop Willie Wells (seventy-seven), and first baseman Mule Suttles (sixty-five). A fourth player was also stuck in line despite a QS above sixty points. Juan Marichal (sixty-two) had been a star pitcher for the San Francisco Giants and two other clubs in the integrated major leagues.

Gibson and Marichal both retired in 1975, which made 1981 their first year of BBWAA eligibility. The former sailed in with 337 votes, 36 above the 75 percent threshold. The latter languished in sixth place with 233 votes. Gibson held a 12-point edge over Marichal on the QS scale, yet other statistics for the two pitchers were remarkably similar: Gibson with 251 wins and a 2.91 ERA for the St. Louis Cardinals, Marichal at 243 and 2.89.

Reporters asked Gibson if he could explain the wide disparity in their election totals. He shook his head. "No," he finally said. "I don't think I'm one hundred votes better than Juan Marichal."[180]

1982

Hall of Fame Summary

New inductees: 4
Category: Player 3, Pioneer/Executive 1
Election: BBWAA 2, Committee 2
Player QS average: 61.7 (BBWAA 86.0, Committee 13.0)
Hall of Famers to date: 180
Category: Player 145, Manager 9, Pioneer/Executive 21, Umpire 5
Election: BBWAA 63, Committee 117
Player QS average: 47.7 (BBWAA 62.1, Committee 36.7)

Inductees

- Henry Aaron. **Category:** Player. **Position:** RF. **QS:** 87 (excellent). **Career:** 1954-1976, G 3,298, HR 755, RBI 2,297, BA .305. **Election:** BBWAA.
- Happy Chandler. **Category:** Pioneer/Executive. **Election:** Veterans Committee.
- Travis Jackson. **Category:** Player. **Position:** SS. **QS:** 13 (poor). **Career:** 1922-1936, G 1,656, HR 135, RBI 929, BA .291. **Election:** Veterans Committee.
- Frank Robinson. **Category:** Player. **Position:** RF. **QS:** 85 (excellent). **Career:** 1956-1976, G 2,808, HR 586, RBI 1,812, BA .294. **Election:** BBWAA.

BBWAA Election Summary

Voters: 415
Votes needed for induction: 312
Candidates receiving votes: 33
Candidates elected: 2
Candidates inducted in future: 14

BBWAA Top Ten

1. Henry Aaron, 406 (97.83%)*
2. Frank Robinson, 370 (89.16%)*
3. Juan Marichal, 305 (73.49%)
4. Harmon Killebrew, 246 (59.28%)
5. Hoyt Wilhelm, 236 (56.87%)
6. Don Drysdale, 233 (56.14%)
7. Gil Hodges, 205 (49.40%)
8. Luis Aparicio, 174 (41.93%)
9. Jim Bunning, 138 (33.25%)
10. Red Schoendienst, 135 (32.53%)

A CLOUD OF SUSPENSE hovered over the BBWAA election in 1982. Everybody knew that Henry Aaron would be admitted to the Hall of Fame, but it was uncertain if the home-run king would be the first player to be chosen unanimously.

Traditionalists already knew the answer. Unanimity just wasn't their thing. Nine writers somehow left Aaron off their ballots, though his support rate of 97.83 percent still ranked as the second-highest in the hall's first forty-seven years, topped only by Ty Cobb's 98.23 percent in 1936.

Aaron was gracious. "I'd be lying if I said I didn't want to be unanimous, but I realized nobody had ever been a unanimous choice," he said. "I was happy to come in second [to Cobb]."[181]

The writers' other honoree, Frank Robinson, would have been the key attraction at most induction ceremonies. Only sixteen Hall of Famers as of 1982 carried quality scores higher than Robinson's eighty-five points. But one of them happened to be Aaron at eighty-seven. "I was always following him in my career," laughed Robinson, "and now I finally caught up with him."[182]

The two sluggers launched 1,341 homers between them: 755 by Aaron, 586 by Robinson. They were first and fourth, respectively, in the all-time home-run standings as of 1982. Both also ranked among the top ten batters for career hits, runs scored, and runs batted in.

The player picked by the Veterans Committee, shortstop Travis Jackson, couldn't match the firepower or overall skill of 1982's dynamic duo, as indicated by his anemic QS of thirteen points. Jackson's selection was especially curious because twelve shortstops eligible for committee consideration had higher scores, some considerably higher. The foremost were Willie Wells at seventy-seven points, Arky Vaughan at fifty-seven, and George Davis at fifty-one.

It was equally surprising that the panel decided to honor Albert "Happy" Chandler, an amiable governor and senator from Kentucky who had served as commissioner from 1945 to 1951. Chandler's verbosity contrasted with the austerity of his predecessor, Kenesaw Mountain Landis, and it had grated on several of the owners. "He was a completely uninhibited man and naturally developed enemies," observed

Shirley Povich of the *Washington Post.*[183] These foes prevented Chandler from securing a second term in office, earning his lasting enmity. "If I'd known the snakepit I was stepping into," he once said of the commissionership, "I'd have passed."[184]

Chandler had done little to justify his selection, as the Hall of Fame discovered when designing his plaque. There was virtually nothing concrete to cite, so Chandler's description—just thirty-eight words long—was padded with a recitation of his political career and a platitudinous salute to "his broad concern for all phases of the game." Admission to the hall gave the eighty-four-year-old honoree a sense of vindication. "I think justice always triumphs in the long run," Chandler crowed.[185]

1983

Hall of Fame Summary

New inductees: 4
Category: Player 3, Manager 1
Election: BBWAA 2, Committee 2
Player QS average: 40.7 (BBWAA 56.0, Committee 10.0)
Hall of Famers to date: 184
Category: Player 148, Manager 10, Pioneer/Executive 21, Umpire 5
Election: BBWAA 65, Committee 119
Player QS average: 47.6 (BBWAA 61.9, Committee 36.3)

Inductees

- Walter Alston. **Category:** Manager. **Career:** 1954-1976, W-L 2,040-1,613, Pennants 7, Titles 4. **Election:** Veterans Committee.
- George Kell. **Category:** Player. **Position:** 3B. **QS:** 10 (poor). **Career:** 1943-1957, G 1,795, HR 78, RBI 870, BA .306. **Election:** Veterans Committee.
- Juan Marichal. **Category:** Player. **Position:** P. **QS:** 62 (excellent). **Career:** 1960-1975, G 471, W-L 243-142, SV 2, ERA 2.89. **Election:** BBWAA.
- Brooks Robinson. **Category:** Player. **Position:** 3B. **QS:** 50 (good). **Career:** 1955-1977, G 2,896, HR 268, RBI 1,357, BA .267. **Election:** BBWAA.

BBWAA Election Summary

Voters: 374
Votes needed for induction: 281
Candidates receiving votes: 31
Candidates elected: 2
Candidates inducted in future: 13

BBWAA Top Ten

1. Brooks Robinson, 344 (91.98%)*
2. Juan Marichal, 313 (83.69%)*
3. Harmon Killebrew, 269 (71.93%)
4. Luis Aparicio, 252 (67.38%)
5. Hoyt Wilhelm, 243 (64.97%)
6. Don Drysdale, 242 (64.71%)
7. Gil Hodges, 237 (63.37%)
8. Nellie Fox, 173 (46.26%)
9. Billy Williams, 153 (40.91%)
10. Red Schoendienst, 146 (39.04%)

JUAN MARICHAL FINALLY MADE IT to Cooperstown on his third try. He was accompanied by the BBWAA's other inductee in 1983, slick-fielding third baseman Brooks Robinson. The pitcher had the higher quality score—sixty-two points to fifty—but Robinson dominated the election, outpacing the runner-up by thirty-one votes. He reveled in becoming the rare Hall of Famer honored primarily for his proficiency with a glove. "If this is a blow struck for the defense, fine," Robinson said.[186]

It was impossible to quibble with the Veterans Committee's choice of Walter Alston, who had managed the Dodgers to four world titles. But the panel's selection of George Kell was puzzling. Brooks Robinson possessed the best QS among all third basemen eligible for the hall in 1983, a list on which Kell (ten points) ranked a distant seventeenth. The writers had never given Kell more than 37 percent support in his thirteen elections, though the committee was more favorably disposed. Two members were friends from his Detroit days—general manager Charlie Gehringer and catcher Birdie Tebbetts—and they helped to wave him through.[187]

Kell broke into tears when he got the call. "These are the players against whom I played. These are my peers. These are the sportswriters who saw me play," he said of the Veterans Committee. "It's as much an honor, if not more, than if I had gone in another way."[188]

His emotion was understandable, though his opinion was shared by few. Players aspired to be elected by the BBWAA, not by the committee. Timing was a key reason. The writers were given first crack at all candidates, which allowed them to cherry-pick the very best. Degree of difficulty also enhanced the honor of a BBWAA selection. It was obviously a greater accomplishment to attain 75 percent support from four hundred writers scattered across the country than to win fourteen votes from eighteen men jammed around a table.

Five contenders came within fifty votes of induction by the writers in 1983, led by slugger Harmon Killebrew, who fell twelve votes short in his third year of eligibility. Killebrew wondered aloud about the logic of a system that required the same candidates to compete year after year. "I'm not going to hit another home run in my life," he said. "What I've done is either enough or it isn't enough."[189]

His point was reinforced by a look back at 1983's election results from four decades in the future. Eleven candidates received at least one hundred votes from the writers that year, with only Robinson and Marichal topping 75 percent. The other nine would all be admitted to the plaque gallery eventually, though three would be forced to wait more than a decade. Gil Hodges, who finished seventh in 1983, wouldn't make it to Cooperstown until 2022.

1984

Hall of Fame Summary

New inductees: 5
Category: Player 5
Election: BBWAA 3, Committee 2
Player QS average: 36.0 (BBWAA 46.0, Committee 21.0)
Hall of Famers to date: 189
Category: Player 153, Manager 10, Pioneer/Executive 21, Umpire 5
Election: BBWAA 68, Committee 121
Player QS average: 47.2 (BBWAA 61.2, Committee 36.0)

Inductees

- Luis Aparicio. **Category:** Player. **Position:** SS. **QS:** 31 (marginal). **Career:** 1956-1973, G 2,599, HR 83, RBI 791, BA .262. **Election:** BBWAA.
- Don Drysdale. **Category:** Player. **Position:** P. **QS:** 51 (good). **Career:** 1956-1969, G 518, W-L 209-166, SV 6, ERA 2.95. **Election:** BBWAA.
- Rick Ferrell. **Category:** Player. **Position:** C. **QS:** 9 (poor). **Career:** 1929-1947, G 1,884, HR 28, RBI 734, BA .281. **Election:** Veterans Committee.
- Harmon Killebrew. **Category:** Player. **Position:** 1B. **QS:** 56 (good). **Career:** 1954-1975, G 2,435, HR 573, RBI 1,584, BA .256. **Election:** BBWAA.
- Pee Wee Reese. **Category:** Player. **Position:** SS. **QS:** 33 (marginal). **Career:** 1940-1958, G 2,166, HR 126, RBI 885, BA .269. **Election:** Veterans Committee.

BBWAA Election Summary

Voters: 403
Votes needed for induction: 303
Candidates receiving votes: 27
Candidates elected: 3
Candidates inducted in future: 8

BBWAA Top Ten

1. Luis Aparicio, 341 (84.62%)*
2. Harmon Killebrew, 335 (83.13%)*
3. Don Drysdale, 316 (78.41%)*
4. Hoyt Wilhelm, 290 (71.96%)
5. Nellie Fox, 246 (61.04%)
6. Billy Williams, 202 (50.12%)

7. Jim Bunning, 201 (49.88%)
8. Orlando Cepeda, 124 (30.77%)
8. Tony Oliva, 124 (30.77%)
10. Roger Maris, 107 (26.55%)

You could make a stronger Hall of Fame case for Wes Ferrell than for his older brother. Not a great case, mind you, but definitely a better one.

Wes pitched fifteen seasons (1927-1941) for six clubs, primarily the Cleveland Indians. Rick caught for three teams between 1929 and 1947, spending eight years apiece with the St. Louis Browns and Washington Senators. Here's how they stacked up:

• Wes was a workhorse who topped the American League in complete games four times and innings pitched three times. His twenty-five wins in 1935 also led the league. Rick never ranked first in the AL in any offensive category.

• Wes placed eighth in balloting for 1934's Most Valuable Player Award, then finished second to Hank Greenberg in the subsequent MVP contest. The latter trophy rightfully should have been his. Wes piled up 10.6 wins above replacement in 1935. No other AL player exceeded 8.8 WAR, and Greenberg ranked sixth at 7.5. Rick never landed among the top ten vote-getters in any season.

• Wes ranked in the top 20 percent of all American League pitchers between 1931 and 1935, as determined by the five-year test. Rick didn't even make it as high as the top 60 percent of the league's batters in any half-decade.

• The BBWAA wasn't overly impressed with either sibling, though it gave an edge to the younger brother. Wes picked up a grand total of twenty-seven Hall of Fame votes from the writers between 1948 and 1962. Rick received three votes in all—single tallies in 1956, 1958, and 1960.

So what did the Veterans Committee do in 1984? It ignored Wes and elected Rick Ferrell to Cooperstown. Sportswriters were stunned by the announcement. "He had not been rumored as a strong candidate," wrote Jack Lang in the *Sporting News*. "But he is a man who exudes class, and his inclusion in the Cooperstown shrine will be greeted warmly by everyone in baseball."[190]

The controversy over the committee's other selection was even more intense. Rumors had been swirling that a pair of postwar short-stops would be admitted simultaneously in 1984. Pee Wee Reese of the Brooklyn Dodgers received the expected call, but Phil Rizzuto of the New York Yankees was left outside.[191]

Several indicators gave Reese a decided edge over Rizzuto, includ-ing quality score (thirty-three vs. fifteen), All-Star Game appearances (ten vs. five), and peak support in a BBWAA election (47.9 percent vs. 38.4 percent). Yet the New York press showed no interest in facts, pre-ferring to bellow its indignation. The Yankees' bombastic owner, George Steinbrenner, announced that his club would not participate in any of the Hall of Fame's exhibition games until Rizzuto was admitted.[192] The candidate himself confessed to entering a state of "semi-shock" after learning of the committee's decision. "I got all choked up," Rizzuto said. "Then I got bombed, and this morning I woke up, and life goes on."[193]

The BBWAA's choices in 1984—Luis Aparicio, Harmon Killebrew, and Don Drysdale—were safe and popular by comparison. It was the first time since 1972 that the writers agreed on at least three inductees in a single year.

1985

Hall of Fame Summary

New inductees: 4
Category: Player 4
Election: BBWAA 2, Committee 2
Player QS average: 42.0 (BBWAA 41.0, Committee 43.0)
Hall of Famers to date: 193
Category: Player 157, Manager 10, Pioneer/Executive 21, Umpire 5
Election: BBWAA 70, Committee 123
Player QS average: 47.1 (BBWAA 60.6, Committee 36.1)

Inductees

- Lou Brock. **Category:** Player. **Position:** LF. **QS:** 32 (marginal). **Career:** 1961-1979, G 2,616, HR 149, RBI 900, BA .293. **Election:** BBWAA.
- Enos Slaughter. **Category:** Player. **Position:** RF. **QS:** 29 (poor). **Career:** 1938-1959, G 2,380, HR 169, RBI 1,304, BA .300. **Election:** Veterans Committee.
- Arky Vaughan. **Category:** Player. **Position:** SS. **QS:** 57 (good). **Career:** 1932-1948, G 1,817, HR 96, RBI 926, BA .318. **Election:** Veterans Committee.
- Hoyt Wilhelm. **Category:** Player. **Position:** P. **QS:** 50 (good). **Career:** 1952-1972, G 1,070, W-L 143-122, SV 228, ERA 2.52. **Election:** BBWAA.

BBWAA Election Summary

Voters: 395
Votes needed for induction: 297
Candidates receiving votes: 36
Candidates elected: 2
Candidates inducted in future: 9

BBWAA Top Ten

1. Hoyt Wilhelm, 331 (83.80%)*
2. Lou Brock, 315 (79.75%)*
3. Nellie Fox, 295 (74.68%)
4. Billy Williams, 252 (63.80%)
5. Jim Bunning, 214 (54.18%)
6. Catfish Hunter, 212 (53.67%)
7. Roger Maris, 128 (32.41%)
8. Harvey Kuenn, 125 (31.65%)
9. Orlando Cepeda, 114 (28.86%)
9. Tony Oliva, 114 (28.86%)

NELLIE FOX DEBUTED ON THE BBWAA's ballot in 1971. The longtime second baseman for the Chicago White Sox received just 10.8 percent support that year, though it would have been foolish to write him off. "Nellie was the greatest competitor I ever played with," said Billy Pierce, who pitched eighteen seasons in the big leagues.[194] Fox displayed the same persistence as a Hall of Fame candidate, slowly gathering momentum. His biggest gain—predictably and sadly—occurred after his death from lymphatic cancer in December 1975, the month in which the writers cast their 1976 ballots. He jumped 23.9 percentage points.

But it wasn't enough. Fox was still pursuing induction in 1985, the last pane in his window of eligibility. Jack Lang, who was supervising the tabulation process, knew it would be a close call. He eagerly scanned the tally sheet, noted the unsurprising victories by relief pitcher Hoyt Wilhelm and left fielder Lou Brock, and picked up the phone. Lang informed Hall of Fame president Ed Stack that Fox might be the BBWAA's third inductee. His final results could be rounded to 75 percent. Would that be good enough? "Did he get a pure 75 percent?" asked Stack. No, Lang admitted. Fox had fallen two votes short of the magic number at 74.68 percent. "You must have a pure 75 percent," Stack said sternly, and that was that.[195]

Chicago sportswriter Jerome Holtzman filed an appeal, but it did no good. Fox's file was sent over to the Veterans Committee, which would delay his admission for another dozen years.[196] The panel's immediate attention was focused on its two selections for 1985, shortstop Arky Vaughan and right fielder Enos Slaughter. The latter had been outspokenly bitter when he slipped off the writers' ballot in 1979—"after giving nineteen years of my life to baseball, this is a poor reward"—but he now insisted that all was forgiven.[197]

Both of the committee's honorees had played ball in New York—Vaughan for the Dodgers, Slaughter for the Yankees—though the city's reporters displayed little interest. An unbylined account in the *Times* unwittingly revealed the foremost concern of the New York press. The lead paragraph briefly named the panel's choices, then made an abrupt shift. "Phil Rizzuto and twenty-seven other candidates," the story said, "did not make it."[198]

1986

Hall of Fame Summary

New inductees: 3
Category: Player 3
Election: BBWAA 1, Committee 2
Player QS average: 35.7 (BBWAA 59.0, Committee 24.0)
Hall of Famers to date: 196
Category: Player 160, Manager 10, Pioneer/Executive 21, Umpire 5
Election: BBWAA 71, Committee 125
Player QS average: 46.8 (BBWAA 60.6, Committee 35.9)

Inductees

- Bobby Doerr. **Category:** Player. **Position:** 2B. **QS:** 29 (poor). **Career:** 1937-1951, G 1,865, HR 223, RBI 1,247, BA .288. **Election:** Veterans Committee.
- Ernie Lombardi. **Category:** Player. **Position:** C. **QS:** 19 (poor). **Career:** 1931-1947, G 1,853, HR 190, RBI 990, BA .306. **Election:** Veterans Committee.
- Willie McCovey. **Category:** Player. **Position:** 1B. **QS:** 59 (good). **Career:** 1959-1980, G 2,588, HR 521, RBI 1,555, BA .270. **Election:** BBWAA.

BBWAA Election Summary

Voters: 425
Votes needed for induction: 319
Candidates receiving votes: 39
Candidates elected: 1
Candidates inducted in future: 9

BBWAA Top Ten

1. Willie McCovey, 346 (81.41%)*
2. Billy Williams, 315 (74.12%)
3. Catfish Hunter, 289 (68.00%)
4. Jim Bunning, 279 (65.65%)
5. Roger Maris, 177 (41.65%)
6. Tony Oliva, 154 (36.24%)
7. Orlando Cepeda, 152 (35.76%)
8. Harvey Kuenn, 144 (33.88%)
9. Maury Wills, 124 (29.18%)
10. Bill Mazeroski, 100 (23.53%)

TED WILLIAMS DIDN'T WAIT CALMLY for other people to take the lead. The self-proclaimed "greatest hitter who ever lived" once admitted (with considerable understatement) that "I have never been regarded especially as a man with great patience." His autobiography offered several adjectives that perfectly described his outspoken personality. Among them: *emotional, explosive, impetuous,* and *tempestuous.*[199]

Williams brought his take-charge attitude to the Veterans Committee in 1986, where his first self-appointed task was securing Bobby Doerr's admission to the hall. Doerr had joined the Boston Red Sox in 1937—two years prior to Williams—and had been a fixture at second base up to 1951. His quality score of twenty-nine points was uncompelling, but his teammate lobbied strenuously on his behalf. "We never had a captain [in Boston], but Bobby was the silent captain of the team," Williams said emphatically. His fellow committee members acquiesced.[200]

The panel's other choice, catcher Ernie Lombardi, carried an even weaker score (nineteen) despite having won National League batting titles in 1938 and 1942. That made 1986 the fifth year—and, up to now, the final year—in which the committee selected at least two candidates whose average QS was worse than twenty-five points.

No voices were raised against the BBWAA's election of powerful first baseman Willie McCovey, who cleared the threshold with twenty-seven votes to spare. The only real controversies in 1986 were inspired by a pair of Yankees.

Roger Maris died from lymphoma a few days before the writers cast their ballots, triggering the usual postmortem avalanche of votes. Maris climbed to fifth place, his best finish in thirteen years of eligibility. But was he truly worthy of Cooperstown? Several influential columnists demurred. They insisted that Maris's candidacy was powered solely by the sixty-one home runs he had hit in 1961. Rule 6, of course, prohibited any induction driven by an exceptional achievement in a single season.

Then there was the case of a certain diminutive infielder, who was once again bypassed by the Veterans Committee. "Phil Rizzuto, the onetime shortstop for the Yankees, and six other contenders did not make it today," wrote Joseph Durso in the second paragraph of his *New York Times* story.[201] The Scooter's floundering Hall of Fame campaign had become an obsession of his hometown press corps.

1987

Hall of Fame Summary

New inductees: 3
Category: Player 3
Election: BBWAA 2, Committee 1
Player QS average: 29.7 (BBWAA 40.5, Committee 8.0)
Hall of Famers to date: 199
Category: Player 163, Manager 10, Pioneer/Executive 21, Umpire 5
Election: BBWAA 73, Committee 126
Player QS average: 46.5 (BBWAA 60.0, Committee 35.6)

Inductees

- Ray Dandridge. **Category:** Player. **Position:** 3B. **QS:** 8 (poor). **Career:** 1933-1944, G 245, HR 4, RBI 148, BA .321. **Election:** Veterans Committee.
- Catfish Hunter. **Category:** Player. **Position:** P. **QS:** 30 (marginal). **Career:** 1965-1979, G 500, W-L 224-166, SV 1, ERA 3.26. **Election:** BBWAA.
- Billy Williams. **Category:** Player. **Position:** LF. **QS:** 51 (good). **Career:** 1959-1976, G 2,488, HR 426, RBI 1,475, BA .290. **Election:** BBWAA.

BBWAA Election Summary

Voters: 413
Votes needed for induction: 310
Candidates receiving votes: 26
Candidates elected: 2
Candidates inducted in future: 7

BBWAA Top Ten

1. Billy Williams, 354 (85.71%)*
2. Catfish Hunter, 315 (76.27%)*
3. Jim Bunning, 289 (69.98%)
4. Orlando Cepeda, 179 (43.34%)
5. Roger Maris, 176 (42.62%)
6. Tony Oliva, 160 (38.74%)
7. Harvey Kuenn, 144 (34.87%)
8. Bill Mazeroski, 125 (30.27%)
9. Maury Wills, 113 (27.36%)
10. Ken Boyer, 96 (23.24%)
10. Lew Burdette, 96 (23.24%)

CATFISH HUNTER WAS TOUCHINGLY HUMBLE when informed of his election to the Hall of Fame on January 14, 1987. "I don't know if I deserve it," he said. "I was a control pitcher who hit spots. I had players behind me to back me up. If I didn't play on those teams, I wouldn't have won as many as I did, and I wouldn't have been in the World Series six times."[202]

He was absolutely right.

Hunter spent a decade (1965-1974) with the Kansas City and Oakland Athletics, followed by five seasons with the New York Yankees. Each of those franchises made the World Series three times. The A's won all three, the Yankees two.

Hunter was an important cog in those championship machines. He won 224 regular-season games, another 9 in postseason play. But two facts must be acknowledged. Hunter benefited from the support of great lineups, as he admitted, as well as the comfort of pitching in friendly ballparks. The vast Oakland-Alameda County Coliseum remains a nightmare for hitters to this day, while Yankee Stadium statistically favored pitchers in the late 1970s. Hunter, as a result, was 31 percent better at home (2.70 ERA) than on the road (3.92). No other Hall of Fame pitcher enjoyed such a decided home-field advantage throughout his career.

And yet, even under such favorable conditions, Hunter's record wasn't all that great. It's true that he twice led the American League in wins, but he also allowed the most earned runs and the most home runs two years apiece. "You can argue Hunter was a Hall-of-Fame-caliber pitcher for five seasons—and I'd agree—but other than that, he was either average or below average," said BBWAA member Matt Snyder.[203] His conclusion was buttressed by Hunter's quality score of thirty points, right at the very bottom of the marginal range.

The voters were swayed by all of those World Series rings, of course, and by the extensive media exposure that Hunter received in his New York years. Peter Ueberroth jokingly suggested another factor, the bizarre and highly publicized behavior of the tyrants who owned the Athletics and Yankees in those years. "Catfish Hunter had the distinction of playing for both Charlie Finley and George Steinbrenner," said the commissioner, "which is enough in itself to put a player in the Hall of Fame."[204]

If the writers truly wanted to elect the best available pitcher in 1987, they should have focused on Jim Bunning, who had precisely the same number of victories as Hunter (224) and a quality score nearly twice as high (53 points). But Bunning fell twenty-one votes short of induction in his eleventh year on the BBWAA's ballot.

The other honorees in 1987—left fielder Billy Williams of the Cubs and Athletics, third baseman Ray Dandridge of the Negro leagues— didn't stir up the doubts that Hunter did. Both choices were widely applauded. (Dandridge's true value was not reflected in his quality score of eight points, as explained in a previous chapter.)

"As a sixteen-year member of the Chicago Cubs, I had become accustomed to hearing the deriding phrase, 'Wait until next year,'" said Williams, chosen by the writers in his sixth year of eligibility. "But now, all of that is behind me because I'm here in Cooperstown."[205]

1988

Hall of Fame Summary

New inductees: 1
Category: Player 1
Election: BBWAA 1
Player QS average: 59.0 (BBWAA 59.0)
Hall of Famers to date: 200
Category: Player 164, Manager 10, Pioneer/Executive 21, Umpire 5
Election: BBWAA 74, Committee 126
Player QS average: 46.6 (BBWAA 60.0, Committee 35.6)

Inductees

- Willie Stargell. **Category:** Player. **Position:** LF. **QS:** 59 (good). **Career:** 1962-1982, G 2,360, HR 475, RBI 1,540, BA .282. **Election:** BBWAA.

BBWAA Election Summary

Voters: 427
Votes needed for induction: 321
Candidates receiving votes: 30
Candidates elected: 1
Candidates inducted in future: 7

BBWAA Top Ten

1. Willie Stargell, 352 (82.44%)*
2. Jim Bunning, 317 (74.24%)
3. Tony Oliva, 202 (47.31%)
4. Orlando Cepeda, 199 (46.60%)
5. Roger Maris, 184 (43.09%)
6. Harvey Kuenn, 168 (39.34%)
7. Bill Mazeroski, 143 (33.49%)
8. Luis Tiant, 132 (30.91%)
9. Maury Wills, 127 (29.74%)
10. Ken Boyer, 109 (25.53%)
10. Mickey Lolich, 109 (25.53%)

AN INCONCEIVABLE EVENT OCCURRED on March 1, 1988. The Veterans Committee met for four and a half hours in Tampa, argued about dozens of Hall of Fame candidates, and elected absolutely no one. It was the first shutout in the panel's thirty-five-year history.[206]

The deadlock occurred despite—or perhaps because of—a glut of worthy contenders. Three Negro leaguers who carried excellent quality scores were eligible for committee consideration in 1988: Turkey Stearnes (seventy-nine points), Willie Wells (seventy-seven), and Mule Suttles (sixty-five). Another twelve candidates were grouped between fifty and fifty-nine points.

And then there was Phil Rizzuto with his puny QS of fifteen. New Yorkers were again outraged by the panel's unwillingness to induct their favorite shortstop. "Maybe it's time the commissioner stepped in and took a look at that committee," snapped Yankees manager Billy Martin, a onetime teammate of Rizzuto's.[207]

The writers saved the day, guaranteeing that the induction ceremony would feature a star attraction, perhaps two. They elected left fielder Willie Stargell of the Pittsburgh Pirates in his first year of BBWAA eligibility. Jim Bunning also seemed to be destined for the hall. The pitcher was named on 317 of 418 completed forms, apparently putting him over the top with 75.8 percent support.

But nine other writers submitted blank ballots, which were included in the official count. Bunning dropped to 74.2 percent (317 of 427) and remained outside the plaque gallery. The rebels described themselves as purists. Moss Klein of the *Newark Star-Ledger* called his empty ballot "a vote for exercising higher standards for the game's most prestigious honor," and Bill Madden of the *New York Daily News* sniffed that his nonvote was "a statement of my Hall of Fame philosophy."[208]

Seven of the nine blanks, interestingly enough, were submitted by writers from New York. All of them suggested that they were trying to save the hall from itself. "I think we have slowly eroded the standards of the men we put in, and I don't want to further contribute to that erosion," declared Phil Pepe, one of Madden's colleagues at the *Daily News*.[209]

Columnists from the very same New York market, of course, were fervently leading the Hall of Fame campaign for Phil Rizzuto.

1989

Hall of Fame Summary

New inductees: 4
Category: Player 3, Umpire 1
Election: BBWAA 2, Committee 2
Player QS average: 49.3 (BBWAA 65.0, Committee 18.0)
Hall of Famers to date: 204
Category: Player 167, Manager 10, Pioneer/Executive 21, Umpire 6
Election: BBWAA 76, Committee 128
Player QS average: 46.6 (BBWAA 60.2, Committee 35.4)

Inductees

- Al Barlick. **Category:** Umpire. **Election:** Veterans Committee.
- Johnny Bench. **Category:** Player. **Position:** C. **QS:** 60 (excellent). **Career:** 1967-1983, G 2,158, HR 389, RBI 1,376, BA .267. **Election:** BBWAA.
- Red Schoendienst. **Category:** Player. **Position:** 2B. **QS:** 18 (poor). **Career:** 1945-1963, G 2,216, HR 84, RBI 773, BA .289. **Election:** Veterans Committee.
- Carl Yastrzemski. **Category:** Player. **Position:** LF. **QS:** 70 (excellent). **Career:** 1961-1983, G 3,308, HR 452, RBI 1,844, BA .285. **Election:** BBWAA.

BBWAA Election Summary

Voters: 447
Votes needed for induction: 336
Candidates receiving votes: 30
Candidates elected: 2
Candidates inducted in future: 10

BBWAA Top Ten

1. Johnny Bench, 431 (96.42%)*
2. Carl Yastrzemski, 423 (94.63%)*
3. Gaylord Perry, 304 (68.01%)
4. Jim Bunning, 283 (63.31%)
5. Fergie Jenkins, 234 (52.35%)
6. Orlando Cepeda, 176 (39.37%)
7. Tony Oliva, 135 (30.20%)
8. Bill Mazeroski, 134 (29.98%)
9. Harvey Kuenn, 115 (25.73%)
10. Maury Wills, 95 (21.25%)

THE ELECTION OF 1989 was a no-brainer for the writers, even for Moss Klein. "There shouldn't be any blank Hall of Fame ballots this year," the BBWAA's king of abstention conceded.[210]

Boston Red Sox left fielder Carl Yastrzemski and Cincinnati Reds catcher Johnny Bench had retired after the 1983 season, so their eligibility windows opened simultaneously in 1989. Both ranked among baseball's 25 greatest sluggers through 1988: Yastrzemski 18th with 452 home runs, Bench 25th with 389. Both had been fixtures in the All-Star Game, making thirty-two appearances between them. Both possessed excellent quality scores: Yastrzemski seventy points, Bench sixty.

Few writers dissented from their selections. Just 16 of the 447 voters declined to list Bench, and only 24 skipped Yastrzemski. Klein voted for both, ending his three-year run of blank ballots. It marked the first time since the BBWAA's inaugural election in 1936 that at least two candidates received more than 90 percent support.[211]

Most observers had assumed that Jim Bunning would be joining Bench and Yastrzemski in the Hall of Fame, finally making it after falling just four votes shy a year earlier. But a substantial number of writers inexplicably jumped off of Bunning's bandwagon. He dropped from 74.2 percent in 1988 to 63.3 percent in 1989, fifty-three votes short of the threshold with only two years of eligibility remaining. "I am compelled to ask how a candidate can be less qualified now than he was in the previous balloting," said Carl Lundquist, a BBWAA member who continued to support Bunning's induction.[212]

The Veterans Committee argued for nearly six hours before agreeing to admit Al Barlick, an umpire, and Red Schoendienst, a second baseman with a quality score of eighteen points.[213] Most fans responded with a collective yawn, though a few were outraged. *Sporting News* reader Barry Considine of Troy, New York, dashed off a letter to the paper's editor, pronouncing himself "appalled" by the choice of Schoendienst. "As for the other selection," Considine wrote. "An umpire? Come on!"[214]

1990

Hall of Fame Summary

New inductees: 2
Category: Player 2
Election: BBWAA 2
Player QS average: 60.5 (BBWAA 60.5)
Hall of Famers to date: 206
Category: Player 169, Manager 10, Pioneer/Executive 21, Umpire 6
Election: BBWAA 78, Committee 128
Player QS average: 46.8 (BBWAA 60.2, Committee 35.4)

Inductees

- Joe Morgan. **Category:** Player. **Position:** 2B. **QS:** 64 (excellent). **Career:** 1963-1984, G 2,649, HR 268, RBI 1,133, BA .271. **Election:** BBWAA.
- Jim Palmer. **Category:** Player. **Position:** P. **QS:** 57 (good). **Career:** 1965-1984, G 558, W-L 268-152, SV 4, ERA 2.86. **Election:** BBWAA.

BBWAA Election Summary

Voters: 444
Votes needed for induction: 333
Candidates receiving votes: 34
Candidates elected: 2
Candidates inducted in future: 10

BBWAA Top Ten

1. Jim Palmer, 411 (92.57%)*
2. Joe Morgan, 363 (81.76%)*
3. Gaylord Perry, 320 (72.07%)
4. Fergie Jenkins, 296 (66.67%)
5. Jim Bunning, 257 (57.88%)
6. Orlando Cepeda, 211 (47.52%)
7. Tony Oliva, 142 (31.98%)
8. Bill Mazeroski, 131 (29.50%)
9. Harvey Kuenn, 107 (24.10%)
10. Ron Santo, 96 (21.62%)

THE BBWAA GAVE A collective thumbs-down to most candidates appearing on the Hall of Fame ballot for the first time, even if they possessed impressive credentials. Every single newcomer between 1937 and 1961, regardless of quality, was forced to wait at least another year for induction. Bob Feller and Jackie Robinson finally broke the barrier in 1962, yet one-shot triumphs remained rare. Only fifteen initial-ballot victories were recorded in the twenty-four elections from 1964 through 1988.

Moss Klein—yes, again—was among the self-appointed guardians who barred induction to all but a handful of fresh candidates. "The honor of gaining admission in that first year is a special privilege, and should be granted only to the truly overwhelming," Klein insisted.[215] He failed to explain the importance of such a distinction. Every plaque in the hall, after all, was the same size and shape, no matter if an honoree was elected by the writers in his initial year of eligibility or by the Veterans Committee after four decades of retirement.

Many BBWAA members had begun to question the logic behind the informal ban on new contenders, as indicated by the results of recent elections. Two first-timers had been inducted in 1989—Johnny Bench and Carl Yastrzemski—and two more were poised for victory in 1990. Even Klein caught the spirit. "Voting for Jim Palmer and Joe Morgan on the Hall of Fame ballot was easy," he admitted.[216] Never before had a pair of new candidates been elected to the hall in consecutive years.

The 1990 inductees possessed strong quality scores—second baseman Morgan at sixty-four points, pitcher Palmer at fifty-seven—yet they found it difficult to picture themselves among the game's immortals. "Mays, Musial, and Morgan in the same breath. I'm not sure I'll ever get used to that," said Morgan. Palmer posed a question: "Am I as good as a lot of pitchers here?" He paused to consider. "Probably not," he went on. "But I would have voted for myself."[217]

The Veterans Committee ultimately was unable to identify anybody worthy of its support in 1990. It began with a list of twenty-five candidates, reduced it to eleven, cut it again to five, and ended in a stalemate. The panel finally gave up after five hours, announcing its second shutout in three years. "We were not going to stay until we were able to elect somebody," said Hall of Fame president Ed Stack. "I have no apologies."[218]

1991

Hall of Fame Summary

New inductees: 5
Category: Player 4, Pioneer/Executive 1
Election: BBWAA 3, Committee 2
Player QS average: 51.0 (BBWAA 62.7, Committee 16.0)
Hall of Famers to date: 211
Category: Player 173, Manager 10, Pioneer/Executive 22, Umpire 6
Election: BBWAA 81, Committee 130
Player QS average: 46.9 (BBWAA 60.3, Committee 35.2)

Inductees

- Rod Carew. **Category:** Player. **Position:** 2B. **QS:** 59 (good). **Career:** 1967-1985, G 2,469, HR 92, RBI 1,015, BA .328. **Election:** BBWAA.
- Fergie Jenkins. **Category:** Player. **Position:** P. **QS:** 68 (excellent). **Career:** 1965-1983, G 664, W-L 284-226, SV 7, ERA 3.34. **Election:** BBWAA.
- Tony Lazzeri. **Category:** Player. **Position:** 2B. **QS:** 16 (poor). **Career:** 1926-1939, G 1,740, HR 178, RBI 1,194, BA .292. **Election:** Veterans Committee.
- Gaylord Perry. **Category:** Player. **Position:** P. **QS:** 61 (excellent). **Career:** 1962-1983, G 777, W-L 314-265, SV 10, ERA 3.11. **Election:** BBWAA.
- Bill Veeck. **Category:** Pioneer/Executive. **Election:** Veterans Committee.

BBWAA Election Summary

Voters: 443
Votes needed for induction: 333
Candidates receiving votes: 34
Candidates elected: 3
Candidates inducted in future: 9

BBWAA Top Ten

1. Rod Carew, 401 (90.52%)*
2. Gaylord Perry, 342 (77.20%)*
3. Fergie Jenkins, 334 (75.40%)*
4. Rollie Fingers, 291 (65.69%)
5. Jim Bunning, 282 (63.66%)
6. Orlando Cepeda, 192 (43.34%)
7. Tony Oliva, 160 (36.12%)
8. Bill Mazeroski, 142 (32.05%)
9. Ron Santo, 116 (26.19%)
10. Harvey Kuenn, 100 (22.57%)

A SENSE OF IMPENDING DOOM enveloped the Hall of Fame's board of directors at the start of 1991. Baseball's all-time hit leader, Pete Rose, had played his final game in 1986, which meant he was on track to join the BBWAA's ballot in January 1992, just twelve months in the future. Most of the board members considered it a chilling prospect.

The problem, of course, was that Rose had been slapped with a life-time suspension in 1989 for repeatedly betting on baseball games. How would it look if such a miscreant gained admission to Cooperstown's hallowed gallery? The board moved swiftly to prevent such an unhappy occurrence, voting on February 4, 1991, to bar the induction of any per-manently suspended player. "I was fearful that [Rose] could have been elected by a combination of those who thought he should go in and those who reacted by saying, 'They can't tell me what to do,'" said a board member, *St. Louis Post-Dispatch* columnist Bob Broeg.[219]

The ban was announced less than four weeks after the BBWAA's election of three players with impressive quality scores. The newcom-ers were Rose's contemporaries, so reporters naturally asked them to weigh in. Their answers did not please the baseball establishment. Second baseman Rod Carew (fifty-nine points): "Pete is baseball. You hate to see it taken away from him." Pitcher Gaylord Perry (sixty-one): "If Pete's inducted, I'm going to be the first one to go up and shake his hand." Pitcher Fergie Jenkins (sixty-eight): "I feel adamantly he belongs in the hall."[220]

The Veterans Committee enhanced 1991's festivities with two post-humous selections—one as excellent as it was unexpected, the other as unwarranted as it was predictable.

It had always been difficult to imagine Bill Veeck in the plaque gallery, despite his status as the game's most dynamic owner between the mid-1940s and the early 1960s. American League officials and club executives had disliked almost everything about Veeck—his boister-ous promotions, his outspoken criticism of the status quo, his refusal to wear ties to league meetings. "My fellow club owners haven't exactly lavished their affection on me," he once admitted.[221]

Yet it was impossible to ignore Veeck's ability to win championships and attract capacity crowds. Even the *Sporting News*, notorious for its conservative editorials, had once hailed him as a role model for competing owners. "Let the other magnates tear a page out of the Veeck book," the paper recommended in 1948, "and send already impressive big-league box-office figures soaring to empyrean heights."[222] Such admiration finally triumphed over long-held grudges in 1991's committee room. "Somewhere, I know Bill is happy—and astounded," said his widow.[223]

The choice of Tony Lazzeri was almost impossible to defend. The second baseman, who carried a weak quality score of sixteen points, never led the majors in any single-season category except most strikeouts by a batter. Yet Lazzeri had held down the sixth spot in the batting order for the immortal 1927 Yankees, and that seemed to be good enough for the committee. He was destined to be the Hall of Fame's final inductee from the white major leagues of the 1920s, a group heavily overrepresented in Cooperstown.

1992

Hall of Fame Summary

New inductees: 4
Category: Player 3, Umpire 1
Election: BBWAA 2, Committee 2
Player QS average: 65.3 (BBWAA 71.0, Committee 54.0)
Hall of Famers to date: 215
Category: Player 176, Manager 10, Pioneer/Executive 22, Umpire 7
Election: BBWAA 83, Committee 132
Player QS average: 47.2 (BBWAA 60.5, Committee 35.4)

Inductees

- Rollie Fingers. **Category:** Player. **Position:** P. **QS:** 59 (good). **Career:** 1968-1985, G 944, W-L 114-118, SV 341, ERA 2.90. **Election:** BBWAA.
- Bill McGowan. **Category:** Umpire. **Election:** Veterans Committee.
- Hal Newhouser. **Category:** Player. **Position:** P. **QS:** 54 (good). **Career:** 1939-1955, G 488, W-L 207-150, SV 26, ERA 3.06. **Election:** Veterans Committee.
- Tom Seaver. **Category:** Player. **Position:** P. **QS:** 83 (excellent). **Career:** 1967-1986, G 656, W-L 311-205, SV 1, ERA 2.86. **Election:** BBWAA.

BBWAA Election Summary

Voters: 430
Votes needed for induction: 323
Candidates receiving votes: 31
Candidates elected: 2
Candidates inducted in future: 8

BBWAA Top Ten

1. Tom Seaver, 425 (98.84%)*
2. Rollie Fingers, 349 (81.16%)*
3. Orlando Cepeda, 246 (57.21%)
4. Tony Perez, 215 (50.00%)
5. Bill Mazeroski, 182 (42.33%)
6. Tony Oliva, 175 (40.70%)
7. Ron Santo, 136 (31.63%)
8. Jim Kaat, 114 (26.51%)
9. Maury Wills, 110 (25.58%)
10. Ken Boyer, 71 (16.51%)

TOM SEAVER WAS A LOCK for the Hall of Fame in 1992, though the ubiquitous Moss Klein warned against excessive expectations. "He won't be a unanimous choice, because no one ever is," wrote Klein, "but there's no logical reason not to vote for him."[224]

Five members of the BBWAA's electorate defied this conventional wisdom, though the other 425 backed Seaver, the winner of 311 games as a pitcher for the New York Mets, Cincinnati Reds, and 2 other clubs. His resulting support level was 98.84 percent, breaking Ty Cobb's fifty-six-year-old record of 98.23 percent. Seaver was succinct when reporters asked for his reaction. "Total disbelief," he said.[225]

Seaver (eighty-three) was the first new Hall of Famer with a quality score of eighty points or better since the joint entrance of Henry Aaron and Frank Robinson ten years earlier, and he was just the eighth inductee since 1952 to hail from the eighty-plus club. Nobody else on 1992's ballot came close to Seaver's QS, though the candidate with the second-highest score, relief pitcher Rollie Fingers (fifty-nine points), also received the writers' stamp of approval.

Pete Rose would have been a strong contender, too, if not for the unfortunate matter of his gambling suspension. His quality score of 56 points not only exceeded the ratings for all BBWAA candidates except Seaver and Fingers, but it also outstripped the scores for more than 60 percent of the players who had already been enshrined (109 of 176). His 4,256 hits, as everybody knew, were the most by any batter in big-league history.

Baltimore Sun columnist Mike Littwin was so incensed by Rose's ban that he resigned from the BBWAA's pool of eligible voters. Forty-one writers registered protests by casting write-in votes for Rose. Bob Hunter of the *Los Angeles Daily News* wrote the hit king's name three times. "That was my way to emphasize that Rose should be on there," he said.

It didn't matter. "Pete Rose's name can be written in from now until the end of time," said Hall of Fame president Ed Stack. "But it's pointless unless the rules of the game are changed."[226]

The Veterans Committee added a third highly rated pitcher, Hal Newhouser (54 points), to the class of 1992, yielding an average quality score of 65.3 points. It was the first time since 1937—fifty-five years earlier—that a group of at least three players entered the hall with a joint QS of sixty-five or better.

1993

Hall of Fame Summary

New inductees: 1
Category: Player 1
Election: BBWAA 1
Player QS average: 65.0 (BBWAA 65.0)
Hall of Famers to date: 216
Category: Player 177, Manager 10, Pioneer/Executive 22, Umpire 7
Election: BBWAA 84, Committee 132
Player QS average: 47.3 (BBWAA 60.6, Committee 35.4)

Inductees

- Reggie Jackson. **Category:** Player. **Position:** RF. **QS:** 65 (excellent). **Career:** 1967-1987, G 2,820, HR 563, RBI 1,702, BA .262. **Election:** BBWAA.

BBWAA Election Summary

Voters: 423
Votes needed for induction: 318
Candidates receiving votes: 28
Candidates elected: 1
Candidates inducted in future: 8

BBWAA Top Ten

1. Reggie Jackson, 396 (93.62%)*
2. Phil Niekro, 278 (65.72%)
3. Orlando Cepeda, 252 (59.57%)
4. Tony Perez, 233 (55.08%)
5. Steve Garvey, 176 (41.61%)
6. Tony Oliva, 157 (37.12%)
7. Ron Santo, 155 (36.64%)
8. Jim Kaat, 125 (29.55%)
9. Dick Allen, 70 (16.55%)
10. Ken Boyer, 69 (16.31%)

NOBODY EVER ACCUSED REGGIE JACKSON of modesty.

Jackson first came to public attention as a hard-hitting, fast-talking right fielder for the Oakland Athletics, winners of three world titles from 1972 to 1974. But his fame—and his ego—shifted into overdrive when he entered free agency in late 1976. "If I played in New York," Jackson mused, "they'd name a candy bar after me." He signed with the

Yankees, and sure enough, the Reggie Bar soon appeared on supermarket shelves. It took only three months for Jackson to declare himself the greatest star on a New York club that was destined to win consecutive World Series in 1977 and 1978. "I'm the straw that stirs the drink," he famously insisted.[227]

Jackson wrapped up his 21-year career in 1987 with 563 home runs, the 6th-highest total at the time. He was elected to the Hall of Fame in 1993 with 93.6 percent support, a level topped by only nine previous inductees. Jack Lang of the BBWAA phoned Jackson's California home to pass along the glad tidings. The formal press conference was slated the next day in New York, so Lang urged Jackson to rush to the airport.

The reaction from the other end of the line was unexpected. No ego-fueled exultation, just a quiet tone of worry. "I don't have a bag packed," said Jackson. "I don't have any clothes."

Lang gently chided him. "You knew you were going to get in," he said.

The newest Hall of Famer was almost meek in response. "Well," he said, "I was hoping."[228]

Jackson regained his sense of majesty by the August 1 induction ceremony, thanks in part to the Veterans Committee's inability to do its job. Seventeen of the old-timers being considered by the panel had quality scores of 48 points or better, surpassing the average QS (47.3 points) for all 177 players who had already been inducted. How many of these promising candidates were selected? Not a single one.

Ed Stack, the hall's president, skillfully put a positive spin on the committee's inadequacies, noting that Jackson would be taking the stage all alone. "He will have his day in the stars, so to speak, to perform on the platform by himself," Stack said. "I'm sure he'll enjoy that very much."[229]

1994

Hall of Fame Summary

New inductees: 3
Category: Player 2, Manager 1
Election: BBWAA 1, Committee 2
Player QS average: 41.0 (BBWAA 67.0, Committee 15.0)
Hall of Famers to date: 219
Category: Player 179, Manager 11, Pioneer/Executive 22, Umpire 7
Election: BBWAA 85, Committee 134
Player QS average: 47.3 (BBWAA 60.6, Committee 35.1)

Inductees

- Steve Carlton. **Category:** Player. **Position:** P. **QS:** 67 (excellent). **Career:** 1965-1988, G 741, W-L 329-244, SV 2, ERA 3.22. **Election:** BBWAA.
- Leo Durocher. **Category:** Manager. **Career:** 1939-1973, W-L 2,008-1,709, Pennants 3, Titles 1. **Election:** Veterans Committee.
- Phil Rizzuto. **Category:** Player. **Position:** SS. **QS:** 15 (poor). **Career:** 1941-1956, G 1,661, HR 38, RBI 563, BA .273. **Election:** Veterans Committee.

BBWAA Election Summary

Voters: 456
Votes needed for induction: 342
Candidates receiving votes: 34
Candidates elected: 1
Candidates inducted in future: 11

BBWAA Top Ten

1. Steve Carlton, 436 (95.61%)*
2. Orlando Cepeda, 335 (73.46%)
3. Phil Niekro, 273 (59.87%)
4. Tony Perez, 263 (57.68%)
5. Don Sutton, 259 (56.80%)
6. Steve Garvey, 166 (36.40%)
7. Tony Oliva, 158 (34.65%)
8. Ron Santo, 150 (32.89%)
9. Bruce Sutter, 109 (23.90%)
10. Jim Kaat, 98 (21.49%)

THE HALL OF FAME ISSUED a brief and seemingly trivial announcement on July 31, 1993, welcoming three newcomers to the eighteen-man

Veterans Committee. Yogi Berra, Pee Wee Reese, and Bill White would assume their duties the following February, replacing three members who had died in recent months.

Insiders understood the significance of the appointments. All three men were good friends of Phil Rizzuto. Berra had been his teammate on the Yankees for eleven years, Reese had competed against him in six World Series, and White had shared a broadcast booth with him for eighteen seasons. A headline in the *New York Times* reached the logical conclusion: "Veterans Committee Additions Aid Rizzuto."[230] A roundup in the *Sporting News* was more succinct. "Scooter's a mortal lock," it declared.[231]

And so it came to pass. The Veterans Committee duly voted on February 25, 1994, to admit Rizzuto to the Hall of Fame, thirty-eight years after his final game. Berra was given the honor of making the phone call. "Well, we got you in," he told his old pal.[232] Rizzuto became the eighteenth shortstop enshrined in the plaque gallery. His 17 predecessors carried an average quality score of 34.1 points. He had a QS of fifteen.

Two more inductees made it to the hall in 1994. Both were notorious for their stormy relationships with the press.

The committee's other choice was the late Leo Durocher, who managed four National League clubs over twenty-two seasons, winning his lone world title with the New York Giants in 1954. He was frequently vituperative and abusive in his dealings with reporters. "With Durocher, it was totally adversarial," recalled Roger Kahn, who covered his clubs for the *New York Herald Tribune*.[233] The BBWAA's only honoree, pitcher Steve Carlton, notched 329 victories for 6 clubs, primarily the Philadelphia Phillies and St. Louis Cardinals. The taciturn Carlton steadfastly ignored the questions posed by reporters, no matter their level of persistence.

The writers had punished several ornery candidates for refusing to bow to the power of the press. One of the greatest players in history, Rogers Hornsby, was spurned by 22 percent of the voters in 1942, nearly preventing his election. A career .341 hitter, Bill Terry, was kept out of the hall until 1954, eighteen years after his retirement. The immortal

Ted Williams was left off of twenty ballots in 1966.

So it was noteworthy that 95.6 percent of the writers voted for Carlton in his first year of eligibility. It was equally surprising when the new honoree agreed to participate in a press conference. He joked with reporters about his upcoming remarks at the induction ceremony: "Maybe I'll give one of those Sally Field speeches, like the one she gave at the Oscars a few years ago. Oh, you like me! You like me!" A Hall of Fame official eventually stepped in, noting that the session had run thirty minutes. Carlton waved him off and called for additional questions. "I don't mind," he said. "It's been a long time."[234]

1995

Hall of Fame Summary

New inductees: 5
Category: Player 4, Pioneer/Executive 1
Election: BBWAA 1, Committee 4
Player QS average: 46.0 (BBWAA 91.0, Committee 31.0)
Hall of Famers to date: 224
Category: Player 183, Manager 11, Pioneer/Executive 23, Umpire 7
Election: BBWAA 86, Committee 138
Player QS average: 47.2 (BBWAA 61.0, Committee 35.0)

Inductees

- Richie Ashburn. **Category:** Player. **Position:** CF. **QS:** 31 (marginal). **Career:** 1948-1962, G 2,189, HR 29, RBI 586, BA .308. **Election:** Veterans Committee.
- Leon Day. **Category:** Player. **Position:** P. **QS:** 21 (poor). **Career:** 1934-1946, G 90, W-L 48-21, SV 3, ERA 3.50. **Election:** Veterans Committee.
- William Hulbert. **Category:** Pioneer/Executive. **Election:** Veterans Committee.
- Mike Schmidt. **Category:** Player. **Position:** 3B. **QS:** 91 (excellent). **Career:** 1972-1989, G 2,404, HR 548, RBI 1,595, BA .267. **Election:** BBWAA.
- Vic Willis. **Category:** Player. **Position:** P. **QS:** 41 (marginal). **Career:** 1898-1910, G 513, W-L 249-205, SV 11, ERA 2.63. **Election:** Veterans Committee.

BBWAA Election Summary

Voters: 460
Votes needed for induction: 345
Candidates receiving votes: 35
Candidates elected: 1
Candidates inducted in future: 10

BBWAA Top Ten

1. Mike Schmidt, 444 (96.52%)*
2. Phil Niekro, 286 (62.17%)
3. Don Sutton, 264 (57.39%)
4. Tony Perez, 259 (56.30%)
5. Steve Garvey, 196 (42.61%)
6. Tony Oliva, 149 (32.39%)

7. Ron Santo, 139 (30.22%)
8. Jim Rice, 137 (29.78%)
8. Bruce Sutter, 137 (29.78%)
10. Jim Kaat, 100 (21.74%)

MORE THAN FIFTEEN THOUSAND players competed at the major-league level between 1871 and 1989. Only nine of them—fewer than one-tenth of 1 percent—were so exceptional that their quality scores soared to ninety points or higher.

Eight of these superstars were comfortably ensconced in the Hall of Fame by 1979, when Willie Mays became the latest to join. The ninth was Mike Schmidt (ninety-one points), who played third base for the Philadelphia Phillies between 1972 and 1989. Schmidt topped the National League in home runs eight times, won ten Gold Gloves, and earned three Most Valuable Player Awards. He was "the best third baseman ever, baseball's best player for the last twenty years," in the opinion of *Sporting News* columnist Dave Kindred.[235]

Schmidt scored a landslide victory in 1995, his first year of Hall of Fame eligibility, drawing votes from 96.5 percent of the BBWAA's members. Only three inductees—Tom Seaver, Ty Cobb, and Henry Aaron—had received greater support in the previous fifty-nine years.

Sixteen voters snubbed Schmidt. Some undoubtedly acted to prevent a unanimous election, but Bill Brown of the *Delaware County Times* offered a different reason for ignoring a player he had covered for several years. "I found him to be particularly insensitive to others, especially to children and even to younger teammates who looked up to him as a hero," said Brown.[236] Schmidt attributed any personal deficiencies to an intense focus on the game itself. "I sometimes have probably taken things too seriously in my life," he said, "but that's my nature."[237]

The Hall of Fame's relationship with the Veterans Committee could best be described as cyclical. The hall would keep a tight leash on the panel for several years, loosen its grip for awhile, then pull the tether taut again. A period of relative freedom began in 1995, with the committee receiving permission to name more than two inductees. It chose four. The most famous was another Phillies star, Richie Ashburn, who was as sunny as Schmidt was grim. The *Philadelphia Inquirer's* Jayson

Stark suggested that Ashburn might be the city's most popular resident ever. "If he isn't," Stark wrote, "he's locked in a very tight race with Ben Franklin, Frankie Avalon, and Pat Olivieri, the guy who runs Pat's Steaks."[238]

1996

Hall of Fame Summary

New inductees: 4
Category: Player 2, Manager 2
Election: Committee 4
Player QS average: 52.5 (Committee 52.5)
Hall of Famers to date: 228
Category: Player 185, Manager 13, Pioneer/Executive 23, Umpire 7
Election: BBWAA 86, Committee 142
Player QS average: 47.3 (BBWAA 61.0, Committee 35.4)

Inductees

- Jim Bunning. **Category:** Player. **Position:** P. **QS:** 53 (good). **Career:** 1955-1971, G 591, W-L 224-184, SV 16, ERA 3.27. **Election:** Veterans Committee.
- Bill Foster. **Category:** Player. **Position:** P. **QS:** 52 (good). **Career:** 1923-1937, G 238, W-L 110-56, SV 12, ERA 2.63. **Election:** Veterans Committee.
- Ned Hanlon. **Category:** Manager. **Career:** 1889-1907, W-L 1,313-1,164, Pennants 5, Titles 0. **Election:** Veterans Committee.
- Earl Weaver. **Category:** Manager. **Career:** 1968-1986, W-L 1,480-1,060, Pennants 4, Titles 1. **Election:** Veterans Committee.

BBWAA Election Summary

Voters: 470
Votes needed for induction: 353
Candidates receiving votes: 31
Candidates elected: 0
Candidates inducted in future: 10

BBWAA Top Ten

1. Phil Niekro, 321 (68.30%)
2. Tony Perez, 309 (65.74%)
3. Don Sutton, 300 (63.83%)
4. Steve Garvey, 175 (37.23%)
5. Ron Santo, 174 (37.02%)
6. Tony Oliva, 170 (36.17%)
7. Jim Rice, 166 (35.32%)
8. Bruce Sutter, 137 (29.15%)
9. Tommy John, 102 (21.70%)
10. Jim Kaat, 91 (19.36%)

THE CIRCUMSTANCES IN 1996 may have been unusual, but the rhetoric was familiar.

The BBWAA pitched its first shutout in a quarter-century. No contender came within thirty votes of the 75 percent threshold. The writers had been prolific since their previous goose egg in 1971—picking forty-one Hall of Famers in twenty-four elections—but they found the current crop of candidates unexciting. Clichés from the empty elections of the 1950s and 1960s were dusted off. "The absence of an electee this year emphasizes the exclusivity of membership in the Baseball Hall of Fame," said Donald Marr, the hall's president.

Eight of 1996's top ten vote-getters would eventually be enshrined, though five would wait in line for another decade or longer. (Steve Garvey and Tommy John would never be admitted.) The stalemate was especially frustrating for the three contenders who drew more than 60 percent support in 1996: pitchers Phil Niekro and Don Sutton and first baseman Tony Perez. The latter tried his best to be philosophical. "What can you do," asked Perez, "other than wait until they're ready?"[239]

Jim Bunning knew all about waiting. The right-hander retired in 1971 after pitching seventeen seasons for the Detroit Tigers, Philadelphia Phillies, and two other clubs. The BBWAA debated his Hall of Fame credentials for fifteen years, always giving him at least 33.3 percent support. Bunning climbed as high as 74.2 percent by 1988—just four votes short of the prize—with three years of eligibility remaining. Everybody agreed that he was a cinch to be elected, yet he somehow lost momentum and was eliminated from the ballot in 1991.

The Veterans Committee finally rescued him in 1996. The panel also selected a pitcher from the Negro leagues (Bill Foster) and a pair of managers with Baltimore roots (Ned Hanlon and Earl Weaver). But it was the tart-tongued Bunning, now a congressman from Kentucky, who dominated the induction ceremony on August 4, 1996.

His was not the usual acceptance speech. Bunning barked a series of reprimands and admonitions. He castigated owners and players for their incessant labor disputes: "Get your house in order." He chided owners for leaving the commissioner's post vacant ever since they had forced Fay Vincent's resignation in 1992: "Find a rudder before Congress gives up on you and intervenes." And he saved a few harsh words for the group that had kept him outside the hall for so many years, noting that the BBWAA refused to elect Sutton (324 victories) and Niekro (318), who both ranked among the 14 winningest pitchers to that point. Bunning's exasperation was evident. "Do you baseball writers know how hard it is to win three hundred games?" he asked.[240]

1997

Hall of Fame Summary

New inductees: 4
Category: Player 3, Manager 1
Election: BBWAA 1, Committee 3
Player QS average: 53.0 (BBWAA 53.0, Committee 53.0)
Hall of Famers to date: 232
Category: Player 188, Manager 14, Pioneer/Executive 23, Umpire 7
Election: BBWAA 87, Committee 145
Player QS average: 47.4 (BBWAA 60.9, Committee 35.7)

Inductees

- Nellie Fox. **Category:** Player. **Position:** 2B. **QS:** 29 (poor). **Career:** 1947-1965, G 2,367, HR 35, RBI 790, BA .288. **Election:** Veterans Committee.
- Tommy Lasorda. **Category:** Manager. **Career:** 1976-1996, W-L 1,599-1,439, Pennants 4, Titles 2. **Election:** Veterans Committee.
- Phil Niekro. **Category:** Player. **Position:** P. **QS:** 53 (good). **Career:** 1964-1987, G 864, W-L 318-274, SV 29, ERA 3.35. **Election:** BBWAA.
- Willie Wells. **Category:** Player. **Position:** SS. **QS:** 77 (excellent). **Career:** 1924-1948, G 1,038, HR 140, RBI 879, BA .331. **Election:** Veterans Committee.

BBWAA Election Summary

Voters: 473
Votes needed for induction: 355
Candidates receiving votes: 30
Candidates elected: 1
Candidates inducted in future: 8

BBWAA Top Ten

1. Phil Niekro, 380 (80.34%)*
2. Don Sutton, 346 (73.15%)
3. Tony Perez, 312 (65.96%)
4. Ron Santo, 186 (39.32%)
5. Jim Rice, 178 (37.63%)
6. Steve Garvey, 167 (35.31%)
7. Bruce Sutter, 130 (27.48%)
8. Jim Kaat, 107 (22.62%)
9. Joe Torre, 105 (22.20%)
10. Tommy John, 97 (20.51%)

NELLIE FOX'S JOURNEY TO Cooperstown was lengthy and indirect. The second baseman set off on the BBWAA highway in 1971, though he loitered in the slow lane for thirteen years. His candidacy didn't shift into high gear until 1984, his penultimate year of eligibility. The writers boosted his support level by 14.8 percentage points to 61.0 percent, then up another 13.7 points to 74.7 percent in 1985. Yet he remained two votes short.

So Fox was shunted to the bypass operated by the Veterans Committee, where he immediately ran into heavy traffic. The panel inducted twelve players between 1986 and 1996, including a trio of second basemen: Bobby Doerr, Red Schoendienst, and Tony Lazzeri. None of the three exceeded Fox's quality score of twenty-nine points, yet all were admitted while he remained outside.

Fox's manager on the White Sox, Al Lopez, sat on the committee, which theoretically should have helped his cause. But vague rumors began to circulate that Lopez was blocking his former star's election for unspecified reasons. "He was a good man for me," Lopez said publicly, though unidentified panel members confirmed that the manager never voted for Fox in their closed-door meetings.[241]

Lopez's sixteen-year term ended in 1994, finally removing that impediment, but the Veterans Committee waited until 1997 to admit Fox to the hall. The news excited his widow in Pennsylvania—"we've waited so long, but this makes the wait worthwhile"—and also thrilled a self-appointed lobbying group, the Nellie Fox Society, whose members cheered wildly in the Chicago restaurant where they received the news.[242] The Veterans Committee also inducted shortstop Willie Wells, a Negro leaguer whose selection was long overdue, and manager Tommy Lasorda.

Phil Niekro was the only player elected by the BBWAA in 1997. He crossed the 75 percent threshold with twenty-five votes to spare, while runner-up Don Sutton missed by nine votes. Niekro admitted to being confused by the outcome, given that he narrowly trailed Sutton in several key categories, including wins (318 for Niekro vs. 324 for Sutton), earned-run average (3.35 vs. 3.26), strikeouts (3,342 vs. 3,574) and quality score (53 vs. 63).

The logical move, of course, would have been to induct both men the same year, but that wasn't the Hall of Fame's way. "I was very disappointed for him," Niekro said of Sutton. "I mean, here's a man who's got more wins than I do. I feel for the guy, I really do."[243]

1998

Hall of Fame Summary

New inductees: 5
Category: Player 4, Pioneer/Executive 1
Election: BBWAA 1, Committee 4
Player QS average: 55.0 (BBWAA 63.0, Committee 52.3)
Hall of Famers to date: 237
Category: Player 192, Manager 14, Pioneer/Executive 24, Umpire 7
Election: BBWAA 88, Committee 149
Player QS average: 47.5 (BBWAA 60.9, Committee 36.2)

Inductees

- George Davis. **Category:** Player. **Position:** SS. **QS:** 51 (good). **Career:** 1890-1909, G 2,372, HR 73, RBI 1,440, BA .295. **Election:** Veterans Committee.
- Larry Doby. **Category:** Player. **Position:** CF. **QS:** 50 (good). **Career:** 1942-1959, G 1,670, HR 273, RBI 1,094, BA .287. **Election:** Veterans Committee.
- Lee MacPhail. **Category:** Pioneer/Executive. **Election:** Veterans Committee.
- Bullet Rogan. **Category:** Player. **Position:** P. **QS:** 56 (good). **Career:** 1920-1938, G 214, W-L 120-52, SV 16, ERA 2.65. **Election:** Veterans Committee.
- Don Sutton. **Category:** Player. **Position:** P. **QS:** 63 (excellent). **Career:** 1966-1988, G 774, W-L 324-256, SV 5, ERA 3.26. **Election:** BBWAA.

BBWAA Election Summary

Voters: 473
Votes needed for induction: 355
Candidates receiving votes: 26
Candidates elected: 1
Candidates inducted in future: 8

BBWAA Top Ten

1. Don Sutton, 386 (81.61%)*
2. Tony Perez, 321 (67.86%)
3. Ron Santo, 204 (43.13%)
4. Jim Rice, 203 (42.92%)
5. Gary Carter, 200 (42.28%)
6. Steve Garvey, 195 (41.23%)

7. Bruce Sutter, 147 (31.08%)
8. Tommy John, 129 (27.27%)
8. Jim Kaat, 129 (27.27%)
10. Dave Parker, 116 (24.52%)

DON SUTTON'S 324-256 RECORD didn't change a whit between 1997 and 1998, yet the passage of time somehow enhanced its cachet. A total of 346 BBWAA members had voted for Sutton the previous year—just short of the required 355—but 40 converts scrambled onto his bandwagon once a new set of ballots was sent out. He was the only inductee approved by the writers in 1998.

Sutton had debuted with the Los Angeles Dodgers thirty-two years earlier, pitching in the same rotation as Hall of Famers Sandy Koufax and Don Drysdale. He was never able to match their blazing speed or larger-than-life reputations. "Nothing about Sutton, from his 6-1, 190-pound build to his fastball, which rarely broke 90 miles per hour, was too impressive," recalled Thomas Boswell, one of the great baseball writers of the late twentieth century.[244]

Sutton was all too aware of his reputation. "I always felt like I was never perceived that I was as good as those guys, and I thought realistically that the skills I possessed were not as good as those guys," he said. "That led me to believe that I had to work harder, because I always wanted my end result to be in the same neighborhood."[245] He battled his way to 324 victories, the 12th-highest total for any pitcher as of 1998. Yet a sense of inadequacy seemed to linger. The Dodgers retired Sutton's uniform number that year, and he expressed astonishment when Koufax attended the ceremony. "How could I not? You're the only 300-game winner I ever played with," replied Koufax, who had 165 victories to his credit.[246]

The Veterans Committee enjoyed an unusually strong year in 1998, inducting three players whose quality scores were only a few points shy of the excellent range. All three should have been welcomed to Cooperstown much earlier. Shortstop George Davis was elected in his sixty-third year of eligibility, the longest wait endured by an inductee whose QS was fifty points or better. Center fielder Larry Doby, the first black player in the American League, and Bullet Rogan, one of the top pitchers in the Negro leagues, had been eligible for thirty-four and twenty-eight years, respectively.

The committee's fourth selection, Lee MacPhail, had served as president of the American League and in front-office roles with the Baltimore Orioles and New York Yankees. He was the first son of a Hall of Famer to join his father in the plaque gallery. Larry MacPhail, inducted in 1978, had been a bombastic and creative executive. His son was mild-mannered and patient. "Unfortunately, a person with Dad's talent comes along only once every fifty years," said the younger MacPhail. "I've never thought of imitating him."[247]

1999

Hall of Fame Summary

New inductees: 7
Category: Player 5, Manager 1, Umpire 1
Election: BBWAA 3, Committee 4
Player QS average: 50.8 (BBWAA 63.7, Committee 31.5)
Hall of Famers to date: 244
Category: Player 197, Manager 15, Pioneer/Executive 24, Umpire 8
Election: BBWAA 91, Committee 153
Player QS average: 47.6 (BBWAA 61.0, Committee 36.1)

Inductees

- George Brett. **Category:** Player. **Position:** 3B. **QS:** 69 (excellent). **Career:** 1973-1993, G 2,707, HR 317, RBI 1,596, BA .305. **Election:** BBWAA.
- Orlando Cepeda. **Category:** Player. **Position:** 1B. **QS:** 46 (good). **Career:** 1958-1974, G 2,124, HR 379, RBI 1,365, BA .297. **Election:** Veterans Committee.
- Nestor Chylak. **Category:** Umpire. **Election:** Veterans Committee.
- Nolan Ryan. **Category:** Player. **Position:** P. **QS:** 70 (excellent). **Career:** 1966-1993, G 807, W-L 324-292, SV 3, ERA 3.19. **Election:** BBWAA.
- Frank Selee. **Category:** Manager. **Career:** 1890-1905, W-L 1,284-862, Pennants 5, Titles 0. **Election:** Veterans Committee.
- Joe Williams. **Category:** Player. **Position:** P. **QS:** 17 (poor). **Career:** 1923-1932, G 53, W-L 16-19, SV 2, ERA 3.51. **Election:** Veterans Committee.
- Robin Yount. **Category:** Player. **Position:** SS. **QS:** 52 (good). **Career:** 1974-1993, G 2,856, HR 251, RBI 1,406, BA .285. **Election:** BBWAA.

BBWAA Election Summary

Voters: 497
Votes needed for induction: 373
Candidates receiving votes: 24
Candidates elected: 3
Candidates inducted in future: 8

BBWAA Top Ten

1. Nolan Ryan, 491 (98.79%)*
2. George Brett, 488 (98.19%)*
3. Robin Yount, 385 (77.46%)*
4. Carlton Fisk, 330 (66.40%)
5. Tony Perez, 302 (60.76%)

6. Gary Carter, 168 (33.80%)
7. Steve Garvey, 150 (30.18%)
8. Jim Rice, 146 (29.38%)
9. Bruce Sutter, 121 (24.35%)
10. Jim Kaat, 100 (20.12%)

THE BBWAA HIT THE TRIFECTA in 1999, inducting three popular and highly respected players. The quality scores for pitcher Nolan Ryan (seventy points) and third baseman George Brett (sixty-nine) fit comfortably in the excellent range. Shortstop Robin Yount (fifty-two) wasn't far behind. Their average of 63.7 points was the third-highest QS for three or more players chosen by the writers in a single election during the twentieth century, trailing only the initial two classes of 1936 (92.2) and 1937 (87.0).

Ryan, Brett, and Yount had all retired in 1993, making 1999 their first year of eligibility. The last time the writers tapped three newcomers at the same time was the inaugural election of 1936, inspiring Murray Chass of the *New York Times* to hail "a first-ballot bonanza unseen in more than sixty years."[248] Ryan received votes from 491 of the 497 writers. His support level of 98.79 percent fell just short of the record for the hall's first sixty-four years, Tom Seaver's 98.84 percent in 1992. Brett's 98.19 percent ranked fourth on the same list, an outcome that stunned him. "It just knocked me on the floor," he said.[249]

The Veterans Committee added four honorees at its meeting on March 2, boosting the Hall of Fame's incoming class to seven members, the largest since 1972. The public showed little interest in three of the panel's selections, a nineteenth-century manager (Frank Selee), an umpire (Nestor Chylak), and a Negro leagues pitcher whose meager statistics failed to reflect his skills (Joe Williams). All were deceased.

The committee's fourth inductee, first baseman Orlando Cepeda, not only remained among the living, but was well remembered by fans over the age of forty. Cepeda had blasted 264 homers between 1961 and 1970—topping all but 5 National League batters in that decade—and had been unanimously elected the league's Most Valuable Player in 1967. But his image was tarnished by a ten-month prison sentence for smuggling marijuana in 1975, which undoubtedly dissuaded the writers from voting him into the hall. He peaked at 73.5 percent—just seven votes below the threshold—in 1994, his fifteenth and final year on the BBWAA's ballot.[250]

Cepeda was bitter when the writers spurned him. "To hell with the Hall of Fame. I could care less," he snapped.[251] But he pronounced himself a changed man in 1999. "I wasn't ready to get in before," Cepeda said when the hall finally came calling. "I still had work to do in healing myself."[252]

Fans flocked to Cooperstown for the induction ceremony on July 25, 1999, paying homage to four great stars from the previous four decades, four players who evoked fond memories of younger days. It was impossible to know the exact number of people who jammed into the tiny village on Otsego Lake—the hall's spokesman guessed more than fifty thousand—but everybody agreed that the crowd was the biggest the Hall of Fame had ever seen. "When I first drove up in the bus and got a look at the number of people, I was a bit intimidated," said Yount, who was scheduled to give the first acceptance speech. "I went directly to the bathroom."[253]

2000

Hall of Fame Summary

New inductees: 5
Category: Player 4, Manager 1
Election: BBWAA 2, Committee 3
Player QS average: 46.5 (BBWAA 39.0, Committee 54.0)
Hall of Famers to date: 249
Category: Player 201, Manager 16, Pioneer/Executive 24, Umpire 8
Election: BBWAA 93, Committee 156
Player QS average: 47.6 (BBWAA 60.5, Committee 36.4)

Inductees

- Sparky Anderson. **Category:** Manager. **Career:** 1970-1995, W-L 2,194-1,834, Pennants 5, Titles 3. **Election:** Veterans Committee.
- Carlton Fisk. **Category:** Player. **Position:** C. **QS:** 45 (good). **Career:** 1969-1993, G 2,499, HR 376, RBI 1,330, BA .269. **Election:** BBWAA.
- Bid McPhee. **Category:** Player. **Position:** 2B. **QS:** 29 (poor). **Career:** 1882-1899, G 2,138, HR 53, RBI 1,072, BA .272. **Election:** Veterans Committee.
- Tony Perez. **Category:** Player. **Position:** 1B. **QS:** 33 (marginal). **Career:** 1964-1986, G 2,777, HR 379, RBI 1,652, BA .279. **Election:** BBWAA.
- Turkey Stearnes. **Category:** Player. **Position:** CF. **QS:** 79 (excellent). **Career:** 1923-1940, G 984, HR 186, RBI 997, BA .349. **Election:** Veterans Committee.

BBWAA Election Summary

Voters: 499
Votes needed for induction: 375
Candidates receiving votes: 29
Candidates elected: 2
Candidates inducted in future: 7

BBWAA Top Ten

1. Carlton Fisk, 397 (79.56%)*
2. Tony Perez, 385 (77.15%)*
3. Jim Rice, 257 (51.50%)
4. Gary Carter, 248 (49.70%)
5. Bruce Sutter, 192 (38.48%)
6. Rich Gossage, 166 (33.27%)

7. Steve Garvey, 160 (32.06%)
8. Tommy John, 135 (27.05%)
9. Jim Kaat, 125 (25.05%)
10. Dale Murphy, 116 (23.25%)

FOUR PLAYERS WERE WELCOMED to the Hall of Fame in 2000. Two could be labeled obscure. Bid McPhee was a second baseman for the Cincinnati Reds who had retired a century earlier—101 years earlier, to be exact—with a fairly low quality score of 29 points. He was joined by a little-known Negro leaguer whose QS (seventy-nine) would be the highest for any inductee between 1996 and 2013. "Turkey Stearnes was one of the greatest hitters we ever had," said Satchel Paige. "He was as good as Josh [Gibson]. He was as good as anybody [who] ever played ball."[254]

It was never easy to fathom the inner workings of the Veterans Committee, though it was especially difficult in 2000. What made the panel resurrect McPhee fifty-seven years after his death? Why did it choose him over another nineteenth-century second baseman, Ross Barnes, whose QS (fifty-three) was nearly twice as high? And why had the committee forced Stearnes to wait so long? It was true that few present-day fans knew his name, but his statistics had warranted his induction as far back as the 1970s, when Negro leaguers first became eligible.

The BBWAA's choices couldn't match Stearnes's quality score, but catcher Carlton Fisk (forty-five points) and first baseman Tony Perez (thirty-three) had fame in their favor. The respective stars for the Boston Red Sox and the Reds had participated in one of the greatest (and most heavily watched) World Series of all time, the 1975 battle won by Cincinnati in a pressure-packed seventh game. Fisk made it to the hall in his second year on the ballot, Perez in his ninth. The latter had drawn more than 60 percent support in the previous four elections, only to fall short. "It's sweet now, when I'm in," said Perez. "It doesn't matter how long I had to wait."[255]

Perez's longtime manager, Sparky Anderson, was named the fifth and final member of the class of 2000. Most men who made baseball their career visited Cooperstown at some point in their lives, but

Anderson had deliberately stayed away. "I didn't want to go into the most precious place in baseball unless I belonged there," he explained. "If I got elected, I'll go in and spend hours looking at everything. Then I'll know I'm in a place that's a dream house."[256]

2001

Hall of Fame Summary

New inductees: 4
Category: Player 4
Election: BBWAA 2, Committee 2
Player QS average: 35.0 (BBWAA 40.0, Committee 30.0)
Hall of Famers to date: 253
Category: Player 205, Manager 16, Pioneer/Executive 24, Umpire 8
Election: BBWAA 95, Committee 158
Player QS average: 47.3 (BBWAA 60.1, Committee 36.3)

Inductees

- Bill Mazeroski. **Category:** Player. **Position:** 2B. **QS:** 11 (poor). **Career:** 1956-1972, G 2,163, HR 138, RBI 853, BA .260. **Election:** Veterans Committee.
- Kirby Puckett. **Category:** Player. **Position:** CF. **QS:** 31 (marginal). **Career:** 1984-1995, G 1,783, HR 207, RBI 1,085, BA .318. **Election:** BBWAA.
- Hilton Smith. **Category:** Player. **Position:** P. **QS:** 49 (good). **Career:** 1932-1948, G 148, W-L 66-35, SV 9, ERA 2.86. **Election:** Veterans Committee.
- Dave Winfield. **Category:** Player. **Position:** RF. **QS:** 49 (good). **Career:** 1973-1995, G 2,973, HR 465, RBI 1,833, BA .283. **Election:** BBWAA.

BBWAA Election Summary

Voters: 515
Votes needed for induction: 387
Candidates receiving votes: 30
Candidates elected: 2
Candidates inducted in future: 7

BBWAA Top Ten

1. Dave Winfield, 435 (84.47%)*
2. Kirby Puckett, 423 (82.14%)*
3. Gary Carter, 334 (64.85%)
4. Jim Rice, 298 (57.86%)
5. Bruce Sutter, 245 (47.57%)
6. Rich Gossage, 228 (44.27%)
7. Steve Garvey, 176 (34.17%)
8. Tommy John, 146 (28.35%)
9. Don Mattingly, 145 (28.16%)
10. Jim Kaat, 135 (26.21%)

A PAIR OF CONTROVERSIES—one current, one delayed—shadowed the Hall of Fame's class of 2001.

The immediate bone of contention was the induction of Bill Mazeroski by the Veterans Committee. The second baseman's quality score (eleven points) was the worst for any American or National League honoree since Rick Ferrell in 1984, and his career batting average of .260 was the fourth-lowest for any position player in the plaque gallery. The BBWAA had already deemed Mazeroski's credentials to be unconvincing. Fewer than a quarter of the writers had voted for him in any of his first nine elections, and only 42.3 percent had supported him on his fifteenth and final try in 1992.

Everybody agreed that Mazeroski was wondrous in the field—wide-ranging, sure-handed, quick on the double play—but those skills never swayed a majority of the BBWAA's members. "What he has to sell is lots and lots of defense, and the Hall of Fame isn't buying," wrote Bill James in 1995.[257] What kept Mazeroski's campaign alive, ironically enough, was one stroke of his bat, an iconic (and uncharacteristic) home run that clinched the 1960 World Series for the Pittsburgh Pirates. The glory of that moment was captured in a classic photograph—Mazeroski rounding third base with his right arm high in triumph—and that was how most fans (and most writers) remembered him four decades later.[258]

But another factor would give Mazeroski's candidacy a greater boost. The Veterans Committee was chaired by Joe Brown, the very general manager who had assembled Pittsburgh's 1960 championship roster. Brown had always been a convincing negotiator in trade talks, and he proved to be equally persuasive in the committee room. One of the panel's members, Ted Williams, was reportedly angered by Mazeroski's selection. But open-heart surgery forced Williams to miss the meeting, so he was unable to counter Brown's advocacy.[259]

The year's other controversial selection did not seem undesirable at the time. The BBWAA elected a pair of newcomers to the ballot: right fielder Dave Winfield, who starred for the San Diego Padres, New York Yankees, and four other clubs over twenty-two seasons, and center fielder Kirby Puckett, who spent his entire twelve-year career with the Minnesota Twins. Winfield's statistics were solid: 465 homers, 3,110 hits, and a quality score of 49 points. But Puckett's QS of thirty-one was the lowest for any first-ballot inductee between 1936 and 2001. The average score for the span's other thirty-five first-timers (seventy-one points) was 129 percent higher.

Puckett seemed to fit the profile of a multiyear candidate, such as Luis Aparicio and Lou Boudreau, whose quality scores of thirty-one were identical to his. It took six years for Aparicio to amass the necessary votes, ten elections for Boudreau. But Puckett gained immediate admission because of the malady that had brought his career to a sad and sudden end—irreversible retina damage—and because the voters were cheered by his philanthropic efforts and upbeat disposition. "It may be cloudy in my right eye," he said at the induction ceremony. "But the sun is shining in my left eye."[260]

Voters soon had reason to question their haste. Puckett's wife filed for divorce in 2002, accusing him of threatening to kill her. She alleged that he had choked her with an electric cord and held a pistol to her head. It was revealed that Puckett had a longtime mistress, who eventually sought a protective order against him. He was arrested after a third woman charged him with groping her in a restaurant. Puckett was acquitted in the subsequent trial, but the confluence of events had destroyed his image. "All they really know now in Minnesota is that he was one whale of a baseball player," wrote George Dohrmann in *Sports Illustrated*. "They'll never be so sure of anyone else again."[261]

2002

Hall of Fame Summary

New inductees: 1
Category: Player 1
Election: BBWAA 1
Player QS average: 40.0 (BBWAA 40.0)
Hall of Famers to date: 254
Category: Player 206, Manager 16, Pioneer/Executive 24, Umpire 8
Election: BBWAA 96, Committee 158
Player QS average: 47.3 (BBWAA 59.9, Committee 36.3)

Inductees

- Ozzie Smith. **Category:** Player. **Position:** SS. **QS:** 40 (marginal). **Career:** 1978-1996, G 2,573, HR 28, RBI 793, BA .262. **Election:** BBWAA.

BBWAA Election Summary

Voters: 472
Votes needed for induction: 354
Candidates receiving votes: 24
Candidates elected: 1
Candidates inducted in future: 9

BBWAA Top Ten

1. Ozzie Smith, 433 (91.74%)*
2. Gary Carter, 343 (72.67%)
3. Jim Rice, 260 (55.08%)
4. Bruce Sutter, 238 (50.42%)
5. Andre Dawson, 214 (45.34%)
6. Rich Gossage, 203 (43.01%)
7. Steve Garvey, 134 (28.39%)
8. Tommy John, 127 (26.91%)
9. Bert Blyleven, 124 (26.27%)
10. Jim Kaat, 109 (23.09%)

BILL MAZEROSKI'S ELECTION IN March 2001 triggered a pair of aftershocks in the ten months that followed. The first was the Hall of Fame's decision in August 2001 to restructure the Veterans Committee.

The panel had been making strange choices ever since its creation forty-eight years earlier. A pair of umpires in 1953? Ray Schalk in 1955? Max Carey, Heinie Manush, and Lloyd Waner in the 1960s? Frankie

Frisch's flood of Giants and Cardinals in the 1970s? Travis Jackson, George Kell, Tony Lazzeri, and Phil Rizzuto in subsequent years? All of these picks had stirred up doubts and questions—and justifiably so.

Yet Mazeroski's induction somehow aroused more criticism than any previous selection. Critics accused the panel's chairman, Joe Brown, of exerting excessive pressure on behalf of his former player. "Obviously, Joe spoke very vigorously for him," admitted Leonard Koppett, a sportswriter who sat on the committee.[262] But Brown's advocacy was in no way unusual. Cronyism had been a trait of the Veterans Committee from the very start.

What seemed to matter more, certainly to Ted Williams and other critics, was Mazeroski's relative weakness as a hitter. He simply didn't fit the stereotype of a Hall of Famer. Some critics made this point in mild terms, including statistical guru Bill James: "I don't see Bill Mazeroski as a Hall of Famer; obviously some voters did."[263] Others were caustic. *New York Post* columnist Joel Sherman fired this broadside the day after Mazeroski was chosen: "The Hall of Fame Veterans Committee was created to rectify mistakes. Which means its next act should be self-abolishment."[264]

The hall apparently agreed. It announced in August a sixfold expansion of the committee, which would henceforth consist of all living Hall of Famers, as well as all sportswriters and announcers who had won the Spink and Frick Awards, a pool of ninety voters in all. This enlarged panel would vote by mail—no more meetings in tiny rooms—and only in odd-numbered years.[265] "We didn't do this because we're unhappy with the people the Veterans Committee selected," insisted Joe Morgan, the star second baseman who had become the hall's vice chairman. Nobody was fooled.[266]

The second aftershock rumbled five months later in January, when shortstop Ozzie Smith became the only player elected by the BBWAA—and hence the only member of the hall's class of 2002.

Smith was very much in Mazeroski's mold, a player honored primarily for his glovework. His nickname, "the Wizard of Oz," referred to his lightning-fast reflexes and acrobatic abilities, not any skills he might have displayed at the plate. Smith's career batting average (.262) was the fifth-lowest for any position player inducted to that point, just two points better than Mazeroski's. But his 44.2 defensive wins above replacement were the most in big-league history.

Smith was elected easily—crossing the threshold with seventy-nine votes to spare—and he wondered if the furor over Mazeroski's selection might have inspired the writers to think more deeply about fielding, easing his own journey to Cooperstown. "Bill and myself," Smith said, "are the guys leading the way to remind people how important that aspect of the game always has been and always will be."[267]

2003

Hall of Fame Summary

New inductees: 2
Category: Player 2
Election: BBWAA 2
Player QS average: 47.0 (BBWAA 47.0)
Hall of Famers to date: 256
Category: Player 208, Manager 16, Pioneer/Executive 24, Umpire 8
Election: BBWAA 98, Committee 158
Player QS average: 47.3 (BBWAA 59.6, Committee 36.3)

Inductees

- Gary Carter. **Category:** Player. **Position:** C. **QS:** 45 (good). **Career:** 1974-1992, G 2,296, HR 324, RBI 1,225, BA .262. **Election:** BBWAA.
- Eddie Murray. **Category:** Player. **Position:** 1B. **QS:** 49 (good). **Career:** 1977-1997, G 3,026, HR 504, RBI 1,917, BA .287. **Election:** BBWAA.

BBWAA Election Summary

Voters: 496
Votes needed for induction: 372
Candidates receiving votes: 29
Candidates elected: 2
Candidates inducted in future: 10

BBWAA Top Ten

1. Eddie Murray, 423 (85.28%)*
2. Gary Carter, 387 (78.02%)*
3. Bruce Sutter, 266 (53.63%)
4. Jim Rice, 259 (52.22%)
5. Andre Dawson, 248 (50.00%)
6. Ryne Sandberg, 244 (49.19%)
7. Lee Smith, 210 (42.34%)
8. Rich Gossage, 209 (42.14%)
9. Bert Blyleven, 145 (29.23%)
10. Steve Garvey, 138 (27.82%)

GARY CARTER SEEMED A SAFE BET to join the Hall of Fame in 2002. Support for the catcher had grown by 15.9 percentage points in 2000, his third year on the BBWAA's ballot, and then by another 15.2 points in 2001. Those consecutive gains pushed him up to 64.9 percent. Another increase of similar size would secure his place in the plaque gallery.

Carter's wife was so certain of success that she planned a surprise party for January 8, 2002, the day the results of the writers' election were announced. The big surprise, unfortunately, was that her husband fell eleven votes short of induction. She cried, and he did, too. Carter struggled to understand. "Was I too accommodating?" he asked. "Was I too nice? Was it because I played in Montreal for eleven years? I don't know."[268]

No party was planned in 2003, and the news was much happier. Carter was elected to Cooperstown on his sixth try. "It wasn't the easiest thing to deal with," he said, "but now it seems like these five years went by in a day."[269] He was joined by Eddie Murray, a slugging first base-man who starred for the Baltimore Orioles. Murray was a first-ballot inductee.

Carter posed a dilemma for the Hall of Fame, one it had rarely encountered. He had played the bulk of his career with the Montreal Expos (1,503 of his 2,296 games), yet had attained his greatest fame with the Mets, notably with New York's world-championship squad in 1986. He told the hall's president, Dale Petroskey, that he wanted the portrait on his plaque to show him wearing a Mets cap.

Carter offered a couple of reasons. He appealed to emotion—"my heart is always going to be in New York"—and he expressed concern about the future of the Expos, who were struggling financially. (The franchise would move to Washington two years later.) "If the Expos are no longer in existence," he said, "how is that going to be beneficial to me and my family when we have an opportunity to be part of a family that will be around a long time?"

Reporters and fans assumed that each inductee had the final say on his portrait, but Petroskey denied that such a privilege had ever existed. He ruled that Carter would be depicted with an Expos cap. "Our responsibility is to history and to baseball history, and we looked at it from every angle," he said. "In the end, there was only one answer. It became clear to us he made his major impact to baseball history in Montreal."[270]

The expanded—and supposedly improved—Veterans Committee debuted in 2003. Eighty-five Hall of Famers, sportswriters, and announcers were asked to make selections from two lists—the first consisting of twenty-six players, the second comprising fifteen managers, umpires, and executives. No candidate came close to the necessary 75 percent. Joe Morgan, the hall's vice chairman, praised his fellow voters for their stringent approach. "I think a lot of [them] did look at it that way," he said. "Did this guy deserve to be in Cooperstown with the other immortals? That's the way to judge them."[271]

It was just like old times.

2004

Hall of Fame Summary

New inductees: 2
Category: Player 2
Election: BBWAA 2
Player QS average: 54.0 (BBWAA 54.0)
Hall of Famers to date: 258
Category: Player 210, Manager 16, Pioneer/Executive 24, Umpire 8
Election: BBWAA 100, Committee 158
Player QS average: 47.4 (BBWAA 59.5, Committee 36.3)

Inductees

- Dennis Eckersley. **Category:** Player. **Position:** P. **QS:** 61 (excellent). **Career:** 1975-1998, G 1,071, W-L 197-171, SV 390, ERA 3.50. **Election:** BBWAA.
- Paul Molitor. **Category:** Player. **Position:** 3B. **QS:** 47 (good). **Career:** 1978-1998, G 2,683, HR 234, RBI 1,307, BA .306. **Election:** BBWAA.

BBWAA Election Summary

Voters: 506
Votes needed for induction: 380
Candidates receiving votes: 30
Candidates elected: 2
Candidates inducted in future: 9

BBWAA Top Ten

1. Paul Molitor, 431 (85.18%)*
2. Dennis Eckersley, 421 (83.20%)*
3. Ryne Sandberg, 309 (61.07%)
4. Bruce Sutter, 301 (59.49%)
5. Jim Rice, 276 (54.55%)
6. Andre Dawson, 253 (50.00%)
7. Rich Gossage, 206 (40.71%)
8. Lee Smith, 185 (36.56%)
9. Bert Blyleven, 179 (35.38%)
10. Jack Morris, 133 (26.28%)

THE TWO MEMBERS OF Cooperstown's class of 2004 possessed different skills—one was a dominant pitcher, the other an imposing hitter—yet they shared the gift of versatility.

Dennis Eckersley was a starting pitcher for twelve years and a closer in the dozen that followed. He reached twin peaks in his career—winning twenty games as a starter for the Boston Red Sox in 1978, then earning two of baseball's highest honors (the Most Valuable Player and Cy Young Awards) as a reliever for the Oakland Athletics in 1992. The Hall of Fame classified Paul Molitor as a third baseman, though he played every position but pitcher and catcher during his twenty-one seasons as a big leaguer, fifteen with the Milwaukee Brewers. He led the American League three years apiece in hits and runs scored.

The hall's two newest members had something else in common, an unhappy understanding of the dangers of substance abuse. Eckersley had entered an alcohol-rehabilitation center after the 1986 season. "I hate to talk about it, but guess what? That's part of my story. It's who I am," he said. Cocaine was Molitor's drug of choice early in his big-league career. "It was something that could have easily cut short my career if I didn't get a grip on it quickly," he admitted. The struggles of both men had been heavily publicized in the 1980s.[272]

Pete Rose watched the 2004 election with more than passing interest. He accused the Hall of Fame of a double standard. "If I had been an alcoholic or a drug addict," he said, "baseball would have suspended me for six weeks and paid for my rehabilitation." His eligibility for the hall would not have been affected. But a gambling disorder, classified by the American Psychiatric Association as another form of addiction, was somehow different. "The distinction between drugs, booze, and gambling told me that baseball was interested in punishment—not treatment," Rose said bitterly.[273]

Eckersley reacted impatiently to Rose's diatribe. The pitcher pointed to one key difference. He and Molitor had worked to overcome their problems while still in the major leagues. Rose had not. "Why didn't he get help?" said Eckersley. "There's help for that stuff, isn't there?"[274]

2005

Hall of Fame Summary

New inductees: 2
Category: Player 2
Election: BBWAA 2
Player QS average: 55.0 (BBWAA 55.0)
Hall of Famers to date: 260
Category: Player 212, Manager 16, Pioneer/Executive 24, Umpire 8
Election: BBWAA 102, Committee 158
Player QS average: 47.4 (BBWAA 59.4, Committee 36.3)

Inductees

- Wade Boggs. **Category:** Player. **Position:** 3B. **QS:** 62 (excellent).
  Career: 1982-1999, G 2,439, HR 118, RBI 1,014, BA .328. **Election:** BBWAA.
- Ryne Sandberg. **Category:** Player. **Position:** 2B. **QS:** 48 (good).
  Career: 1981-1997, G 2,164, HR 282, RBI 1,061, BA .285. **Election:** BBWAA.

BBWAA Election Summary

Voters: 516
Votes needed for induction: 387
Candidates receiving votes: 25
Candidates elected: 2
Candidates inducted in future: 8

BBWAA Top Ten

1. Wade Boggs, 474 (91.86%)*
2. Ryne Sandberg, 393 (76.16%)*
3. Bruce Sutter, 344 (66.67%)
4. Jim Rice, 307 (59.50%)
5. Rich Gossage, 285 (55.23%)
6. Andre Dawson, 270 (52.33%)
7. Bert Blyleven, 211 (40.89%)
8. Lee Smith, 200 (38.76%)
9. Jack Morris, 172 (33.33%)
10. Tommy John, 123 (23.84%)

ONLY ONE AMERICAN LEAGUE BATTER amassed more than three thousand hits between the beginning of the 1980s and the end of the 1990s. Third baseman Wade Boggs rapped 2,098 hits in 11 seasons (1982-1992) with the Boston Red Sox, another 702 in 5 years (1993-1997) with the New York Yankees, and the final 210 in a curtain call (1998-1999) with his hometown Tampa Bay Devil Rays. Grand total: 3,010.

That exalted total stamped Boggs as a certain Hall of Famer, as did his quality score of sixty-two points. Officials in Cooperstown found no fault with his credentials, which included five AL batting crowns, fifteen seasons with an average higher than .300, and seven years with at least two hundred hits. But they were troubled by a widespread rumor that had been circulating since 1998.

Boggs had signed his final contract with the expansion Devil Rays in order to continue his pursuit of three thousand hits—"the mountain I wanted to stick my flag into"—and to play in front of his seventy-five-year-old father.[275] The team reportedly asked for one thing in return. It stipulated—so the rumor went—that Boggs must be portrayed in a Devil Rays cap on the plaque that would eventually be installed in the hall.

It was a repeat of the Gary Carter controversy, or so it seemed. Boggs had made his name in Boston. Inducting him as Tampa Bay's first Hall of Famer would have been ludicrous. Officials gingerly broached the subject with Boggs, who denied that his contract with the Devil Rays had contained any such clause.[276] His plaque featured a Red Sox cap. "If the Hall of Fame were to pick my Little League hat," he said, "I would have been very happy with that."[277]

Boggs was joined in the class of 2005 by Ryne Sandberg, a contemporary second baseman with a QS of forty-eight points. The BBWAA passed over several players with higher scores, including right fielder Andre Dawson (fifty-three points) and pitchers Bert Blyleven (sixty-nine), Lee Smith (sixty), and Rich Gossage (fifty-four). All finished among 2005's top eight vote-getters, and all would eventually be inducted.

The Veterans Committee, now limited to activity in odd-numbered years, conducted its second election since the expansion of its membership. The results in 2005 were the same as in 2003. Nobody was chosen. "This should be a difficult process," said Tom Seaver. "The process is not to elect, but to go though the voting process. And it's very subjective. I voted for three, and when I talked to another Hall of Famer, he told me he had voted for three, but neither of us had voted for the same ones."[278]

2006

Hall of Fame Summary

New inductees: 18
Category: Player 12, Pioneer/Executive 6
Election: BBWAA 1, Committee 17
Player QS average: 32.0 (BBWAA 45.0, Committee 30.8)
Hall of Famers to date: 278
Category: Player 224, Manager 16, Pioneer/Executive 30, Umpire 8
Election: BBWAA 103, Committee 175
Player QS average: 46.6 (BBWAA 59.3, Committee 35.8)

Inductees

- Ray Brown. **Category:** Player. **Position:** P. **QS:** 57 (good). **Career:** 1931-1945, G 215, W-L 122-45, SV 13, ERA 3.02. **Election:** Negro Leagues Committee.
- Willard Brown. **Category:** Player. **Position:** CF. **QS:** 59 (good). **Career:** 1937-1948, G 397, HR 49, RBI 354, BA .347. **Election:** Negro Leagues Committee.
- Andy Cooper. **Category:** Player. **Position:** P. **QS:** 21 (poor). **Career:** 1920-1939, G 288, W-L 118-64, SV 24, ERA 3.58. **Election:** Negro Leagues Committee.
- Frank Grant. **Category:** Pioneer/Executive. **Election:** Negro Leagues Committee.
- Pete Hill. **Category:** Player. **Position:** CF. **QS:** 7 (poor). **Career:** 1920-1925, G 159, HR 7, RBI 84, BA .303. **Election:** Negro Leagues Committee.
- Biz Mackey. **Category:** Player. **Position:** C. **QS:** 18 (poor). **Career:** 1920-1947, G 894, HR 52, RBI 603, BA .328. **Election:** Negro Leagues Committee.
- Effa Manley. **Category:** Pioneer/Executive. **Election:** Negro Leagues Committee.
- Jose Mendez. **Category:** Player. **Position:** P. **QS:** 16 (poor). **Career:** 1920-1926, G 69, W-L 30-9, SV 8, ERA 3.46. **Election:** Negro Leagues Committee.
- Alex Pompez. **Category:** Pioneer/Executive. **Election:** Negro Leagues Committee.
- Cumberland Posey. **Category:** Pioneer/Executive. **Election:** Negro Leagues Committee.
- Louis Santop. **Category:** Player. **Position:** C. **QS:** 9 (poor). **Career:** 1923-1926, G 115, HR 7, RBI 65, BA .317. **Election:** Negro Leagues Committee.

- Bruce Sutter. **Category:** Player. **Position:** P. **QS:** 45 (good). **Career:** 1976-1988, G 661, W-L 68-71, SV 300, ERA 2.83. **Election:** BBWAA.
- Mule Suttles. **Category:** Player. **Position:** 1B. **QS:** 65 (excellent). **Career:** 1924-1944, G 906, HR 179, RBI 877, BA .339. **Election:** Negro Leagues Committee.
- Ben Taylor. **Category:** Player. **Position:** 1B. **QS:** 10 (poor). **Career:** 1920-1929, G 627, HR 26, RBI 449, BA .337. **Election:** Negro Leagues Committee.
- Cristobal Torriente. **Category:** Player. **Position:** CF. **QS:** 31 (marginal). **Career:** 1920-1932, G 646, HR 55, RBI 530, BA .340. **Election:** Negro Leagues Committee.
- Sol White. **Category:** Pioneer/Executive. **Election:** Negro Leagues Committee.
- J.L. Wilkinson. **Category:** Pioneer/Executive. **Election:** Negro Leagues Committee.
- Jud Wilson. **Category:** Player. **Position:** 3B. **QS:** 46 (good). **Career:** 1923-1945, G 900, HR 77, RBI 724, BA .352. **Election:** Negro Leagues Committee.

BBWAA Election Summary

Voters: 520
Votes needed for induction: 390
Candidates receiving votes: 27
Candidates elected: 1
Candidates inducted in future: 7

BBWAA Top Ten

1. Bruce Sutter, 400 (76.92%)*
2. Jim Rice, 337 (64.81%)
3. Rich Gossage, 336 (64.62%)
4. Andre Dawson, 317 (60.96%)
5. Bert Blyleven, 277 (53.27%)
6. Lee Smith, 234 (45.00%)
7. Jack Morris, 214 (41.15%)
8. Tommy John, 154 (29.62%)
9. Steve Garvey, 135 (25.96%)
10. Alan Trammell, 92 (17.69%)

NEARLY THREE DECADES HAD PASSED since the Negro Leagues Committee voted to cease operations in 1977, claiming that it couldn't find additional candidates worthy of induction. The absurdity of its dissolution was subsequently proved by the Veterans Committee, which honored another nine black stars from pre-integration days, beginning with

Rube Foster in 1981 and culminating with Hilton Smith in 2001.

The Hall of Fame, to its credit, declined to close the books after Smith's selection. It launched a study in 2001—backed by a grant of $250,000 from baseball's central office—to identify other Negro leaguers who deserved consideration. A list of ninety-four names was eventually compiled. It was slowly whittled to thirty-nine finalists.[279]

The task of picking the winners was assigned to a group of twelve scholars and historians, a reincarnation of the Negro Leagues Committee. The new panel was not intended to be permanent. Its members were to meet only once. Any candidate receiving at least nine votes at the February 2006 session would be inducted. No limit was placed on the number of honorees.

Former commissioner Fay Vincent, who had been forced from office by a group of disgruntled owners in 1992, was the surprising choice to head the committee. He was pleased with the assignment, though he regretted its timing. "This is an effort that is thirty years too late," said Vincent. "This should have been done when a lot [of the finalists] were alive."[280]

Seventeen candidates received the necessary votes from the committee. Eleven were classified as players, six as pioneers/executives. Quality scores don't accurately reflect the accomplishments of all Negro leaguers, as previously explained, yet it was noteworthy that four of the new inductees were in the excellent or good range: first baseman Mule Suttles (sixty-five points), center fielder Willard Brown (fifty-nine), pitcher Ray Brown (fifty-seven), and third baseman Jud Wilson (forty-six).

The seventeen Negro leaguers collectively possessed three other significant characteristics:

• Their group included the first woman to be inducted. Effa Manley co-owned the Newark Eagles with her husband in the 1930s and 1940s, though everybody knew that she called the shots. "While Abe had the money, she was really the one running the show," said historian Leslie Heaphy, a member of the committee.[281]

• Two of them were white: Manley and fellow owner J.L. Wilkinson.[282]

• All were deceased. Only two of the thirty-nine finalists were still alive as of 2006—left fielder Minnie Minoso and first baseman Buck O'Neil—and the committee unconsciously followed tradition in bypassing both.[283]

Bob Feller, a white Hall of Famer known for speaking his mind, was outraged by the omission of O'Neil. "He wasn't a great hitter—a banjo hitter—though he was a Fancy Dan, a good fielder, at first base," said Feller. "But he should have been elected for his contributions, his ambassadorship for baseball and the Negro leagues, the most eloquent spokesman, a real leader."[284] O'Neil died two months after 2006's induction ceremony.

It was never adequately explained why all seventeen Negro leaguers were honored on the same day. If three or four had been enshrined per year, their names and achievements might have been adequately highlighted. But their stories were swamped by the deluge of facts and figures that accompanied 2006's mass induction, a fate that also befell the BBWAA's only choice, relief pitcher Bruce Sutter. Cooperstown's previous record was eleven honorees in 1946, a number that had been derided as much too large. The final count in 2006 was eighteen.

2007

Hall of Fame Summary

New inductees: 2
Category: Player 2
Election: BBWAA 2
Player QS average: 56.5 (BBWAA 56.5)
Hall of Famers to date: 280
Category: Player 226, Manager 16, Pioneer/Executive 30, Umpire 8
Election: BBWAA 105, Committee 175
Player QS average: 46.7 (BBWAA 59.2, Committee 35.8)

Inductees

- Tony Gwynn. **Category:** Player. **Position:** RF. **QS:** 49 (good). **Career:** 1982-2001, G 2,440, HR 135, RBI 1,138, BA .338. **Election:** BBWAA.
- Cal Ripken Jr. **Category:** Player. **Position:** SS. **QS:** 64 (excellent). **Career:** 1981-2001, G 3,001, HR 431, RBI 1,695, BA .276. **Election:** BBWAA.

BBWAA Election Summary

Voters: 545
Votes needed for induction: 409
Candidates receiving votes: 28
Candidates elected: 2
Candidates inducted in future: 8

BBWAA Top Ten

1. Cal Ripken Jr., 537 (98.53%)*
2. Tony Gwynn, 532 (97.61%)*
3. Rich Gossage, 388 (71.19%)
4. Jim Rice, 346 (63.49%)
5. Andre Dawson, 309 (56.70%)
6. Bert Blyleven, 260 (47.71%)
7. Lee Smith, 217 (39.82%)
8. Jack Morris, 202 (37.06%)
9. Mark McGwire, 128 (23.49%)
10. Tommy John, 125 (22.94%)

THE BBWAA ELECTED TWO acclaimed players in 2007. They were first-ballot honorees, the forty-second and forty-third in history.[285]

Both were renowned for feats that seemed almost superhuman. Cal Ripken Jr. shattered Lou Gehrig's immortal record by playing in 2,632 consecutive games; Tony Gwynn won 8 National League batting titles.

Each spent his career with a single club—twenty-one years for Ripken as a shortstop and third baseman for the Baltimore Orioles, twenty seasons for Gwynn as a right fielder for the San Diego Padres—yet both were hailed as stars throughout the baseball world.

Neither was a unanimous choice—the writers could never let that happen—but both came close. Ripken's 98.5 percent was the third-highest level of support received by any inductee to that point. Gwynn's 97.6 percent ranked seventh.

Their overwhelming popularity attracted a throng of excited fans. Attendance at the induction ceremony on July 29, 2007, was estimated at eighty-two thousand, the Hall of Fame's greatest crowd ever. Many of the inductees' admirers displayed signs during the festivities. "My Son is Named Cal Because of You," read a banner unfurled by a Ripken fan. "3,000 Miles for 1 Hero," said a sign held by a Californian who had crossed the country in Gwynn's honor.[286]

There were two notable absences. The first was the lack of old-time honorees. The revamped Veterans Committee—consisting of all living Hall of Famers, as well as selected writers and announcers—again failed to approve any candidates. "The writers voted on these players for fifteen years, and they weren't elected," snapped Joe Morgan. "Why are we being criticized because we haven't elected someone in the last six years?"[287]

The other conspicuous absentee from 2007's ceremony was Mark McGwire, a slugging first baseman for the Oakland Athletics and St. Louis Cardinals. McGwire's 583 home runs—the seventh-highest total through 2006—had established him as a certain first-ballot inductee, but that was before rumors of steroid abuse began to swirl. His downfall was capped by his refusal in 2005 to answer a congressional committee's questions about performance-enhancing drugs. Only 23.5 percent of the BBWAA's members voted for McGwire in his initial year of eligibility, the first signal that a majority of the voters considered steroids a barrier to induction.

The hall's newest members were asked to comment on McGwire's plight. "I don't mind saying I think he's a Hall of Famer," Gwynn said eagerly. But Ripken exhibited a better understanding of the prevailing mood. "I don't think it's my place to actually cast judgment," he said.[288]

2008

Hall of Fame Summary

New inductees: 6
Category: Player 1, Manager 2, Pioneer/Executive 3
Election: BBWAA 1, Committee 5
Player QS average: 54.0 (BBWAA 54.0)
Hall of Famers to date: 286
Category: Player 227, Manager 18, Pioneer/Executive 33, Umpire 8
Election: BBWAA 106, Committee 180
Player QS average: 46.7 (BBWAA 59.2, Committee 35.8)

Inductees

- Barney Dreyfuss. **Category:** Pioneer/Executive. **Election:** Veterans Committee.
- Rich Gossage. **Category:** Player. **Position:** P. **QS:** 54 (good). **Career:** 1972-1994, G 1,002, W-L 124-107, SV 310, ERA 3.01. **Election:** BBWAA.
- Bowie Kuhn. **Category:** Pioneer/Executive. **Election:** Veterans Committee.
- Walter O'Malley. **Category:** Pioneer/Executive. **Election:** Veterans Committee.
- Billy Southworth. **Category:** Manager. **Career:** 1929-1951, W-L 1,044-704, Pennants 4, Titles 2. **Election:** Veterans Committee.
- Dick Williams. **Category:** Manager. **Career:** 1967-1988, W-L 1,571-1,451, Pennants 4, Titles 2. **Election:** Veterans Committee.

BBWAA Election Summary

Voters: 543
Votes needed for induction: 408
Candidates receiving votes: 23
Candidates elected: 1
Candidates inducted in future: 8

BBWAA Top Ten

1. Rich Gossage, 466 (85.82%)*
2. Jim Rice, 392 (72.19%)
3. Andre Dawson, 358 (65.93%)
4. Bert Blyleven, 336 (61.88%)
5. Lee Smith, 235 (43.28%)
6. Jack Morris, 233 (42.91%)
7. Tommy John, 158 (29.10%)

8. Tim Raines, 132 (24.31%)
9. Mark McGwire, 128 (23.57%)
10. Alan Trammell, 99 (18.23%)

THE HALL OF FAME's board of directors raised the white flag in the summer of 2007. The Veterans Committee had just pitched its third straight shutout, a dismal outcome that forced the directors to admit defeat. They scrapped the expanded panel and replaced it with an altered version of the previous system.

The Veterans Committee was divided into three subcommittees, respectively focusing on pioneers and executives, managers and umpires, and players. The first two groups would select inductees for 2008, the latter for 2009.[289]

The new plan broke the logjam, though the initial round of selections was uninspiring. The first subcommittee tapped owners Barney Dreyfuss and Walter O'Malley and former commissioner Bowie Kuhn. The second added a pair of managers, Billy Southworth and Dick Williams. Each choice could be summarized by a single adjective:

• Dreyfuss: obscure. The owner of the Pittsburgh Pirates had been dead for seventy-six years.

• O'Malley: overrated. His plaque hailed him as a "visionary owner who inspired baseball's move west" by shifting the Dodgers from Brooklyn to Los Angeles, a claim that was overly generous. California's economic potential had been evident to everybody long before O'Malley hit the road in 1957. "Capital of the movie industry, center of styles, a city of some million and one-half, Los Angeles cannot be denied its place in the sun," the ever-cautious *Sporting News* had concluded as early as 1941. O'Malley was obviously a successful owner, but he most certainly was not a man of vision.[290]

• Kuhn: overmatched. He served as commissioner from 1969 to 1984, presiding over five work stoppages. Marvin Miller, the executive director of the players' union, frequently outwitted Kuhn, a fact that the Veterans Committee chose to ignore. It rejected Miller during the same meeting at which it elected Kuhn. "That's like putting Wile E. Coyote in the Hall of Fame instead of the Road Runner," said former pitcher Jim Bouton.[291]

• Southworth: underqualified. He managed the St. Louis Cardinals to a pair of world titles, yet both came during World War II, when the level of competition was diluted. Southworth's regular-season victory total (1,044) is still the lowest for any American or National League manager in the hall. The others all had more than 1,280 wins.

• Williams: debatable. The manager of six clubs, notably the world-champion Oakland Athletics in 1972 and 1973, was the best candidate selected by the Veterans Committee in 2008, though a few skeptics dissented. They observed that two managers who retired prior to Williams and remained outside the hall—Gene Mauch and Ralph Houk—won more regular-season games than he did. Houk also matched his total of two World Series titles.

The BBWAA added a single honoree to 2008's induction ceremony, relief pitcher Rich Gossage, who broke through in his ninth year on the ballot. Gossage was a baseball celebrity—remembered for his fiery spirit and Fu Manchu mustache—but the other inductees aroused little public interest. Only fourteen thousand spectators attended the festivities in Cooperstown, a decline of 83 percent from the previous year.[292]

2009

Hall of Fame Summary

New inductees: 3
Category: Player 3
Election: BBWAA 2, Committee 1
Player QS average: 47.7 (BBWAA 56.0, Committee 31.0)
Hall of Famers to date: 289
Category: Player 230, Manager 18, Pioneer/Executive 33, Umpire 8
Election: BBWAA 108, Committee 181
Player QS average: 46.7 (BBWAA 59.1, Committee 35.8)

Inductees

- Joe Gordon. **Category:** Player. **Position:** 2B. **QS:** 31 (marginal). **Career:** 1938-1950, G 1,566, HR 253, RBI 975, BA .268. **Election:** Veterans Committee.
- Rickey Henderson. **Category:** Player. **Position:** LF. **QS:** 65 (excellent). **Career:** 1979-2003, G 3,081, HR 297, RBI 1,115, BA .279. **Election:** BBWAA.
- Jim Rice. **Category:** Player. **Position:** LF. **QS:** 47 (good). **Career:** 1974-1989, G 2,089, HR 382, RBI 1,451, BA .298. **Election:** BBWAA.

BBWAA Election Summary

Voters: 539
Votes needed for induction: 405
Candidates receiving votes: 20
Candidates elected: 2
Candidates inducted in future: 7

BBWAA Top Ten

1. Rickey Henderson, 511 (94.81%)*
2. Jim Rice, 412 (76.44%)*
3. Andre Dawson, 361 (66.98%)
4. Bert Blyleven, 338 (62.71%)
5. Lee Smith, 240 (44.53%)
6. Jack Morris, 237 (43.97%)
7. Tommy John, 171 (31.73%)
8. Tim Raines, 122 (22.63%)
9. Mark McGwire, 118 (21.89%)
10. Alan Trammell, 94 (17.44%)

JOE GORDON WAS NAMED the American League's Most Valuable Player in 1942, though he did not deserve the award.

Boston Red Sox left fielder Ted Williams won his first Triple Crown that year, batting .356 with 36 homers and 137 runs batted in. Gordon scored a dubious Triple Crown of his own, leading the league in strikeouts by a batter (ninety-five), groundouts into double plays (twenty-two), and errors committed by a second baseman (twenty-eight).

A panel of twenty-four sportswriters sifted through the evidence and amazingly decided to give the MVP trophy to Gordon instead of Williams. Three factors seemed to be conclusive: Gordon posted a batting average of .322, which was solid, albeit not in Williams's territory; he had the good fortune to play for the vaunted New York Yankees; and the writers preferred his amiable personality to Williams's fiery temper.

It's strange how one mistake can beget another. Gordon's MVP was always offered as Exhibit A by supporters who felt he belonged in the Hall of Fame. Their campaign failed to convince the BBWAA, which never gave Gordon more than 28.5 percent of its votes. He was eliminated from the writers' ballot in 1970. But the restructured Veterans Committee happily took the bait and welcomed him to the hall thirty-nine years later.[293]

Forty-five players eligible for the committee's consideration in 2009 had quality scores better than Gordon's thirty-one points, yet he somehow emerged as its only selection. It seems safe to make this assertion: If he hadn't snatched Ted Williams's Most Valuable Player Award in 1942, Joe Gordon never would have been admitted to the plaque gallery.

The BBWAA added two left fielders to the hall in 2009. Rickey Henderson, who flashed an excellent QS of sixty-five points, qualified easily in his first attempt, supported by 94.8 percent of the writers. Jim Rice (forty-seven points) inched across the threshold with seven votes to spare in his fifteenth year of trying. "As far as what took so long, I have no idea," said Rice. "The only thing I can say is I'm glad it's over with." BBWAA members cast a total of 3,974 votes for Rice during his odyssey between 1995 and 2009. No other candidate in Hall of Fame history stayed on the ballot long enough (and suffered so many close calls) to receive more than 3,324.[294]

2010

Hall of Fame Summary

New inductees: 3
Category: Player 1, Manager 1, Umpire 1
Election: BBWAA 1, Committee 2
Player QS average: 53.0 (BBWAA 53.0)
Hall of Famers to date: 292
Category: Player 231, Manager 19, Pioneer/Executive 33, Umpire 9
Election: BBWAA 109, Committee 183
Player QS average: 46.8 (BBWAA 59.1, Committee 35.8)

Inductees

- Andre Dawson. **Category:** Player. **Position:** RF. **QS:** 53 (good). **Career:** 1976-1996, G 2,627, HR 438, RBI 1,591, BA .279. **Election:** BBWAA.
- Doug Harvey. **Category:** Umpire. **Election:** Veterans Committee.
- Whitey Herzog. **Category:** Manager. **Career:** 1973-1990, W-L 1,281-1,125, Pennants 3, Titles 1. **Election:** Veterans Committee.

BBWAA Election Summary

Voters: 539
Votes needed for induction: 405
Candidates receiving votes: 22
Candidates elected: 1
Candidates inducted in future: 9

BBWAA Top Ten

1. Andre Dawson, 420 (77.92%)*
2. Bert Blyleven, 400 (74.21%)
3. Roberto Alomar, 397 (73.65%)
4. Jack Morris, 282 (52.32%)
5. Barry Larkin, 278 (51.58%)
6. Lee Smith, 255 (47.31%)
7. Edgar Martinez, 195 (36.18%)
8. Tim Raines, 164 (30.43%)
9. Mark McGwire, 128 (23.75%)
10. Alan Trammell, 121 (22.45%)

ANDRE DAWSON MADE A REASONABLE ASSUMPTION prior to the BBWAA's 2010 election. Dawson, an outfielder for the Montreal Expos and Chicago Cubs, had been one of four candidates to draw more than 60 percent support the previous year. Rickey Henderson and Jim Rice were enshrined in 2009, which left Dawson and pitcher Bert Blyleven on the Hall of Fame's doorstep.

"We were both right there," Dawson said of Blyleven, "and I felt that this is the year we would get in."

He was half-right. Dawson climbed to 77.9 percent in 2010, crossing the threshold by a margin of fifteen votes. But Blyleven, who played for the Minnesota Twins and four other clubs, remained on the other side at 74.2 percent. He received precisely 400 votes, though he needed 405. "Five votes short is a little bit on the sad side," said Blyleven, "but my percentages jumped up a lot from last year, and I really appreciate that."[295]

Blyleven was the fourth candidate in seventy-five years to exceed 74 percent without being inducted. The fates of his predecessors gave cause for concern. Nellie Fox peaked at 74.7 percent in 1985—his final appearance on the writers' ballot—and he remained outside the hall until the Veterans Committee called twelve years later. Jim Bunning inexplicably slipped from 74.2 percent in 1988 to 57.9 percent in 1990. He, too, was forced to wait for the committee. Only Billy Williams ascended directly, climbing from 74.1 percent in 1986 to 85.7 percent in the next election.

Most observers agreed that Blyleven would eventually make it to Cooperstown, but they no longer felt sanguine about the prospects for Mark McGwire, who had once been tagged as a surefire first-ballot honoree. The taint of steroid abuse limited McGwire's support to just 23.8 percent in 2010, his fourth year on the ballot. It would prove to be his high-water mark.

The Veterans Committee's low-key selections—manager Whitey Herzog and umpire Doug Harvey—added little excitement to 2010's induction ceremony. The only drama occurred when Dawson, like Gary Carter before him, objected to appearing in an Expos cap on his plaque. He preferred a Cubs hat, though the hall overruled him.[296] "I never experienced love from a city until I arrived in Chicago," he told the Cubs fans who cheered him at the Cooperstown festivities. "You're the reason I kept playing the game."[297]

2011

Hall of Fame Summary

New inductees: 3
Category: Player 2, Pioneer/Executive 1
Election: BBWAA 2, Committee 1
Player QS average: 50.0 (BBWAA 50.0)
Hall of Famers to date: 295
Category: Player 233, Manager 19, Pioneer/Executive 34, Umpire 9
Election: BBWAA 111, Committee 184
Player QS average: 46.8 (BBWAA 58.9, Committee 35.8)

Inductees

- Roberto Alomar. **Category:** Player. **Position:** 2B. **QS:** 31 (marginal). **Career:** 1988-2004, G 2,379, HR 210, RBI 1,134, BA .300. **Election:** BBWAA.
- Bert Blyleven. **Category:** Player. **Position:** P. **QS:** 69 (excellent). **Career:** 1970-1992, G 692, W-L 287-250, SV 0, ERA 3.31. **Election:** BBWAA.
- Pat Gillick. **Category:** Pioneer/Executive. **Election:** Era Committee.

BBWAA Election Summary

Voters: 581
Votes needed for induction: 436
Candidates receiving votes: 27
Candidates elected: 2
Candidates inducted in future: 9

BBWAA Top Ten

1. Roberto Alomar, 523 (90.02%)*
2. Bert Blyleven, 463 (79.69%)*
3. Barry Larkin, 361 (62.13%)
4. Jack Morris, 311 (53.53%)
5. Lee Smith, 263 (45.27%)
6. Jeff Bagwell, 242 (41.65%)
7. Tim Raines, 218 (37.52%)
8. Edgar Martinez, 191 (32.87%)
9. Alan Trammell, 141 (24.27%)
10. Larry Walker, 118 (20.31%)

THE HALL OF FAME GAVE UP on the Veterans Committee on July 26, 2010. The panel had gone through several permutations since its creation in 1953, evolving from a compact group of eleven members to an enormous pool of as many as ninety voters. Yet it had rarely functioned effectively, and the hall's board decided at long last to dissolve it.

The final box score credited the Veterans Committee with 120 inductees in 58 years. Its honorees included nine umpires, sixteen managers, seventeen pioneers and executives, and seventy-eight players. Only six of the latter came with quality scores in the excellent range of sixty points or better. They were heavily outnumbered by the thirty-seven players who were selected despite wallowing under thirty points on the QS scale.

But a lack of quality wasn't the biggest complaint lodged against the Veterans Committee in its twilight years. The major grievance concerned its insufficient quantity. The committee selected only one player (Joe Gordon) in its final nine years of existence, a pace that even the mossbacks on the hall's board considered glacial. There was general agreement that something had to be done.

The new plan was to create three separate panels, assigning a distinct span to each: 1871 to 1946, 1947 to 1972, 1973 to the present. One of these Era Committees would meet each winter, adhering to a three-year cycle.[298] "In identifying candidates by era, as opposed to by category, the board feels this change will allow for an equal review of all eligible candidates," said Jane Forbes Clark, the hall's chairwoman.[299]

The new system's debut failed to satisfy the critics. The Era Committee for the seasons since 1973 came first in the rotation, and its sixteen members elected Pat Gillick to the hall's class of 2011. Gillick had been a successful general manager of four clubs—guiding the Toronto Blue Jays and Philadelphia Phillies to world titles—yet few fans knew much about him. A more logical choice would have been union executive Marvin Miller, who had been famous and heavily influential. He fell one vote short of the necessary 75 percent. "They decided a long time ago that they would downgrade any impact the union has had," the ninety-three-year-old Miller said bitterly. "And part of that plan was to keep me out of it."[300]

The largest number of writers to participate in any BBWAA election (581) cast ballots in 2011. They inducted Gillick's second baseman with the Blue Jays, Roberto Alomar, and pitcher Bert Blyleven. Alomar made it on his second try, but Blyleven had been facing the voters ever since 1998, despite an excellent quality score of sixty-nine points. "It's been fourteen years of praying and waiting," he said. "I thank the baseball writers of America for, I'm going to say, finally getting it right."[301]

2012

Hall of Fame Summary

New inductees: 2
Category: Player 2
Election: BBWAA 1, Committee 1
Player QS average: 40.0 (BBWAA 40.0, Committee 40.0)
Hall of Famers to date: 297
Category: Player 235, Manager 19, Pioneer/Executive 34, Umpire 9
Election: BBWAA 112, Committee 185
Player QS average: 46.7 (BBWAA 58.8, Committee 35.8)

Inductees

- Barry Larkin. **Category:** Player. **Position:** SS. **QS:** 40 (marginal). **Career:** 1986-2004, G 2,180, HR 198, RBI 960, BA .295. **Election:** BBWAA.
- Ron Santo. **Category:** Player. **Position:** 3B. **QS:** 40 (marginal). **Career:** 1960-1974, G 2,243, HR 342, RBI 1,331, BA .277. **Election:** Era Committee.

BBWAA Election Summary

Voters: 573
Votes needed for induction: 430
Candidates receiving votes: 21
Candidates elected: 1
Candidates inducted in future: 7

BBWAA Top Ten

1. Barry Larkin, 495 (86.39%)*
2. Jack Morris, 382 (66.67%)
3. Jeff Bagwell, 321 (56.02%)
4. Lee Smith, 290 (50.61%)
5. Tim Raines, 279 (48.69%)
6. Alan Trammell, 211 (36.82%)
7. Edgar Martinez, 209 (36.47%)
8. Fred McGriff, 137 (23.91%)
9. Larry Walker, 131 (22.86%)
10. Mark McGwire, 112 (19.55%)

RON SANTO DISTINGUISHED HIMSELF in the field and at the plate. He earned five Gold Gloves in fourteen seasons as a third baseman for the Chicago Cubs, and he twice led the National League in on-base percentage. He never won a Most Valuable Player Award, though he did finish among the top eight vote-getters on four occasions. His resumé may not have been exceptional, but it was undeniably solid, and the same could be said of his quality score of forty points.

The Hall of Fame had already inducted 137 players when Santo became eligible in January 1980. Sixty-one of those honorees—nearly half of the group—ranked below Santo on the QS scale. Yet the BBWAA showed no interest. Only 15 writers voted for him in 1980, just 3.9 percent of the 385 who cast ballots. The 5 percent floor had been adopted a year earlier, so Santo was immediately eliminated as a candidate.

Members of the hall's board weren't happy. They insisted that the dismissals of Santo and several other contenders had been abrupt and unfair. Lengthy negotiations with the BBWAA yielded a reprieve, with Santo and ten others receiving amnesty. They were restored to the ballot in 1985.[302]

The writers were a bit more receptive this time. Santo received 13.4 percent support in his second debut and eventually climbed to 43.1 percent. (A majority of the other reinstated candidates were swiftly ejected a second time. None ever did better than Ken Boyer's 25.5 percent in 1988.) But the clock ran out for Santo in 1998, and he was eliminated again. The Veterans Committee showed interest in subsequent years, even giving more votes to Santo than to any other player on its ballot in 2007. But he never attained the necessary 75 percent, so he remained outside the hall.[303]

Death provided the final boost for Santo, as for so many inductees who preceded him. Bladder cancer claimed his life in December 2010, almost precisely one year prior to the initial meeting of the Era Committee for his period (1947-1972). He was elected easily. "I believe he was meant to be in the hall," said his widow. "Unfortunately, it didn't happen in his lifetime."[304]

The other member of Cooperstown's class of 2012, ironically enough, carried the same quality score (forty points) as Santo. Shortstop Barry Larkin, who played his entire nineteen-season career with the Cincinnati Reds, won an MVP trophy in 1995, a feat that Santo did not accomplish. But Larkin trailed his classmate in other respects. He owned three Gold Gloves (vs. Santo's five), and he never led the league in a major offensive category.

Yet the BBWAA's voters, for reasons known only to them, were as enthusiastic about Larkin as they were apathetic about Santo. They elected the younger player to the hall in just his third year on the ballot.

2013

Hall of Fame Summary

New inductees: 3
Category: Player 1, Pioneer/Executive 1, Umpire 1
Election: Committee 3
Player QS average: 47.0 (Committee 47.0)
Hall of Famers to date: 300
Category: Player 236, Manager 19, Pioneer/Executive 35, Umpire 10
Election: BBWAA 112, Committee 188
Player QS average: 46.7 (BBWAA 58.8, Committee 35.9)

Inductees

- Hank O'Day. **Category:** Umpire. **Election:** Era Committee.
- Jacob Ruppert. **Category:** Pioneer/Executive. **Election:** Era Committee.
- Deacon White. **Category:** Player. **Position:** 3B. **QS:** 47 (good). **Career:** 1871-1890, G 1,560, HR 24, RBI 988, BA .312. **Election:** Era Committee.

BBWAA Election Summary

Voters: 569
Votes needed for induction: 427
Candidates receiving votes: 26
Candidates elected: 0
Candidates inducted in future: 9

BBWAA Top Ten

1. Craig Biggio, 388 (68.19%)
2. Jack Morris, 385 (67.66%)
3. Jeff Bagwell, 339 (59.58%)
4. Mike Piazza, 329 (57.82%)
5. Tim Raines, 297 (52.20%)
6. Lee Smith, 272 (47.80%)
7. Curt Schilling, 221 (38.84%)
8. Roger Clemens, 214 (37.61%)
9. Barry Bonds, 206 (36.20%)
10. Edgar Martinez, 204 (35.85%)

ONLY 9 BIG LEAGUERS posted quality scores of 90 points or better during the first 130 years of organized baseball, a span that ran from 1871 to 2000. All nine were swiftly admitted to the Hall of Fame. Six entered in their first year of eligibility. The other three—Nap Lajoie, Rogers

Hornsby, and Lefty Grove—were slightly delayed, largely because of the hall's early logjam of top-flight candidates. The median level of support for a player with a ninety-plus QS—based on each contender's first BBWAA election after retirement—was 94.7 percent.

Mike Schmidt, who retired in 1989 and entered the Hall of Fame in 1995, was the ninth and final player in the twentieth century to post a quality score in the nineties. The hall's ballot didn't feature a comparable star until 2013, when left fielder Barry Bonds and pitcher Roger Clemens simultaneously reached eligibility. They carried identical quality scores of ninety points, making them the tenth and eleventh players in history to reach that exalted level.

It would have been easy to predict 2013's election results under normal circumstances. Schmidt had received 444 of 460 votes in 1995, a support level of 96.5 percent. Bonds and Clemens probably would have fared even better, given the increased willingness of the BBWAA's members to rally behind the game's top players. Four candidates since 1995 had exceeded Schmidt's vote percentage, even though none had a QS higher than Nolan Ryan's seventy points.

But 2013, of course, was not a normal election. Clemens and Bonds were dogged by widespread, albeit unconfirmed, rumors of steroid abuse. Both received less than 40 percent support in "the most resounding referendum yet on the legacy of steroids in baseball," as Tyler Kepner of the *New York Times* described it.[305] Clemens finished eighth among the thirty-seven candidates on the ballot. Bonds was ninth.

Bonds, who was vacationing in Hawaii, offered no immediate reaction, while Clemens affected nonchalance. "After what has been written and said over the last few years, I'm not overly surprised," he said.[306] But several Hall of Famers hastened to voice their approval. Some spoke in moderate tones. "I would've felt a little uneasy sitting up there on the stage, listening to some of these new guys talk about how great they were," said Al Kaline. Others were tersely emphatic. "Wow! Baseball writers make a statement. Feels right," tweeted Dennis Eckersley.[307] Fellow pitcher Rich Gossage drew a line in the sand. "If any of these guys ever get in, I probably will never go back to the Hall of Fame," he said.[308]

The firestorm ignited by Bonds and Clemens consumed most of the oxygen in 2013. Relatively little was written or said about the other candidates. Craig Biggio, a twenty-year second baseman for the Houston Astros, emerged as the frontrunner, though he fell thirty-nine votes short of induction. "I wish we had an electee," said Jeff Idelson, the hall's president. "But I'm not surprised, given how volatile this era has been."[309]

Idelson had to content himself with three new Hall of Famers selected by the Era Committee that covered the period from 1871 to 1946. A total of 123 years had passed since the retirement of third baseman Deacon White, whose wait for induction was the longest in the hall's history. White died in 1939. His classmates passed away in the same decade—umpire Hank O'Day in 1935, New York Yankees owner Jacob Ruppert in 1939.

Plaques were presented to White's great-grandson, O'Day's great-nephew, and Ruppert's great-grandniece at the induction festivities on July 28, 2013. It was Cooperstown's first ceremony without a living honoree since 1965, and America's baseball fans reacted accordingly. The attendance was estimated—quite generously—at just twenty-five hundred.[310]

2014

Hall of Fame Summary

New inductees: 6
Category: Player 3, Manager 3
Election: BBWAA 3, Committee 3
Player QS average: 65.3 (BBWAA 65.3)
Hall of Famers to date: 306
Category: Player 239, Manager 22, Pioneer/Executive 35, Umpire 10
Election: BBWAA 115, Committee 191
Player QS average: 47.0 (BBWAA 58.9, Committee 35.9)

Inductees

- Bobby Cox. **Category:** Manager. **Career:** 1978-2010, W-L 2,504-2,001, Pennants 5, Titles 1. **Election:** Era Committee.
- Tom Glavine. **Category:** Player. **Position:** P. **QS:** 52 (good). **Career:** 1987-2008, G 682, W-L 305-203, SV 0, ERA 3.54. **Election:** BBWAA.
- Tony La Russa. **Category:** Manager. **Career:** 1979-2011#, W-L 2,728-2,365, Pennants 6, Titles 3. **Election:** Era Committee.
- Greg Maddux. **Category:** Player. **Position:** P. **QS:** 82 (excellent). **Career:** 1986-2008, G 744, W-L 355-227, SV 0, ERA 3.16. **Election:** BBWAA.
- Frank Thomas. **Category:** Player. **Position:** 1B. **QS:** 62 (excellent). **Career:** 1990-2008, G 2,322, HR 521, RBI 1,704, BA .301. **Election:** BBWAA.
- Joe Torre. **Category:** Manager. **Career:** 1977-2010, W-L 2,326-1,997, Pennants 6, Titles 4. **Election:** Era Committee.

#: *La Russa's record does not include his post-induction stint with the White Sox.*

BBWAA Election Summary

Voters: 571
Votes needed for induction: 429
Candidates receiving votes: 30
Candidates elected: 3
Candidates inducted in future: 10

BBWAA Top Ten

1. Greg Maddux, 555 (97.20%)*
2. Tom Glavine, 525 (91.94%)*
3. Frank Thomas, 478 (83.71%)*
4. Craig Biggio, 427 (74.78%)
5. Mike Piazza, 355 (62.17%)
6. Jack Morris, 351 (61.47%)

7. Jeff Bagwell, 310 (54.29%)
8. Tim Raines, 263 (46.06%)
9. Roger Clemens, 202 (35.38%)
10. Barry Bonds, 198 (34.68%)

ROGER CLEMENS AND BARRY BONDS stumbled in 2014, their second year of eligibility. Clemens's support dropped 2.2 percentage points from the previous election, and Bonds suffered a decline of 1.5 points. Both were mired more than 225 votes below the induction threshold. The BBWAA clearly was not in a forgiving mood.

But the sad tale of these two tarnished superstars wasn't the dominant story in 2014. Cooperstown had happier news. The writers elected three well-respected players who had retired in the previous decade, and the Era Committee added three high-profile managers of recent vintage. Hall of Fame officials were especially pleased that all six inductees were still alive.

The class of 2014 was led by Greg Maddux, the eighth-winningest pitcher in big-league history. He notched 355 victories for the Atlanta Braves, Chicago Cubs, and 2 other teams over 23 seasons, and his quality score of 82 points was the highest for any inductee since Mike Schmidt in 1995. Maddux received 555 votes, the biggest raw total for any candidate in the Hall of Fame's history. His share of 97.2 percent was the eighth-largest in seventy-nine years.

The writers also elected Maddux's Atlanta teammate, pitcher Tom Glavine (QS of fifty-two points), and a first baseman and designated hitter for the Chicago White Sox, Frank Thomas (sixty-two). The heavily muscled Thomas refused to entertain questions about Bonds, Clemens, and other alleged steroid abusers. "As for what they did, I don't think any of us will ever really know," Thomas said. "But I can just tell you, what I did was real, and that's why I've got this smile on my face right now."[311]

The hall's three new players carried an average quality score of 65.3 points, which ranked as the best joint QS for any group of three or more BBWAA inductees since 1937. The Era Committee's new choices were equally solid. Only five big-league managers had registered more than twenty-three hundred wins, and all three of 2014's honorees belonged to that elite club. Bobby Cox, Tony La Russa, and Joe Torre had collectively won 7,558 regular-season games, 17 league pennants, and 8 World Series titles. (La Russa returned to the dugout in 2021 to manage the White Sox, pushing his win total higher.)

The fans registered their approval of 2014's star-studded lineup. An estimated crowd of forty-eight thousand jammed the grounds of the Clark Sports Center on July 27, 2014.[312] A large number were fans of the Braves, there to cheer Maddux, Glavine, and their manager, Cox. But it was a tearful Thomas who stole the show. "As soon as I stood up," he told the crowd, "my knees started knocking, and the first thing I looked at was my mom. It hit me right in my heart."[313]

2015

Hall of Fame Summary

New inductees: 4
Category: Player 4
Election: BBWAA 4
Player QS average: 68.0 (BBWAA 68.0)
Hall of Famers to date: 310
Category: Player 243, Manager 22, Pioneer/Executive 35, Umpire 10
Election: BBWAA 119, Committee 191
Player QS average: 47.3 (BBWAA 59.2, Committee 35.9)

Inductees

- Craig Biggio. **Category:** Player. **Position:** 2B. **QS:** 34 (marginal). **Career:** 1988-2007, G 2,850, HR 291, RBI 1,175, BA .281. **Election:** BBWAA.
- Randy Johnson. **Category:** Player. **Position:** P. **QS:** 89 (excellent). **Career:** 1988-2009, G 618, W-L 303-166, SV 2, ERA 3.29. **Election:** BBWAA.
- Pedro Martinez. **Category:** Player. **Position:** P. **QS:** 84 (excellent). **Career:** 1992-2009, G 476, W-L 219-100, SV 3, ERA 2.93. **Election:** BBWAA.
- John Smoltz. **Category:** Player. **Position:** P. **QS:** 65 (excellent). **Career:** 1988-2009, G 723, W-L 213-155, SV 154, ERA 3.33. **Election:** BBWAA.

BBWAA Election Summary

Voters: 549
Votes needed for induction: 412
Candidates receiving votes: 27
Candidates elected: 4
Candidates inducted in future: 8

BBWAA Top Ten

1. Randy Johnson, 534 (97.27%)*
2. Pedro Martinez, 500 (91.07%)*
3. John Smoltz, 455 (82.88%)*
4. Craig Biggio, 454 (82.70%)*
5. Mike Piazza, 384 (69.95%)
6. Jeff Bagwell, 306 (55.74%)
7. Tim Raines, 302 (55.01%)
8. Curt Schilling, 215 (39.16%)
9. Roger Clemens, 206 (37.52%)
10. Barry Bonds, 202 (36.79%)

THE TREND WAS CLEAR to almost everyone. Barry Bonds and Roger Clemens had drawn fewer than 40 percent of the writers' votes in 2014, falling slightly below their mediocre debuts in 2013. Both were marooned in the lagoon of BBWAA indifference. It seemed unlikely that they would make landfall in Cooperstown anytime soon.

The Hall of Fame's board wished that both of the alleged steroid abusers would simply disappear. A perpetual fog of publicity enveloped Bonds and Clemens—and consequently the hall itself—as reporters and broadcasters speculated ceaselessly about the duo's odds of eventual redemption. Board members fretted that the media's endless barrage would tarnish the hall's reputation and obscure the candidacies of other distinguished players.

The long-term forecast envisioned more of the same. The fifteen-year window for Bonds and Clemens wouldn't close until 2027. How would the Hall of Fame survive such a long stretch of unwanted controversy? And what would happen if the tainted candidates eventually began to inch toward induction? An annual gain of just three percentage points would put both on the cusp by their fifteenth year.

The obvious solution was to shut the window more rapidly, so the board voted on July 26, 2014, to pare the eligibility period from fifteen to ten years, effective in 2015. Exemptions were granted to Don Mattingly, Alan Trammell, and Lee Smith, serious contenders who had already been on the ballot for more than a decade. They would be allowed their promised fifteen-year runs. All other current or future candidates—most definitely including Bonds and Clemens—would be subject to the ten-year cutoff.[314]

Officials offered a benign explanation, though nobody was fooled. "It's become evident, especially over the past thirty years or so, that the likelihood of election after ten years is incredibly minimal," said Jeff Idelson, the hall's president.[315] His point was contradicted by several plaques displayed near his office. Bert Blyleven, Jim Rice, and Bruce Sutter had been elected by the BBWAA during the thirty-year period that Idelson cited (1985-2014) after languishing on the ballot for more than a decade. Ralph Kiner, Bob Lemon, and Duke Snider had achieved the same feat between 1965 and 1984.

But the hall was lucky. The controversy over its rule change was dissipated by the 2015 election, which proved to be historic in several ways:

• The writers chose pitchers Randy Johnson, Pedro Martinez, and John Smoltz, and second baseman Craig Biggio. It was the first time in sixty years that they inducted more than three candidates.[316]

• Johnson and Martinez received more than 90 percent support in 2015, a year after Greg Maddux and Tom Glavine had done similarly well. Never before had multiple players exceeded 90 percent in consecutive elections.

• Johnson, Martinez, and Smoltz emerged as first-ballot honorees, making 2014-2015 the only span with at least three first-timers in back-to-back elections. (Maddux, Glavine, and Frank Thomas had succeeded in their initial appearances in 2014.)

• Johnson's quality score of eighty-nine points established him as the top-rated inductee since Mike Schmidt two decades earlier.

• Martinez (eighty-four points) and Smoltz (sixty-five) also rated above sixty on the QS scale, which meant that 2015 was the first year since 1976 with three honorees in the excellent range.

The sixteen-member Era Committee decided not to add anyone to 2015's distinguished class. The panel rejected all ten candidates on its ballot, though Dick Allen and Tony Oliva did come within one vote of the necessary twelve. Jane Forbes Clark pronounced the requisite benediction upon the committee's latest shutout: "The results today are a reminder that election to the Hall of Fame is incredibly difficult."[317]

2016

Hall of Fame Summary

New inductees: 2
Category: Player 2
Election: BBWAA 2
Player QS average: 59.5 (BBWAA 59.5)
Hall of Famers to date: 312
Category: Player 245, Manager 22, Pioneer/Executive 35, Umpire 10
Election: BBWAA 121, Committee 191
Player QS average: 47.4 (BBWAA 59.2, Committee 35.9)

Inductees

- Ken Griffey Jr. **Category:** Player. **Position:** CF. **QS:** 72 (excellent). **Career:** 1989-2010, G 2,671, HR 630, RBI 1,836, BA .284. **Election:** BBWAA.
- Mike Piazza. **Category:** Player. **Position:** C. **QS:** 47 (good). **Career:** 1992-2007, G 1,912, HR 427, RBI 1,335, BA .308. **Election:** BBWAA.

BBWAA Election Summary

Voters: 440
Votes needed for induction: 330
Candidates receiving votes: 25
Candidates elected: 2
Candidates inducted in future: 8

BBWAA Top Ten

1. Ken Griffey Jr., 437 (99.32%)*
2. Mike Piazza, 365 (82.95%)*
3. Jeff Bagwell, 315 (71.59%)
4. Tim Raines, 307 (69.77%)
5. Trevor Hoffman, 296 (67.27%)
6. Curt Schilling, 230 (52.27%)
7. Roger Clemens, 199 (45.23%)
8. Barry Bonds, 195 (44.32%)
9. Edgar Martinez, 191 (43.41%)
10. Mike Mussina, 189 (42.95%)

THE TURNOUT HAD BEEN STRONG for recent Hall of Fame elections—too strong, as far as the hall's board was concerned.

Fewer than 200 writers participated in many of the elections between the late 1940s and early 1960s, bottoming out at 121 in 1948. But the number of voters had been on the rise ever since, topping three hundred in 1966, four hundred in 1979, five hundred in 2001. The 5 largest vote totals were recorded between 2011 and 2015, peaking at 581 in the former year.

The problem, as Hall of Fame officials saw it, was the inability of quantity to guarantee quality. Perpetual voting rights were granted to anybody who had possessed a BBWAA card for at least ten years. Dozens of members continued to participate in the hall's elections even though they no longer covered baseball on a regular basis. Some didn't watch games at all.

So the board decided in July 2015 to partially drain the voting pool, straining out the older members who had retired or moved on to other beats. A new registration system would determine each cardholder's status. Only those who had been directly involved with baseball within the past decade would be allowed to vote in 2016 and subsequent elections.

Jane Forbes Clark insisted that the change would guarantee "the most active electorate possible."[318] She angered many of the old-timers who were stripped of their voting privileges, though retiree Michael Gee, formerly of the *Boston Herald*, was an exception. "I know her diplomatic language actually meant, 'We'd like voters who have actually been at a damn ballgame sometime during the Obama administration.' Fair enough," Gee wrote.[319] It was assumed that a smaller, younger pool of voters would be more receptive to players who had recently left the game. "That move could help the electoral causes of some popular candidates, including Tim Raines and Jeff Bagwell," predicted analyst Jay Jaffe.[320]

The number of voters dropped to 440 in 2016—the lowest total since 1993—but Raines and Bagwell weren't immediate beneficiaries. Both remained on the short side of 75 percent as catcher Mike Piazza and center fielder Ken Griffey Jr. sailed into the hall. Griffey, who carried a quality score of seventy-two points, was named on all but three ballots, a state of near-unanimity facilitated by the removal of intransigent elderly voters. His support level of 99.3 percent set a new record, breaking Tom Seaver's 98.8 percent. "I'm truly honored to be elected, and to have the highest percentage is definitely a shock," Griffey said. "I don't think that way. The big thing is to get into the Hall of Fame."[321]

2017

Hall of Fame Summary

New inductees: 5
Category: Player 3, Pioneer/Executive 2
Election: BBWAA 3, Committee 2
Player QS average: 47.3 (BBWAA 47.3)
Hall of Famers to date: 317
Category: Player 248, Manager 22, Pioneer/Executive 37, Umpire 10
Election: BBWAA 124, Committee 193
Player QS average: 47.4 (BBWAA 58.9, Committee 35.9)

Inductees

- Jeff Bagwell. **Category:** Player. **Position:** 1B. **QS:** 68 (excellent). **Career:** 1991-2005, G 2,150, HR 449, RBI 1,529, BA .297. **Election:** BBWAA.
- Tim Raines. **Category:** Player. **Position:** LF. **QS:** 34 (marginal). **Career:** 1979-2002, G 2,502, HR 170, RBI 980, BA .294. **Election:** BBWAA.
- Ivan Rodriguez. **Category:** Player. **Position:** C. **QS:** 40 (marginal). **Career:** 1991-2011, G 2,543, HR 311, RBI 1,332, BA .296. **Election:** BBWAA.
- John Schuerholz. **Category:** Pioneer/Executive. **Election:** Era Committee.
- Bud Selig. **Category:** Pioneer/Executive. **Election:** Era Committee.

BBWAA Election Summary

Voters: 442
Votes needed for induction: 332
Candidates receiving votes: 23
Candidates elected: 3
Candidates inducted in future: 6

BBWAA Top Ten

1. Jeff Bagwell, 381 (86.20%)*
2. Tim Raines, 380 (85.97%)*
3. Ivan Rodriguez, 336 (76.02%)*
4. Trevor Hoffman, 327 (73.98%)
5. Vladimir Guerrero, 317 (71.72%)
6. Edgar Martinez, 259 (58.60%)
7. Roger Clemens, 239 (54.07%)
8. Barry Bonds, 238 (53.85%)
9. Mike Mussina, 229 (51.81%)
10. Curt Schilling, 199 (45.02%)

Tim Raines was caught short by the reduction of the Hall of Fame's eligibility window from fifteen years to ten.

The left fielder for the Montreal Expos and five other clubs always knew that his journey to Cooperstown would be arduous. He posted nice stats during his 23-year career—2,605 hits, 808 stolen bases, a quality score of 34 points—yet he lacked the aura of a first-ballot inductee. Raines received 24.3 percent support in 2008, his initial year of eligibility, and slowly began to climb. He passed 50 percent in 2013. His eventual success began to seem likely, given that he had nine more years to cross the threshold.

Only he didn't. Raines was blindsided by the hall's decision to impose a ten-year cutoff in 2015, which meant he suddenly faced elimination in 2017, not 2022. He worked his way up to 69.8 percent in 2016, setting the stage for a do-or-die election. "Last night was probably the worst night I've had over the ten years," he said after securing admission on January 18, 2017. "I knew I was close, but I wasn't sure. Everything is out of control. You have to wait."[322]

First baseman Jeff Bagwell knew the feeling. His quality score (sixty-eight points) was compelling, though he was dogged by unsubstantiated rumors of steroid abuse. The resulting air of uncertainty delayed his induction until his seventh appearance on the ballot. But the BBWAA's third honoree in 2017, catcher Ivan Rodriguez, was elected in his first try despite similar whispers about performance-enhancing drugs. *New York Times* columnist Tyler Kepner speculated that Rodriguez's swift victory "will most likely help the cases of Bonds and Clemens."[323]

And, indeed, the candidacies of Barry Bonds and Roger Clemens seemed to gain new life in their fifth year. Both soared above 50 percent for the first time—Clemens to 54.1 percent, Bonds to 53.9 percent. Two factors seemed to be at play. Young writers who had recently joined the voting pool appeared to be more forgiving of PED use. And several older voters were angered by the Era Committee's decision in December 2016—a month prior to the BBWAA election—to induct Bud Selig, who had served as commissioner during the so-called steroid era.

Susan Slusser of the *San Francisco Chronicle* accused Selig of turning a blind eye to baseball's PED crisis. She called it "senseless to keep steroid guys out when the enablers are in the Hall of Fame. I now will hold my nose and vote for players I believe cheated."[324] Peter Botte of the *New York Daily News* echoed Slusser's willingness to support Bonds and Clemens in the wake of Selig's admission. "I always thought it would take a proven user getting in for me to reconsider my stance," Botte wrote. "It turns out the impetus was much higher on baseball's masthead."[325]

Subtle adjustments were made to both of Cooperstown's induction tracks during the 2017 cycle. The BBWAA proposed that all ballots cast in its annual election be publicly released, an idea rejected by the hall's board. A compromise was hammered out, giving writers the option of having their votes posted on the BBWAA's website. An overwhelming majority of 309 consented to release in 2017, while 133 retained privacy.[326] The Era Committee's change was less momentous. The tripartite panel was redivided into groups covering four spans: 1871-1949, 1950-1969, 1970-1987, and 1988-present. (An unbalanced rotation guaranteed that the latter two panels would meet more frequently.) Selig and executive John Schuerholz were elected by the new subcommittee for the period since 1988.[327]

2018

Hall of Fame Summary

New inductees: 6
Category: Player 6
Election: BBWAA 4, Committee 2
Player QS average: 51.0 (BBWAA 58.8, Committee 35.5)
Hall of Famers to date: 323
Category: Player 254, Manager 22, Pioneer/Executive 37, Umpire 10
Election: BBWAA 128, Committee 195
Player QS average: 47.5 (BBWAA 58.9, Committee 35.9)

Inductees

- Vladimir Guerrero. **Category:** Player. **Position:** RF. **QS:** 50 (good). **Career:** 1996-2011, G 2,147, HR 449, RBI 1,496, BA .318. **Election:** BBWAA.
- Trevor Hoffman. **Category:** Player. **Position:** P. **QS:** 77 (excellent). **Career:** 1993-2010, G 1,035, W-L 61-75, SV 601, ERA 2.87. **Election:** BBWAA.
- Chipper Jones. **Category:** Player. **Position:** 3B. **QS:** 64 (excellent). **Career:** 1993-2012, G 2,499, HR 468, RBI 1,623, BA .303. **Election:** BBWAA.
- Jack Morris. **Category:** Player. **Position:** P. **QS:** 37 (marginal). **Career:** 1977-1994, G 549, W-L 254-186, SV 0, ERA 3.90. **Election:** Era Committee.
- Jim Thome. **Category:** Player. **Position:** 1B. **QS:** 44 (marginal). **Career:** 1991-2012, G 2,543, HR 612, RBI 1,699, BA .276. **Election:** BBWAA.
- Alan Trammell. **Category:** Player. **Position:** SS. **QS:** 34 (marginal). **Career:** 1977-1996, G 2,293, HR 185, RBI 1,003, BA .285. **Election:** Era Committee.

BBWAA Election Summary

Voters: 422
Votes needed for induction: 317
Candidates receiving votes: 27
Candidates elected: 4
Candidates inducted in future: 3

BBWAA Top Ten

1. Chipper Jones, 410 (97.16%)*
2. Vladimir Guerrero, 392 (92.89%)*
3. Jim Thome, 379 (89.81%)*
4. Trevor Hoffman, 337 (79.86%)*

5. Edgar Martinez, 297 (70.38%)
6. Mike Mussina, 268 (63.51%)
7. Roger Clemens, 242 (57.35%)
8. Barry Bonds, 238 (56.40%)
9. Curt Schilling, 216 (51.18%)
10. Omar Vizquel, 156 (36.97%)

THE BBWAA ELECTED FOUR PLAYERS to the Hall of Fame in 2018, led by Chipper Jones, a longtime third baseman for the Atlanta Braves. He received the votes of 97.2 percent of the writers, the eleventh-best share for any candidate since 1936. Jones's quality score was in the excellent range (sixty-four points), he had been the National League's Most Valuable Player in 1999, and he was among the top ten vote-getters for MVP in five other seasons.

Jones was a first-ballot inductee, as was Jim Thome (forty-four points), a first baseman and designated hitter for six clubs, notably the Cleveland Indians. Thome was the 8th player to hit more than 600 home runs, finishing his 22-year career with 612. Right fielder Vladimir Guerrero (fifty points), who spent most of his time with the Montreal Expos and Los Angeles Angels, was elected in his second year of eligibility, shooting up from 71.7 percent in 2017 to 92.9 percent. Relief pitcher Trevor Hoffman of the San Diego Padres led 2018's quartet with a quality score of seventy-seven points, yet he received the fewest votes (79.9 percent) and waited the longest to be inducted (three years).

The 1970-1987 version of the Era Committee added a pair of Tigers to the class of 2018. Pitcher Jack Morris and shortstop Alan Trammell had starred on Detroit's 1984 world-championship club. "It's going to be a warm and fuzzy day for Tigers fans," said Morris. "The tradition of Tiger baseball is magnified because of finally getting acknowledgment for that great '84 team."[328]

Skeptics wondered if the recognition was warranted. Nine pitchers who had been active between 1970 and 1987 (and who remained outside the Hall of Fame) possessed quality scores better than Morris's thirty-seven points, led by Lee Smith with sixty. Morris's career earned-run average of 3.90 was the worst for any of the seventy-eight pitchers inducted through 2018. Only ten of the others carried ERAs higher than 3.50.

Eight non-pitching contenders from the same era outrated Trammell's QS of thirty-four. One of them, ironically enough, was his long-time double-play partner, second baseman Lou Whitaker, whose score of thirty-five was a single point better. Trammell had a slight edge over Whitaker in batting average (.285 vs. .276) and Gold Gloves (four vs. three), but Whitaker had more hits (2,369 vs. 2,365) and homers (244 vs. 185) and a better on-base percentage (.363 vs. .352).

The two were virtually carbon copies of each other, yet the voters inexplicably perceived a massive difference. The BBWAA had kept Trammell's candidacy alive for the maximum of fifteen years, pushing him as high as 40.9 percent, before the Era Committee swooped in to induct him. But the writers eliminated Whitaker in his very first ballot appearance in 2001, giving him just 2.9 percent support, and little was said about his chances thereafter.

It was a crazy disconnect. "If Tram is in, Sweet Lou should be next. Like the start of a double play, from Tram to Lou. That only seems right," wrote *Detroit Free Press* columnist Jeff Seidel.[329] Trammell conceded the point in his induction speech. He gestured toward Whitaker in the audience. "It's my hope that you'll be up here someday," he said.[330]

Perhaps the most important thing about the ceremony on July 29, 2018, was that all of the Hall of Fame's new members were present. Not since 1955 had six living players been inducted. The resulting crowd of fifty-three thousand fans was the second-largest to that point.[331]

2019

Hall of Fame Summary

New inductees: 6
Category: Player 6
Election: BBWAA 4, Committee 2
Player QS average: 57.0 (BBWAA 64.8, Committee 41.5)
Hall of Famers to date: 329
Category: Player 260, Manager 22, Pioneer/Executive 37, Umpire 10
Election: BBWAA 132, Committee 197
Player QS average: 47.7 (BBWAA 59.1, Committee 36.0)

Inductees

- Harold Baines. **Category:** Player. **Position:** DH. **QS:** 23 (poor). **Career:** 1980-2001, G 2,830, HR 384, RBI 1,628, BA .289. **Election:** Era Committee.
- Roy Halladay. **Category:** Player. **Position:** P. **QS:** 62 (excellent). **Career:** 1998-2013, G 416, W-L 203-105, SV 1, ERA 3.38. **Election:** BBWAA.
- Edgar Martinez. **Category:** Player. **Position:** DH. **QS:** 39 (marginal). **Career:** 1987-2004, G 2,055, HR 309, RBI 1,261, BA .312. **Election:** BBWAA.
- Mike Mussina. **Category:** Player. **Position:** P. **QS:** 69 (excellent). **Career:** 1991-2008, G 537, W-L 270-153, SV 0, ERA 3.68. **Election:** BBWAA.
- Mariano Rivera. **Category:** Player. **Position:** P. **QS:** 89 (excellent). **Career:** 1995-2013, G 1,115, W-L 82-60, SV 652, ERA 2.21. **Election:** BBWAA.
- Lee Smith. **Category:** Player. **Position:** P. **QS:** 60 (excellent). **Career:** 1980-1997, G 1,022, W-L 71-92, SV 478, ERA 3.03. **Election:** Era Committee.

BBWAA Election Summary

Voters: 425
Votes needed for induction: 319
Candidates receiving votes: 24
Candidates elected: 4
Candidates inducted in future: 1

BBWAA Top Ten

1. Mariano Rivera, 425 (100.00%)*
2. Roy Halladay, 363 (85.41%)*
2. Edgar Martinez, 363 (85.41%)*
4. Mike Mussina, 326 (76.71%)*

5. Curt Schilling, 259 (60.94%)
6. Roger Clemens, 253 (59.53%)
7. Barry Bonds, 251 (59.06%)
8. Larry Walker, 232 (54.59%)
9. Omar Vizquel, 182 (42.82%)
10. Fred McGriff, 169 (39.76%)

A THREAD OF DEFIANCE ran through the Hall of Fame's elections from 1936 through 2018. The BBWAA's members steadfastly refused to endorse any player unanimously, no matter how skilled or popular he might have been. That's simply the way things were, and everybody knew it.

The pattern was established in the very first year. Honus Wagner, then and now the leader in quality score (98 points), was ignored by 11 writers in 1936, as was Babe Ruth, whose 714 home runs topped the majors until 1974. Ty Cobb, the career batting-average champion at .366, was spurned by four voters.

Several columnists, themselves BBWAA cardholders, howled about the absurdity of the organization's informal prohibition. They insisted that Wagner, Ruth, and Cobb had been robbed, and they subsequently demanded unanimity for superstars such as Henry Aaron, Willie Mays, and Tom Seaver. Joe Falls, then with the *Detroit News,* openly campaigned for Aaron in 1982: "How could anyone not vote for this man?" But Falls conceded that at least one of his fellow writers would certainly defy logic. "It has never happened—nobody has ever been a unanimous choice—and I'm afraid it's going to happen again," he wrote, and he was right. Nine voters declined to include Aaron on their ballots.[332]

A few writers believed that the BBWAA's tradition was shameful. "It's an embarrassment to our association," said the group's secretary/treasurer, Jack Lang, after twenty-three writers refused to vote for Mays in 1979.[333] But most members shrugged it off as a fact of life. Moss Klein of the *Newark Star-Ledger* avidly supported Seaver in 1992, though he knew there would be holdouts. "He won't be a unanimous choice, because no one ever is," Klein accurately predicted. Five voters gave Seaver a pass.[334]

This silly custom persisted through 2018, though there were signs of its eventual demise. Modern writers seemed more likely than their predecessors to coalesce behind outstanding candidates. Eight contenders received better than 95 percent support in the twenty years from 1999 through 2018, matching the eight who had topped 95 percent during the sixty-three years that came before (1936-1998). The heightened glare of publicity was another factor. Most writers now released their ballots on the BBWAA's website, making it easier to identify a spoilsport.

The question of unanimity was relevant in 1999 because New York Yankees reliever Mariano Rivera was appearing on the ballot for the first time. The all-time leader in saves (652) carried a quality score of 89 points, a figure topped by only 11 players since 1871. The resulting ingredients—the BBWAA's evolving attitude, blended with Rivera's outstanding statistics—seemed to be an ideal recipe for a history-making event.

And so it proved to be. Rivera was listed on all 425 ballots, establishing him as the writers' first unanimous selection, an honor that had escaped Wagner, Ruth, Cobb, and all the rest. "After my career, I was thinking that I had a shot to be a Hall of Famer," he said. "But this was beyond my imagination."[335]

Rivera was the biggest story in 2019, of course, though not the only one. The writers elected three other players: pitchers Roy Halladay and Mike Mussina and designated hitter Edgar Martinez. The Era Committee added two more: relief pitcher Lee Smith and DH Harold Baines. Four of these inductees carried quality scores of sixty points or better—Rivera, Mussina (sixty-nine points), Halladay (sixty-two), and Smith (sixty)—making 2019 the first class since 1936 to be blessed with so many players in the excellent range.

2020

Hall of Fame Summary

New inductees: 4
Category: Player 3, Pioneer/Executive 1
Election: BBWAA 2, Committee 2
Player QS average: 48.3 (BBWAA 58.5, Committee 28.0)
Hall of Famers to date: 333
Category: Player 263, Manager 22, Pioneer/Executive 38, Umpire 10
Election: BBWAA 134, Committee 199
Player QS average: 47.7 (BBWAA 59.1, Committee 35.9)

Inductees

- Derek Jeter. **Category:** Player. **Position:** SS. **QS:** 41 (marginal). **Career:** 1995-2014, G 2,747, HR 260, RBI 1,311, BA .310. **Election:** BBWAA.
- Marvin Miller. **Category:** Pioneer/Executive. **Election:** Era Committee.
- Ted Simmons. **Category:** Player. **Position:** C. **QS:** 28 (poor). **Career:** 1968-1988, G 2,456, HR 248, RBI 1,389, BA .285. **Election:** Era Committee.
- Larry Walker. **Category:** Player. **Position:** RF. **QS:** 76 (excellent). **Career:** 1989-2005, G 1,988, HR 383, RBI 1,311, BA .313. **Election:** BBWAA.

BBWAA Election Summary

Voters: 397
Votes needed for induction: 298
Candidates receiving votes: 25
Candidates elected: 2
Candidates inducted in future: 0

BBWAA Top Ten

1. Derek Jeter, 396 (99.75%)*
2. Larry Walker, 304 (76.57%)*
3. Curt Schilling, 278 (70.03%)
4. Roger Clemens, 242 (60.96%)
5. Barry Bonds, 241 (60.71%)
6. Omar Vizquel, 209 (52.64%)
7. Scott Rolen, 140 (35.26%)
8. Billy Wagner, 126 (31.74%)
9. Gary Sheffield, 121 (30.48%)
10. Todd Helton, 116 (29.22%)

JANE FORBES CLARK WRAPPED UP the Hall of Fame's annual festivities on July 21, 2019, with an open invitation. The next induction ceremony, she told the crowd, would take place in 371 days—on July 26, 2020—and she encouraged everybody to make plans to attend.

Fans of the New York Yankees had packed the grounds in Cooperstown to cheer 2019's unanimous honoree, Mariano Rivera. But Clark's announcement caused them to look ahead. They began to chant: "Deh-rick Jee-tur!" Clap, clap, clap-clap-clap. "Deh-rick Jee-tur!" Clap, clap, clap-clap-clap.[336]

It was taken for granted that Derek Jeter, a twenty-year shortstop for the Yankees, would be a first-ballot choice the following year, as indeed he proved to be. Jeter received votes from 396 of the 397 writers who participated in the 2020 election. His support level of 99.75 percent was the second-highest in history, trailing only Rivera.

The writers also elected Larry Walker, a right fielder for the Colorado Rockies and Montreal Expos, though by a considerably tighter margin. Jeter exceeded the 75 percent threshold with ninety-eight votes to spare, but Walker squeaked across by a six-vote margin. "As great as Derek is, remember those old forty-fives we used to listen to?" laughed Walker. "They had the song on the A side and the [other] side you didn't really know about? I'm the song on the B side."[337]

Walker actually had a better quality score than Jeter (seventy-six vs. forty-one points) and a somewhat higher batting average (.313 vs. .310). But Jeter towered over his 2020 classmate for two reasons: He owned five World Series rings—five more than Walker—and he had attained iconic status in the nation's largest media market.

The Era Committee added labor leader Marvin Miller and catcher Ted Simmons to the mix. Miller, who had died in 2012, was long overdue for induction. Hanging his plaque in the same gallery where his adversary, Bowie Kuhn, had resided since 2008 was an act of "subversive greatness," said Jeff Katz, a baseball author and former mayor of Cooperstown.[338] No such aura surrounded Simmons, who had played for the St. Louis Cardinals and two other clubs. His QS of twenty-eight was the second-lowest for any player inducted since 2006.

The ceremony in July 2020 was destined to be the Derek Jeter Show, with the other honorees playing supporting roles. An enormous crowd was anticipated—perhaps the largest ever—though the onset of the Covid-19 pandemic in March upset those expectations. Tim Mead, the Hall of Fame's president, waited until late April before bowing to reality and pulling the plug. There would be no ceremony in 2020, not in Cooperstown or any other venue. "We would not have a made-for-television or a virtual program," Mead said. "The induction ceremony is a special moment for the baseball community across the country and beyond."[339]

2021

Hall of Fame Summary

New inductees: 0
Hall of Famers to date: 333
Category: Player 263, Manager 22, Pioneer/Executive 38, Umpire 10
Election: BBWAA 134, Committee 199
Player QS average: 47.7 (BBWAA 59.1, Committee 35.9)

BBWAA Election Summary

Voters: 401
Votes needed for induction: 301
Candidates receiving votes: 20
Candidates elected: 0
Candidates inducted in future: 0

BBWAA Top Ten

1. Curt Schilling, 285 (71.07%)
2. Barry Bonds, 248 (61.85%)
3. Roger Clemens, 247 (61.60%)
4. Scott Rolen, 212 (52.87%)
5. Omar Vizquel, 197 (49.13%)
6. Billy Wagner, 186 (46.38%)
7. Todd Helton, 180 (44.89%)
8. Gary Sheffield, 163 (40.65%)
9. Andruw Jones, 136 (33.92%)
10. Jeff Kent, 130 (32.42%)

NOBODY WAS CHOSEN FOR the Hall of Fame in 2021, the fourth election year in which the writers and the committee failed to produce an honoree, joining 1950, 1958, and 1960. It was the first complete shutout in more than six decades.

Covid was one of the reasons. The Era Committee's meeting in December 2020 was canceled because its members couldn't gather in person.[340] Controversy was another factor. The BBWAA's four runners-up in 2020—the contenders who came closest to 75 percent without being elected—were befouled by unfavorable publicity that damaged their candidacies in 2021. Barry Bonds and Roger Clemens still lugged their steroid baggage, Curt Schilling continued to outrage critics with his political outspokenness, and Omar Vizquel faced allegations of sexual abuse.[341] The lack of fresh faces also hurt. None of 2021's new candidates had a quality score higher than twenty-six points.

Schilling fared the best, inching up from 70.0 percent in 2020 to 71.1 percent. He missed induction in 2021 by sixteen votes, though he had the solace of another year of eligibility. He opted to chuck it away. "I will not participate in the final year of voting," Schilling announced. "I am requesting to be removed from the ballot. I'll defer to the [Era] Committee and men whose opinions actually matter and who are in a position to actually judge a player." The BBWAA refused to pull his name from its list.[342]

Bonds and Clemens also had one year left on the ballot. Both reached personal highs in 2021—Bonds at 61.9 percent, Clemens at 61.6 percent—yet they remained more than fifty votes short of their goal. It was difficult to imagine either of them breaking through in 2022.[343]

That, however, was an issue for the future. The matter at hand was the Hall of Fame's 2021 induction festivities, featuring the four honorees who had been selected a year earlier. The Covid pandemic remained a concern, so the event was slated for the Wednesday following Labor Day, a ploy to reduce attendance. More than fifty thousand fans had been anticipated for the original ceremony on a midsummer Sunday in 2020. Twenty thousand still showed up on a September weekday in 2021.

The darling of the crowd, of course, was Derek Jeter. The applause he received wasn't as intense as it would have been a year earlier, though he didn't seem to mind. "It's humbling," he said of the cheers. "It's a special feeling, and you tend to miss it when you don't hear it anymore."[344]

2022

Hall of Fame Summary

New inductees: 7
Category: Player 5, Pioneer/Executive 2
Election: BBWAA 1, Committee 6
Player QS average: 35.2 (BBWAA 52.0, Committee 31.0)
Hall of Famers to date: 340
Category: Player 268, Manager 22, Pioneer/Executive 40, Umpire 10
Election: BBWAA 135, Committee 205
Player QS average: 47.5 (BBWAA 59.1, Committee 35.8)

Inductees

- Bud Fowler. **Category:** Pioneer/Executive. **Election:** Era Committee.
- Gil Hodges. **Category:** Player. **Position:** 1B. **QS:** 15 (poor). **Career:** 1943-1963, G 2,071, HR 370, RBI 1,274, BA .273. **Election:** Era Committee.
- Jim Kaat. **Category:** Player. **Position:** P. **QS:** 36 (marginal). **Career:** 1959-1983, G 898, W-L 283-237, SV 17, ERA 3.45. **Election:** Era Committee.
- Minnie Minoso. **Category:** Player. **Position:** LF. **QS:** 47 (good). **Career:** 1946-1980, G 1,946, HR 195, RBI 1,093, BA .299. **Election:** Era Committee.
- Buck O'Neil. **Category:** Pioneer/Executive. **Election:** Era Committee.
- Tony Oliva. **Category:** Player. **Position:** RF. **QS:** 26 (poor). **Career:** 1962-1976, G 1,676, HR 220, RBI 947, BA .304. **Election:** Era Committee.
- David Ortiz. **Category:** Player. **Position:** DH. **QS:** 52 (good). **Career:** 1997-2016, G 2,408, HR 541, RBI 1,768, BA .286. **Election:** BBWAA.

BBWAA Election Summary

Voters: 394
Votes needed for induction: 296
Candidates receiving votes: 28
Candidates elected: 1
Candidates inducted in future: 0

BBWAA Top Ten

1. David Ortiz, 307 (77.92%)*
2. Barry Bonds, 260 (65.99%)
3. Roger Clemens, 257 (65.23%)
4. Scott Rolen, 249 (63.20%)
5. Curt Schilling, 231 (58.63%)

6. Todd Helton, 205 (52.03%)
7. Billy Wagner, 201 (51.02%)
8. Andruw Jones, 163 (41.37%)
9. Gary Sheffield, 160 (40.61%)
10. Alex Rodriguez, 135 (34.26%)

WE ALREADY DISCUSSED 2022'S ELECTION in Chapter 1 of this book, and in exceptionally close detail. Little more needs to be said.

Seven honorees were added to the Hall of Fame: David Ortiz by the BBWAA; Bud Fowler, Gil Hodges, Jim Kaat, Minnie Minoso, Buck O'Neil, and Tony Oliva by two Era Committees. The class of 2022 was the largest since the admission of seventeen Negro leaguers and Bruce Sutter in 2006.

A crowd of thirty-five thousand attended the induction ceremony in Cooperstown on July 24, 2022. Ortiz was the big draw, as evidenced by the large number of fans wearing Boston Red Sox hats and jerseys. The first-ballot inductee became emotional at the podium, especially when referring to his late mother. "Going through this speech and putting it together, I cried a lot, to be honest with you, even this morning, every time I touched base about my mom," Ortiz said.[345]

Barry Bonds, Roger Clemens, and Curt Schilling all reached the end of the line in 2022, at least as far as the BBWAA was concerned. They fell short of 75 percent for the tenth straight year. Their dossiers were transferred to an Era Committee, which would decide their fate in a meeting (or series of meetings) yet to be scheduled.

The committee, which had already been restructured several times in the twenty-first century, received another facelift in 2022. The hall's board voted to consolidate the four subcommittees into three. One portion would now focus on candidates associated with baseball prior to 1980. The remaining panels would cover the period from 1980 to the present, one concentrating on players, the other on managers, executives, and umpires. The new groups would meet on a three-year rotation, beginning with the 2023 cycle.[346]

These changes may streamline the induction process—that's the professed goal—yet they are unlikely to reduce the level of controversy that currently envelopes the Hall of Fame. Steroids and the larger question of character will cast a shadow over elections for years to come, as the hall's president has acknowledged. But Josh Rawitch prefers to view this ongoing debate in a positive light. "We believe that character matters in life, not just the voting process for the Hall of Fame," he said. "Some industries are probably held to higher standards, baseball being one of those, and has always been one of those. We actually think that that's a good thing."[347]

CHAPTER FOUR

Action

THERE WAS A TIME when baseball deserved the title of America's favorite game.

The Gallup Poll documented its preeminence in 1948, a dozen years after the Hall of Fame's initial election. Gallup's interviewers asked a cross-section of Americans to name the sport they preferred to watch. These were the top three responses:

- Baseball, 39 percent
- Football, 17 percent
- Basketball, 10 percent[1]

Gallup released its survey results in April 1948, the same month in which a *Sporting News* editorial proclaimed baseball to be "the sport of the people, the fun of the common man, the national pastime of America."[2] The praise may have been a touch excessive, but who could honestly dispute the conclusion? Baseball had scored a veritable rout in the nationwide poll, winning by a margin of better than two to one. Its supremacy seemed secure, its future bright.

Yet there were people in the sport—influential people—who worried about its status. Branch Rickey, the sharpest executive ever to grace a front office, had warned as early as 1943 that professional football was destined to emerge as a serious threat. Arthur Daley, a stolid columnist for the *New York Times*, chuckled at the very idea. "What challenge," he asked, "can a 20-game sport ever make to a 154-game one?"[3]

He would eventually find out. Baseball remained the nation's favorite game throughout the 1950s, yet football steadily narrowed the gap, a trend exacerbated by the contrasting styles of their commissioners.

Baseball lagged under the lethargic Ford Frick, while the frenetic Bert Bell propelled the National Football League forward. "Professional football's attendance has been going straight up in the same decade that baseball's attendance has been going straight down," moaned Bill Veeck, "because Bert Bell gave the NFL such aggressive leadership."[4] Bell kept pushing, exhorting, and scheming until a fatal heart attack struck in October 1959 at Philadelphia's Franklin Field, where he was watching the Eagles play the Pittsburgh Steelers.[5]

Insiders predicted that Bell's demise would curb football's momentum, but Branch Rickey sensed that the younger sport would not be easily shaken. "I am alarmed at the subtle invasion of professional football, which is gaining preeminence over baseball. It's unthinkable," he grumbled in 1959.[6] Rickey's concerns were echoed by Larry MacPhail, another future Hall of Famer renowned for his innovative spirit. "Baseball is in real trouble," he said. "I regret to say that it is no longer the national pastime."[7]

MacPhail's gloom was slightly premature. Gallup reported in 1960 that baseball retained a lead of thirteen percentage points over football—down from 1948's margin of twenty-two points, yet substantial nonetheless.[8] Football's new commissioner, thirty-three-year-old Pete Rozelle, was pleased by his sport's steady progress, though he acknowledged its underdog status. The NFL launched its schedule each September, but Rozelle made a point of waiting until the mid-October conclusion of the World Series to pop the cork on a bottle of champagne. "Here's to the beginning of football season," he would say.[9]

Rozelle dispensed with this quaint tradition only after firmly establishing himself as Bell's successor. The cover story of a December 1962 issue of *Time* declared football to be "The Sport of the '60s," and Rozelle did his best to convert the hype to reality.[10] He launched the Super Bowl four years later, signed massive television contracts with the major networks, and gradually transformed Bell's vision into reality. Gallup detected a new leader by 1972:

- Football, 32 percent
- Baseball, 24 percent
- Basketball, 9 percent[11]

Baseball has continued to lose its hold on the American heart ever since Gallup reported those unhappy results. The reasons have been well-documented.

Games have steadily grown longer—from an average of two hours and twenty-seven minutes in 1972 to three hours and seven minutes in 2022—yet the amount of action has declined. There were 16.7 strikeouts in a typical contest during the most recent season, up 50 percent from 11.1 per game in 1972.[12] The rise of analytics has inspired bizarre defensive shifts, quick hooks for starting pitchers, and a nightly glut of relievers, all of which have deadened the product. "Analytics has had a deleterious effect on the way the game is being played on the field," admitted Rob Manfred, the current commissioner.[13] And, of course, the steroid crisis has shaken the public's confidence.

My aim here is not to dwell on the factors that have caused baseball to slip, but to stress the severity of its decline.

"Take a look at the empty seats in ballparks and the empty ballfields in playgrounds. It concerns me, and for those in baseball, it should scare you," warned Mike Schmidt in 1995.[14] The problem has grown considerably worse since then. Big-league attendance declined in nine of the twelve seasons preceding the Covid-19 outbreak, resulting in an overall drop of 13.7 percent.[15] An average of twelve million viewers tuned into World Series telecasts in 2021, a pitiful fraction of the forty to fifty million who routinely watched in the 1980s and early 1990s. The February 2022 audience for Pete Rozelle's shining legacy, football's Super Bowl, was nine times bigger—112 million.[16]

It came as no surprise, then, that Gallup's most recent survey on America's favorite sport, which it conducted in December 2017, found football occupying a position of dominance and baseball suffering a free fall:

- Football, 37 percent
- Basketball, 11 percent
- Baseball, 9 percent[17]

But, you ask, what does this lamentable history have to do with the National Baseball Hall of Fame?

The answer should be obvious. Baseball's problems are the hall's problems. The empty seats and fields that troubled Mike Schmidt might, with the passage of time, translate to a plaque gallery devoid of fans, a museum with no reason to exist. Cooperstown has good reason to worry.

Rob Manfred has promised an aggressive response to baseball's on-field shortcomings. Big changes will be implemented for the 2023 season, including a pitch clock and limitations on defensive shifting. Theo Epstein, the executive who assembled world-championship squads for the Boston Red Sox and Chicago Cubs, collaborated with Manfred in planning this rescue mission. "The goal," said Epstein, "is to move closer to the very best version of baseball."[18]

The Hall of Fame is saddled with its own deficiencies, which have been detailed in previous chapters of this book, yet it lacks a similar focus on self-improvement. It has no discernible master plan for the decades ahead, no Theo Epstein at the wheel, no stated goal of becoming its "very best version."

Bill James, the statistical guru and baseball historian, issued his own warning in 1995, coincidentally the same year in which Mike Schmidt sounded his alarm. "If the Hall of Fame's administrators don't take seriously their problems," wrote James, "something else will come along and push them aside, within the course of a few decades."[19]

That critical moment may soon be at hand. The Hall of Fame was born at the apogee of baseball's popularity, and it prospered greatly from its link to the unchallenged national pastime. But the sport and the hall have fallen considerably in public esteem. They now face stark options—evolution or irrelevance.

Baseball appears, at long last, to be taking steps to embrace the former option and avoid the latter. The Hall of Fame must do the same. It must reinvigorate itself, inspiring new levels of excitement and engagement among the game's millions of fans. This chapter offers a way forward, a nine-part action plan.

1. General Amnesty

JAY JAFFE, A THOUGHTFUL BASEBALL ANALYST, wrote a book about the Hall of Fame in 2017. He chose a safe, straightforward title: *The Coo-*

perstown Casebook. Then he cranked up the voltage with a subtitle that hinted at real controversy: *Who's in the Baseball Hall of Fame, Who Should Be In, and Who Should Pack Their Plaques.*

It turned out to be a very interesting book, though it didn't deliver the promised sizzle. Jaffe pointed out the weak choices made by the hall's electorate over the years, but he stopped short of recommending expulsions. His subtitle raised the prospect of a wholesale housecleaning, yet he failed to carry his concept to its logical conclusion.

Jaffe wasn't the first to broach such an idea. John Leo, a syndicated newspaper columnist, suggested in 1988 that the Hall of Fame should follow the lead of art museums that "deaccession"—a polite word for "unload"—paintings and sculptures they no longer want. Leo posed this question: "Who wouldn't like to deaccession players like Sunny Jim Bottomley, Zack Wheat, Jesse Haines, Chick Hafey, or George Kell, who was mistakenly accessioned a few years ago by the perennially woeful Committee on Veterans?"[20] But Leo didn't follow through. He didn't suggest a procedure to achieve his goal.

Peter Clark, an editor at the *San Diego Union-Tribune,* was similarly caustic in a piece he wrote for the *Sporting News* in 2002. Clark expressed disdain for several of the honorees who share the plaque gallery with Babe Ruth, Ty Cobb, and other all-time greats. "Ruth and Cobb," he said, "should not be surrounded by Phil Rizzuto, George Kelly, Ray Schalk, Rick Ferrell, Jimmy Collins, Lloyd Waner, and Tommy McCarthy." Clark suggested the removal of an unworthy member upon any admission of a new inductee—a one-for-one trade—though he didn't discuss the mechanics.[21]

It's remarkably easy—and tempting—to assemble a list of Hall of Famers who might deserve to be drummed out. So easy, in fact, that I put together a full twenty-five-man roster of possibilities. It features the current members who carry the two lowest quality scores at each position, except for pitchers (the eight lowest) and designated hitters (the one lowest). I excluded Negro leaguers from this exercise, given the unreliability of some of their QS ratings.

Everybody on this squad was a fine player, of course, yet twenty-four of them rate lower than thirty points on the QS scale, an indication of their low status in the plaque gallery. The highest score on the list is Catfish Hunter's thirty, which puts him at the very bottom of the marginal range. Here's the complete roster, with each player's big-league span and quality score in parentheses:

Lowest QS by Position

P: Jesse Haines (1918-1937, 11)
P: Jack Chesbro (1899-1909, 13)
P: Rube Marquard (1908-1925, 20)
P: Bob Lemon (1941-1958, 20)
P: Waite Hoyt (1918-1938, 27)
P: Herb Pennock (1912-1934, 28)
P: Mickey Welch (1880-1892, 29)
P: Catfish Hunter (1965-1979, 30)
C: Rick Ferrell (1929-1947, 9)
C: Ray Schalk (1912-1929, 10)
1B: George Kelly (1915-1932, 5)
1B: Gil Hodges (1943-1963, 15)
2B: Bill Mazeroski (1956-1972, 11)
2B: Johnny Evers (1902-1929, 12)
SS: Joe Sewell (1920-1933, 12)
SS: Travis Jackson (1922-1936, 13)
3B: Freddie Lindstrom (1924-1936, 4)
3B: George Kell (1943-1957, 10)
LF: Chick Hafey (1924-1937, 13)
LF: Heinie Manush (1923-1939, 17)
CF: Lloyd Waner (1927-1945, 10)
CF: Earle Combs (1924-1935, 14)
RF: Tommy McCarthy (1884-1896, 1)
RF: Ross Youngs (1917-1926, 12)
DH: Harold Baines (1980-2001, 23)

Let's not stop with players. Our Hall of Fame squad needs a manager, doesn't it? I nominate Bucky Harris (.493 career winning percentage) or Wilbert Robinson (one game above .500). The general manager could be Lee MacPhail, a nice man who didn't accomplish anything special at the helm of the Yankees and Orioles. The owner's box could be occupied by the amiable (yet ineffectual) Tom Yawkey or the relatively anonymous Barney Dreyfuss. A plethora of uninspiring candidates—from Morgan Bulkeley to Bud Selig—could fill the top administrative posts of league president and commissioner.

So, yes, it's a simple matter to nominate Hall of Famers for eviction. But it's not so easy to proceed from the general concept to a specific process, as several writers before me have discovered. Who would decide which honorees would be removed? What public explanation would be given? Would some kind of a farewell ceremony be held? How frequently would expulsions be conducted? Could an ex-inductee be reinstated to the hall at some point in the future?

And there's an even bigger question to ponder.

Every player, manager, executive, and umpire who was admitted to the Hall of Fame was assured of permanent enshrinement. There is no provision in the hall's rules for the reconsideration of past election results or the removal of members. The accolade was intended to be perpetual. How could such a promise be broken?[22]

Revocation, quite simply, would be dishonorable. Hence my proposal of a general amnesty. The rest of this chapter will suggest major changes in many of the Hall of Fame's procedures and operations. Almost everything should—and will—be open to question. Except, that is, for the hall's current membership. It should be sacrosanct.

All 340 plaques in Cooperstown's gallery can rest easy.

2. New Committee

THE HALL OF FAME'S ELECTION SYSTEM made sense when it was devised in 1936.

The Baseball Writers' Association of America was assigned the task of inducting the twentieth century's best players. Most big-league sportswriters had been covering baseball for ten to twenty years, many even longer. They had seen a majority (if not all) of their era's greats in action, and they were (presumably) impartial. The hall's plan called for roughly two hundred BBWAA members to pool their wisdom in annual elections. Who better to make such fateful decisions?

The nineteenth century was a different matter. Current writers hadn't seen players of such ancient vintage, so a special panel of elderly experts was created. It would go by various names—the Old-Timers Committee, the Centennial Commission, the Veterans Committee—but the principle was always the same. A small group would meet in a small room and select honorees from long ago.

The assumption, of course, was that the committee was a stopgap, a short-lived necessity. It would be phased out in a decade or so, perhaps around 1950. The nineteenth century's icons would have been inducted by then, as would the outstanding players from the period between 1900 and 1920. The distant past would therefore be a settled matter, and the BBWAA's members could carry on with the task of judging the stars they had actually covered.

But reality failed to adhere to this scenario. It was rerouted by the adjustments that the Hall of Fame ceaselessly made to its election procedures. Ken Smith, an unapologetic cheerleader who eventually became the hall's director, counted more than twenty rule changes in the first two decades. Critics snorted at this instability, but Smith detected only the pursuit of excellence. "Nobody in baseball, from the commissioner, executives, and Cooperstown people to the men on the field and in the press box and the multitude of fans," Smith insisted, "would stand for any carelessness in electing people to the Hall of Fame. It required wise, judicious guidance to keep the doors guarded."[23]

Say what?

The Old-Timers Committee didn't hold a meeting after 1949, tacitly acknowledging that it had outlived its usefulness. But the hall kept tinkering, somehow embedding a new Veterans Committee into the process.[24] The new panel heralded its arrival in 1953 by making six mediocre and uninteresting choices, thereby establishing the unhappy pattern that has persisted to this day. The hall's various committees have admitted 133 players, carrying an average quality score of 35.8 points. That's 39 percent below the average QS of 59.1 points for the BBWAA's 135 inductions. Here's another way to view this enormous gap: Fifty-nine of the committees' honorees had quality scores in the poor range, but the same was true of only six players picked by the writers.

The conclusion is obvious. The committee (now a tripartite structure collectively known as the Era Committees) has no reason to exist, and it never did a good job, anyway. It should be eliminated.

The other major player in the selection process, the BBWAA, also should be relieved of its duties, though for a different reason. It's difficult to find fault with the choices the writers have made over the years, but their monopoly can no longer be justified.

The BBWAA was the logical foundation for the Hall of Fame's electorate in 1936. Broadcasters weren't given serious consideration back then, nor did they deserve it. Radio play-by-play was in its infancy, and television was in its experimental phase. Other sources of potential voters were essentially nonexistent. Few authors were writing about baseball's history back then, and sabermetric analysis and the internet were decades away from creation. Sportswriters were the only independent observers who dealt with baseball on a daily basis in the 1930s. It made perfect sense to give them the vote.

But that rationale hasn't applied for a long time. Hundreds of broadcasters, for instance, spend as much time at the ballpark as beat writers do. Tyler Kepner of the *New York Times* posed the obvious question in 2013: "Why should people like Vin Scully, Joe Buck, and Jon Miller have no chance to vote for the Hall of Fame?"[25] Why not, indeed? And why aren't knowledgeable people in other fields brought into the process, too?

I propose the creation of a multifaceted Hall of Fame Selection Committee, vested with the sole authority to induct candidates into the plaque gallery. It will cover baseball's history in its entirety, uniting the spans previously divided between the BBWAA and the Era Committees. The new panel's one hundred members will be allocated among these groups:

- BBWAA members (twenty)
- Radio and television broadcasters (twenty)
- Hall of Famers (twenty)
- Statistical analysts (ten)
- Authors and historians (ten)
- Past players, managers, and executives not in the hall (ten)
- Current players, managers, and executives (nine)
- Fans (one)

Members will serve five-year terms. Twenty panelists will depart annually, replaced by twenty newcomers. A designated subcommittee will nominate the new members, keeping within the quotas above, subject to the approval of the hall's board. (The annual rotation will be launched with staggered terms during the Selection Committee's initial phase. Twenty of the inaugural members, chosen by lot, will serve for only one year, another twenty for two years, and so on.)

The quotas are self-explanatory, except perhaps for the final entry. Baseball fans will be invited to vote online, submitting a new form each day (if they wish) during a specified voting period. The tabulated results will be converted into a single ballot that reflects the collective opinions of the public. A similar system has been used to great effect by the Rock and Roll Hall of Fame since 2012. More than five million ballots were submitted by music fans in its 2022 election.[26]

The quota system ensures a broadly representative and inclusive committee. The size of the panel will be manageable—not so large that its members become anonymous, yet not so small that they can be easily manipulated.

Voters will cast individual ballots, just as BBWAA members do today. There will be no meetings in cramped rooms, no opportunities for an overbearing chairman (a reincarnated Frankie Frisch or Joe Brown) to exert his influence on behalf of the latest version of Jesse Haines or Bill Mazeroski, no chances for a carefully constructed cabal to push another Phil Rizzuto through Cooperstown's gates.

Tyler Kepner's 2013 critique, mentioned a few paragraphs back, identified the serious flaws that plague the Hall of Fame's elections: "There are too many unqualified voters—too many voters, period—and too many segments of the baseball world with no say in the process."[27] The new Selection Committee addresses—and resolves—those complaints.

3. Streamlined Process

THE HALL OF FAME HAS COCOONED its voting system in a crazy quilt of rules and regulations.

A player must have been an active big leaguer for a minimum of ten seasons to be certified as a Hall of Fame candidate. He must have been retired for five years to become eligible for BBWAA consideration. He must receive at least 5 percent support from the writers to qualify for the subsequent year's ballot. If he is not elected to the hall, he cannot appear on more than ten ballots before his case is shunted to an Era Committee.

Few of these rules are logical. Not one of them is necessary. Let's consider them case by case.

The Hall of Fame has been willing to play fast and loose with **the ten-season requirement** on occasion. Ross Youngs fulfilled it in a technical sense, though only if his seven-game debut in 1917 counted as a full year. The Veterans Committee inducted him in 1972 after ruling that Youngs had indeed participated in "ten league championship seasons."[28] Addie Joss pitched nine years for Cleveland before being felled by tubercular meningitis in 1911. The committee remained eager to admit him, so the hall's board simply granted a waiver in 1978.[29]

Other players have entered the plaque gallery despite relatively short periods of success, with Sandy Koufax a prime example. "My career lasted twelve years," he once said, "but only six were good ones."[30] Koufax's excellence was undisputed, though the same couldn't be said of other short-timers. Tommy McCarthy—the QS scale's one-point wonder—spent 13 years in the majors, though he played at least 130 games in only 5 of them. Chick Hafey was a step worse in his 13 seasons, topping the 130 mark only 4 times. And Hack Wilson's 12-year career included 6 of fewer than 120 games.

If the hall hasn't demanded a full decade of excellence from all of its current members, why should future candidates be held to such an arbitrary standard? Cooperstown should open its doors to any player who is capable of attracting support from three-quarters of the voters, no matter how long (or short) his career.

The **five-season retirement rule** seems equally unnecessary. Babe Ruth was elected to the hall in 1936, just a year after his final at-bat. Joe DiMaggio, Carl Hubbell, and Mel Ott spent only three years as retirees before being inducted, back when restrictions were looser than today's. Immediate waivers were granted to Lou Gehrig after the onset of his fatal illness and Roberto Clemente after his death in a plane crash.

The voters didn't require five years of detailed study and rumination before electing these six superstars. Their brilliance was undisputed. Just look at their quality scores, all solidly in the excellent range. Only one of these early arrivals finished below seventy-eight on the QS scale—Clemente at sixty-nine points—and his career was cut short while he was still batting at a .300 clip.

Six players received votes from more than 98 percent of the writers during the past quarter-century. What purpose was served by making Nolan Ryan, George Brett, Cal Ripken Jr., Ken Griffey Jr., Mariano Rivera, and Derek Jeter cool their heels for five years after hanging up their cleats? What new information about their careers was unearthed during those half-decades? You know the answers.

The **5 percent threshold** was instituted in 1979 to clear deadwood from the ballot. It proved to be overly effective, not only removing minor candidates, but often wiping out contenders who were promising, yet slow-blooming.

This side effect was entirely predictable. Ninety-three players had been inducted during the three decades (1949-1978) prior to the threshold's implementation. Precisely one-third of those candidates—thirty-one—received fewer than 5 percent of the BBWAA's votes at some point during the thirty-year span, yet all of them joined the plaque gallery in due course. Twenty-six eventually took the committee route, but the other five gradually accumulated the votes of 75 percent of the writers. Luke Appling, for instance, started with 0.8 percent and 1.2 percent support in his first two elections. He was approved by the BBWAA a decade later. Ralph Kiner made a fifteen-year trek from 1.1 percent in 1960 to 75.4 percent in 1975.

If the 5 percent threshold had existed in their time, Appling and Kiner would have been wiped from the BBWAA's ballot the very first year. That's precisely what happened to third baseman Ron Santo, who was disqualified after his 1980 debut at 3.9 percent. A small group of writers campaigned persistently for Santo's reinstatement, arguing that a player of his quality deserved another chance. The hall capitulated in 1985, restoring Santo and another ten eliminated players to the ballot. Santo finally earned his place in Cooperstown in 2012. (Two of his reinstated colleagues, Dick Allen and Curt Flood, might possibly be inducted by the Era Committee in the 2020s.)[31]

No lesson was learned from this debacle. The hall has opted to retain the 5 percent threshold, even after it temporarily derailed another pair of eventual Hall of Famers, Ted Simmons and Harold Baines.

An enormous **eligibility window for BBWAA elections**—twenty-five years—was implemented in 1957. This rule stipulated that a candidate would join the ballot five years after the end of his playing days, and he would remain on it for a quarter-century, unless (of course) he was inducted in the meantime. An unsuccessful contender wouldn't be transferred to the Veterans Committee's purview until he had completed thirty years of retirement.

The hall's officials eventually came to consider this window too generous, so they trimmed it to fifteen years as of 1963. And that remained its length until July 2014, when it was shortened to ten years, effective in 2015.

I have already cited the rationale advanced by Jeff Idelson, the hall's president at the time, but it bears repeating. "It's become evident, especially over the past thirty years or so," said Idelson, "that the likelihood of election after ten years is incredibly minimal."[32]

Which is absurd, of course. A dozen players—not an insignificant number—clawed their way through eleven elections (or even more) before securing the writers' approval. Bill Terry (1954), Rabbit Maranville (also 1954), and Bert Blyleven (2011) reached 75 percent on their fourteenth attempts. Red Ruffing (1967) and Jim Rice (2009) needed fifteen years apiece. Dazzy Vance (1955) finally broke through in his sixteenth election.[33]

The real reason for the shortened window was transparent. The hall wished to rid itself as quickly as possible of Barry Bonds, Roger Clemens, and other alleged steroid abusers. "Deadlines are a good thing," BBWAA president LaVelle Neal III said in defense of the change.[34] That's true to a point, of course, but a deadline that is too short will inevitably force the elimination of worthy candidates. Ten years is too short.

It's time to jettison all of these rules, thresholds, and floors.

Here's a streamlined process that has logic in its favor: Every player will become eligible for the ballot twenty years after his first big-league game. Every manager, executive, or umpire will qualify for consideration twenty years after the beginning of his professional involvement with baseball.

It doesn't matter if a prospective candidate is still active. If he reaches his twentieth anniversary, he will automatically become eligible for the hall. Albert Pujols would have qualified on April 2, 2021, the day he started his twenty-first year in the big leagues, thereby putting him in line for 2022's ballot. We know—*everybody* knows—that Pujols is destined for Cooperstown. Imagine the excitement if he were elected to the hall while still playing for the Cardinals. The benefits to baseball are obvious, the harm is nonexistent. Was the hall injured when an inducted manager, Tony La Russa, returned to the dugout with the White Sox in 2021? Of course not.

Eligibility will be open-ended. If the Selection Committee wants to debate the merits of Ross Barnes or Bobby Mathews, a couple of solid players whose careers ended before 1890, it will be free to do so. If it wishes to consider active veterans who have reached the twenty-year mark, it can do it. Anybody who was connected to major-league baseball for at least twenty years—no matter when—will swim in the pool of possibilities.

But we can't conduct an open vote on the thousands of players, managers, executives, and umpires who are theoretically eligible. The result would be chaos. That's why a screening subcommittee will be assigned the task of nominating a maximum of twenty candidates for each annual election.

Recent Hall of Fame ballots have contained as many as thirty-seven names, even though relatively few were serious contenders. The 2019 election, for example, featured thirty-five candidates. Nineteen received less than 10 percent support; eleven didn't draw any votes at all. The subcommittee will avoid such sideshows. It will nominate only those candidates who possess strong credentials, taking care to encompass a wide range of positions and eras.

Each year's ballot will be constructed anew. If a contender falls just short of induction, the subcommittee might allow him a return engagement the following year, though it will not be required to do so. The panel also will be allowed to reinstate a candidate to the ballot after a hiatus of one or several years.

4. Broader Reach

THE HALL OF FAME EXHIBITED an early willingness to induct men who had made diverse contributions to baseball's development. This open spirit reached full flower in 1938, when the Centennial Commission honored Alexander Cartwright and Henry Chadwick for achievements beyond the playing field.

Cartwright was hailed as the "father of modern baseball" for codifying the game's rules in 1845 and spreading the gospel of baseball to the West Coast and Hawaii, a resumé that might have been padded just a touch. "The fullness of his contribution to the game's origins remains one of baseball's greatest mysteries," wrote historian Monica Nucciarone.[35] Yet Cartwright retains the distinction of being one of the first two inductees not celebrated for a career as a player, manager, or league president. The other was his 1938 classmate, Chadwick, a journalist who was credited with creating the box score and compiling baseball's first rulebook.

The Centennial Commission made an additional pair of esoteric choices in 1939, tapping Al Spalding for being an "organizational genius" and Candy Cummings for inventing the curveball. Spalding probably deserved induction for his success as a pitcher, though the commission seemed to be equally impressed with the eponymous sporting-goods firm he founded after his playing days.[36] Cummings never would have made it to Cooperstown without his innovation. Other pitchers claimed to have devised the curve, but the *Sporting News* settled the dispute. "The preponderance of proof would seem to be in Cummings's favor," it ruled.[37]

The Hall of Fame thereafter refrained from making such unusual choices. Cartwright remains the only honoree who was enshrined as a founding father, Chadwick the only journalist, Spalding the only entrepreneur, Cummings the only pitch inventor. Every inductee after 1939 was voted into the hall solely because of his or her record as a player, manager, club or league executive, or umpire.

That doesn't mean the hall has been totally oblivious to contributions of other sorts. Its first postwar attempt to broaden its scope was unveiled in 1946. The idea behind the Honor Rolls of Baseball, according to Ken Smith, was to salute "representatives from important departments other than actual play." The four Honor Rolls included five managers, eleven umpires, eleven executives, and twelve sportswriters, none of whom had qualified for the main gallery. These thirty-nine men weren't classified as members of the hall, but were placed on a somewhat lower level. (Nine have since been inducted.) The Honor Rolls were widely ridiculed—the *Sporting News* dubbed them the "Array of Almosts"—and completely ignored. Nothing was ever said of them again.[38]

The Honor Rolls were important in only one regard. They constituted the hall's first systematic attempt to honor journalists. Two subsequent efforts were more successful—creation of the J.G. Taylor Spink Award for sportswriters (now known as the BBWAA Career Excellence Award) in 1962 and the Ford C. Frick Award for Broadcasting Excellence in 1978. Seventy-three writers and forty-six broadcasters had received these annual prizes as of 2022.[39]

Winners of these awards, just like the men listed on 1946's Honor Rolls, are technically not members of the hall. But they sit on the platform and make speeches at the induction ceremony, just as the honored players do, and they're treated as equals by many of those players. Peter Gammons, who won the Spink Award in 2004, was rendered virtually speechless when Willie Mays asked him to sign a baseball at that summer's ceremony.

"I'm not a Hall of Fame player," Gammons reminded him.

"You're one of us," Mays replied, "and if you don't sign, I'll kick you in the behind." Gammons quickly scrawled his signature on a ball.[40]

If the great Willie Mays, the oldest living Hall of Famer, believes that the 119 honored writers and broadcasters are full members of Cooperstown's exclusive club, who are we to disagree? So let's make their elevation official.

And let's not stop there. It's time to widen the array of occupations represented on the Hall of Fame ballot. The screening subcommittee, of course, will draw candidates from the usual fields—players, managers, executives, and umpires—but it will also consider writers, broadcasters, scouts, statistical analysts, groundskeepers, agents, and doctors, among other professions.

This expansion—this broadening of the hall's scope—will open the doors to deserving honorees who previously had little or no hope of induction. Let me offer a few suggestions. This isn't a comprehensive list by any stretch of the imagination, just a hint of the various types of contributors who could be included on the Selection Committee's ballot:

• Clyde Sukeforth was the scout who advised Branch Rickey that Jackie Robinson would be the ideal trailblazer to integrate the major leagues. "I consider your role, next to Mr. Rickey's and my wife's—yes, bigger than any other person with whom I came in contact," Robinson later wrote to Sukeforth. The latter, for good measure, was also the scout who discovered Roberto Clemente for the Pittsburgh Pirates.[41]

• Allan Roth served as the Dodgers' statistician from 1947 to 1964, but he is better described as baseball's first sabermetrician, even though the term didn't exist in his heyday. Roth invented the save as a statistical category in 1951, and he devised an eight-part equation in 1954 to measure a player's full worth, a precursor of wins above replacement. Rickey called the formula "the most constructive thing to come into baseball in my memory."[42]

• Bill James advanced Roth's work exponentially. It was James who brought statistical analysis into baseball's mainstream, and it was he who coined "sabermetrics" to name the burgeoning field he inspired. *Time* included James on its 2006 list of one hundred people who were transforming the world, and author Jamie Malanowski later hailed him as "the man who has had the greatest influence on baseball in the last forty years."[43]

• George Toma became known as the "Sultan of Sod" for his stellar work as the head groundskeeper for the Athletics and Royals in Kansas City, always finding ways to give the home team an edge. "He does his damage with a set of gardening tools, not with a bat," the *New York Times* said in 1976. Toma grew to be so famous in his field—pun fully intended—that the National Football League recruited him to prepare the playing surface for each year's Super Bowl.[44]

• Many current owners hate Scott Boras, though his clients dearly love him. Both sides can agree on only one thing: Boras is the most powerful agent in today's game, probably the most powerful ever. He negotiated 13 contracts in excess of $100 million in 2020 alone, according to a *Forbes* study, and he secured a total of $3.2 billion for his clients during that 12-month period.[45]

• A Hall of Fame case can be made for pitcher Tommy John, based partly on his 288 victories over 26 seasons, and partly on the groundbreaking surgery that carries his name. But what about Frank Jobe, the doctor who devised the operation that has saved hundreds of pitching careers? Jobe seems to be a logical candidate for Cooperstown, though he always insisted that his patient's courage was the most important component of the story. "So it's Tommy John surgery," the doctor once said. "And I like the way it sounds, don't you?"[46]

You get the idea. There are dozens of worthy contenders out there in what we might call nontraditional fields. The Selection Committee will have the responsibility of adding these newcomers to the mix, ensuring that the Hall of Fame salutes greatness in all aspects of baseball.

It's essential that these additions be made as efficiently as possible. My proposals will greatly increase the hall's membership, an expansion that could easily overwhelm visitors. If there are five or six hundred plaques, their sheer volume and diversity might prove to be intimidating. If fans can't easily locate their favorite players, why should they even bother going to Cooperstown?

The solution is to divide the inductees into two separate wings. The 268 members honored for their on-field performances will be given their own gallery, known (naturally) as the players' wing. These stars attract most of the hall's tourist traffic, so it makes perfect sense to assemble their plaques in a single hall.

The others will be placed in the contributors' wing, which will initially contain 10 umpires, 22 managers, 40 pioneers/executive, 46 broadcasters, and 73 writers—a total of 191 honorees. Representatives of the other fields cited above will also be welcomed to this gallery.

5. Separate Ratings

HARMON KILLEBREW WAS ONE of baseball's most feared sluggers between the late 1950s and the early 1970s, renowned for his incredible strength. "The homers he hit against us would be homers in any park, including Yellowstone," said Baltimore manager Paul Richards.[47] Killebrew retired in 1975 with 573 home runs, the fifth-highest total at the time.

But the longtime star for the Washington Senators and Minnesota Twins wasn't simply a power hitter. Killebrew also had a finely tuned batting eye, which allowed him to lead the American League four times in walks and once in on-base percentage. He was named the AL's Most Valuable Player in 1969, he finished among the four highest vote-getters for MVP in five other seasons, and he became the first player to be voted an All-Star Game starter at three different positions (first base, third base, and left field).

A first-ballot Hall of Famer, right? Well, no.

Only 22 percent of the players enshrined in the plaque gallery (58 of 268) were admitted in their first year of eligibility. The rest—roughly four of every five—were forced to wait. And Killebrew was among them.[48]

His made his initial appearance on the ballot in 1981, the year that Bob Gibson's ticket was punched. Killebrew finished fourth at 59.6 percent, leaving him sixty-two votes away from induction. Henry Aaron and Frank Robinson were the clear choices in 1982, while Killebrew treaded water in fourth place at 59.3 percent. Brooks Robinson and Juan Marichal pushed to the front of the line a year later. Killebrew was right behind them, though his 71.9 percent support left him twelve votes short of the prize.

It was all incredibly frustrating and difficult to understand, causing Killebrew to utter a mournful complaint that I have previously cited. "I'm not going to hit another home run in my life," he said in 1983. "What I've done is either enough or it isn't enough."[49]

Killebrew finally made it to the plaque gallery in 1984, as everybody knew he eventually would, though his objection remains relevant today. The BBWAA's election system is patently illogical. Requiring the same candidates to compete against each other in a ceaseless cycle—year after year after year—is a pointless exercise. The same adjective can be applied to the hall's habit of delaying candidates who are widely acknowledged to be virtual locks for induction.

But the BBWAA isn't the only guilty party. The committees have been just as bad. Marvin Miller was a fixture on the Veterans Committee's ballots during the first two decades of the twenty-first century, usually facing the same opponents. "The next time they have an election like this, it should only be among the people who didn't appear on this ballot," he said on one occasion. "It's ridiculous to say let's do this again for the people who have been retired for many years and failed to get the necessary votes."[50]

The hall, as it frequently does, waited until Miller was dead before inducting him, an unhappy (and inevitable) byproduct of its monotonous cycle. "It takes them too long to vote on these players," said Edd Roush after he was finally ushered into the plaque gallery in 1962.[51] At least Roush was still among the living when his time came. Several of his predecessors were repeatedly spurned while alive, only to be accepted in the first election after they passed away, including Roger Bresnahan and Jimmy Collins in 1945, Herb Pennock in 1948, Harry Heilmann in 1952, and Rabbit Maranville in 1954.

Purists describe the Hall of Fame's election system as a careful winnowing process, which supposedly provides the "wise, judicious guidance" extolled by Ken Smith.[52] No candidate is admitted until his accomplishments have been carefully compared to a series of eternal benchmarks—that's what we're told—and if several years of study are required, so be it. "Hall of Fame candidates don't compete against each other," BBWAA voter Moss Klein insisted in 1988. "They compete against all-time standards."[53]

That, of course, is nonsense. If Harmon Killebrew had been matched against the commonly accepted definition of a Hall of Famer, he would have been inducted immediately in 1981. But candidates *do* compete against each other, no matter what Klein and other traditionalists might contend. The system required Killebrew to step aside for the likes of Bob Gibson and Henry Aaron. It forced him—for no particular reason—to wait his turn. Hundreds of worthy contenders have done the same.

Enough already. It's time to convert Klein's ideals from empty rhetoric to actual practice. Here's how the new process will work:

• The screening subcommittee will produce a list of twenty candidates, which will be distributed to the ninety-nine voting members of the Selection Committee by mid-November. The ballot will be accompanied by a packet that contains detailed information about every contender. The subcommittee will recruit a variety of experts to participate in a series of online panel discussions, offering different perspectives on the twenty finalists. Voters will be encouraged to watch.

• The ballot, information packet, and panel discussions will be posted on the Hall of Fame's website, making it possible for fans to collectively participate as the Selection Committee's hundredth member.

• Voters will be asked to rate the absolute merits of each candidate separately, in contrast to the current practice of matching all finalists against each other on a relative basis. The ballot will instruct the voter to grade each contender on the four-point scale that is so familiar to students everywhere. A score of four points denotes a candidate who is definitely worthy of induction. Three points, slightly lower in quality, yet still a borderline Hall of Famer. Two, a bit below Cooperstown's standards. One, well off the mark. Zero, not at all deserving of consideration.

• Voters will be encouraged to give their honest assessments of all finalists. No candidate is guaranteed a return trip to the following year's ballot, so it would be foolish for a voter to follow the old practice of downgrading a solid first-time candidate.

• The scores from all one hundred voters—the ninety-nine panel members and the collective vote of the fans—will be averaged for each candidate. Anybody with an average of 3.00 points or better will be admitted to the hall, since 3.00 is the equivalent of 75 percent of the highest possible score. Results will be announced in January, just as they are now.

The hall's previous guidelines prohibited a BBWAA member from voting for more than ten candidates, but the new process will impose no such limits. If a member of the Selection Committee wants to award four-point ratings to all twenty finalists, he or she is free to do so. Nor will there be a maximum number of inductees. The hall welcomed an enormous group of eighteen newcomers without a fuss in 2006, so why should anybody object if eight or ten candidates—or even more—are admitted under this new system?

6. Team Honors

ERIC DAVIS HAD A nice career—17 seasons, 1,430 hits, .269 batting average—though it wasn't sufficiently impressive to pave his way to the Hall of Fame. He received only three votes from BBWAA members in 2007 and dropped off the ballot.

Yet Davis eagerly awaited the election results five years later, and he was excited to learn of Barry Larkin's induction. The two had been teammates on Cincinnati's 1990 world champions, with Davis supplying the power (a team-leading 86 runs batted in) and Larkin the consistency (185 hits and a .301 average). Davis knew that every World Series titlist between 1903 and 1993 was represented (as of 2012) by a player, manager, or executive in Cooperstown, with the sole exception of the 1990 Reds. It pleased him that Larkin would be filling the gap.

"By him going to the Hall of Fame," Davis said happily, "it's like *we* made the Hall of Fame."[54]

Which begs the question: Baseball is a team game, so why does the hall confine itself to individual honorees?

Basketball's shrine, the Naismith Memorial Basketball Hall of Fame, has followed a different path from the start. Its inaugural class of 1959 comprised fifteen individuals and two teams. The latter were the First Team, an informal name for the eighteen students who played the first basketball game in 1891 under the tutelage of James Naismith, the sport's inventor; and the Original Celtics, the first successful professional club, which traveled the country during the 1920s and 1930s. Another ten teams were welcomed to the basketball hall between 1961 and 2022.[55]

This is an example that baseball would do well to emulate. Thousands upon thousands of the tourists who flock to Cooperstown wear the hats and jerseys of their favorite clubs. They're drawn to the hall by the outstanding players honored within, but their excitement would be magnified if baseball's greatest teams were honored, too.

Basketball's hall has admitted an unusual array of teams, including early barnstormers (the All-American Red Heads and Buffalo Germans), noteworthy college squads (Immaculata, Tennessee A&I, Texas Western), a pair of U.S. Olympic teams (1960 and 1992), and the incomparable Harlem Globetrotters. Yet it has opted, for whatever reason, not to include the standout clubs of recent generations. Bill Russell and John Wooden are honored as individuals, but their respective dynasties, the Boston Celtics and UCLA Bruins, have not been inducted.[56]

I suggest a different approach for Cooperstown. Rule 6 prohibits the induction of a player based on accomplishments confined to a single season, and the same restriction should apply to teams. The Hall of Fame, under my system, will honor ballclubs that have sustained a level of excellence for at least three consecutive years.

Teams will be chosen in a separate annual election, though the procedure will be similar to that for individuals. The screening sub-committee will assemble a list of ten nominated clubs, and it will distribute ballots and supporting material to the Selection Committee in mid-January. The same four-point scale will be used, with an average score of 3.00 as the threshold for induction. Results will be announced in late February.

It's tempting to say that the hall should add a third wing for teams, though that seems a step too far. I doubt there's sufficient room or money for such an expansion project in Cooperstown. So let's add the inducted teams to the contributors' wing for now, and we'll see what happens in the future.

I have assembled my own list of thirty possibilities for team honors, based on a formula that I devised to grade every big-league club between 1871 and 2020. It compared each team's regular-season statistics to the norms for its particular league and year in four categories:

Team Ratings

- Winning percentage (30 percent)
- Run differential per game (30 percent)
- Bases per outs (batters, 20 percent)
- Earned-run average (pitchers, 20 percent)

I used standard deviations and z-scores, weighting the four factors according to the percentages above. There's no need to delve into the specifics, but it's important to understand what the results mean. My formula assigned a relative score to each team, indicating the degree to which it was better or worse than the average club of its time. I used those scores to compile top-to-bottom ratings of 3,236 big-league squads over 150 seasons.

Thirty franchises ranked among the top 324 clubs of all time—the very highest 10 percent—for at least three years in a row. Those are the teams that are profiled on the pages that follow. I don't present these ratings as the final word on this subject—not in the least—but I do believe they offer a reasonable glimpse at the clubs that might be worthy of induction.

Each profile includes a team's collective win-loss record and winning percentage for its designated span, as well as its per-game averages of runs scored and allowed. The win-loss record for each particular season is also shown, along with the percentage of all 1871-2020 clubs that the given team outranked. The concluding list of Hall of Famers includes any inductee who played for or managed the team during the span, no matter how briefly.

Some of these thirty entries were truly dominant, while others fell a tiny bit short. But they have two qualities in common: They all played excellent ball for a protracted period, and they all deserve to be included in the Hall of Fame discussion.

1873-1875 Boston Red Stockings

League: National Association
Span: 3 years
Overall record: 166-42, .798
Overall runs per game: 10.82 scored, 5.72 allowed
Individual seasons: 1873 (43-16, 91.50%), 1874 (52-18, 95.43%), 1875 (71-8, 96.01%)
Hall of Famers: Jim O'Rourke, Al Spalding, Deacon White, George Wright, Harry Wright (manager)

The *Boston Journal* rejoiced when the Red Stockings were founded in 1871. "Boston," it exulted, "can now boast of possessing a first-class professional baseball club."[57] The claim proved to be a touch premature.

The team finished second in the National Association's initial season before fashioning a run of four straight pennants. The first championship team fell just short of the threshold at 89.89 percent, but the final three (1873-1875) qualified easily.

1880-1882 Chicago White Stockings

League: National League
Span: 3 years
Overall record: 178-74, .706
Overall runs per game: 6.66 scored, 4.13 allowed
Individual seasons: 1880 (67-17, 98.08%), 1881 (56-28, 99.72%), 1882 (55-29, 97.40%)
Hall of Famers: Cap Anson (manager), King Kelly

Don't be fooled. The Chicago White Stockings were the lineal ancestors of the Cubs, not the White Sox. They swept to three straight National League pennants between 1880 and 1882, led by Cap Anson, their fiery manager and first baseman. The White Stockings' winning percentage of .798 in 1880 remains the single-season record for the American and National Leagues.

1885-1888 St. Louis Browns

League: American Association
Span: 4 years
Overall record: 359-162, .689
Overall runs per game: 6.73 scored, 4.40 allowed
Individual seasons: 1885 (79-33, 96.75%), 1886 (93-46, 99.23%), 1887 (95-40, 95.92%), 1888 (92-43, 93.82%)
Hall of Famers: Charles Comiskey (manager), Tommy McCarthy

They carried different names and played in different leagues, yet the St. Louis Browns of the American Association and the St. Louis Cardinals of the National League were one and the same. Manager Charles Comiskey's Browns won four AA pennants and almost 70 percent of their regular-season games from 1885 to 1888. They skipped to the NL and changed names after the AA folded. Comiskey went on to found the Chicago White Sox.

1891-1893 Boston Beaneaters

League: National League
Span: 3 years

Overall record: 275-142, .659
Overall runs per game: 6.42 scored, 4.97 allowed
Individual seasons: 1891 (87-51, 98.11%), 1892 (102-48, 90.02%), 1893 (86-43, 90.54%)
Hall of Famers: John Clarkson, Hugh Duffy, Joe Kelley, King Kelly, Tommy McCarthy, Kid Nichols, Frank Selee (manager)

Manager Frank Selee stressed the importance of team chemistry, a quality that his Beaneaters possessed in abundance in the early 1890s. "It was my good fortune," Selee said, "to be surrounded by a lot of good, clean fellows who got along finely together."[58] They also won with great regularity, taking three consecutive National League pennants between 1891 and 1893.

1894-1898 Baltimore Orioles

League: National League
Span: 5 years
Overall record: 452-214, .679
Overall runs per game: 7.43 scored, 5.01 allowed
Individual seasons: 1894 (89-39, 96.57%), 1895 (87-43, 96.72%), 1896 (90-39, 98.70%), 1897 (90-40, 96.51%), 1898 (96-53, 96.45%)
Hall of Famers: Dan Brouthers, Ned Hanlon (manager), Hughie Jennings, Willie Keeler, Joe Kelley, John McGraw, Wilbert Robinson

Baltimore's teams were renowned for their feisty spirit and scrappy play during the mid to late 1890s. Umpire John Heydler, who later became president of the National League, accused the Orioles of being "mean, vicious, ready to maim a rival player or umpire."[59] They battled their way to three NL pennants (1894-1896), then finished second in 1897 and 1898. All five of those clubs posted winning percentages above .640.

1909-1911 Philadelphia Athletics

League: American League
Span: 3 years
Overall record: 298-156, .656
Overall runs per game: 4.65 scored, 3.16 allowed
Individual seasons: 1909 (95-58, 92.27%), 1910 (102-48, 97.09%), 1911 (101-50, 95.77%)
Hall of Famers: Home Run Baker, Charles Bender, Eddie Collins, Connie Mack (manager), Eddie Plank

The Philadelphia Athletics moved in 1909 from Columbia Park, a tiny, wooden structure, to Shibe Park, the first big-league stadium constructed of concrete and steel. Manager Connie Mack assembled a roster worthy of his franchise's new palace. The Athletics, who had posted a weak 68-85 record in 1908, soared to second place with 95 victories in 1909. But the best was yet to come —a pair of World Series titles in 1910 and 1911.[60]

1911-1913 New York Giants

League: National League
Span: 3 years
Overall record: 303-153, .664
Overall runs per game: 4.88 scored, 3.51 allowed
Individual seasons: 1911 (99-54, 94.81%), 1912 (103-48, 98.86%), 1913 (101-51, 96.20%)
Hall of Famers: Rube Marquard, Christy Mathewson, John McGraw (manager)

John McGraw had been the Orioles' sparkplug in the 1890s, always ready to lay down a bunt, steal a base, or start a fight. He built the New York Giants in his image, a hustling squad that impressed a fellow field boss. "There has been only one manager, and his name is McGraw," said Connie Mack.[61] The Giants won consecutive National League pennants from 1911 to 1913, yet lost all three World Series.

1923-1925 Kansas City Monarchs

League: Negro National League
Span: 3 years
Overall record: 170-77, .688
Overall runs per game: 6.48 scored, 4.24 allowed
Individual seasons: 1923 (54-32, 92.49%), 1924 (57-22, 97.74%), 1925 (59-23, 90.39%)
Hall of Famers: Jose Mendez (manager), Bullet Rogan

The Monarchs dominated the Negro National League during its first decade as a recognized major league. Kansas City secured six NNL championships between 1920 and 1929, while finishing second in three of the four remaining seasons. The club reached its peak in the stretch from 1923 to 1925, when it won almost 69 percent of its games and outscored opponents by an average of 2.24 runs.

1928-1931 Philadelphia Athletics

League: American League
Span: 4 years
Overall record: 411-198, .675
Overall runs per game: 5.79 scored, 4.27 allowed
Individual seasons: 1928 (98-55, 97.16%), 1929 (104-46, 99.41%), 1930 (102-52, 92.06%), 1931 (107-45, 94.59%)
Hall of Famers: Ty Cobb, Mickey Cochrane, Eddie Collins, Jimmie Foxx, Lefty Grove, Waite Hoyt, Connie Mack (manager), Al Simmons, Tris Speaker

Connie Mack's first Philadelphia dynasty crumbled under financial pressure in 1915. "If you win," he said unhappily, "the players all expect raises." He bartered some of his stars for much-needed cash. Others escaped to the upstart Federal League.[62] But Mack slowly built a new club that was even stronger. The Athletics averaged 102.8 victories per season between 1928 and 1931, winning three American League titles and two world championships along the way.

1934-1939 New York Yankees

League: American League
Span: 6 years
Overall record: 592-321, .648
Overall runs per game: 6.10 scored, 4.30 allowed
Individual seasons: 1934 (94-60, 91.25%), 1935 (89-60, 91.93%), 1936 (102-51, 98.45%), 1937 (102-52, 97.96%), 1938 (99-53, 97.43%), 1939 (106-45, 99.01%)
Hall of Famers: Earle Combs, Bill Dickey, Joe DiMaggio, Lou Gehrig, Lefty Gomez, Joe Gordon, Burleigh Grimes, Tony Lazzeri, Joe McCarthy (manager), Red Ruffing, Babe Ruth

Ten Hall of Famers starred for the Yankees during the final six seasons of the 1930s, including such all-time greats as Babe Ruth (released in 1935), Joe DiMaggio (promoted in 1936), and Lou Gehrig (felled by amyotrophic lateral sclerosis in 1939). The Yanks finished second to the Tigers in 1934 and 1935, then powered their way to four straight world titles. They won sixteen World Series games and lost only three between 1936 and 1939.

1937-1941 Kansas City Monarchs

League: Negro American League
Span: 5 years
Overall record: 198-90, .688
Overall runs per game: 4.12 scored, 2.53 allowed
Individual seasons: 1937 (52-19, 97.37%), 1938 (45-25, 92.98%),
  1939 (46-25, 90.88%), 1940 (30-10, 99.44%), 1941 (25-11, 96.17%)
Hall of Famers: Willard Brown, Andy Cooper (manager), Buck O'Neil,
  Satchel Paige, Bullet Rogan, Hilton Smith, Turkey Stearnes

The Monarchs truly ruled the Negro American League from 1937 to 1941, claiming five consecutive championships. Two of those teams (1937 and 1940) posted winning percentages higher than .730; the others all finished above .620. Kansas City's pitching staff—paced by Hilton Smith and Satchel Paige—allowed only 2.53 runs per game during the half-decade, the stingiest rate for any of the thirty dynasties profiled in this section.

1937-1943 Homestead Grays

League: Negro National League
Span: 7 years
Overall record: 307-124, .712
Overall runs per game: 5.57 scored, 3.32 allowed
Individual seasons: 1937 (45-18, 98.83%), 1938 (41-13, 99.32%),
  1939 (36-19, 96.04%), 1940 (34-19, 90.20%), 1941 (51-22, 91.62%),
  1942 (47-19, 90.26%), 1943 (53-14, 98.24%)
Hall of Famers: Cool Papa Bell, Ray Brown, Ray Dandridge, Leon Day,
  Josh Gibson, Buck Leonard, Willie Wells, Jud Wilson

No big-league club has ever matched the Homestead Grays' level of dominance in the 1930s and 1940s. The Grays, who split their time between home fields in Pittsburgh and Washington, won nine straight Negro National League titles from 1937 to 1945. Homestead's first seven squads ranked above 90 percent in the all-time standings—the longest run of excellence for any franchise—but the 1944 Grays broke the spell by slipping to 85.13 percent.

1941-1943 New York Yankees

League: American League
Span: 3 years
Overall record: 302-160, .654

Overall runs per game: 4.95 scored, 3.61 allowed
Individual seasons: 1941 (101-53, 98.76%), 1942 (103-51, 97.59%), 1943 (98-56, 93.79%)
Hall of Famers: Bill Dickey, Joe DiMaggio, Lefty Gomez, Joe Gordon, Joe McCarthy (manager), Phil Rizzuto, Red Ruffing

The Yankees stumbled to third place in 1940, bringing a sudden end to the 1934-1939 streak noted above. They rebounded with three American League pennants (1941-1943) and two world championships before the wartime draft depleted their roster. St. Louis Browns manager Luke Sewell was stunned by the weak lineup New York fielded in 1944. "Those big bats weren't there," Sewell said. "They were in the army." The Yankees tumbled back to third.[63]

1942-1944 St. Louis Cardinals

League: National League
Span: 3 years
Overall record: 316-146, .684
Overall runs per game: 4.69 scored, 3.07 allowed
Individual seasons: 1942 (106-48, 96.29%), 1943 (105-49, 98.98%), 1944 (105-49, 99.51%)
Hall of Famers: Stan Musial, Enos Slaughter, Billy Southworth (manager)

The St. Louis Cardinals notched 106 wins in 1942—a franchise record—vaulting them two games ahead of the National League's defending champions, the Brooklyn Dodgers. The Cards went on to defeat the Yankees in the World Series. The next two wartime seasons yielded identical 105-49 records, a pair of NL titles, and the 1944 world title. The Cardinals secured the latter crown by defeating St. Louis's other team, the usually hapless Browns.

1951-1953 New York Yankees

League: American League
Span: 3 years
Overall record: 292-167, .636
Overall runs per game: 5.07 scored, 3.76 allowed
Individual seasons: 1951 (98-56, 92.70%), 1952 (95-59, 94.40%), 1953 (99-52, 96.23%)
Hall of Famers: Yogi Berra, Joe DiMaggio, Whitey Ford, Mickey Mantle, Johnny Mize, Phil Rizzuto, Casey Stengel (manager)

No franchise had won more than two consecutive World Series before the Yankees breezed to four (1936-1939). It seemed to be a feat that couldn't be topped. And it wasn't—for fourteen years. A new set of Yanks stormed to five straight championships from 1949 to 1953. The first two squads fell short of the dynasty threshold—86.18 percent (1949) and 87.36 percent (1950)—but the final three were comfortably above.

1956-1958 Milwaukee Braves

League: National League
Span: 3 years
Overall record: 279-183, .604
Overall runs per game: 4.65 scored, 3.71 allowed
Individual seasons: 1956 (92-62, 93.85%), 1957 (95-59, 96.35%), 1958 (92-62, 97.00%)
Hall of Famers: Henry Aaron, Eddie Mathews, Red Schoendienst, Warren Spahn

The Braves boasted an enthusiastic fan base and a core of young stars. They finished a single game behind the National League champion Brooklyn Dodgers in 1956, won two pennants (and one World Series title) the next two seasons, and tied for first place in 1959. "We were sure—everybody in Milwaukee was sure—that we were the superior team," said Henry Aaron.[64] But the budding dynasty collapsed in a play-off loss to Los Angeles.

1956-1958 New York Yankees

League: American League
Span: 3 years
Overall record: 287-175, .621
Overall runs per game: 5.05 scored, 3.76 allowed
Individual seasons: 1956 (97-57, 90.82%), 1957 (98-56, 95.95%), 1958 (92-62, 98.27%)
Hall of Famers: Yogi Berra, Whitey Ford, Mickey Mantle, Phil Rizzuto, Enos Slaughter, Casey Stengel (manager)

The Yankees slipped (ever so slightly) following their 1949-1953 streak of five consecutive world championships. Their ratings fell to 89.24 percent in 1954 (second place in the American League) and 88.59 percent in 1955 (a World Series defeat) before rebounding above 90 percent. New York won three AL pennants and two major-league titles from 1956 to 1958, splitting the final two World Series with the previously mentioned Milwaukee Braves.

1960-1963 New York Yankees

League: American League
Span: 4 years
Overall record: 406-233, .635
Overall runs per game: 4.84 scored, 3.85 allowed
Individual seasons: 1960 (97-57, 93.69%), 1961 (109-53, 97.65%), 1962 (96-66, 95.73%), 1963 (104-57, 93.14%)
Hall of Famers: Yogi Berra, Whitey Ford, Mickey Mantle, Casey Stengel (manager)

The 1959 season went badly for the defending world champions. New York plummeted to third place with a 79-75 record, fifteen games behind the American League champion Chicago White Sox. But the Yankees reverted to form with impressive speed, taking every AL championship between 1960 and 1964, along with World Series trophies in 1961 and 1962. The '64 pennant winner (84.70 percent) didn't rate highly enough to be included in the span above.

1969-1971 Baltimore Orioles

League: American League
Span: 3 years
Overall record: 318-164, .660
Overall runs per game: 4.80 scored, 3.36 allowed
Individual seasons: 1969 (109-53, 99.63%), 1970 (108-54, 99.20%), 1971 (101-57, 99.10%)
Hall of Famers: Jim Palmer, Brooks Robinson, Frank Robinson, Earl Weaver (manager)

The 1969 Orioles seemed unstoppable. They won 109 games, then swept Minnesota in the American League Championship Series. The only remaining obstacle to a world title was the upstart New York Mets, who proved to be more formidable than expected. "They just pitched better than us," Baltimore manager Earl Weaver said glumly after the Mets prevailed.[65] The Orioles rebounded to win the 1970 World Series decisively, then lost the 1971 version in seven games.

1971-1975 Oakland Athletics

League: American League
Span: 5 years
Overall record: 476-326, .594
Overall runs per game: 4.36 scored, 3.48 allowed
Individual seasons: 1971 (101-60, 90.23%), 1972 (93-62, 96.26%), 1973 (94-68, 90.32%), 1974 (90-72, 98.49%), 1975 (98-64, 95.02%)
Hall of Famers: Orlando Cepeda, Rollie Fingers, Catfish Hunter, Reggie Jackson, Tony La Russa, Billy Williams, Dick Williams (manager)

The free-spirited Athletics were united by their dislike of Charlie Finley, the club's irascible, tight-fisted owner. "Finley takes all the fun out of winning," groused Reggie Jackson.[66] Yet the A's nonetheless kept piling up victories. They won five straight divisional titles between 1971 and 1975, capping the span with three consecutive World Series triumphs (1972-1974). The latter streak remains the longest for any club not named the New York Yankees.

1972-1976 Cincinnati Reds

League: National League
Span: 5 years
Overall record: 502-300, .626
Overall runs per game: 4.88 scored, 3.77 allowed
Individual seasons: 1972 (95-59, 91.75%), 1973 (99-63, 93.29%), 1974 (98-64, 90.73%), 1975 (108-54, 99.60%), 1976 (102-60, 97.22%)
Hall of Famers: Sparky Anderson (manager), Johnny Bench, Joe Morgan, Tony Perez

A few dynasties—no more than a handful—are so dominant and colorful that they go down in history with distinctive nicknames. The New York Yankees of the 1930s, a/k/a the Bronx Bombers, are a prime example. Cincinnati's Big Red Machine of the 1970s is another.[67] The Reds hit their stride between 1972 and 1976, averaging 100.4 victories per year. They ended that half-decade with back-to-back World Series triumphs over the Red Sox and Yankees.

1986-1988 New York Mets

League: National League
Span: 3 years
Overall record: 300-184, .620

Overall runs per game: 4.77 scored, 3.74 allowed
Individual seasons: 1986 (108-54, 99.85%), 1987 (92-70, 94.34%),
1988 (100-60, 99.38%)
Hall of Famers: Gary Carter

The 1986 and 1988 versions of the New York Mets were two of the greatest clubs in history, both scoring above 99 percent. The '86 Mets achieved lasting fame by winning 108 games and the World Series. "It was a team that I think typified New York's grit, and the fans took to us," said first baseman Keith Hernandez.[68] The '88 squad was derailed in the seventh game of the National League Championship Series.

1988-1990 Oakland Athletics

League: American League
Span: 3 years
Overall record: 306-180, .630
Overall runs per game: 4.62 scored, 3.63 allowed
Individual seasons: 1988 (104-58, 97.68%), 1989 (99-63, 96.82%),
1990 (103-59, 99.94%)
Hall of Famers: Harold Baines, Dennis Eckersley, Rickey Henderson,
Tony La Russa (manager)

The 1988-1990 Athletics didn't have the panache of their Oakland forerunners from the 1970s, yet they duplicated the earlier generation's feat of reigning as American League champions three years in a row. The key difference was in their World Series records. The A's won three big-league titles from 1972 to 1974, but only one (1989) in the span between 1988 and 1990.

1990-1992 Pittsburgh Pirates

League: National League
Span: 3 years
Overall record: 289-197, .595
Overall runs per game: 4.51 scored, 3.80 allowed
Individual seasons: 1990 (95-67, 95.24%), 1991 (98-64, 98.55%),
1992 (96-66, 91.84%)
Hall of Famers: (none)

This is the twenty-fourth entry on the chronological list of baseball's dynasties—and the very first without a Hall of Fame player. It's a technical distinction, really, since Barry Bonds starred for the Pirates during this stretch, winning the National League's Most Valuable Player

Award in 1990 and 1992. Pittsburgh made it to the NL Championship Series in '90, '91, and '92—only to lose each time.

1991-1993 Atlanta Braves

League: National League
Span: 3 years
Overall record: 296-190, .609
Overall runs per game: 4.52 scored, 3.65 allowed
Individual seasons: 1991 (94-68, 92.33%), 1992 (98-64, 96.69%), 1993 (104-58, 95.52%)
Hall of Famers: Bobby Cox (manager), Tom Glavine, Chipper Jones, Greg Maddux, John Smoltz

Nobody envisioned the Braves as contenders in 1991. They had wallowed below .500 the previous seven seasons, but their new manager, Bobby Cox, swiftly turned them around. "Bobby just had this ability to believe in people," said John Smoltz, who blossomed as a pitcher under Cox.[69] The Braves won a pair of National League pennants in 1991 and 1992—defeating the aforementioned Pirates in both championship series—though a World Series title remained elusive.

1994-1996 Cleveland Indians

League: American League
Span: 3 years
Overall record: 265-153, .634
Overall runs per game: 5.91 scored, 4.64 allowed
Individual seasons: 1994 (66-47, 93.38%), 1995 (100-44, 99.88%), 1996 (99-62, 96.88%)
Hall of Famers: Jack Morris, Eddie Murray, Jim Thome, Dave Winfield

The Indians won the American League Central Division in 1995 by thirty games over Kansas City, still the biggest gap between first- and second-place finishers. A jubilant fan brandished a sign at the division-clinching celebration: "Deal With It, America. Cleveland Indians: Best Team in Baseball."[70] The dream ended with a World Series loss to Atlanta. The '97 Indians, who rated below 90 percent, clawed back to the series, but lost again.

1995-1999 Atlanta Braves

League: National League
Span: 5 years

Overall record: 496-296, .626
Overall runs per game: 4.89 scored, 3.80 allowed
Individual seasons: 1995 (90-54, 95.15%), 1996 (96-66, 94.53%),
1997 (101-61, 99.29%), 1998 (106-56, 99.07%), 1999 (103-59,
93.17%)
Hall of Famers: Bobby Cox (manager), Tom Glavine, Chipper Jones,
Greg Maddux, John Smoltz

The Braves endured a brief hiccup after the triumphant span from 1991 to 1993. Their rating dipped to 87.98 percent in 1994's strike-shortened season, then rebounded above 90 percent the next five years, which is why the great Atlanta clubs of the 1990s have two separate listings. The latter half of the decade featured three World Series appearances, bringing a big-league championship in 1995 and heartbreaks in 1996 and 1999.

1997-1999 New York Yankees

League: American League
Span: 3 years
Overall record: 308-178, .634
Overall runs per game: 5.67 scored, 4.27 allowed
Individual seasons: 1997 (96-66, 98.21%), 1998 (114-48, 99.97%),
1999 (98-64, 96.60%)
Hall of Famers: Wade Boggs, Derek Jeter, Tim Raines, Mariano Rivera,
Joe Torre (manager)

The 1998 Yankees are frequently hailed as the greatest team ever. They won 70 percent of their regular-season games—a total of 114—and 11 of 13 postseason contests. "You were literally shocked if they didn't win," said play-by-play man Michael Kay.[71] New York's 1999 and 2000 squads weren't as good, though they emulated their predecessor by winning world titles. (The 2000 club is excluded from this span because it scored below 90 percent.)

2017-2019 Houston Astros

League: American League
Span: 3 years
Overall record: 311-175, .640
Overall runs per game: 5.38 scored, 3.86 allowed
Individual seasons: 2017 (101-61, 97.13%), 2018 (103-59, 94.13%),
2019 (107-55, 98.02%)
Hall of Famers: (none)

A gigantic asterisk is appended to this entry. Every baseball fan is aware that Houston secured its first world title in 2017 with the help of an elaborate (and illegal) sign-stealing scheme. "That's not playing the game the right way," said former Astros pitcher Mike Fiers, who blew the whistle in 2019.[72] Opponents vehemently agreed, openly questioning Houston's 2017-2019 run of three divisional championships and two World Series appearances.

2017-2020 Los Angeles Dodgers

League: National League
Span: 4 years
Overall record: 345-202, .631
Overall runs per game: 5.14 scored, 3.69 allowed
Individual seasons: 2017 (104-58, 98.33%), 2018 (92-71, 95.98%), 2019 (106-56, 99.69%), 2020 (43-17, 99.91%)
Hall of Famers: (none)

The end of this four-year span is artificial—and premature—because all statistical analysis for this book stopped after 2020. (Anybody playing beyond that season won't be eligible for the Hall of Fame for several years.) Yet the Dodgers kept rolling past the deadline, exceeding 100 regular-season victories in 2021 and 2022. The relevant period here (2017-2020) featured three visits to the World Series—a victory in 2020, losses in 2017 and 2018.

7. Elite Recognition

JOE MORGAN WAS UNFAMILIAR with failure. He tackled—and succeeded at—a variety of baseball-related jobs. Morgan played twenty-two seasons in the big leagues, winning two Most Valuable Player Awards, amassing an excellent quality score (sixty-four points), and entrenching himself as one of the greatest second basemen of all time. He spent two decades at ESPN, serving as an announcer on its primary television crew. He joined the Hall of Fame's board of directors, rising to become its vice chairman.[73]

It's easy to understand why Morgan never seemed to be threatened by the success of others, why he felt comfortable at any gathering of baseball people, why he considered Cooperstown an idyllic place where everybody was equally deserving of respect. "Here," he said expansively, "no player was better than anyone else. We are all peers."[74]

He painted a pleasant picture, though not an accurate one. Most of Morgan's fellow inductees—especially those who failed to match his high level of achievement—were more realistic. They acknowledged that the Hall of Fame's roster has always been stratified, rather than uniform. Listen to these witnesses:

• Sam Rice (1963): "If it were a real Hall of Fame, you'd say [Ty] Cobb, [Tris] Speaker, Walter Johnson, Babe Ruth, Lou Gehrig, and a few others belonged, and then you'd let your voice soften to a mere whisper."[75]

• Earl Averill (1975): "I'm convinced my record speaks for itself and that I was qualified to become a member. Not that I think of myself walking in the light of Babe Ruth, Ty Cobb, or Rogers Hornsby. But then, who else could stand beside those giants?"[76]

• Pee Wee Reese (1984): "I always looked at the Hall of Fame as the DiMaggios, the Cobbs, the Ruths, the Ted Williamses."[77]

• Reggie Jackson (1993): "There's Hall of Famers, and then there's *really* Hall of Famers."[78]

• Bruce Sutter (2006): "It still doesn't sound right to me: Nolan Ryan, Sandy Koufax, and Bruce Sutter. But I guess I'm going to be there with them."[79]

• Jim Kaat (2022): "There's got to be degrees of the Hall of Fame. I think they probably have a back row for me, and I'll wave to those guys up there."[80]

Critics have seized on these statements, citing them to support proposals for the hall's downsizing. Peter Clark, writing in the *Sporting News* in 2002, suggested a drastic cut that would have exiled all but twenty-five members. "The Hall of Fame should be reserved only for the greatest of the great," he insisted.[81] A 2014 *Newsweek* article called for the elimination of any inductee who wasn't a certified legend. "We know who baseball's legends are," wrote John Walters. "They're surnames: Cobb, Speaker, DiMaggio, Feller, Koufax, Gibson, Rose (yes, Rose), Maddux. They're nicknames: Babe, the Iron Horse, Teddy Ballgame, Hammerin' Hank, the Say Hey Kid, the Big Hurt."[82] Everybody else, by implication, was supposed to hit the bricks.

My new system doesn't go as far as Clark or Walters would have liked—don't forget that we've already imposed a general amnesty—but it does recognize the underlying validity of their assertions. Yes, they're right. The Hall of Fame *has* gotten too big. It had 340 members after the 2022 election, and that was before we elevated 119 writers and broadcasters to official status, hiking the total to 459. It's possible that the number of honorees will pass five hundred by 2030.

That leaves us with this dilemma: How can we maintain such a large (and growing) Hall of Fame without eclipsing the radiance of its most brilliant members? How can we properly acknowledge the players at the apex of what Jim Kaat calls the "degrees of the Hall of Fame," ensuring that they don't become lost in the crowd?

The answer can be found in an obscure historical episode that involved academia and its arcane internal politics.

Let me briefly explain. The National Institute of Arts and Letters was founded in 1898. Its stated goal was to promote the "advancement of art and literature" in the United States, though its actual purpose was to serve as an honor society. Two hundred and fifty architects, artists, musicians, and writers were elected as lifetime members. They luxuriated in their status as the nation's intellectual and creative paragons, the outstanding men and women in their chosen fields.[83]

But their excitement faded rather quickly. Many members, according to literary historian Malcolm Cowley, came to believe that two hundred and fifty was simply too big a number. "One of the first arguments was occasioned by the size of the institute," Cowley wrote. "Wasn't it too large to confer enough dignity on its individual members?"[84]

A solid consensus gradually emerged on this ticklish question, with most members agreeing that the institute was insufficiently exclusive. It was simply too big. But advocates understood that a reduction would not be easily accomplished. Expelling honorees was an unthinkable option, given that they possessed lifetime tenure. And nobody was offering to step aside for the benefit of his or her colleagues.

The institute's sharpest minds eventually fashioned a solution. They proposed the creation of a second body, the American Academy of Arts and Letters, which would be restricted to fifty members. All academy members would be drawn from the institute's roster of two hundred and fifty. The chosen fifty would constitute the *crème de la crème*, the highest intellectual echelon in the United States. This new two-tiered system—institute and academy—was implemented in 1904.[85]

Here is a model for baseball to emulate. The Hall of Fame will continue its inexorable growth toward five hundred members and beyond—there's no reason to stop it—but the very best will be elevated to another tier. Exceptional inductees will retain their plaques in the main gallery, while also being welcomed to an exclusive club restricted to the greatest players of all time, known as the Elite 100.

There will be a separate display, of course. I hesitate to recommend the construction of yet another wing—previous proposals in this chapter have already taxed the Hall of Fame's budget and available territory—but the Elite 100 will quickly become the hall's prime attraction. It will definitely need its own space.

The Elite 100 will be confined to players, since they are the stars who draw a large majority of Cooperstown's annual visitors. The Selection Committee will scrutinize the records of all players in the hall—268 at current count—and tap 100 for this ultimate honor. The basic principle is the one that the National Institute of Arts and Letters followed in spinning off the smaller, more exclusive American Academy.

Yet there's also a key difference. Members of the academy received lifetime tenure, but players in the Elite 100 will serve ten-year terms, subject to reelection. (They will retain perpetual membership in the hall itself, regardless of any success or failure at the elite level.) The screening subcommittee will construct the ballot, nominating a group of ten players from a common era and set of positions. The Selection Committee will render its verdict in the early spring, after each voter has designated his five choices. (This will be a straight pick-five-of-ten election, not involving the four-point scale.) The top five vote-getters in each group will be admitted to the Elite 100. Elections for two groups will be conducted simultaneously on a yearly basis.

The initial membership of the Elite 100 will be determined during its first decade, as ten new inductees are added annually. The reelection cycle will begin in the eleventh year, with the incumbents in the first two groups returning to face challengers picked by the subcommittee.

Imagine the excitement that will be stirred by each year's balloting for the Elite 100—the media profiles of great players from the past, the heated debates over their relative merits, the intense anticipation of the election results. The annual enshrinement of ten elite honorees will become an important element of the induction ceremony in July.

I have presumed to simulate these elections, making my own nominations within twenty groups that are detailed on the following pages. I matched the distribution of positional groups to the breakdown of the hall's 268 players:

- Infielders, including catchers: 108 (40 percent)
- Outfielders, including designated hitters: 77 (29 percent)
- Pitchers: 83 (31 percent)

Eight groups, as a result, consist of infielders, while six apiece are allocated to outfielders and pitchers. All of these groups are divided by eras, with the middle year of each player's career serving as a rough guide. First baseman Cap Anson, for instance, entered the major leagues in 1871 and played through 1897, giving him a midpoint of 1884. That qualified him for Group A, which comprises ten infielders with midpoints between 1871 and 1901. (I chose time spans that were roughly equivalent in their distributions of Hall of Famers. The subcommittee, I imagine, will be more subjective when it assigns a span to each group.)

Players elected to the Elite 100 will not be listed as representatives of specific groups. They will installed as peers, very much in the spirit voiced by Joe Morgan. The only purpose of the groups is to guarantee a fair representation of all positions and eras. The Selection Committee will be instructed to consider all of a player's accomplishments, even if he played different positions or extended his career beyond his given span.

Any candidate for the Elite 100, of course, must already be a member of the Hall of Fame. You'll notice that I nominated a few nonmembers, who are indicated by carats (^). They were included because the hall has numerical shortages in given groups, and because I assumed that these contenders might be inducted during the next few years.

So let's take a closer look at my lists of potential candidates for the Elite 100. Players are listed alphabetically within each group. Their names are followed in parentheses by their primary positions and quality scores.

Group A (Infielders, 1871-1901 Midpoints)

Cap Anson (1B, 83)
Jake Beckley (1B, 37)
Dan Brouthers (1B, 86)
Jimmy Collins (3B, 19)
Roger Connor (1B, 77)
George Davis (SS, 51)
Buck Ewing (C, 33)
Bid McPhee (2B, 29)
John Ward (SS, 37)
Deacon White (3B, 47)

Cap Anson, Dan Brouthers, and Roger Connor are clearly deserving of Elite 100 membership. Their skills have long been recognized—all three were enshrined in Cooperstown by 1976—and they stand apart as the only nineteenth-century infielders with quality scores in the excellent range. One minor drawback is that all three were first basemen. Shortstop George Davis and third baseman Deacon White infuse Group A with a touch of positional diversity.

Group B (Infielders, 1902-1925 Midpoints)

Home Run Baker (3B, 49)
Frank Chance (1B, 26)
Eddie Collins (2B, 72)
Nap Lajoie (2B, 90)
John Henry Lloyd (2B, 15)
Rabbit Maranville (SS, 21)
Louis Santop (C, 9)
George Sisler (1B, 42)
Honus Wagner (SS, 98)
Bobby Wallace (SS, 32)

These infielders from the early 1900s don't stack up well. Their average QS (45.4 points) is the second-lowest among all 20 groups. Three contenders are cinches for the Elite 100—the greatest shortstop ever (Honus Wagner) and a pair of outstanding second basemen (Eddie Collins and Nap Lajoie). After that, who knows? Consideration must be given to John Henry Lloyd and Louis Santop, two highly regarded Negro leaguers whose scores were depressed by segregation.

Group C (Infielders, 1926-1936 Midpoints)

Mickey Cochrane (C, 21)
Jimmie Foxx (1B, 85)
Frankie Frisch (2B, 46)
Lou Gehrig (1B, 87)
Charlie Gehringer (2B, 61)
Gabby Hartnett (C, 33)
Rogers Hornsby (2B, 96)
Mule Suttles (1B, 65)
Willie Wells (SS, 77)
Jud Wilson (3B, 46)

This is the first of four groups with more candidates in the excellent range (six) than available slots in the Elite 100 (five). Who should be left out? Certainly not Rogers Hornsby, Lou Gehrig, or Jimmie Foxx, three outstanding hitters with quality scores of eighty-five or better. And not Willie Wells, who earned a QS of seventy-seven in the Negro leagues. That leaves Mule Suttles and Charlie Gehringer to battle for the final spot.

Group D (Infielders, 1937-1951 Midpoints)

Luke Appling (SS, 42)
Roy Campanella (C, 33)
Ray Dandridge (3B, 8)
Josh Gibson (C, 76)
Hank Greenberg (1B, 53)
Buck Leonard (1B, 68)
Johnny Mize (1B, 66)
Pee Wee Reese (SS, 33)
Jackie Robinson (2B, 48)
Arky Vaughan (SS, 57)

Infield talent was a bit sparse in the middle of the twentieth century, as evidenced by this list and the one that follows. Group D's average quality score is 48.4. Only three groups are lower. The obvious selections here are catcher Josh Gibson and first basemen Buck Leonard and Johnny Mize, all above sixty-five on the QS scale. Hank Greenberg and Jackie Robinson are solid choices to join them in the Elite 100.

Group E (Infielders, 1952-1966 Midpoints)

Luis Aparicio (SS, 31)
Ernie Banks (SS, 57)
Yogi Berra (C, 48)
Orlando Cepeda (1B, 46)
Nellie Fox (2B, 29)
Gil Hodges (1B, 15)
Harmon Killebrew (1B, 56)
Eddie Mathews (3B, 60)
Brooks Robinson (3B, 50)
Red Schoendienst (2B, 18)

This is perhaps the weakest group on the Elite 100 ballot. Its average quality score (41.0) is easily the lowest, 4.4 points behind runner-up Group B (45.4). Third baseman Eddie Mathews is the only candidate with an excellent QS, and he barely earned that distinction with a score of sixty. Every other group has at least two players in the excellent range. Group E's top contenders after Mathews are Ernie Banks and Harmon Killebrew.

Group F (Infielders, 1967-1981 Midpoints)

Dick Allen (1B, 54)^
Johnny Bench (C, 60)
Rod Carew (2B, 59)
Carlton Fisk (C, 45)
Willie McCovey (1B, 59)
Joe Morgan (2B, 64)
Tony Perez (1B, 33)
Ron Santo (3B, 40)
Mike Schmidt (3B, 91)
Ted Simmons (C, 28)

Only nine infielders from this period are in the Hall of Fame. Should the Elite 100 ballot for Group F be limited to those nine, or should a tenth candidate be appended? I opted for the latter, adding Dick Allen, who is likely to be welcomed to Cooperstown someday. The group's top contenders are the five with quality scores of fifty-nine points or better:

Mike Schmidt, Joe Morgan, Johnny Bench, Rod Carew, and Willie McCovey.

Group G (Infielders, 1982-1995 Midpoints)

Wade Boggs (3B, 62)
George Brett (3B, 69)
Gary Carter (C, 45)
Barry Larkin (SS, 40)
Paul Molitor (3B, 47)
Eddie Murray (1B, 49)
Cal Ripken Jr. (SS, 64)
Ryne Sandberg (2B, 48)
Ozzie Smith (SS, 40)
Robin Yount (SS, 52)

Let's start with the easy part. Three of Group G's players—George Brett, Cal Ripken Jr., and Wade Boggs—possess quality scores in the excellent range. All three belong in the Elite 100. But the battle for the remaining two slots will be fierce. The group's other seven players are bunched between fifty-two and forty on the QS scale. A decent case could be made for any of them.

Group H (Infielders, 1996-2016 Midpoints)

Roberto Alomar (2B, 31)
Jeff Bagwell (1B, 68)
Craig Biggio (2B, 34)
Derek Jeter (SS, 41)
Chipper Jones (3B, 64)
Mike Piazza (C, 47)
Alex Rodriguez (SS, 85)^
Ivan Rodriguez (C, 40)
Frank Thomas (1B, 62)
Jim Thome (1B, 44)

Alex Rodriguez has been added to Group H's ballot because only nine infielders from recent times have been welcomed to Cooperstown—so far. Others are likely to arrive soon, with Scott Rolen and Todd Helton being real possibilities. Either one would knock Rodriguez off this list. The members of Group H with the best chances of being voted into the Elite 100 are Chipper Jones, Frank Thomas, and the ever-popular Derek Jeter.

Group I (Outfielders, 1871-1908 Midpoints)

Jesse Burkett (LF, 51)
Fred Clarke (LF, 45)
Sam Crawford (RF, 68)
Ed Delahanty (LF, 73)
Hugh Duffy (CF, 38)
Billy Hamilton (CF, 49)
Willie Keeler (RF, 45)
King Kelly (RF, 49)
Jim O'Rourke (LF, 49)
Sam Thompson (RF, 52)

Ed Delahanty and Sam Crawford tower above the other players in this group. Their respective quality scores of seventy-three and sixty-eight points easily outdistance the competition. Who else has a chance to make the Elite 100? Group I's next five players are neck and neck. All have compelling stories, and all fall between fifty-two and forty-nine points in terms of QS. Flip a coin, perhaps?

Group J (Outfielders, 1909-1930 Midpoints)

Oscar Charleston (CF, 80)
Ty Cobb (CF, 90)
Goose Goslin (LF, 43)
Harry Heilmann (RF, 67)
Pete Hill (CF, 7)
Babe Ruth (RF, 90)
Tris Speaker (CF, 85)
Cristobal Torriente (CF, 31)
Zack Wheat (LF, 40)
Hack Wilson (CF, 30)

Many experts acclaim Babe Ruth as the greatest player of all time. Others heap the same praise on Ty Cobb. Dozens of Negro leaguers—and several white scouts—insist that Oscar Charleston was the equal of both. All three should go directly to the Elite 100. Two other members of Group J also carry quality scores above sixty points—Tris Speaker and Harry Heilmann—and they round out the picture nicely.

Group K (Outfielders, 1931-1949 Midpoints)

Cool Papa Bell (CF, 34)
Willard Brown (CF, 59)
Joe DiMaggio (CF, 78)

Chuck Klein (RF, 50)
Joe Medwick (LF, 56)
Mel Ott (RF, 81)
Al Simmons (LF, 63)
Turkey Stearnes (CF, 79)
Paul Waner (RF, 51)
Ted Williams (LF, 89)

Group K, like its predecessor, features five players with excellent quality scores. Which makes things easy, right? That was the case in Group J, whose five QS leaders were clearly the best candidates for the Elite 100. But not here. Ted Williams, Mel Ott, Turkey Stearnes, and Joe DiMaggio surely deserve to be picked. But the fifth man in QS, Al Simmons, is not necessarily superior to Willard Brown or Joe Medwick.

Group L (Outfielders, 1950-1972 Midpoints)

Henry Aaron (RF, 87)
Roberto Clemente (RF, 69)
Al Kaline (RF, 68)
Mickey Mantle (CF, 84)
Willie Mays (CF, 95)
Stan Musial (LF, 87)
Frank Robinson (RF, 85)
Duke Snider (CF, 60)
Willie Stargell (LF, 59)
Carl Yastrzemski (LF, 70)

Group L boasts the deepest talent pool of all. Nine players carry quality scores in the excellent range. The only one who doesn't, Willie Stargell, is a single point short. The average QS (76.4) is the best for any group. So who should be picked? Willie Mays, Henry Aaron, Stan Musial, Frank Robinson, and Mickey Mantle are frontrunners, though a plausible case could be made for any of the other five candidates.

Group M (Outfielders, 1973-1991 Midpoints)

Harold Baines (DH, 23)
Andre Dawson (RF, 53)
Tony Gwynn (RF, 49)
Rickey Henderson (LF, 65)
Reggie Jackson (RF, 65)
Dave Parker (RF, 41)^
Kirby Puckett (CF, 31)

Tim Raines (LF, 34)
Jim Rice (LF, 47)
Dave Winfield (RF, 49)

Only eight outfielders and one designated hitter have been sum-moned to Cooperstown from this span in the late twentieth century. One player not in the hall, Dave Parker, rounds out the ten-man ballot. Group M, which is relatively weak, features only two candidates with quality scores above sixty points: Rickey Henderson and Reggie Jack-son. Both are obvious choices for the Elite 100, as is eight-time batting champ Tony Gwynn.

Group N (Outfielders, 1992-2016 Midpoints)

Barry Bonds (LF, 90)^
Ken Griffey Jr. (CF, 72)
Vladimir Guerrero (RF, 50)
Andruw Jones (CF, 37)^
Kenny Lofton (CF, 39)^
Edgar Martinez (DH, 39)
David Ortiz (DH, 52)
Manny Ramirez (LF, 66)^
Gary Sheffield (RF, 47)^
Larry Walker (RF, 76)

The Hall of Fame includes three outfielders and two DHs of recent vintage, leaving five slots here. BBWAA support for Andruw Jones and Gary Sheffield has exceeded 40 percent, raising hopes for eventual induc-tion. The outlook is murkier for additions Barry Bonds, Kenny Lofton, and Manny Ramirez. Four current Hall of Famers in Group N have quality scores of fifty or better, led by Larry Walker and Ken Griffey Jr.

Group O (Pitchers, 1871-1908 Midpoints)

John Clarkson (SP, 56)
Pud Galvin (SP, 45)
Tim Keefe (SP, 69)
Christy Mathewson (SP, 87)
Kid Nichols (SP, 82)
Old Hoss Radbourn (SP, 42)
Amos Rusie (SP, 55)
Rube Waddell (SP, 59)
Vic Willis (SP, 41)
Cy Young (SP, 86)

Christy Mathewson and Cy Young sailed to Cooperstown in the hall's first two elections. They should be voted into the Elite 100 with similar ease. Another pair of pitchers from baseball's early years—Kid Nichols and Tim Keefe—also boast excellent ratings on the QS scale. The final slot is up for grabs among three pitchers with virtually identical scores: John Clarkson, Amos Rusie, and Rube Waddell.

Group P (Pitchers, 1909-1930 Midpoints)

Pete Alexander (SP, 86)
Mordecai Brown (SP, 51)
Stan Coveleski (SP, 34)
Red Faber (SP, 42)
Bill Foster (SP, 52)
Walter Johnson (SP, 96)
Eddie Plank (SP, 58)
Bullet Rogan (SP, 56)
Dazzy Vance (SP, 67)
Ed Walsh (SP, 59)

Only three members of Group P have quality scores higher than sixty points, the thinnest representation of excellence on any of the six pitching ballots. That trio—Walter Johnson, Pete Alexander, and Dazzy Vance—heads directly to the Elite 100. Five other contenders, including Negro leaguers Bullet Rogan and Bill Foster, are clumped together with scores in the fifties.

Group Q (Pitchers, 1931-1949 Midpoints)

Ray Brown (SP, 57)
Dizzy Dean (SP, 48)
Bob Feller (SP, 70)
Lefty Gomez (SP, 49)
Lefty Grove (SP, 90)
Carl Hubbell (SP, 78)
Hal Newhouser (SP, 54)
Satchel Paige (SP, 73)
Red Ruffing (SP, 44)
Hilton Smith (SP, 49)

Group Q is dominated by four superstars who merit instant admission to the Elite 100. Bob Feller, Lefty Grove, Carl Hubbell, and Satchel Paige carry quality scores of seventy points or greater. But a consensus is unlikely on the fifth and final choice. The remaining six pitchers on this ballot have been squeezed into a thirteen-point envelope, with scores between fifty-seven and forty-four.

Group R (Pitchers, 1950-1972 Midpoints)

Jim Bunning (SP, 53)
Don Drysdale (SP, 51)
Whitey Ford (SP, 54)
Bob Gibson (SP, 74)
Sandy Koufax (SP, 53)
Juan Marichal (SP, 62)
Gaylord Perry (SP, 61)
Robin Roberts (SP, 69)
Warren Spahn (SP, 72)
Hoyt Wilhelm (RP, 50)

The average QS for this midcentury collection is 59.9 points, the worst score for any of the six pitching groups. But don't get the wrong impression. There's still an impressive array of talent here, headed by Bob Gibson and Warren Spahn. Sandy Koufax also seems to be certain of selection. That leaves two available slots for the likes of Whitey Ford, Juan Marichal, Gaylord Perry, and Robin Roberts. Not an easy decision.

Group S (Pitchers, 1973-1991 Midpoints)

Bert Blyleven (SP, 69)
Steve Carlton (SP, 67)
Dennis Eckersley (SP/RP, 61)
Rollie Fingers (RP, 59)
Fergie Jenkins (SP, 68)
Jim Palmer (SP, 57)
Nolan Ryan (SP, 70)
Tom Seaver (SP, 83)
Lee Smith (RP, 60)
Don Sutton (SP, 63)

Eight of the pitchers on Group S's ballot have quality scores of sixty points or better, putting them in the excellent range. Rollie Fingers and Jim Palmer, the two exceptions, are barely off the mark. So who should be picked for the Elite 100? The highest scorers, Tom Seaver and Nolan Ryan, are obvious choices, as is Steve Carlton. The other seven finalists are worthy contenders for the remaining two positions.

Group T (Pitchers, 1992-2016 Midpoints)

Roger Clemens (SP, 90)^
Tom Glavine (SP, 52)
Roy Halladay (SP, 62)
Trevor Hoffman (RP, 77)
Randy Johnson (SP, 89)
Greg Maddux (SP, 82)
Pedro Martinez (SP, 84)
Mike Mussina (SP, 69)
Mariano Rivera (RP, 89)
John Smoltz (SP/RP, 65)

Ballots for recent periods tend to lack a full complement of Hall of Famers, since it takes time for the induction process to fill the ranks. (See Group N for an extreme example.) But that's not a problem here. Group T contains nine pitchers from the twenty-first century who have already been enshrined, plus outsider Roger Clemens. The top candidates for the Elite 100 are Randy Johnson, Greg Maddux, Pedro Martinez, and Mariano Rivera.

8. Character Guidance

Ozzie Smith was an ever-smiling embodiment of humility, always quick to applaud others, always slow to accept praise. Contemporaries hailed him as the slickest shortstop in history—a fielder without peer—yet he expressed doubts. "People who get to see me all the time may say I'm the best, but I don't know," he said. "I've never even had a chance to see some great shortstops like Mark Belanger or Luis Aparicio or Marty Marion."[86]

Few writers shared his reticence. They whisked Smith into the Hall of Fame on his first try in 2002, giving him an overwhelming level of support (91.7 percent). The induction thrilled him, though Smith remained true to his nature. He reminded fans that he and the other Hall of Famers were not perfect individuals, far from it. "Of course, the people that have plaques in there, it's all going to be about the good stuff," Smith said. "But there's some bad stuff, too, and that's for all of us. I think we all have a dark side of our lives."[87]

Several Hall of Famers, Smith not among them, have been shadowed by backgrounds of exceptional darkness, as noted at several points in the previous chapter. Let's wade through Cooperstown's checklist of character flaws—some previously mentioned, some not—with induction dates in parentheses:

• Babe Ruth (1936), the greatest ballplayer of all time, was often asked the secret of his success. "Good, clean living," he always answered with a laugh. The Babe was notorious in the baseball world as a serial philanderer with a seemingly endless capacity for Prohibition-era liquor.[88]

• Several of Ruth's Hall of Fame colleagues were flat-out alcoholics, notably Pete Alexander (1938), Paul Waner (1952), and Hack Wilson (1979). Reporters were baffled when Casey Stengel called Waner graceful, and they asked the manager why he felt the adjective was appropriate. "Because he could slide into second base without breaking the bottle in his hip pocket," Stengel replied.[89]

• Addiction became the unofficial theme of Cooperstown's 2004 ceremony. Both of that year's inductees had battled substance-abuse problems in the early stages of their careers—Paul Molitor with cocaine, Dennis Eckersley with alcohol.[90]

• Wade Boggs (2005) blamed a different form of addiction after a long-standing extramarital affair was revealed. He suggested that his problem might have been an excessive desire for sex. "It's not like I did drugs, or shot someone, or ended up in prison," Boggs said.[91]

• Fergie Jenkins (1991) and Orlando Cepeda (1999) were both arrested on drug charges. Jenkins was detained at Toronto's airport with four grams of cocaine in his luggage. "They weren't mine. They were found in my bag," he said vaguely after a judge granted him an absolute discharge. Cepeda served a ten-month prison sentence in Puerto Rico for smuggling marijuana.[92]

• Rube Waddell (1946) was briefly jailed in 1903 for failing to support his wife financially. He was suspended from the majors twice the same year, once for climbing into the stands to attack a spectator, the other time for skipping out on his team, the Philadelphia Athletics.[93]

• Duke Snider (1980) was sentenced to two years of probation and fined five thousand dollars for income tax evasion. "We're in the world of choice, and I made the wrong choice," he said.[94]

• Kirby Puckett (2001) and Roberto Alomar (2011) were both accused of domestic abuse. Puckett's wife charged him with choking her with a cord and threatening her with a gun. A woman described as a "baseball industry employee" accused Alomar of sexual misconduct.[95]

• Cap Anson (1939) was a virulent racist who spearheaded the drive to segregate the National League in the 1880s. He was, in essence, the father of baseball's color barrier. The N-word was so deeply ingrained in Anson's vocabulary that he even used it in his autobiography.[96]

• Sportswriter Fred Lieb reported that Tris Speaker (1937) and Rogers Hornsby (1942) told him they were members of the Ku Klux Klan. Lieb also suspected Ty Cobb (1936) of being connected to the KKK: "His general attitude toward black fellow citizens and his unreasoning dislike for the Church of Rome and its hierarchy clearly made him eligible for Klan membership."[97]

• Speaker and Cobb were accused of conspiring to fix a game in September 1919. The case eventually landed on the desk of the commissioner, Kenesaw Mountain Landis, who cleared them both. But historian Lowell Blaisdell came to a different conclusion after digging through the records in 2005. "Unless all the indicators, the clues, and the hints are misleading," he wrote, "Cobb and Speaker, though exonerated, were probably guilty."[98]

• The irascible Hornsby showed no respect for the rulebook. "You've got to cheat," he wrote in 1961. "I know if I had played strictly by the rules, I'd have been home feeding my bird dogs a long time ago instead of earning a good living in baseball."[99] Hornsby was an inveterate gambler, eventually running up such huge debts at the racetrack that his farm was forced into foreclosure.[100]

• Gaylord Perry (1991) was far from alone in his reliance on the spitball—a pitch that had been banned in 1920—though he was unusually proud of the connection. He titled his autobiography *Me and the Spitter.* "I reckon I tried everything on the old apple, but salt and pepper and chocolate sauce topping," he admitted.[101]

These sins vary in intensity. Some are clearly reprehensible; others might be considered forgivable. The degree of tolerance depends on the beholder, and most BBWAA members have proven to be very tolerant indeed. That's why every single player listed above remains a member in good standing of the Hall of Fame, no matter the severity of his transgressions.

The hall has issued only a couple of pronouncements on character issues. The first was its 1944 adoption of Rule 5, which vaguely implored voters to consider each candidate's "integrity, sportsmanship, [and] character," among other factors.[102] The second was its 1991 edict barring Pete Rose from membership.

Wayward behavior has surfaced as a minor issue in several BBWAA elections, including the very first. The failure of two frontrunners to receive unanimous support in 1936 was widely attributed to their personal flaws. "Ruth and Cobb may have failed in the character test," as sportswriter John Kieran put it.[103] But the C-word never became a significant factor during the hall's first fifty-five years. Rule 5 never prevented an otherwise worthy contender from entering the plaque gallery.

Pete Rose presented a special case. Rose gambled on the Cincinnati Reds while serving as their manager, a direct violation of major-league rules. He was slapped with a lifetime suspension in August 1989, two and a half years before he was scheduled to appear on the Hall of Fame ballot. The hall's board subsequently acted to prevent Rose's debut, voting in February 1991 to bar him (and any other permanently ineligible player) from consideration.[104]

Cooperstown slipped back into peaceful repose for twenty years or so. It didn't confront another character issue of truly serious dimensions until 2013, when alleged steroid abusers Barry Bonds and Roger Clemens made their way to the ballot. The debate over performance-enhancing drugs has continued at a fevered pitch ever since.

The hall, which acted so swiftly in Rose's case, offered no help at all to voters ensnared in the PED controversy. I've already cited a 2022 *New York Times* interview with Josh Rawitch, the hall's president, but his quote bears repeating. "Once you try to start giving guidance on character in one instance, you probably have to start giving it in all instances," he said. "We just think it's far more important to leave that up to the electorate, whether that's the BBWAA or the Era Committees, because it means something different to every person."[105]

That's called passing the buck.

Character has become too big an issue to be handled in such a cavalier manner. The time has come for the Hall of Fame's leaders to cut through the confusion and demonstrate leadership. These are the necessary steps:

• Pete Rose's hall eligibility will be restored.

• Selection Committee members will be instructed to assess a candidate's on-field accomplishments, but not his character, when voting for the Hall of Fame.

• Those same committee members will be allowed to take character into account, if they wish, when voting for the Elite 100.

Rose's ineligibility, to be blunt, is absolutely senseless. Yes, he violated a rule and, yes, he should have been suspended for a time. But an eternal ban is ridiculous, especially in light of baseball's current eagerness to cozy up to online gambling services.

The National Football League faced an identical problem in 1963, when investigators discovered that star players Paul Hornung and Alex Karras were regularly betting on NFL games. Commissioner Pete Rozelle suspended them indefinitely, a ban he lifted eleven months later. "This is a move that can be applauded with the same fervor as his original action," *New York Times* columnist Arthur Daley wrote of the reinstatement. "The commissioner proved his point and hammered home a stunning object lesson. There was no need for its continuance."[106]

Anybody who ever threw a game—like Shoeless Joe Jackson (quality score of forty-four points) or Eddie Cicotte (thirty-six points)—deserves to be permanently barred from baseball's Hall of Fame. But Pete Rose was totally unlike the notorious Black Sox. He always bet on his own team, and he always tried to win. He belongs in Cooperstown. Paul Hornung and Alex Karras, after all, were both enshrined in the Pro Football Hall of Fame. The world did not stop spinning.

The issue of performance-enhancing drugs is trickier.

Ballplayers and other athletes have always been intrigued by the mysteries of chemistry. Pud Galvin, who pitched between 1875 and 1892, reportedly consumed an elixir made from monkey testicles. Babe Ruth allegedly injected himself on at least one occasion with an extract from sheep testicles. It's unknown if either of these Hall of Famers received the testosterone boost he was hoping for.[107]

Drugs of greater effectiveness made their way into baseball clubhouses after World War II, as documented by a pair of players who doubled as authors. Jim Brosnan joked in his 1960 bestseller, *The Long Season*, about the importance of "nine-inning pills" for starting pitchers.[108] Jim Bouton dealt with the subject of amphetamines more directly in 1970's *Ball Four*, using their popular nickname at the time: "Greenies are pep pills—dextroamphetamine sulfate—and a lot of baseball players couldn't function without them."[109]

Stronger PEDs reportedly hit baseball in the 1970s, though athletes in other sports had been experimenting with them since the middle of the twentieth century. Russian weightlifters reportedly began taking anabolic steroids around 1954. The first documented doping case in the Olympics occurred in 1960, when a Danish cyclist died after being injected with roniacol. "Danish sports have been dragged down into the mud by criminal cheaters in cycling," wailed a Copenhagen newspaper.[110]

Olympic officials were slow to recognize the danger, and the same was true of their baseball counterparts. Steroid abuse in the major leagues was an open secret by the 1990s. "All you all knew," Tony Gwynn said to reporters in 2007. "We knew. Players knew. Owners knew. Everybody knew. And we didn't say anything about it."[111]

Mark McGwire, who set a new record with seventy home runs in 1998, lied and equivocated for twelve years before admitting PED use. "It's something I'm certainly not proud of," he said in 2010. "I'm certainly sorry for having done it." Other high-profile suspects, notably Bonds and Clemens, adamantly denied all accusations. They were never suspended, and their criminal records were clean. (Barry Bonds's 2011 conviction on a charge of obstruction of justice was overturned in 2015.)[112]

It's tempting to shut Cooperstown's doors to any candidate who ever used PEDs, or was overwhelmingly suspected of having done so. "The game of baseball has no place for cheaters," said Henry Aaron. "There's no place in the Hall of Fame for people who cheat."[113] But avowed cheater Rogers Hornsby is already in the plaque gallery, and so are several players who experimented with earlier forms of chemical assistance. Who knows how much their careers were helped—if at all—by testicular elixirs or amphetamines?

It's similarly impossible to know who really used steroids—absent a confession—or what benefits the users might have received. BBWAA members tacitly acknowledged this point when they began inducting players who had been the subjects of unconfirmed PED rumors, including Mike Piazza (2016), Jeff Bagwell (2017), Ivan Rodriguez (2017), and David Ortiz (2022).

The Hall of Fame's mission statement lays out three aims: "preserve the sport's history, honor excellence within the game, and make a connection between the generations of people who enjoy baseball."[114] It says nothing about protecting the purity of the sport, which is why so many miscreants reside comfortably within its gallery.

Members of the Selection Committee should not attempt to be private investigators, pharmaceutical analysts, or public ethicists—three jobs they are totally unqualified to fill. They should confine themselves to the hall's mission of honoring excellence. They should base their assessments of candidates on what is reliably known about those players—namely, their records. Former commissioner Fay Vincent, who was decidedly old school on many issues, stands with the newer generation on this one. "Bonds and Clemens may not have been saints, but they were great players," he said. "Pretending anything else is hypocrisy."[115]

So yes, all of baseball's outstanding players should be enshrined in the Hall of Fame. But it's important to remember that a higher honor, the Elite 100, has been added to the structure. The hall's ethical standards have varied widely—extremely loose for decades, rather tight these days—resulting in the strange gaps that currently plague its membership. The Elite 100 must avoid such inconsistency.

Selection Committee members will be given a choice. They will be permitted to take character into account when electing players to the elite chamber, or they will be allowed to ignore the C-word as a factor. The Elite 100 will be baseball's highest honor, so it seems reasonable to give greater latitude to the voters who are responsible for choosing the winners. But committee members must pledge to conduct their character analysis in a uniform manner. If they opt to bar PED users, they should also be willing to vote against racists, domestic abusers, cheaters, and other malefactors.

It will be interesting to see what choices they make.

9. Updated Look

DAVID ORTIZ WAS NO DIFFERENT from other baseball fans. He found the hall's plaque gallery to be an awe-inspiring place.

Ortiz paid his first visit to Cooperstown on May 2, 2022, almost three months prior to his induction ceremony. He donned the appropriate uniform—a Hall of Fame cap and jersey—and made his way through the exhibits. He enjoyed privileges that would never be extended to the average tourist, including a chance to heft the bat that Ted Williams used to hit his final home run in 1960.

But the gallery was the highlight of Ortiz's visit. He paused when he reached the entrance, taking a moment to gaze at the 333 bronze plaques neatly arrayed in marble-columned alcoves along the side walls and semicircular back wall. Each plaque was secured to a marble backing board by small screws with heads shaped like baseballs. The backing, in turn, was affixed to oak walls soaring more than twenty feet to a series of skylights.

"This is like a dream come true, to be honest with you," Ortiz finally said. "I still can't believe it. It's gonna take me a minute to get there. This is it. This is it." He examined the plaques of friends and contemporaries: Pedro Martinez, Juan Marichal, Vladimir Guerrero, Frank Thomas, Kirby Puckett. He lingered in front of the space for Puckett, whom Ortiz had met as a prospect with the Minnesota Twins. "That was my guy," he said brokenly, wiping his eyes.

Ortiz gradually made his way to the spot reserved for him. His plaque wouldn't be hung until induction week, but the backing board was already in place. He scrawled his signature on a portion of the marble that would eventually be covered. "Man, it has been a long road," he said. "This is my first time ever being in this room, and when you walk around, you get goosebumps."[116]

Who could possibly find fault with such an amazing place?

Well, if we're going to be honest, there are a few long-standing problems that need to be addressed.

The first is the erratic quality of the plaques themselves. The *Sporting News* began complaining as early as 1936, three years before the hall opened its doors. The plaques for the original five inductees had already been prepared, and the newspaper groused about "an unfortunate lack of consistency" in their wording. Babe Ruth's plaque hailed him as the "greatest drawing card in [the] history of baseball," though it said little about his accomplishments. Walter Johnson's plaque called him the "fastest ball pitcher in [the] history of [the] game," but devoted only two sentences to his magnificent twenty-one-year pitching career.

The *Sporting News* called for fewer adjectives and greater detail. "Perhaps it would be just as well to omit the superlatives and the flowers and confine the citations to simple statements of facts, instead of calling one individual the 'greatest of all' and ignoring the greatness of others," the paper said. The editorial suggested that future players were likely to exceed the records set by the first inductees, rendering the initial descriptions inaccurate.[117]

Some of the early listings were maddeningly vague. Connie Mack was still managing when he was inducted in 1937. This is what his thirty-word plaque said then—and still says today: "A star catcher, but famed more as manager of the Philadelphia Athletics since 1901. Winner of 9 pennants and 5 world championships. Received the Bok Award in Philadelphia for 1929." Mack's catching career and civic prize, which had no impact on his induction, weren't worth mentioning. His pennants and world titles were greatly important, of course, but the plaque said nothing of Mack's all-time records for managerial wins and losses or his key role in establishing the American League. An update after his retirement in 1950 would have been useful.

Sixteen men were admitted to the Hall of Fame in its first three years, 1936 to 1938. The average length of their plaque descriptions was just 30.7 words. Nap Lajoie received the shortest shrift, only twenty-two words to summarize twenty-one seasons of excellence. Even Morgan Bulkeley received greater coverage—twenty-four words—and he hadn't accomplished a single thing.

The hall has rotated its approach 180 degrees since those early days of excessive superlatives and rigid brevity. Plaques of recent vintage are crammed with bureaucratic phraseology and copious statistics. Harold Baines, for example, is described as a "respected and clutch left-handed hitter whose professional approach and humble demeanor made him one of the most consistent and reliable players of the 1980s and 1990s." That's a twenty-six-word sentence—exceeding Lajoie's entire plaque—and there are sixty-two more words after that. The typeface used for Baines's description is so small and compact that some fans find it difficult to read.

Baines was among sixteen honorees who entered the hall between 2018 and 2020, matching the total for 1936-1938. The average text length for the newer group was 94.7 words, roughly triple the average of 30.7 words for the original inductees. A similar degree of inflation can be seen in a comparison of the plaques for the five commissioners in the gallery. Their years of induction are in parentheses:

- Kenesaw Mountain Landis (1944): 25 words
- Ford Frick (1970): 19 words
- Happy Chandler (1982): 38 words
- Bowie Kuhn (2008): 81 words
- Bud Selig (2017): 102 words

Landis was allotted one word for each of his twenty-four years as commissioner, with one additional word as a bonus. Selig's description is four times longer. The text on his plaque is so tightly squeezed that it's nearly illegible.

This generational disparity does not extend to the upper half of each plaque, the place where each member's portrait is displayed. Old and new inductees have suffered equally at the hands of the hall's artists. Many of the bronze images of legendary players—not all, but a surprisingly large number—are remarkably unlike their photographs.

Just take a walk through the gallery. A grim, bloated Babe Ruth stares bleakly as you pass by. Christy Mathewson's face is unexpectedly fleshy for such a trim athlete. Tris Speaker appears to be a heavy middle-aged man, not a fleet outfielder. Cy Young looks to be aged and dour. Joe DiMaggio bares his teeth as if he senses a foul odor. Faces purported to be those of Mickey Mantle, Sandy Koufax, Bob Gibson, and Marvin Miller are virtually unrecognizable.

An additional peculiarity is evident in several instances. Some players are depicted in caps with unexpected logos, others in hats without any identifying marks.

The Hall of Fame prefers to link an inductee to a single team whenever possible, even if he starred for two franchises or even more. Gary Carter and Andre Dawson respectively believed that they had played their best ball for the New York Mets and Chicago Cubs, yet the hall portrayed both in Montreal Expos caps. "Here I am, representing this team as a Hall of Famer," Carter said unhappily in 2003, "and we don't know where their future is."[118] (It turned out to be in Washington, where the Expos relocated in 2005.) Reggie Jackson, Dave Winfield, Vladimir Guererro, and Wade Boggs were other honorees whose hat choices were widely discussed before the hall issued its final edicts.

A few Hall of Famers have avoided controversy by donning blank caps. Catfish Hunter, Greg Maddux, and Tony La Russa prospered with multiple franchises. They didn't express preferences for their hats, and the hall let them slide. La Russa, who had managed the Chicago White Sox, Oakland Athletics, and St. Louis Cardinals, explained his neutrality as a conscious decision, attributing his induction to "the totality of the success of each of those teams."[119]

The plaque gallery—despite its shortcomings—still manages to project a sense of majesty, as David Ortiz discovered during his tour. But several improvements must be made. Here is the plan of attack:

• Plaques for players will be grouped in one wing, as noted in a previous part of this chapter. Other contributors will be placed in a separate gallery.

• Plaques will be redesigned. They will have a fresher appearance, using photos instead of sculpted images. The text will be livelier, more expressive, and solidly based in fact. Descriptions for different honorees will be of similar length.

• The ideal plaque design will be sufficiently large to include more than one picture, allowing a mixture of action photos and head shots. If an inductee played a prominent role with multiple clubs, there will be space to represent them.

• Plaques will be produced for the 119 writers and broadcasters who are being elevated to official status.

• Separate plaques, perhaps of a larger size, will be designed for the clubs that are inducted. The extra space will allow the display of team photos.

There is one final question to address: What about the Elite 100?

Membership in Cooperstown's most exclusive gallery will be the highest possible honor for any Hall of Famer, a distinction that must be reinforced by its display. Plaques would be too pedestrian, too reminiscent of the players' and contributors' wings. The one hundred honorees deserve something greater, which is why they will be immortalized in small busts.

Let's hope the hall's artists do a better job than they did on the plaques.

Toward the Centennial

THOUSANDS OF HALLS OF FAME dot the American landscape, celebrating national, regional, and local excellence in a myriad of fields, occupations, and sports. They span the alphabet from the Alabama Jazz Hall of Fame, Burlesque Hall of Fame, Candy Hall of Fame, and Disc Golf Hall of Fame to the Television Academy Hall of Fame, United States Figure Skating Hall of Fame, Vocal Group Hall of Fame, and Women in Aviation International Pioneer Hall of Fame.

All of these organizations share a common godfather, Henry Mac-Cracken, who served as chancellor of New York University more than a century ago. MacCracken was the driving force behind America's very first hall, which he conceived to honor the nation's preeminent artists, authors, educators, inventors, politicians, scientists, and soldiers. The

Hall of Fame for Great Americans conducted its first election in 1900 and established itself on the Bronx campus of NYU.

"Hall" was actually a misnomer, since MacCracken's brainchild was an outdoor colonnade, previously described in the second chapter of this book. Its setting along the Harlem River—and the busts of honorees lining its walk—attracted a steady stream of tourists from the start. Its elections and installation ceremonies were heavily covered by newspapers across the country. The hall was accepted with surprising rapidity as an institution of national significance.

MacCracken had good reason to be satisfied. "It is, by itself, a most delightful memorial to great Americans—not only in its architecture and the names inscribed, but also in the surpassing landscape which it commands throughout its five hundred feet of length," he wrote happily. The Hall of Fame for Great Americans seemed to be perfectly situated for long-term prominence.[120]

Other fields paid tribute to MacCracken's creation by copying it. Ford Frick admitted that the idea for the National Baseball Hall of Fame popped into his head as he strolled through the Bronx colonnade.[121] It was the first of thousands of imitations. "If athletes could have their own halls of fame, why couldn't cowboys, policemen, businessmen? Today they do, in Oklahoma City, Miami Beach, and Chicago, respectively," wrote author Richard Rubin.[122]

MacCracken's concept remains as popular today as ever, with dozens of fledgling halls joining the ranks each year. But his prototype has not been as fortunate. The Hall of Fame for Great Americans, despite its early success, has lapsed into disrepair and irrelevance.

Its decline was evident as early as 1970, when its latest election went virtually unnoticed. The imperious Robert Moses, the former economic-development czar of New York City, voiced his dismay. "The truth is that this shrine is neglected," he wrote in 1971. "Meanwhile, the National Baseball Hall of Fame at Cooperstown, an out-of-the-way place, attracts immense crowds."[123] It was a distressing comparison for him to make, given his disdain for spectator sports.

Moses was a man of action. He had been directly responsible for the construction of 7 major bridges, 15 expressways, 658 playgrounds,

20,000 acres of parks, and 148,000 apartments during his reign as New York's chief developer between 1924 and 1968.[124] He now exhorted New York University—and the public at large—to save the Hall of Fame for Great Americans, a challenge that he posed as a question: "Is there no one sufficiently interested in the makers of our America to provide a Westminster Abbey to celebrate them, at least as significant, attractive, and inspiring as a waxworks dedicated to muscle-bound gladiators?"[125]

The answer was no.

NYU abandoned its Bronx campus in 1973, selling it to the City University of New York, which located a community college on the site. Funding for the hall of fame dwindled to a trickle after the sale, as did the flow of tourists. No elections were held after 1976. The busts of four of the final inductees were never commissioned. Hopes were briefly rekindled by restoration efforts in the 1990s, but deterioration soon regained the upper hand.

The Cultural Landscape Foundation added the Hall of Fame for Great Americans to its list of "at-risk landscapes" in 2018. The preservation group reported that MacCracken's beloved structure had been ravaged by "water damage, pollutants, and the effects of weathering," while the colonnade had been discolored by "deep stains from biological contaminants," a polite term for bird droppings. The hall remains open to visitors to this day, though hardly anybody ever comes—and, indeed, nobody really cares.[126]

This sad story is not offered as a prediction; it does not imply a direct link between the Bronx and Cooperstown. But it does serve as a cautionary tale. The Hall of Fame for Great Americans once enjoyed remarkably robust health. It took its prominence for granted, it failed to keep pace with the times, and it eventually paid the price. Halls of fame may promise eternal glory, but they are not guaranteed eternal life.

The National Baseball Hall of Fame and Museum would seem to be fairly well-situated. Its elections continue to draw wide media coverage. Its induction ceremonies still attract thousands of fans. Its plaque gallery remains a year-round tourist attraction.

But clouds are gathering over Cooperstown, as we have discussed throughout this book. Baseball has lost its central place in the nation's heart. The Hall of Fame has become more a subject of controversy than an object of veneration. The plaque gallery has failed to adequately convey the greatness of its inhabitants or the excitement of the game they played.

The nine-point plan outlined in this chapter offers a way for the hall to retool itself. The sooner the process can be started, the better. A pair of centennials are on the horizon: 2036 (one hundred years since the hall's first election) and 2039 (a century since its grand opening). It would be ideal if all of the proposed changes—the Selection Committee, the separate galleries for players and contributors, the inductions of great teams, the Elite 100—could be implemented by then.

Baseball has been in the doldrums, but recent rule changes offer hope. The major leagues are finally facing their shortcomings; they are finally laying the groundwork for a renaissance. The shrine in Cooperstown must do the same.

Bill James has been correct about so many things during his long career as a baseball analyst and historian. His 1995 warning, cited earlier in this chapter, was especially prescient. If the Hall of Fame doesn't seriously address its problems, he predicted, "something else will come along and push them aside."[127]

The danger is real. The time for action is now.

Notes

1. January

1. Zev Chafets, *Cooperstown Confidential: Heroes, Rogues, and the Inside Story of the Baseball Hall of Fame* (New York: Bloomsbury, 2009), pp. 5-6.

2. *2022 National Baseball Hall of Fame Announcement*, MLB Network, January 25, 2022, 4:00 p.m. (EST); Kyle Eustice, "Public Enemy's Chuck D Preps MLB Network for 2022 Hall of Fame Election," *HipHopDX* (January 25, 2022).

3. Tyler Kepner, "Knowing Score if Hall Voters Pitch a Shutout," *New York Times* (January 25, 2022); Jon Tayler, "Manny Ramirez Opens Up on PED Suspensions, Wants to Return to Baseball," *Sports Illustrated* (March 13, 2014).

4. "Hall of Fame Election Requirements," Baseball Writers' Association of America; Chafets, *Cooperstown Confidential*, p. 49.

5. Jeff Schultz, "Hank Aaron Was Right," *The Athletic* (January 25, 2022).

6. Bob Nightengale, "Two Greatest Players of Steroid Era Left Out," *USA Today* (January 26, 2022).

7. Chafets, *Cooperstown Confidential*, p. 49.

8. David Gordon, "Racial Parity in the Hall of Fame," *Baseball Research Journal* (Fall 2018).

9. Tyler Kepner, "Putting Baseball's Racism in Context," *New York Times* (December 22, 2020).

10. *2022 Hall of Fame Announcement*, MLB Network, 4:01 p.m. (EST).

11. *Ibid.*, 4:02 p.m. (EST).

12. *Ibid.*, 4:03 p.m. (EST).

13. "A Timeline of MLB's Drug-Testing Rules," *USA Today* (March 28, 2014); Nightengale, "Two Greatest Players," *USA Today*.

14. Michael Schmidt and Duff Wilson, "Steroid Report Implicates Top U.S. Baseball Players," *New York Times* (December 14, 2007).

15. Ira Berkow, "Bonds Arrives Under Cloud of Scandal," *New York Times* (February 24, 2004).

16. Jack Curry and Duff Wilson, "Clemens Strongly Denies Allegations by His Ex-Trainer," *New York Times* (December 19, 2007).

17. Steve West, "Barry Bonds," Society for American Baseball Research; Frederick Bush, "Roger Clemens," Society for American Baseball Research.

18. G. Scott Thomas, *The Best (and Worst) of Baseball's Modern Era: The Top (and Bottom) Teams and Players From 1961 Through 2016* (Buffalo: Niawanda), p. 230.

19. Mark Faller, "It's End of the Line for Barry Bonds, Roger Clemens on Baseball Hall of Fame Ballot," *Arizona Republic* (January 7, 2022).

20. Bill Shaikin, "Barry Bonds Didn't Make the Hall of Fame. Get Over It," *Los Angeles Times* (January 25, 2022).

21. Tyler Kepner, "Immortals on a Pedestal, Many With Feet of Clay," *New York Times* (January 27, 2022).

22. Kepner, "Knowing Score," *New York Times*.

23. *2022 Hall of Fame Announcement*, MLB Network, 5:48 p.m. (EST).

24. Connie Mack, *My 66 Years in the Big Leagues: The Great Story of America's National Game* (Philadelphia: John C. Winston, 1950), p. 107.

25. Jay Jaffe, *The Cooperstown Casebook: Who's in the Baseball Hall of Fame, Who Should Be In, and Who Should Pack Their Plaques* (New York: Thomas Dunne Books, 2017), p. ix.

26. Chafets, *Cooperstown Confidential*, pp. 5-6.

27. *2022 Hall of Fame Announcement*, MLB Network, 6:15 p.m. (EST).

28. James Vail, *Outrageous Fortune: What's Wrong with Hall of Fame Voting and How to Make it Statistically Sound* (Jefferson, North Carolina: McFarland & Co., 2001), p. 34.

29. Benjamin Hoffman, "Before Robinson, There Was Fowler," *New York Times* (December 7, 2021).

30. Joe Posnanski, "The Outsiders: No. 1, Minnie Minoso," *The Athletic* (January 26, 2021).

31. Dan Hayes, "Twins Celebrate Cooperstown 'Getting Things Right,'" *The Athletic* (December 7, 2021).

32. John Leo, "Housecleaning Plan for the Hall," *New York Times* (January 24, 1988).

33. Tyler Kepner, "Passed-Over Greats of the Game Elected to the Hall of Fame," *New York Times* (December 6, 2021).

34. *2022 Hall of Fame Announcement*, MLB Network, 6:18 p.m. (EST).

35. *Ibid.*, 6:20 p.m. (EST).

36. *Pardon the Interruption*, ESPN, January 26, 2022, 5:38 p.m. (EST).

37. Michael Schmidt, "Ortiz and Ramirez Said to Be on '03 Doping List," *New York Times* (July 30, 2009).

38. Tom Verducci, "Integrity Still Matters for the Hall of Fame," *Sports Illustrated* (January 25, 2022); Hayden Bird, "David Ortiz Was Asked About the Reported 2003 PED Test Following His Hall of Fame Election," *Boston Globe* (January 26, 2022).

39. Richard Sandomir, "Hall Cuts Window for Election by 5 Years," *New York Times* (July 27, 2014).

40. Jayson Stark, "What Kind of Hall of Fame Do We Want to Have?" *The Athletic* (January 27, 2022).

41. Tom Westerholm, "David Ortiz Voted Into Baseball Hall of Fame," *Boston Globe* (January 25, 2022).

42. *2022 Hall of Fame Announcement*, MLB Network, 7:05 p.m. (EST).

43. Tom Westerholm, "Barry Bonds, Former Players Congratulate David Ortiz on Hall of Fame Vote," *Boston Globe* (January 25, 2022).

44. Nick Selbe, "Roger Clemens on Not Getting Voted Into Hall of Fame," *Sports Illustrated* (January 25, 2022).

45. *2022 Hall of Fame Announcement*, MLB Network, 7:59 p.m. (EST).

46. "History of the Museum," National Baseball Hall of Fame and Museum.

47. Kepner, "Immortals on a Pedestal," *New York Times*.

48. Joseph Durso, "Robinson, Marichal Gain Hall," *New York Times* (January 13, 1983).

49. Chafets, *Cooperstown Confidential*, p. 194.

50. Dave Kindred, "The Right to Vote," *Sporting News* (January 24, 2000).

51. *2022 Hall of Fame Announcement*, MLB Network, 4:01 p.m. (EST).

2. Yardsticks

1. Doug Simpson, "The Earl of Snohomish," Society for American Baseball Research.

2. Michael Strauss, "Averill Assails Hall of Fame Selectors," *New York Times* (August 19, 1975).

3. Dave Anderson, "Ruffing is Named to Baseball Hall of Fame in Special Runoff Election," *New York Times* (February 17, 1967).

4. Bill James, *Whatever Happened to the Hall of Fame?: Baseball, Cooperstown, and the Politics of Glory* (New York: Fireside, 1995), p. 71.

5. "LPGA Hall of Fame Criteria," Ladies Professional Golf Association; "LPGA Announces Changes to LPGA Hall of Fame Criteria," Ladies Professional Golf Association (March 29, 2022).

6. "LPGA Hall of Fame History," Ladies Professional Golf Association; Lisa Mickey, "Inbee Park's Up-and-Down Year," *New York Times* (September 14, 2016).

7. James, *Whatever Happened*, pp. 74-75.

8. Tom Verducci, "Remembering the Fame of the Baseball Hall," *Sports Illustrated* (December 6, 2021).

9. Tyler Kepner, "Baseball Rights a Wrong by Adding Negro Leagues to Official Records," *New York Times* (December 16, 2020).

10. Bill Ryczek, "Why the National Association Was a Major League," Society for American Baseball Research.

11. "Cap Anson," National Baseball Hall of Fame and Museum.

12. "Cap Anson," Baseball Reference.

13. "BBWAA Election Rules," National Baseball Hall of Fame and Museum.

14. James, *Whatever Happened*, p. 77.

15. "Don Drysdale," Baseball Reference.

16. Warren Corbett, "Milt Pappas," Society for American Baseball Research; Joseph Durso, "Follies of Hall of Fame Balloting," *New York Times* (January 28, 1979).

17. Joseph Durso, "Koufax, Berra, and Wynn Are Voted Into Baseball's Hall of Fame," *New York Times* (January 20, 1972).

18. G. Scott Thomas, *Leveling the Field: An Encyclopedia of Baseball's All-Time Great Performances as Revealed Through Adjusted Statistics* (New York: Black Dog & Leventhal, 2002), p. 9.

19. Tim Kurkjian, "How the 'K' Became the Most Destructive Letter in Major League Baseball," ESPN.com (May 19, 2021).

20. David Schoenfield, "How Much Has Baseball Really Changed Over the Years?" ESPN.com (January 28, 2019).

21. Thomas, *Leveling the Field*, p. 11.

22. "Park Factor," *Total Baseball: The Official Encyclopedia of Major League Baseball* (New York: Total Sports, 1999), pp. 2532-2533.

23. G. Scott Thomas, *A Brand New Ballgame: Branch Rickey, Bill Veeck, Walter O'Malley, and the Transformation of Baseball, 1945-1962* (Jefferson, North Carolina: McFarland & Co., 2022), pp. 194-195.

24. Duke Snider and Bill Gilbert, *The Duke of Flatbush* (New York: Zebra, 1988), pp. 201-202.

25. "Caught on the Fly," *Sporting News* (February 20, 1936).

26. Ray Dandridge oral history, National Baseball Hall of Fame and Museum; Ray Dandridge oral history, University of Kentucky Special Collections Research Center.

27. George Vecsey, "Ray Dandridge, the Hall of Fame, and 'Fences,'" *New York Times* (May 10, 1987); G. Richard McKelvey, *Mexican Raiders in the Major Leagues, 1946* (Jefferson, North Carolina: McFarland & Co., 2006), p. 45.

28. John Holway, "Dandy at Third: Ray Dandridge," *National Pastime* (1982).

29. Robert Peterson, *Only the Ball Was White* (Englewood Cliffs, New Jersey: Prentice-Hall, 1970), p. 74.

30. Thomas Kern, "John Henry 'Pop' Lloyd," Society for American Baseball Research.

3. Elections

1. Zev Chafets, *Cooperstown Confidential: Heroes, Rogues, and the Inside Story of the Baseball Hall of Fame* (New York: Bloomsbury, 2009), pp. 26-27; James Mallinson, "A.G. Mills," Society for American Baseball Research; Jay Jaffe, *The Cooperstown Casebook: Who's in the Baseball Hall of Fame, Who Should Be In, and Who Should Pack Their Plaques* (New York: Thomas Dunne Books, 2017), pp. 29-30.

2. William Guilfoile, "Why Cooperstown?" Society for American Baseball Research.

3. Ken Smith, *Baseball's Hall of Fame* (New York: Grosset & Dunlap, 1970 revised), pp. 33-34, 45-47.

4. "Why Not a Memorial to Game?" *Sporting News* (May 31, 1934).

5. Chafets, *Cooperstown Confidential*, p. 29; "Stephen C. Clark, Art Patron, Dead," *New York Times* (September 18, 1960).

6. Ford Frick, *Games, Asterisks, and People: Memoirs of a Lucky Fan* (New York: Crown, 1973), pp. 201-203.

7. Victor Danilov, *Hall of Fame Museums: A Reference Guide* (Westport, Connecticut: Greenwood, 1997), pp. 17-20; Henry Mitchell MacCracken, "The Hall of Fame," *American Monthly Review of Reviews* (November 1900); Richard Rubin, "The Mall of Fame," *Atlantic* (July 1997).

8. Chafets, *Cooperstown Confidential*, pp. 32-34; Bill James, *Whatever Happened to the Hall of Fame?: Baseball, Cooperstown, and the Politics of Glory* (New York: Fireside, 1995), p. 34.

9. Arthur Daley, "Baseball Pageant Thrills 10,000 at Game's 100th Birthday Party," *New York Times* (June 13, 1939).

10. Connie Mack, *My 66 Years in the Big Leagues: The Great Story of America's National Game* (Philadelphia: John C. Winston, 1950), p. 116.

11. Smith, *Baseball's Hall of Fame*, p. 19.

12. *Ibid.*, p. 15.

13. Frick, *Games, Asterisks, and People*, pp. 196-199.

14. Richard Sandomir, "In Cooperstown, A Baseball Author Is Also the Manager," *New York Times* (July 25, 2014).

15. Arthur Schlesinger Jr. and Fred Israel, editors, *History of American Presidential Elections, 1789-1968* (New York: Chelsea House, 1971), volume 1, p. 4.

16. James, *Whatever Happened*, p. 31; James Vail, *Outrageous Fortune: What's Wrong With Hall of Fame Voting and How to Make it Statistically Sound* (Jefferson, North Carolina: McFarland & Co., 2001), pp. 18-19.

17. "Ty Cobb Achieves Highest Niche in Modern Baseball Hall of Fame," *New York Times* (February 3, 1936).

18. John Kieran, "A Probe of the Baseball Balloting," *New York Times* (February 4, 1936).

19. James, *Whatever Happened*, p. 33.

20. Michael Haupert, "William Hulbert and the Birth of the National League," *Baseball Research Journal* (Spring 2015); Donald Dewey and Nicholas Acocella, *The Ball Clubs: Every Franchise, Past and Present, Officially Recognized by Major League Baseball* (New York: HarperCollins, 1996), pp. 256-257.

21. "Lajoie, Speaker, Cy Young Named for Baseball Hall of Fame," *New York Times* (January 20, 1937).

22. Jan Finkel, "Pete Alexander," Society for American Baseball Research.

23. Ray Zardetto, *'30: Major League Baseball's Year of the Batter* (Jefferson, North Carolina: McFarland & Co., 2008), p. 59.

24. Frick, *Games, Asterisks, and People*, p. 76.

25. James Lincoln Ray, "Lou Gehrig," Society for American Baseball Research.

26. "Scribes Honor Gehrig," *Sporting News* (December 14, 1939); "Writers Move to Place Gehrig in Hall of Fame," *New York Times* (December 8, 1939).

27. James, *Whatever Happened*, pp. 38-40.

28. John Drebinger, "Hornsby Enters Baseball Hall of Fame," *New York Times* (January 21, 1942).

29. Bill James, *The New Bill James Historical Baseball Abstract* (New York: Free Press, 2003), p. 486.

30. Danny Peary, *We Played the Game: 65 Players Remember Baseball's Greatest Era, 1947-1964.* (New York: Hyperion, 1994), p. 195.

31. Rogers Hornsby and Bill Surface, *My War With Baseball* (New York: Coward-McCann, 1962), p. 248.

32. Dan Daniel, "Landis Named to Hall of Fame," *Sporting News* (December 14, 1944); John Drebinger, "Baseball Pays Tribute to Landis by Picking Him for Hall of Fame," *New York Times* (December 11, 1944).

33. "Landis Leaves Lasting Monument," *Sporting News* (November 30, 1944).

34. Shirley Povich, "Griffith Favors 'Outside Man," *Sporting News* (November 30, 1944).

35. Bruce Watson, "The Judge Who Ruled Baseball," *Smithsonian* (October 2000).

36. David Pietrusza, *Judge and Jury: The Life and Times of Judge Kenesaw Mountain Landis* (South Bend, Indiana: Diamond, 1998), p. 388.

37. "National Intercensal Tables: 1900-1990," United States Census Bureau.

38. Watson, "Judge Who Ruled Baseball," *Smithsonian.*

39. Albert "Happy" Chandler oral history, University of Kentucky Special Collections Research Center.

40. Frederick Lieb, "Ten More Old-Time Stars Added to Game's Shrine," *Sporting News* (May 3, 1945); James, *New Historical Baseball Abstract,* pp. 377-379.

41. Alex Semchuck, "Wilbert Robinson," Society for American Baseball Research.

42. "BBWAA Election Rules," National Baseball Hall of Fame and Museum.

43. Arthur Daley, "Into the Hall of Fame," *New York Times* (December 4, 1945).

44. Jack Bales and Tim Wiles, "Franklin P. Adams's 'Trio of Bear Cubs,'" *Nine* (Spring 2011).

45. Paul Staudohar, "Tinker to Evers to Chance: Poetry in Motion," *Nine* (Fall 2005).

46. Frick, *Games, Asterisks, and People,* p. 21.

47. Chafets, *Cooperstown Confidential,* p. 40.

48. "Hall of Fame Committee Invites Criticism," *Sporting News* (May 2, 1946).

49. Jaffe, *Cooperstown Casebook,* p. 51; "Voting Rules History," National Baseball Hall of Fame and Museum; Roscoe McGowen, "Hubbell, Frisch, Cochrane, Grove Named to Baseball's Hall of Fame," *New York Times* (January 22, 1947).

50. Dan Daniel, "Four Voted in Hall of Fame by Less Than Half of BBWAA," *Sporting News* (January 29, 1947).

51. "Herb Pennock Dies; Starred for Yanks," *New York Times* (January 31, 1948).

52. Roscoe McGowen, "Pennock, Traynor Into Hall of Fame," *New York Times* (February 28, 1948).

53. "Hall of Fame Poll is Divided Widely," *New York Times* (February 12, 1949); "Brown and Nichols Gain Hall of Fame," *New York Times* (May 9, 1949).

54. "All Fall Short in Hall of Fame Vote," *Sporting News* (February 22, 1950).

55. "Another Hall of Fame Stalemate," *Sporting News* (March 1, 1950).

56. "Baseball Typical of 4 Freedoms, Says Ford Frick at Cooperstown," *New York Times* (July 25, 1950); Dick Conners, "Cooperstown's Top Crowd Sees New Wing Dedicated," *Sporting News* (August 2, 1950).

57. J.G. Taylor Spink, "Big Poison Pounds on Door of Shrine," *Sporting News* (February 7, 1951).

58. "Two Worthy New Members of Shrine," *Sporting News* (February 7, 1951).

59. Dan D'Addona, "Harry Heilmann," Society for American Baseball Research; John Drebinger, "Heilmann and Paul Waner Named to Baseball's Hall of Fame at Cooperstown," *New York Times* (February 1, 1952).

60. Drebinger, "Heilmann and Paul Waner Named," *New York Times.*

61. Dan Daniel, "Action Sought on Selection of Early Stars," *Sporting News* (February 11, 1953).

62. James, *Whatever Happened,* p. 51

63. Roscoe McGowen, "Dizzy Dean and Al Simmons Named to Baseball Hall of Fame at Cooperstown," *New York Times* (January 22, 1953).

64. Frederick Lieb, "New Veterans Committee Picks Six for Shrine," *Sporting News* (October 7, 1953).

65. Dan Daniel, "Will Terry Make It? Dickey? Maranville?" *Sporting News* (January 13, 1954).

66. Arthur Daley, "Among the Missing," *New York Times* (January 27, 1947).

67. Roscoe McGowen, "Terry, Dickey, and Maranville Are Elected to Baseball's Hall of Fame," *New York Times* (January 21, 1954); Louis Effrat, "Terry and Dickey Inducted Into Hall of Fame," *New York Times* (August 10, 1954).

68. "Voting Rules History," National Baseball Hall of Fame and Museum; John Drebinger, "Joe DiMaggio, Lyons, Vance, and Hartnett Elected to Baseball's Hall of Fame," *New York Times* (January 27, 1955).

69. Dan Daniel, "Select Six Welcomed Into Game's Hall of Fame," *Sporting News* (August 3, 1955).

70. Joseph Sheehan, "DiMaggio Makes Another Hit at Hall of Fame Induction," *New York Times* (July 26, 1955).

71. William Briordy, "Home Run Baker and Ray Schalk Named to Baseball Hall of Fame," *New York Times* (February 1, 1955).

72. Dan Daniel, "Biggest Group Elected to Shrine Since '47," *Sporting News* (February 2, 1955).

73. Carol McMains and Frank Ceresi, "Hank Gowdy," Society for American Baseball Research.

74. Ray Gillespie, "Changes Adopted in Balloting Rules for Hall of Fame," *Sporting News* (July 25, 1956); "Baseball's Hall of Fame Rules Are Changed to Cut Admissions," *New York Times* (July 23, 1956).

75. "Worthy Addition to a Great Group," *Sporting News* (February 13, 1957).

76. Hy Hurwitz, "Hall of Fame Vote Results in First Shutout Since '50," *Sporting News* (February 12, 1958).

77. "Hall of Fame Hoots, Howls," *Sporting News* (February 12, 1958).

78. Arthur Daley, "Without a Welcome Mat," *New York Times* (February 6, 1958).

79. "Hall of Fame Hoots, Howls," *Sporting News*.

80. Joe King, "Zack Wheat Unanimous Hall of Fame Choice," *Sporting News* (February 11, 1959).

81. Hy Hurwitz, "Shrine Shutout May End Ballot Setup," *Sporting News* (February 10, 1960); "Hyman Hurwitz, 56, Dies; Baseball Writers Officer," *New York Times* (May 2, 1966).

82. "Is There a Doctor in the House?" *Sporting News* (February 10, 1960).

83. Richard Sandomir, "A Flawless Swing, But 3 Votes Shy of a Perfect Ballot," *New York Times* (January 7, 2016).

84. Dan Daniel, "Directors of Shrine List Revised Rules on Voting Methods," *Sporting News* (August 24, 1960); "Voting Rule Changed," *New York Times* (August 18, 1960).

85. Dan Daniel, "Vet Group Elects Hamilton, Carey to Shrine," *Sporting News* (February 8, 1961).

86. Hy Hurwitz, "Writers' Ballots Put Feller, Robinson Plaques in Shrine," *Sporting News* (January 31, 1962).

87. "Feller and Jackie Robinson Elected to Baseball Hall of Fame on First Ballot," *New York Times* (January 24, 1962).

88. Arthur Daley, "On Fringe of Immortality," *New York Times* (January 5, 1962); Dave Anderson, "A Fine Piece of Editing in Cooperstown," *New York Times* (June 26, 2008).

89. "Roush and McKechnie Named to Baseball Hall of Fame by Old-Timers Group," *New York Times* (January 29, 1962).

90. Andrew Schiff, "Henry Chadwick," Society for American Baseball Research.

91. David Fleitz, "The Honor Rolls of Baseball," *Baseball Research Journal* (2005); Bob Burnes, "Writers Choose Spink for Dual Honor With New Shrine Award," *Sporting News* (October 20, 1962).

92. Robert Lipsyte, "Baseball's Hall of Fame Inducts Robinson, Feller, McKechnie, and Roush," *New York Times* (July 24, 1962); Dick Conners, "Fans, Game's Brass Hail New Hall of Famers," *Sporting News* (August 4, 1962).

93. "Roush and McKechnie Named," *New York Times*.

94. Peter Clark, "Outta Here," *Sporting News* (January 21, 2002).

95. Jan Finkel, "Eppa Rixey," Society for American Baseball Research; "Rixey Dead at 72; Made Hall of Fame," *New York Times* (March 2, 1963).

96. "Luke Appling, White Sox Shortstop for 21 Years, Named to Hall of Fame," *New York Times* (February 18, 1964).

97. Bill Lamb, "John Montgomery Ward," Society for American Baseball Research.

98. Stuart Banner, *The Baseball Trust: A History of Baseball's Antitrust Exemption* (New York: Oxford University Press, 2013), pp. 6-8.

99. Dan Daniel, "Grimes, Faber, Manush, 3 Others Enter Shrine," *Sporting News* (February 15, 1964).

100. "Vets Group Selects Galvin for Shrine," *Sporting News* (February 13, 1965).

101. Dick Conners, "Ground Broken for Library at Hall of Fame," *Sporting News* (August 7, 1965); Gordon White Jr., "Baseball Honors $300-a-Year Man," *New York Times* (July 27, 1965).

102. "Heroes Should Meet High Standards," *Sporting News* (January 8, 1966).

103. "Vets Committee Adds Lieb; Hall of Fame Rules Change," *Sporting News* (August 14, 1965).

104. Michael Holley, "A Fitting Send-Off for Ted Williams," *Boston Globe* (July 23, 2002).

105. Arthur Daley, "A Triumph for Justice," *New York Times* (January 23, 1966).

106. "New Rules for Shrine Make Rickey and Stengel Eligible," *Sporting News* (February 12, 1966).

107. Joseph Durso, "Stengel Elected to Hall of Fame in Surprise Balloting," *New York Times* (March 9, 1966).

108. Dick Conners, "Ted and Casey Stars of Shrine Show," *Sporting News* (August 6, 1966); Joseph Durso, "Stengel and Williams Inducted Into Baseball Hall of Fame," *New York Times* (July 26, 1966).

109. James Gould, "What Makes Rickey Tick?" *Esquire* (March 1943).

110. Mack, *My 66 Years*, pp. 201-202.

111. "Rightful Honor for Rickey," *Sporting News* (January 8, 1966).

112. "Rickey, Lloyd Waner Tapped for Hall of Fame," *Sporting News* (February 11, 1967).

113. "Shrine Heroes Introduced; Frisch New Veteran Voter," *Sporting News* (August 6, 1966).

114. Dave Anderson, "Ruffing is Named to Baseball Hall of Fame in Special Runoff Election," *New York Times* (February 17, 1967).

115. Joseph Durso, "Medwick, Ruffing, and Campanella Close, but Nobody Attains Hall of Fame," *New York Times* (January 26, 1967).

116. Russell Schneider, "Ruffing Gains Shrine in 'Last of Ninth,'" *Sporting News* (March 4, 1967).

117. Jack Lang, "Board Okays Annual Hall of Fame Voting for Writers' Group," *Sporting News* (October 14, 1967).

118. Lawrence Ritter, *The Glory of Their Times: The Story of the Early Days of Baseball Told by the Men Who Played It* (New York: Macmillan, 1966), p. xvi.

119. Wilfrid Sheed, "Take Me Back to the Ballgame," *New York Times Book Review* (September 18, 1966).

120. Thomas Lask, "Books of the Times: All of It They Saw, Part They Were," *New York Times* (September 17, 1966).

121. Gregory Wolf, "Waite Hoyt," Society for American Baseball Research.

122. "Shrine Heroes Introduced," *Sporting News.*

123. Leo Durocher and Ed Linn, *Nice Guys Finish Last* (New York: Simon and Schuster, 1975), p. 90.

124. Fred Stein, "Frankie Frisch," Society for American Baseball Research; James, *Whatever Happened,* pp. 162-166.

125. "Gone…And Perhaps Forgotten," *Sporting News* (January 9, 1971).

126. Hy Turkin, "Frick Surveys His 'Quiet' First Year as Boss," *Sporting News* (October 1, 1952).

127. Bill Veeck and Ed Linn, *Veeck—As in Wreck* (New York: G.P. Putnam's Sons, 1962), p. 240.

128. Joseph Durso, "Berra Comes Closest, But No Player Gains Enough Votes for Hall of Fame," *New York Times* (January 22, 1971).

129. Joe Falls, "A Salute to Voters," *Sporting News* (February 6, 1971).

130. Daniel Levitt, "George Weiss," Society for American Baseball Research.

131. Jack Lang, "Seven Seniors Enter Hall Via Vet Group's Vote," *Sporting News* (February 13, 1971); "Marquard, 6 Others in Hall of Fame," *New York Times* (February 1, 1971).

132. "Old-Time Negro Stars Get Shrine Boost," *Sporting News* (August 9, 1969).

133. Jules Tygiel, *Baseball's Great Experiment: Jackie Robinson and His Legacy* (New York: Oxford University Press, 1997), p. 27.

134. Arthur Daley, "Ol' Satch Looks Back and Gains," *New York Times* (February 10, 1971).

135. Chafets, *Cooperstown Confidential,* pp. 129-130.

136. Bowie Kuhn, *Hardball: The Education of a Baseball Commissioner* (New York: Times Books, 1987), pp. 109-110; Joseph Durso, "Baseball to Admit Negro Stars of Pre-Integration Era Into Hall of Fame," *New York Times* (February 4, 1971); "Baseball's Front Door Opens to Satchel Paige," *New York Times* (July 8, 1971).

137. Jack Lang, "Sandy, Yogi, Early Make the Grade," *Sporting News* (February 5, 1972).

138. Joseph Durso, "Koufax, Berra, and Wynn Are Voted Into Baseball's Hall of Fame," *New York Times* (January 20, 1972).

139. Joseph Durso, "Gibson and Leonard Gain Baseball's Hall of Fame," *New York Times* (February 9, 1972); Jack Lang, "Gibson, Leonard Win Shrine Spots," *Sporting News* (February 19, 1972).

140. Robert Peterson, *Only the Ball Was White* (Englewood Cliffs, New Jersey: Prentice-Hall, 1970), p. 158.

141. Murray Chass, "Spahn Elected to Hall of Fame," *New York Times* (January 25, 1973).

142. Joseph Durso, "Clemente Is in Hall of Fame," *New York Times* (March 21, 1973).

143. "Enshrinement is Voted for 'Highpockets' Kelly," *New York Times* (January 29, 1973).

144. James, *New Historical Baseball Abstract*, pp. 455-456.

145. "Frisch, One of Baseball's All-Time Stars, Dies at 75," *Sporting News* (March 24, 1973).

146. Bill Johnson, "Jim Bottomley," Society for American Baseball Research.

147. Joseph Durso, "Mantle and Ford Voted Into Hall of Fame," *New York Times* (January 17, 1974).

148. Joseph Durso, "Mick, Slick, and Cool Papa," *New York Times* (August 13, 1974).

149. Michael Strauss, "Averill Assails Hall of Fame Selectors," *New York Times* (August 19, 1975).

150. Joseph Durso, "Kiner Edges Into Hall of Fame," *New York Times* (January 24, 1975).

151. Strauss, "Averill Assails," *New York Times.*

152. John Holway, "Appreciation: Judy Johnson," *Washington Post* (June 25, 1989).

153. John Contois, "Bucky Harris," Society for American Baseball Research.

154. Joseph Durso, "Two Pitchers Voted Into Hall," *New York Times* (January 23, 1976).

155. Jeremy Beer, "Hothead: How the Oscar Charleston Myth Began," *Baseball Research Journal* (Spring 2017).

156. Jack Lang, "Connor, Lindstrom, Hubbard Enter Hall of Fame," *Sporting News* (February 14, 1976).

157. Joseph Durso, "Banks in Baseball Hall of Fame; Hodges, Mathews Fail in Ballot," *New York Times* (January 20, 1977).

158. Charles Faber, "Amos Rusie," Society for American Baseball Research.

159. Peter Bjarkman, "Martin Dihigo," Society for American Baseball Research.

160. Clark, "Outta Here," *Sporting News.*

161. Jack Lang, "BBWAA Threatens Shrine Vote Boycott," *Sporting News* (August 20, 1977).

162. Jaffe, *Cooperstown Casebook*, pp. 57-58; "New Shrine Rules Could Spell Peace," *Sporting News* (October 15, 1977).

163. Jack Lang, "Dihigo and Lloyd Voted Into Shrine," *Sporting News* (February 19, 1977); John Holway, "Shutting the Door on Negro League Stars," *New York Times* (July 31, 1977).

164. Red Smith, "The Last Outcasts," *New York Times* (February 6, 1977).

165. Alex Semchuck, "Addie Joss," Society for American Baseball Research; "New Shrine Rules," *Sporting News*.

166. Joe Marcin, "Mel Allen, Red Barber Share Frick Award," *Sporting News* (August 5, 1978); Michael Strauss, "Hall of Fame Day: It's Baseball's 'Greatest,'" *New York Times* (August 8, 1978).

167. "Pappas Perplexed," *Sporting News* (December 9, 1978); Joseph Durso, "Follies of Hall of Fame Balloting," *New York Times* (January 28, 1979).

168. Jack Lang, "Mays Top Name on Shrine Ballot," *Sporting News* (December 30, 1978).

169. Joseph Durso, "A Legend Named Willie," *New York Times* (August 6, 1979).

170. "BBWAA Election Rules," National Baseball Hall of Fame and Museum.

171. Red Smith oral history, University of Kentucky Special Collections Research Center.

172. Joseph Durso, "Snider and Kaline Elected to Baseball Hall of Fame," *New York Times* (January 10, 1980); Jack Lang, "Shrine Welcomes Willie, Rebuffs the Duke and Eno," *Sporting News* (February 10, 1979).

173. James Lincoln Ray, "Chuck Klein," Society for American Baseball Research.

174. Dewey and Acocella, *Ball Clubs,* pp. 61-62.

175. Mark Armour, "Tom Yawkey," Society for American Baseball Research.

176. "Yawkey and Klein in Hall," *New York Times* (March 13, 1980).

177. Tim Odzer, "Rube Foster," Society for American Baseball Research.

178. Peterson, *Only the Ball*, p. 115.

179. "Mize, Foster Elected to Hall," *New York Times* (March 12, 1981).

180. Joseph Durso, "Gibson Voted to Hall," *New York Times* (January 16, 1981).

181. Dave Anderson, "Nine Votes From Unanimous," *New York Times* (January 14, 1982).

182. Jack Lang, "Hank Settles for 97.8 Percent," *Sporting News* (January 30, 1982).

183. Shirley Povich oral history, University of Kentucky Special Collections Research Center.

184. Albert Chandler and Vance Trimble, *Heroes, Plain Folks, and Skunks: The Life and Times of Happy Chandler* (Chicago: Bonus, 1989), p. 3.

185. Joseph Durso, "Chandler, Jackson to Join Hall," *New York Times* (March 11, 1982).

186. Joseph Durso, "Robinson, Marichal Gain Hall," *New York Times* (January 13, 1983).

187. Jaffe, *Cooperstown Casebook*, p. 236.

188. "Alston, Kell Join Hall of Fame," *New York Times* (March 11, 1983).

189. Durso, "Robinson, Marichal Gain," *New York Times*.

190. James, *Whatever Happened,* p. 301; Jack Lang, "Vets Committee Taps Reese, Ferrell for Hall," *Sporting News* (March 12, 1984).

191. Joseph Durso, "Hall of Fame Picks Reese and Ferrell," *New York Times* (March 5, 1984).

192. "Steinbrenner Impedes Rizzuto," *New York Times* (March 11, 1984).

193. "Rizzuto's Consolation," *New York Times* (March 6, 1984); Stan Isle, "No Consolation Prize for Rizzuto," *Sporting News* (March 19, 1984).

194. Don Zminda and Robert Bigelow, "Nellie Fox," Society for American Baseball Research.

195. Joseph Durso, "Wilhelm, Brock Elected to Hall," *New York Times* (January 8, 1985).

196. Dick Young, "Only BBWAA Has the Authority to Appeal Verdict in Fox Case," *Sporting News* (February 4, 1985).

197. Joseph Durso, "Mays, on First Try, Elected to Hall of Fame," *New York Times* (January 24, 1979); Dave Anderson, "Country's Life Complete Now," *New York Times* (March 7, 1985).

198. "2 Elected to Hall of Fame," *New York Times* (March 7, 1985).

199. Ted Williams and John Underwood, *My Turn at Bat: The Story of My Life* (New York: Fireside, 1988), p. 11.

200. Joseph Durso, "Doerr, Lombardi Make Hall of Fame," *New York Times* (March 11, 1986); Jack Lang, "Glove Men Don't Seem to Fit Cooperstown," *Sporting News* (March 24, 1986).

201. Durso, "Doerr, Lombardi," *New York Times*.

202. Joseph Durso, "Hunter in Hall With Williams," *New York Times* (January 15, 1987).

203. G. Scott Thomas, *The Best (and Worst) of Baseball's Modern Era: The Top (and Bottom) Teams and Players From 1961 Through 2016* (Buffalo: Niawanda, 2016), p. 229.

204. Ira Berkow, "History and Hope Given Their Due at Cooperstown," *New York Times* (July 27, 1987).

205. *Ibid.*

206. "Old-Timers Are Shut Out," *New York Times* (March 2, 1988).

207. "AL East: Yankees," *Sporting News* (March 21, 1988).

208. Moss Klein, "Hall of Fame for Very Best, Not the Very Good," *Sporting News* (January 4, 1988); Dave Anderson, "Blank Ballots By Writers Burn Bunning," *New York Times* (January 14, 1988).

209. Jack Lang, "Was Bunning Blanked?" *Sporting News* (January 25, 1988).

210. Moss Klein, "The Blanks Stop Here: Bench and Yaz for Hall," *Sporting News* (January 9, 1989).

211. Michael Martinez, "Yastrzemski and Bench Voted to Baseball Hall," *New York Times* (January 10, 1989).

212. Carl Lundquist, "Bizarre Balloting," *Sporting News* (February 13, 1989).

213. "Schoendienst and Barlick Voted Into Hall of Fame," *New York Times* (March 1, 1989).

214. Barry Considine, "Hall of Famers," *Sporting News* (March 27, 1989).

215. Klein, "Hall of Fame for Very Best," *Sporting News*.

216. Moss Klein, "Remembering Billy: Excitement Personified," *Sporting News* (January 8, 1990).

217. "Palmer, Morgan Inducted Into Hall," *New York Times* (August 7, 1990).

218. "No Old-Timers Voted Into the Hall of Fame," *New York Times* (February 28, 1990).

219. Murray Chass, "Hall of Fame Panel Moves to Keep Pete Rose Out," *New York Times* (January 11, 1991); Murray Chass, "Board Says Rose is Ineligible for Hall of Fame," *New York Times* (February 5, 1991).

220. Claire Smith, "New Hall of Famers Keep Rose On Minds," *New York Times* (January 10, 1991).

221. Bill Veeck and Gordon Cobbledick, "So You Want to Run a Ball Club?" *Saturday Evening Post* (April 23, 1949).

222. "Veeck Again Shows His Fellow Magnates," *Sporting News* (June 2, 1948).

223. Ira Berkow, "A Rumble in Valhalla," *New York Times* (July 22, 1991).

224. Moss Klein, "Seaver Aces Key Hall Test: He Belongs," *Sporting News* (January 6, 1992).

225. Joe Sexton, "Seaver Marvels at His Latest Stat: 98.8," *New York Times* (January 9, 1992).

226. Joe Sexton, "Seaver in Hall on a Truly Terrific Reception," *New York Times* (January 8, 1992); "For Pure Polling Power, Seaver is No. 1," *Sporting News* (January 20, 1992).

227. Phil Pepe, "Steinbrenner 'Humanism' Won Reggie For Yanks," *Sporting News* (December 18, 1976); Phil Pepe, "Peace Pipe or Exit Sign for Yanks' Martin?" *Sporting News* (July 2, 1977).

228. Murray Chass, "Jackson Makes the Hall of Fame on First Swing," *New York Times* (January 6, 1993).

229. "No Additions to Hall," *New York Times* (February 24, 1993).

230. "Veterans Committee Additions Aid Rizzuto," *New York Times* (August 1, 1993); Mark Newman, "The Other Voters," *Sporting News* (January 24, 1994).

231. "Caught on the Fly: An Artificial Argument," *Sporting News* (August 16, 1993).

232. Robert Thomas Jr., "At Long Last, Rizzuto Makes Hall of Fame," *New York Times* (February 26, 1994).

233. Steve Gietschier, "Covering the Bases in This Era," *Sporting News* (April 11, 1994).

234. Claire Smith, "Carlton Will Enter Hall Alone," *New York Times* (January 13, 1994); Jack Curry, "His Fame Speaks Volumes: Carlton Talks," *New York Times* (January 14, 1994).

235. Dave Kindred, "No One Did It Like Mike," *Sporting News* (January 23, 1995).

236. Bill Brown, "A Dissenting Voice," *Sporting News* (January 23, 1995).

237. Claire Smith, "Schmidt Again Puts Up Big Numbers," *New York Times* (January 10, 1995).

238. Jayson Stark, "A Day Even Philadelphians Will Love," *Sporting News* (July 31, 1995).

239. Claire Smith, "Shutout at Cooperstown: Niekro Leads List of Rejected," *New York Times* (January 9, 1996).

240. Dave Kindred, "Fans, You Have Been Heard," *Sporting News* (August 19, 1996); Ira Berkow, "Bunning Stands on the Bully Pulpit," *New York Times* (August 5, 1996).

241. Zminda and Bigelow, "Nellie Fox," Society for American Baseball Research; Ira Berkow, "The Phone Rings for Fox's Widow," *New York Times* (March 6, 1997).

242. Fred Mitchell, "For the Fox Family, A Day of Joy," *Chicago Tribune* (March 6, 1997).

243. Claire Smith, "Phil Niekro Voted to Hall; Sutton Misses," *New York Times* (January 7, 1997).

244. Thomas Boswell, "Carlton, Sutton: Dissimilar Styles, Similar Results," *Washington Post* (June 28, 1986).

245. Claire Smith, "Hard Work, Hard Times Lifted Sutton and Doby," *New York Times* (July 27, 1998).

246. Jane Leavy, *Sandy Koufax: A Lefty's Legacy* (New York: HarperCollins, 2002), pp. 259-260.

247. Mark Armour, "Lee MacPhail," Society for American Baseball Research; "Lee MacPhail," National Baseball Hall of Fame and Museum.

248. Murray Chass, "Ryan, Brett, and Yount Are Named to the Hall," *New York Times* (January 6, 1999).

249. Richard Justice, "Ryan, Brett, Yount Elected to Hall," *Washington Post* (January 6, 1999).

250. Murray Chass, "No Margin of Error: Cepeda Elected to Hall," *New York Times* (March 3, 1999).

251. Joe Lapointe, "Reverence and the Thrills of Hall of Fame Rookies," *New York Times* (July 26, 1999).

252. Mark Armour, "Orlando Cepeda," Society for American Baseball Research.

253. Peter Schmuck, "Hall of Fame Numbers in Crowd; Record 50,000 See Induction Ceremonies," *Baltimore Sun* (July 26, 1999).

254. Thomas Kern, "Turkey Stearnes," Society for American Baseball Research.

255. Buster Olney, "Fisk and Perez, Rivals in '75, Both Gain Hall," *New York Times* (January 12, 2000).

256. Jack Curry, "Anderson Saunters In as Doors to Hall Open," *New York Times* (March 1, 2000).

257. James, *Whatever Happened*, p. 337.

258. Thomas, *The Best (and Worst)*, pp. 15-17.

259. Chafets, *Cooperstown Confidential*, pp. 92-93; Jaffe, *Cooperstown Casebook*, pp. 58-59.

260. Ira Berkow, "Honor Hits Home for Hall Inductees," *New York Times* (August 6, 2001).

261. Stew Thornley, "Kirby Puckett," Society for American Baseball Research; George Dohrmann, "The Rise and Fall of Kirby Puckett," *Sports Illustrated* (March 17, 2003).

262. Joel Sherman, "Vets Vote Him In, But No Way Maz Deserves Hall," *New York Post* (March 7, 2001).

263. Bill James, "The Hall of Fame's Original Sin," Bill James Online (February 20, 2017).

264. Sherman, "Vets Vote Him In," *New York Post*.

265. Jaffe, *Cooperstown Casebook*, pp. 58-59; Murray Chass, "More Vets Eligible for Hall in Baseball," *New York Times* (August 7, 2001).

266. Peter Schmuck, "Hall Changes How it Picks Its Veterans," *Baltimore Sun* (August 7, 2001).

267. Dave Sheinin, "O. Smith Elected to Hall of Fame," *Washington Post* (January 9, 2002).

268. Jack Curry, "Hall of Fame Welcomes Smith, But Carter is Left on Doorstep," *New York Times* (January 9, 2002).

269. Murray Chass, "Next Stop Cooperstown for Carter and Murray," *New York Times* (January 8, 2003).

270. Rafael Hermoso, "Carter Will Enter Hall of Fame as Expo," *New York Times* (January 17, 2003).

271. Murray Chass, "New, Improved Hall Panel Elects No One," *New York Times* (February 27, 2003).

272. Tyler Kepner, "Molitor and Eckersley Had Their Own Battles," *New York Times* (January 8, 2004); Doug Skipper and Daniel Levitt, "Paul Molitor," Society for American Baseball Research.

273. "What Is Gambling Disorder?" American Psychiatric Association; Pete Rose and Rick Hill, *My Prison Without Bars* (Emmaus, Pennsylvania: Rodale Press, 2004), p. 148.

274. Kepner, "Molitor and Eckersley," *New York Times*.

275. Marc Topkin, "Rays to Celebrate a Blast From the Past: Wade Boggs' Historic Home Run," *Tampa Bay Times* (August 23, 2018).

276. Steve West, "Wade Boggs," Society for American Baseball Research; Bernie Augustine, "Mike Piazza Probably Wants to Go Into the Hall of Fame in a Mets Cap, But if He Doesn't, Blame Wade Boggs," *New York Daily News* (January 7, 2016).

277. Jack Curry, "Boggs Counts Blessings; Sandberg Also in Hall," *New York Times* (January 5, 2005).

278. Dave Anderson, "Committee is Stranding Too Many on Base," *New York Times* (March 3, 2005).

279. Andrea Williams, "A 15-Year Drought for Negro Leaguers in Cooperstown," *New York Times* (September 7, 2021).

280. Murray Chass, "A Special Election for Rediscovered Players," *New York Times* (February 26, 2006).

281. Amy Essington, "Effa Manley," Society for American Baseball Research; Jack Curry, "Woman Among 17 Elected to Hall of Fame," *New York Times* (February 28, 2006).

282. Essington, "Effa Manley," Society for American Baseball Research; Bill Young and Charles Faber, "J.L. Wilkinson," Society for American Baseball Research.

283. Curry, "Woman Among 17," *New York Times*.

284. Ira Berkow, "17 From Black Baseball Included in Hall at Last," *New York Times* (July 31, 2006).

285. Daniel Kramer and Do-Hyoung Park, "Every First-Ballot Hall of Famer in MLB History," MLB.com (January 25, 2022). (Lou Gehrig and Roberto Clemente are not counted as first-ballot honorees because they were chosen in special elections.)

286. "2000-2009," National Baseball Hall of Fame and Museum; Richard Sandomir, "At Hall of Fame, Day Dedicated to Two Icons," *New York Times* (July 30, 2007).

287. Tyler Kepner, "Veterans' Hall of Fame Vote May Be Subject to Change," *New York Times* (February 28, 2007).

288. Jack Curry, "Two Elected to Hall of Fame; McGwire Misses," *New York Times* (January 9, 2007).

289. Chafets, *Cooperstown Confidential*, p. 138; Joe Lapointe, "Kuhn is Elected to Hall, But Miller is Not," *New York Times* (December 4, 2007); Murray Chass, "Strange Pairing on Hall Ballot," *New York Times* (December 2, 2007).

290. "A Dream Today, Perhaps—But a Reality Tomorrow," *Sporting News* (December 18, 1941); G. Scott Thomas, *A Brand New Ballgame: Branch Rickey, Bill Veeck, Walter O'Malley, and the Transformation of Baseball, 1945-1962* (Jefferson, North Carolina: McFarland & Co., 2022), pp. 193-195.

291. Vince Guerrieri, "Bowie Kuhn," Society for American Baseball Research; Murray Chass, "Marvin Miller, They Love Him or They Hate Him," *New York Times* (December 4, 2007); Jorge Arangure Jr., "Miller Remembered for His Place in Game, and His Absence From the Hall," *New York Times* (January 22, 2013).

292. Richard Sandomir, "At Baseball Hall of Fame, Links Are Cherished," *New York Times* (July 28, 2008).

293. Tyler Kepner, "Yankees' Joe Gordon Elected to Hall of Fame," *New York Times* (December 8, 2008).

294. Jack Curry, "Henderson Cruises Into Hall; Rice Also Slips In," *New York Times* (January 12, 2009); Alexander Edelman, "Jim Rice," Society for American Baseball Research.

295. Tyler Kepner, "Following Long Wait, Dawson Enters Hall Alone," *New York Times* (January 6, 2010).

296. Justin Sablich, "Against Wishes, Dawson Will Enter Hall as an Expo," *New York Times* (January 27, 2010).

297. Richard Sandomir, "In Hall Speeches, Thanks to Family, Mentors, and a Knee Surgeon," *New York Times* (July 25, 2010).

298. Jaffe, *Cooperstown Casebook,* pp. 45-46.

299. Tyler Kepner, "Rule Change Could Put Steinbrenner Up for Hall This Year," *New York Times* (July 27, 2010).

300. Tyler Kepner, "Steinbrenner and Miller Fall Short of Hall," *New York Times* (December 6, 2010).

301. Tyler Kepner, "Alomar and Blyleven Elected to Hall of Fame," *New York Times* (January 5, 2011).

302. Jack Lang, "Brock Tops Hall of Fame List," *Sporting News* (December 10, 1984); James, *Whatever Happened,* p. 343.

303. Kepner, "Veterans' Hall of Fame Vote," *New York Times*; Richard Goldstein, "Ron Santo, Stalwart for Cubs, Dies at 70," *New York Times* (December 3, 2010).

304. Richard Sandomir, "Bittersweet Moment as Santo is Elected to the Hall," *New York Times* (December 5, 2011); Paul Sullivan, "Santo's Family, Friends Celebrate Hall of Fame Voting," *Chicago Tribune* (December 5, 2011).

305. Tyler Kepner, "Bonds (and Everyone) Strikes Out," *New York Times* (January 10, 2013).

306. Nick Cafardo, "No One From 'Steroid Class' Elected to Hall of Fame," *Boston Globe* (January 10, 2013).

307. Houston Mitchell, "Many Hall of Famers Seem Glad Clemens, Bonds Were Snubbed," *Los Angeles Times* (January 10, 2013).

308. Anthony Sulla-Heffinger, "Yankees Great Gossage Says He Won't Go Back to Hall of Fame if Bonds, Clemens Elected," *New York Post* (January 10, 2013).

309. Kepner, "Bonds (and Everyone)," *New York Times.*

310. Richard Sandomir, "Only Echoes of Past Glory Stir the Quiet at Cooperstown," *New York Times* (July 29, 2013).

311. Tyler Kepner, "Greg Maddux, Tom Glavine, and Frank Thomas Elected to Hall of Fame," *New York Times* (January 9, 2014).

312. Richard Sandomir, "Braves Rule Crowds on Cooperstown's Podium and Lawn," *New York Times* (July 28, 2014).

313. Des Bieler, "Emotional Speech by Frank Thomas Highlights Hall of Fame Inductions," *Washington Post* (July 28, 2014).

314. "Voting Rules History," National Baseball Hall of Fame and Museum; Andrew Baggarly, "Barry Bonds Times Out on the BBWAA Hall of Fame Ballot—And Now It's About to Get Really Messy," *The Athletic* (January 26, 2022).

315. Richard Sandomir, "Hall Cuts Window for Election by 5 Years," *New York Times* (July 27, 2014).

316. Tyler Kepner, "Baseball Writers Elect Three Aces and a Doubles Machine," *New York Times* (January 7, 2015).

317. Richard Sandomir, "Golden Era Committee Selects No One for the Hall," *New York Times* (December 9, 2014).

318. Jaffe, *Cooperstown Casebook*, pp. 405-407; Andrew Simon, "Hall Implements Change for BBWAA Voters," MLB.com (July 28, 2015).

319. Michael Gee, "What It Feels Like to be Aged Out of Your Baseball Hall of Fame Vote," *Boston Globe* (August 5, 2015).

320. Jay Jaffe, "Hall of Fame's Cull of Inactive Voters Could Enhance Election Transparency," *Sports Illustrated* (July 29, 2015).

321. Tyler Kepner, "Two Sluggers Trot to Cooperstown," *New York Times* (January 7, 2016).

322. Eduardo Encina, "Tim Raines, An Oriole for a Week, Finally Reaches Hall of Fame," *Baltimore Sun* (January 18, 2017).

323. Tyler Kepner, "Hall of Fame Welcomes Tim Raines, Jeff Bagwell, and Ivan Rodriguez," *New York Times* (January 18, 2017).

324. Alex Reimer, "Years Ago, Bernie Sanders Exposed the Hypocrisy of Electing Bud Selig to the Hall of Fame," *Forbes* (December 5, 2016).

325. Peter Botte, "With Bud Selig Voted Into Hall of Fame, Now Barry Bonds and Roger Clemens Will Get My Vote," *New York Daily News* (December 5, 2016).

326. Cash Kruth, "Starting in 2018, HOF Votes to be Public," MLB.com (December 6, 2016); "Voting FAQ," Baseball Writers' Association of America.

327. Jay Jaffe, "Hall of Fame's Era Committees Changes Are Welcome, Needed Move," *Sports Illustrated* (July 26, 2016).

328. Anthony Fenech, "Detroit Tigers Stars Alan Trammell, Jack Morris Make Baseball Hall of Fame," *Detroit Free Press* (December 10, 2017).

329. Jeff Seidel, "1984 Detroit Tigers Finally Getting the Respect They Deserve From Hall," *Detroit Free Press* (December 10, 2017).

330. Richard Sandomir, "Newest Class of Hall of Famers Carries Records and Memories Into Cooperstown," *New York Times* (July 30, 2018).

331. Tyler Kepner, "Power at the Plate and From the Pen Leads to Cooperstown," *New York Times* (January 25, 2018); "2010-Present," National Baseball Hall of Fame and Museum.

332. Joe Falls, "Joe High on Longevity," *Sporting News* (January 9, 1982).

333. Victor Mather, "Can We All Agree Mariano Rivera Belongs in the Hall? History Says No," *New York Times* (January 17, 2019).

334. Klein, "Seaver Aces Key Hall Test," *Sporting News*.

335. Tyler Kepner, "It's Unanimous: Mariano Rivera is a Hall of Famer," *New York Times* (January 23, 2019).

336. Tyler Kepner, "A Weekend in Cooperstown Produces a Treasury of Memories," *New York Times* (July 23, 2019).

337. James Wagner, "The Head of the Class," *New York Times* (January 22, 2020).

338. Tyler Kepner, "At Last, Hall Honors the Creator of a Colossus," *New York Times* (December 10, 2019).

339. Tyler Kepner, "Baseball Hall of Fame Inductions Will Wait Till Next Year," *New York Times* (April 30, 2020).

340. Tyler Kepner, "The Hall of Fame Kept Dick Allen Waiting. He Ran Out of Time," *New York Times* (December 9, 2020).

341. Tyler Kepner, "Knowing Score if Hall Voters Pitch a Shutout," *New York Times* (January 25, 2022).

342. Tyler Kepner, "Hall of Fame Voters Send a Message: You Are Not Worthy," *New York Times* (January 27, 2021).

343. Kerry Crowley, "Barry Bonds Falls Short of Hall of Fame Again, Will Voters Eventually Listen to Willie Mays?" *San Jose Mercury News* (January 26, 2021).

344. Tyler Kepner, "The Journey Is Complete," *New York Times* (September 9, 2021).

345. Tyler Kepner, "For the Hall of Fame's New Class, Timing Was Everything," *New York Times* (July 24, 2022).

346. "Hall of Fame Restructures Era Committee, Frick Award Voting," National Baseball Hall of Fame and Museum (April 22, 2022).

347. Tyler Kepner, "Immortals on a Pedestal, Many With Feet of Clay," *New York Times* (January 27, 2022).

4. Action

1. "In Depth: Sports," Gallup.

2. "Play Ball—And May the Best Teams Win," *Sporting News* (April 21, 1948).

3. G. Scott Thomas, *A Brand New Ballgame: Branch Rickey, Bill Veeck, Walter O'Malley, and the Transformation of Baseball, 1945-1962* (Jefferson, North Carolina: McFarland & Co., 2022), p. 61; Arthur Daley, "Disagreeing With the Deacon of the Dodgers," *New York Times* (January 5, 1944).

4. Bill Veeck and Ed Linn, *Veeck—As in Wreck* (New York: G.P. Putnam's Sons, 1962), pp. 243-244.

5. "Bert Bell, Pro Football Head, Dies After Collapsing at Game," *New York Times* (October 12, 1959).

6. Arthur Daley, "The Spellbinder," *New York Times* (August 20, 1959).

7. Larry MacPhail, "A Pulmotor for Baseball," *Life* (February 24, 1958).

8. "In Depth: Sports," Gallup.

9. Michael MacCambridge, *America's Game: The Epic Story of How Pro Football Captured a Nation* (New York: Random House, 2004), p. 192.

10. "Vinnie, Vidi, Vici," *Time* (December 21, 1962).

11. "In Depth: Sports," Gallup.

12. "Major League Miscellaneous Year-by-Year Averages and Totals," Baseball Reference; "Major League Batting Year-by-Year Averages," Baseball Reference.

13. Ken Rosenthal, "Rod Carew Has Something to Say on the State of Baseball. And He Said it to Rob Manfred," *The Athletic* (August 26, 2022).

14. Ira Berkow, "Both New Inductees Sound an Alarm for Game," *New York Times* (July 31, 1995).

15. "Major League Miscellaneous Year-by-Year Averages and Totals," Baseball Reference.

16. Tyler Kepner, "Fighting Over the Short Term, With Long-Term Problems Looming," *New York Times* (February 8, 2022); Bill Shea, "World Series Had 2nd Smallest TV Viewership, But the Money Continues to Flow," *The Athletic* (November 4, 2021); Bill Shea, "Why L.A.'s 26th-Best Super Bowl Rating is Better Than it Looks," *The Athletic* (February 15, 2022).

17. "In Depth: Sports," Gallup.

18. David Waldstein, "Baseball, Popular But No Longer Dominant, Seeks to Reclaim Its Cool," *New York Times* (October 25, 2021).

19. Bill James, *Whatever Happened to the Hall of Fame?: Baseball, Cooperstown, and the Politics of Glory* (New York: Fireside, 1995), p. 287.

20. John Leo, "Housecleaning Plan for the Hall," *New York Times* (January 24, 1988).

21. Peter Clark, "Outta Here," *Sporting News* (January 21, 2002).

22. "BBWAA Election Rules," National Baseball Hall of Fame and Museum.

23. Ken Smith, *Baseball's Hall of Fame* (New York: Grosset & Dunlap, 1970 revised), p. 62.

24. "Shutdown of Wire Offices Delays Cooperstown Story," *Sporting News* (August 5, 1953).

25. Tyler Kepner, "A Voting Process Overdue for Reform," *New York Times* (January 8, 2013).

26. Troy Smith, "Rock & Roll Hall of Fame Induction Process: How Do Acts Get Chosen?" *Cleveland Plain Dealer* (August 22, 2016); "2022 Nominees," Rock and Roll Hall of Fame; Daniel Kreps, "Duran Duran, Eminem, Pat Benatar Dominate Rock Hall Fans' Ballot Final Tally," *Rolling Stone* (April 30, 2022).

27. Kepner, "A Voting Process," *New York Times*.

28. Jack Lang, "Gomez, Youngs, Harridge Join Elite in Hall of Fame," *Sporting News* (February 12, 1972).

29. Alex Semchuck, "Addie Joss," Society for American Baseball Research; Bob Broeg, "Gloss Was the Word for Joss," *Sporting News* (March 4, 1978).

30. Joseph Durso, "Koufax, Berra, and Wynn Are Voted Into Baseball's Hall of Fame," *New York Times* (January 20, 1972).

31. Jack Lang, "Brock Tops Hall of Fame List," *Sporting News* (December 10, 1984).

32. Richard Sandomir, "Hall Cuts Window for Election by 5 Years," *New York Times* (July 27, 2014).

33. Barry Bloom, "Hall Reduces Eligibility From 15 Years to 10," MLB.com (July 27, 2014).

34. Sandomir, "Hall Cuts Window," *New York Times*.

35. Monica Nucciarone, "Alexander Cartwright," Society for American Baseball Research.

36. Bill McMahon, "Al Spalding," Society for American Baseball Research.

37. Harold Burr, "Candy Cummings: He Started Something Away Back in Days of '64," *Sporting News* (November 19, 1942).

38. David Fleitz, "The Honor Rolls of Baseball," *Baseball Research Journal* (2005); Smith, *Baseball's Hall of Fame,* pp. 70-71; James, *Whatever Happened,* p. 46.

39. "BBWAA Career Excellence Award," Baseball Writers' Association of America; "Ford C. Frick Award," National Baseball Hall of Fame and Museum.

40. Peter Gammons, "David Ortiz Joined a Brotherhood of Equals, With a Bond Beyond Numbers," *The Athletic* (July 29, 2022).

41. Karl Lindholm, "Clyde Sukeforth: The Dodgers' Yankee and Branch Rickey's Maine Man," *Baseball Research Journal* (Spring 2014); James Lincoln Ray, "Clyde Sukeforth," Society for American Baseball Research.

42. Andy McCue, "Allan Roth," *Baseball Research Journal* (Spring 2014).

43. John Henry, "Bill James," *Time* (May 8, 2006); Jamie Malanowski, "Bill James Has the Required Numbers," *New York Times* (January 21, 2019).

44. Marc Carig, "The Sultan of Sod: At Age 90, Famed Groundskeeper George Toma Still Rakes," *The Athletic* (March 20, 2019); "Groundwork to Foil Hunter and Yanks in Kansas City Being Laid by Toma, the Royals' Nonroster Asset," *New York Times* (October 5, 1976).

45. Jason Belzer, "The World's Most Powerful Sports Agents 2020: Scott Boras Shows His Clients the Money," *Forbes* (December 22, 2020).

46. Doug Miller, "Frank Jobe's Hall of Fame Life," MLB.com (July 22, 2013).

47. Joseph Wancho, "Harmon Killebrew," Society for American Baseball Research.

48. Daniel Kramer and Do-Hyoung Park, "Every First-Ballot Hall of Famer in MLB History," MLB.com (January 25, 2022).

49. Joseph Durso, "Robinson, Marichal Gain Hall," *New York Times* (January 13, 1983).

50. Murray Chass, "New, Improved Hall Panel Elects No One," *New York Times* (February 27, 2003).

51. "Roush and McKechnie Named to Baseball Hall of Fame by Old-Timers Group," *New York Times* (January 29, 1962).

52. Smith, *Baseball's Hall of Fame,* p. 62.

53. Jack Lang, "Was Bunning Blanked?" *Sporting News* (January 25, 1988).

54. Tyler Kepner, "At Long Last, the 1990 Reds Make the Hall of Fame," *New York Times* (January 10, 2012).

55. "Hall of Famers," Naismith Memorial Basketball Hall of Fame; "Full List of Teams Enshrined at Springfield," *Sporting News* (September 9, 2021).

56. "Hall of Famers," Naismith Memorial Basketball Hall of Fame.

57. Bob LeMoine, "Boston Braves Team Ownership History," Society for American Baseball Research.

58. David Fleitz, "Frank Selee," Society for American Baseball Research.

59. Donald Dewey and Nicholas Acocella, *The Ball Clubs: Every Franchise, Past and Present, Officially Recognized by Major League Baseball* (New York: HarperCollins, 1996), p. 14.

60. Bruce Kuklick, *To Every Thing a Season: Shibe Park and Urban Philadelphia, 1909-1976* (Princeton, New Jersey: Princeton University Press, 1991), pp. 25-26; G. Edward White, *Creating the National Pastime: Baseball Transforms Itself, 1903-1953* (Princeton, New Jersey: Princeton University Press, 1996), pp. 21-24.

61. Don Jensen, "John McGraw," Society for American Baseball Research.

62. L. Jon Wertheim, "Remembering the Pathetics," *Sports Illustrated* (June 6, 2016).

63. Bill Gilbert, *They Also Served: Baseball and the Home Front, 1941-1945* (New York: Crown, 1992), p. 132.

64. Henry Aaron and Lonnie Wheeler, *I Had a Hammer: The Hank Aaron Story* (New York: HarperCollins, 1991), pp. 141-142.

65. Warren Corbett, "Earl Weaver," Society for American Baseball Research.

66. Dewey and Acocella, *Ball Clubs,* p. 409.

67. "Big Red Machine," *Time* (August 24, 1970).

68. Anthony DiComo, "Looking Back on the Mets' 1986 Title Run," MLB.com (February 27, 2022).

69. Tim Deale, "Bobby Cox," Society for American Baseball Research.

70. Rich Exner, "1995 Cleveland Indians Hold Their Place in History, Even 20 Years Later," *Cleveland Plain Dealer* (October 2, 2015); Zack Meisel, *Cleveland Rocked: The Personalities, Sluggers, and Magic of the 1995 Indians* (Chicago: Triumph, 2020), p. 7.

71. Sam Borden, "The Yankees, Overshadowed? Why the 'Best Team Ever' Never Got Its Due," ESPN.com (June 15, 2020).

72. Edward Sutelan, "Astros' Cheating Scandal Explained: How Houston's 2017 Sign-Stealing Scheme Shook Up MLB," *Sporting News* (October 29, 2021).

73. Bruce Weber, "Joe Morgan, Hall of Fame Second Baseman, Is Dead at 77," *New York Times* (October 12, 2020).

74. Gammons, "David Ortiz Joined," *The Athletic.*

75. Dave Brady, "'Shrine Fine, But Can't Say That I'm Too Thrilled,' Declares Rice," *Sporting News* (February 9, 1963).

76. Michael Strauss, "Averill Assails Hall of Fame Selectors," *New York Times* (August 19, 1975).

77. Dave Anderson, "The Captain is Saluted," *New York Times* (March 5, 1984).

78. Tyler Kepner, "Hall of Famer Was in a Class All His Own," *New York Times* (January 23, 2021).

79. Jack Curry, "Sutter Still Coming to Grips With Being a Hall of Famer," *New York Times* (January 12, 2006).

80. Tyler Kepner, "Passed-Over Greats of the Game Elected to the Hall of Fame," *New York Times* (December 6, 2021).

81. Clark, "Outta Here," *Sporting News.*

82. John Walters, "In Baseball, Everyone's Famous," *Newsweek* (January 10, 2014).

83. "History," American Academy of Arts and Letters.

84. Malcolm Cowley, *And I Worked at the Writer's Trade: Chapters of Literary History, 1918-1978* (New York: Penguin, 1978), pp. 161-162.

85. "History," American Academy of Arts and Letters; Julia Carmel, "The American Academy of Arts and Letters Unveils Expanded Roster," *New York Times* (March 9, 2021).

86. Dave Anderson, "The Cardinals' Oz of Wizardry," *New York Times* (October 9, 1982).

87. Tyler Kepner, "Putting Baseball's Racism in Context," *New York Times* (December 22, 2020).

88. Jane Leavy, *The Big Fella: Babe Ruth and the World He Created* (New York: HarperCollins, 2018), p. xxix.

89. Bill Pennington, "Hall of Fame Has Always Made Room for Infamy," *New York Times* (January 9, 2013).

90. Tyler Kepner, "Molitor and Eckersley Had Their Own Battles," *New York Times* (January 8, 2004).

91. Dianne Klein, "On the Road Again: Wade Boggs' Former Traveling Companion, Margo Adams, Crisscrosses Country 'Telling All,'" *Los Angeles Times* (March 10, 1989).

92. Murray Chass, "Carew, Perry, and Jenkins Are Voted Into Hall of Fame," *New York Times* (January 9, 1991); Claire Smith, "New Hall of Famers Keep Rose On Minds," *New York Times* (January 10, 1991); Murray Chass, "No Margin of Error: Cepeda Elected to Hall," *New York Times* (March 3, 1999).

93. Alan Levy, *Rube Waddell: The Zany, Brilliant Life of a Strikeout Artist* (Jefferson, North Carolina: McFarland & Co., 2000), pp. 143-144; Dan O'Brien, "Rube Waddell," Society for American Baseball Research.

94. Joseph Fried, "Snider Gets Probation and a Fine in Tax Scheme," *New York Times* (December 2, 1995).

95. Stew Thornley, "Kirby Puckett," Society for American Baseball Research; Jason Foster, "MLB, Blue Jays Fire Roberto Alomar After Investigation Into Sexual Misconduct," *Sporting News* (April 30, 2021).

96. Robert Peterson, *Only the Ball Was White* (Englewood Cliffs, New Jersey: Prentice-Hall, 1970), p. 30; Kevin Blackistone, "It's Time for Baseball to Acknowledge Cap Anson's Role in Erecting its Color Barrier," *Washington Post* (December 2, 2015).

97. Fred Lieb, *Baseball As I Have Known It* (Lincoln, Nebraska: University of Nebraska Press, 1996 reprint), pp. 57-58; Marty Appel, "Historian Puts Spotlight on Cobb and Speaker," *Sports Collectors Digest* (December 21, 2007).

98. Lowell Blaisdell, "The Cobb-Speaker Scandal: Exonerated But Probably Guilty," *Nine* (Spring 2005).

99. Ira Berkow, "The Spitter Versus the Hustler," *New York Times* (July 28, 1991).

100. C. Paul Rogers III, "Rogers Hornsby," Society for American Baseball Research.

101. Mark Armour, "Gaylord Perry," Society for American Baseball Research.

102. "BBWAA Election Rules," National Baseball Hall of Fame and Museum.

103. John Kieran, "A Probe of the Baseball Balloting," *New York Times* (February 4, 1936).

104. Jeffrey Standen, "Pete Rose and Baseball's Rule 21," *Nine* (Spring 2010).

105. Tyler Kepner, "Immortals on a Pedestal, Many With Feet of Clay," *New York Times* (January 27, 2022).

106. Arthur Daley, "Tempered by Mercy," *New York Times* (March 18, 1964).

107. Jay Jaffe, *The Cooperstown Casebook: Who's in the Baseball Hall of Fame, Who Should Be In, and Who Should Pack Their Plaques* (New York: Thomas Dunne Books, 2017), p. 90.

108. Jim Brosnan, *The Long Season* (Chicago: Ivan R. Dee, 2002 reprint), p. 155.

109. Jim Bouton, *Ball Four: The Final Pitch* (Nashville: Turner, 2014), p. 84.

110. "Research Report: Steroids and Other Appearance and Performance Enhancing Drugs," National Institute on Drug Abuse (February 2018); David Maraniss, *Rome 1960: The Summer Olympics That Stirred the World* (New York: Simon & Schuster, 2008), pp. 138-142.

111. Jack Curry, "Two Elected to Hall of Fame; McGwire Misses," *New York Times* (January 9, 2007).

112. Tyler Kepner, "McGwire Admits That He Used Steroids," *New York Times* (January 11, 2010); Steve West, "Barry Bonds," Society for American Baseball Research.

113. Jeff Schultz, "Hank Aaron Was Right," *The Athletic* (January 25, 2022).

114. "Mission," National Baseball Hall of Fame and Museum.

115. Fay Vincent, "Dump the Character Standard for Baseball's Hall of Fame," *Wall Street Journal* (January 29-30, 2022).

116. Peter Abraham, "David Ortiz Visits Hall of Fame Ahead of Induction in July," *Boston Globe* (May 2, 2022); Bill Francis, "Ortiz Overwhelmed by Visit to Hall of Fame," National Baseball Hall of Fame and Museum (May 2, 2022).

117. "A Nominee for the Hall of Fame," *Sporting News* (December 31, 1936).

118. Harvey Araton, "Time to Induct Carter, and Save His Team," *New York Times* (July 23, 2003).

119. Richard Sandomir, "At Hall, a Blank Look Is In Style," *New York Times* (July 24, 2014).

120. Henry Mitchell MacCracken, "The Hall of Fame," *American Monthly Review of Reviews* (November 1900).

121. Ford Frick, *Games, Asterisks, and People: Memoirs of a Lucky Fan* (New York: Crown, 1973), pp. 201-203.

122. Richard Rubin, "The Mall of Fame," *Atlantic* (July 1997).

123. Robert Moses, "Hall of Fame: A Neglected Pantheon," *Newsday* (January 9, 1971).

124. Robert Caro, *Working: Researching, Interviewing, Writing* (New York: Alfred A. Knopf, 2019), pp. 31-34.

125. Moses, "Hall of Fame," *Newsday.*

126. Sam Dolnick, "A Hall of Fame, Forgotten and Forlorn," *New York Times* (December 5, 2009); Rubin, "Mall of Fame," *Atlantic*; James Barron, "Hard to Circle This Hall of Fame and Not Notice the Disrepair," *New York Times* (November 5, 2018).

127. James, *Whatever Happened*, p. 287.

Bibliography

Books

Aaron, Henry, and Lonnie Wheeler. *I Had a Hammer: The Hank Aaron Story.* New York: HarperCollins, 1991.

Banner, Stuart. *The Baseball Trust: A History of Baseball's Antitrust Exemption.* New York: Oxford University Press, 2013.

Bouton, Jim. *Ball Four: The Final Pitch.* Nashville: Turner, 2014.

Brosnan, Jim. *The Long Season.* Chicago: Ivan R. Dee, 2002 reprint.

Caro, Robert. *Working: Researching, Interviewing, Writing.* New York: Alfred A. Knopf, 2019.

Chafets, Zev. *Cooperstown Confidential: Heroes, Rogues, and the Inside Story of the Baseball Hall of Fame.* New York: Bloomsbury, 2009.

Chandler, Albert, and Vance Trimble. *Heroes, Plain Folks, and Skunks: The Life and Times of Happy Chandler.* Chicago: Bonus, 1989.

Cowley, Malcolm. *And I Worked at the Writer's Trade: Chapters of Literary History, 1918-1978.* New York: Penguin, 1978.

Danilov, Victor. *Hall of Fame Museums: A Reference Guide.* Westport, Connecticut: Greenwood, 1997.

Dewey, Donald, and Nicholas Acocella. *The Ball Clubs: Every Franchise, Past and Present, Officially Recognized by Major League Baseball.* New York: HarperCollins, 1996.

Durocher, Leo, and Ed Linn. *Nice Guys Finish Last.* New York: Simon and Schuster, 1975.

Frick, Ford. *Games, Asterisks, and People: Memoirs of a Lucky Fan.* New York: Crown, 1973.

Gilbert, Bill. *They Also Served: Baseball and the Home Front, 1941-1945.* New York: Crown, 1992.

Hornsby, Rogers, and Bill Surface. *My War With Baseball.* New York: Coward-McCann, 1962.

Jaffe, Jay. *The Cooperstown Casebook: Who's in the Baseball Hall of Fame, Who Should Be In, and Who Should Pack Their Plaques.* New York: Thomas Dunne Books, 2017.

James, Bill. *The New Bill James Historical Baseball Abstract.* New York: Free Press, 2003.

_____. *Whatever Happened to the Hall of Fame?: Baseball, Cooperstown, and the Politics of Glory.* New York: Fireside, 1995.

Kuhn, Bowie. *Hardball: The Education of a Baseball Commissioner.* New York: Times Books, 1987.

Kuklick, Bruce. *To Every Thing a Season: Shibe Park and Urban Philadelphia, 1909-1976.* Princeton, New Jersey: Princeton University Press, 1991.

Leavy, Jane. *The Big Fella: Babe Ruth and the World He Created.* New York: HarperCollins, 2018.

_____. *Sandy Koufax: A Lefty's Legacy.* New York: HarperCollins, 2002.

Levy, Alan. *Rube Waddell: The Zany, Brilliant Life of a Strikeout Artist.* Jefferson, North Carolina: McFarland & Co., 2000.

Lieb, Fred. *Baseball As I Have Known It.* Lincoln, Nebraska: University of Nebraska Press, 1996 reprint.

MacCambridge, Michael. *America's Game: The Epic Story of How Pro Football Captured a Nation.* New York: Random House, 2004.

Mack, Connie. *My 66 Years in the Big Leagues: The Great Story of America's National Game.* Philadelphia: John C. Winston, 1950.

Maraniss, David. *Rome 1960: The Summer Olympics That Stirred the World.* New York: Simon & Schuster, 2008.

McKelvey, G. Richard. *Mexican Raiders in the Major Leagues, 1946.* Jefferson, North Carolina: McFarland & Co., 2006.

Meisel, Zack. *Cleveland Rocked: The Personalities, Sluggers, and Magic of the 1995 Indians.* Chicago: Triumph, 2020.

Peary, Danny. *We Played the Game: 65 Players Remember Baseball's Greatest Era, 1947-1964.* New York: Hyperion, 1994.

Peterson, Robert. *Only the Ball Was White.* Englewood Cliffs, New Jersey: Prentice-Hall, 1970.

Pietrusza, David. *Judge and Jury: The Life and Times of Judge Kenesaw Mountain Landis.* South Bend, Indiana: Diamond, 1998.

Ritter, Lawrence. *The Glory of Their Times: The Story of the Early Days of Baseball Told by the Men Who Played It.* New York: Macmillan, 1966.

Rose, Pete, and Rick Hill. *My Prison Without Bars.* Emmaus, Pennsylvania: Rodale Press, 2004.

Schlesinger, Arthur Jr., and Fred Israel, editors. *History of American Presidential Elections, 1789-1968.* New York: Chelsea House, 1971.

Smith, Ken. *Baseball's Hall of Fame.* New York: Grosset & Dunlap, 1970 revised.

Snider, Duke, and Bill Gilbert. *The Duke of Flatbush.* New York: Zebra, 1988.

Thomas, G. Scott. *The Best (and Worst) of Baseball's Modern Era: The Top (and Bottom) Teams and Players From 1961 Through 2016.* Buffalo: Niawanda, 2016.

_____. *A Brand New Ballgame: Branch Rickey, Bill Veeck, Walter O'Malley, and the Transformation of Baseball, 1945-1962.* Jefferson, North Carolina: McFarland & Co., 2022.

_____. *Leveling the Field: An Encyclopedia of Baseball's All-Time Great Performances as Revealed Through Adjusted Statistics.* New York: Black Dog & Leventhal, 2002.

Total Baseball: The Official Encyclopedia of Major League Baseball. New York: Total Sports, 1999.

Tygiel, Jules. *Baseball's Great Experiment: Jackie Robinson and His Legacy.* New York: Oxford University Press, 1997.

Vail, James. *Outrageous Fortune: What's Wrong with Hall of Fame Voting and How to Make it Statistically Sound.* Jefferson, North Carolina: McFarland & Co., 2001.

Veeck, Bill, and Ed Linn. *Veeck—As in Wreck.* New York: G.P. Putnam's Sons, 1962.

White, G. Edward. *Creating the National Pastime: Baseball Transforms Itself, 1903-1953.* Princeton, New Jersey: Princeton University Press, 1996.

Williams, Ted, and John Underwood. *My Turn at Bat: The Story of My Life.* New York: Fireside, 1988.

Zardetto, Ray. *'30: Major League Baseball's Year of the Batter.* Jefferson, North Carolina: McFarland & Co., 2008.

Oral Histories

National Baseball Hall of Fame and Museum (Cooperstown, New York)
  • Ray Dandridge
University of Kentucky Special Collections Research Center (Lexington, Kentucky)
  • Albert "Happy" Chandler
  • Ray Dandridge
  • Shirley Povich
  • Red Smith

Newspapers

Arizona Republic
Baltimore Sun
Boston Globe
Chicago Tribune
Cleveland Plain Dealer
Detroit Free Press
Los Angeles Times
New York Daily News
New York Post
New York Times
Newsday
San Jose Mercury News
Sporting News
Tampa Bay Times
USA Today
Wall Street Journal
Washington Post

Magazines and Journals

American Monthly Review of Reviews
Atlantic
Baseball Research Journal
Esquire
Forbes
Life
National Pastime
New York Times Book Review
Newsweek
Nine
Rolling Stone
Saturday Evening Post
Smithsonian
Sports Collectors Digest
Sports Illustrated
Time

Television Networks

ESPN
MLB Network

News Websites

The Athletic, https://theathletic.com
Baseball Reference, https://www.baseball-reference.com
Bill James Online, https://www.billjamesonline.com
ESPN.com, https://www.espn.com
HipHopDX, https://hiphopdx.com
MLB.com, https://www.mlb.com

Organization Websites

American Academy of Arts and Letters, https://artsandletters.org
American Psychiatric Association, https://psychiatry.org
Baseball Writers' Association of America, https://bbwaa.com
Gallup, https://www.gallup.com
Ladies Professional Golf Association, https://www.lpga.com
Naismith Memorial Basketball Hall of Fame, https://www.hoophall.com
National Baseball Hall of Fame and Museum, https://baseballhall.org
National Institute on Drug Abuse, https://nida.nih.gov
Rock and Roll Hall of Fame, https://www.rockhall.com
Society for American Baseball Research, https://sabr.org
United States Census Bureau, https://www.census.gov

Index

Made in the USA
Middletown, DE
04 May 2023

29909889R00248